ALSO BY RONALD GOLDFARB

The Contempt Power

Ransom: A Critique of the American Bail System

Crime and Publicity: The Impact of News on the Administration of Justice
(with Alfred Friendly)

After Conviction: A Review of the American Correction System
(with Linda Singer)

Jails: The Ultimate Ghetto

Migrant Farm Workers: A Caste of Despair

Clear Understandings: A Guide to Legal Writing
(with James Raymond)

The Writer's Lawyer
(with Gail E. Ross)

PERFECT VILLAINS,

IMPERFECT HEROES

John F. Kennedy and Robert F. Kennedy

Ronald Goldfarb

PERFECT VILLAINS,
IMPERFECT HEROES

Robert F. Kennedy's War

Against Organized

Crime

RANDOM HOUSE

NEW YORK

Library of Congress Cataloging-in-Publication Data
Goldfarb, Ronald L.
Perfect villains, imperfect heroes: Robert F. Kennedy's war
against organized crime / Ronald Goldfarb.—1st ed.
        p.   cm.
Includes bibliographical references and index.
ISBN 0-679-43565-4
1. Kennedy, Robert F., 1925–1968. 2. Organized crime—United States.   I. Title.
E840.8.K4G6   1995   973.922′092—dc20
        [B]   95-8495

Manufactured in the United States of America on acid-free paper
Book design by J. K. Lambert
2 4 6 8 9 7 5 3
First Edition

In memory of my father.

With love to my mother.

. . . the seed never explains the flower.

—Edith Hamilton, *The Greek Way*

ACKNOWLEDGMENTS

Many people helped me with this book in various ways.

Harry Alexander, Herb Bates, G. Robert Blakey, Mortimer Caplin, John Cassidy, John Diuguid, Courtney Evans, Jay Goldberg, Ed Guthman, Bill Hundley, Earl Johnson, John Keeney, Bill Lynch, Tom McBride, Dougald McMillan, Jack Miller, John Nolan, Angie Novello, Henry Ruth, John Seigenthaler, Walter Sheridan, Charles Z. Smith, John Sprizzo, James Symington, and Jake Tanzer, all of whom were colleagues in the organized crime section and the Department of Justice, recalled what we did, and shared their thoughts and papers.

Sherry North and Tom Comerford assisted with miscellaneous research. Anne Clark and Sharon Kirby managed the manuscript production. My law partner, Nina Graybill, was always encouraging and helpful. Kate Lehrer and Joan V. Schroeder applied their novelists' eyes to evolving versions of the manuscript and made important creative suggestions. My friend Dr. George Moraitis made interesting contributions about the psychoanalytical possibilities of some of the subjects in this book. My friend and colleague Hodding Carter III read the manuscript and along with Max Holland and Jan Cook offered useful editorial suggestions. Staff at the JFK Library provided helpful research assistance.

At Random House, Harry Evans's enthusiasm for the idea of this book and Sam Vaughan's editing and friendly encouragements have been deeply appreciated. Thanks, too, to Beth Pearson and Karen McGuinness for their helpful attentions. Originally, Alan Williams was to be my editor, and while illness prevented his completing what was started, I am grateful to have had his collaboration, even for a short time.

James H. Lesar of the Assassination Archives and Research Center, Washington, D.C., provided helpful access to its archives. Dan Moldea generously provided information and photos.

Several times, I was able to work at the Virginia Center for the Creative Arts for brief but very productive and pleasant periods of time. All the staff there, and its director, Bill Smart, have my thanks for their kindnesses and friendship.

RONALD GOLDFARB
Washington, D.C., 1995

CONTENTS

Acknowledgments . . . . *xi*

Author's Note . . . . *xv*

Introduction . . . . *xvii*

1 The Father Within *3*

2 Recruitment of a Rookie Prosecutor *15*

3 The Emergence of Robert Kennedy *22*

4 Learning on the Job *53*

5 My Turn, in Newport, Kentucky *82*

6 A Respite in Washington *124*

7 Politics in Justice *155*

8 Labor and the Rackets *177*

9 Round Two in Newport *203*

10 A Meeting in Kennedy's Office *244*

11 Hidden Villains, Tragic Heroes *258*

12 Justice and Passion: A Portrait of
   Robert Kennedy as Attorney General *300*

Notes *331*

Selected Bibliography *339*

Index *345*

AUTHOR'S NOTE

For almost four years, 1961–1964, the lawyers in the Organized Crime and Racketeering Section of the Justice Department met regularly in the office of the chief of the section, and also in Robert Kennedy's office, to discuss our investigations. Those sessions were informative and exciting for all of us. They provided an opportunity to see the big picture, to learn what others were up to, and to observe the department's leaders in action. Those meetings captured the style and nature of our work.

I have attempted to describe those meetings accurately in this book, despite the fact that there were no transcripts of conversations. To assure the integrity of my recapitulation of each lawyer's comments, I've used the following two techniques:

In most instances, I went back to my colleagues, reviewed their records, and interviewed them, on tape when they agreed. Then I asked them to edit my retelling of their stories. I am grateful for their help in assuring the accuracy of each of their reports. As much as possible, every detail is stated as correctly as they and I can remember them.

We prepared a daily report of our work, which went first to the head of the Criminal Division, and then to Kennedy himself. Through a Freedom of Information Act request, I was able to retrieve copies of those daily reports—over one thousand pages of them—and I drew upon the facts in those reports in appropriate parts of this book to supplement my and my colleagues' recollections.

In addition, I was fortunate to find journalist Miriam Ottenberg's interviews of some of my colleagues. We all knew and respected

Miriam, and were encouraged by Justice Department officials to assist her because her reporting was deemed responsible, fair, and true. Her interviews were done close in time to the events described to her, and they were edited by each attorney, whose records were available to double-check facts. Miriam's estate gave me permission to use this Pulitzer Prize winner's material, which is housed at the Wisconsin State Historical Society Archives Collection.

A final note about references to the main character in this book. His close family and strangers called him Bobby. His colleagues at work called him Bob. Formal references to him usually were to Robert Kennedy, Robert F. Kennedy, or sometimes RFK. In this book, I followed those varied, if inconsistent, forms of reference.

INTRODUCTION

This book focuses on a relatively unreported part of an otherwise much-reported life. It is the inside story of a public adventure whose chief character is Robert F. Kennedy and whose subject is the extraordinary effort he led against organized crime, one that was unmatched in law enforcement history. It also examines an evolving subplot to this government crusade against social demons, one which is haunting to contemplate.

Could there possibly be anything left to say that hasn't already been said about Robert F. Kennedy and his special role in the New Frontier–Camelot days of the early 1960s? Is there any chapter in his already intensely and exhaustively examined life open for fresh examination? This book's answers to these questions should surprise most readers; in unexpected ways they surprised the author, who was a participant in many of the events considered. The story about to be told is essentially historical biography—an attempt to present the fullest possible inside view of one important part of Robert Kennedy's public life. It is also somewhat autobiographical—at once its value and its limitation—in that it describes that experience from the viewpoint of one on-the-line warrior who knew things that the public could not know, but who can only speculate about some of the more intriguing things the hero of this story knew and did. The book will explore lingering and confounding questions about this historic man's important career. Hovering over the story is the profound question: How should we judge heroes when they are human beings, too?

———

In 1965, shortly after I left the U.S. Department of Justice and before starting my law practice, I considered writing a book about my experiences working for Robert F. Kennedy. Ours had been an extraordinary adventure, and one of the cases I had tried was akin to a swashbuckling legal thriller. Robert Kennedy's organized crime program had been his special passion for years, and my own investigatory and trial experiences provided an inside view of how this national law enforcement program evolved, and knowledge of some of what it accomplished. Kennedy, for whom I'd worked throughout his tenure at Justice as well as on his Senate campaign in New York, would write a foreword. It might be an interesting, worthwhile book.

But I'd also worked on a national bail-reform conference during my final months in the Department of Justice, and an article I'd written about it for *The New Republic* led to an offer to do a book on that subject. I wasn't sure which book to write. My friend Victor Navasky suggested I discuss these two prospective projects with a friend of his, a bright young editor at Dial Press. We did so over a drink in New York City, and that editor persuaded me that the bail-reform book was more timely, and the Kennedy Justice Department book could wait; in fact it would be better to write that history with the distance that time would provide. That's what I did. When Senator Robert Kennedy was killed several years later, my impetus to write the history waned.

One thing after another prevented my returning to that subject in the intervening years, though people who knew about my experiences at Kennedy's Justice Department continued to urge me to write about it. For decades, I wondered whether the fateful choice I'd made in 1965 was the right one, and whether it made sense so many years later to write about a crusade that had occurred in the early 1960s. At a party of Kennedy's Justice alumni a few years ago, I was reminded that no one had written the definitive book about this part of Kennedy's career and that some of the people who were key participants in the story were aging. The opportunity might disappear if the book wasn't done soon.

The magnification of Kennedy's reputation in the intervening years, along with my lingering fascination with the episode, led me to return to this project. When I did, I realized that the former Dial editor in New York—Ed Doctorow—was right; the book in the mid-1990s is much different and in several unpredictable respects more interesting than the one I would have written three decades earlier. Some of the records might have been easier to find in 1965, but my colleagues, as noted, have been able to refresh my own recollections of those days.

Time does not change the heart of this story, but distance has provided intriguing perspectives that were not evident earlier. The era I will write about, spanning the years from the end of the 1950s to the middle of the 1960s, has been described often by perceptive authors and from many perspectives, but this one story has been told neither thoroughly nor from the inside. Moreover, some parts of the story could not have been told before because certain critical facts were not revealed until recently. A series of disclosures, combined with what a small group of insiders know from personal experience, provides a new view on what we were doing then.

It seems unlikely that there is a chapter of John Kennedy's administration that has not been fully explored. But that is the case, and this chapter is a vital, indeed in some respects harrowing, one. Other books and documentaries have revealed aspects by describing particular episodes: David Halberstam's *The Best and the Brightest* discloses the first chapter in our country's involvement in Vietnam through descriptions of the early escapades of the Defense Department and intelligence-agency whiz kids; the book and television series *Eyes on the Prize* described the history of the socially wrenching, dynamic days of the civil rights revolution in the South. The frightening Cuban Missile Crisis and the high-minded Peace Corps experiment are important and well-documented stories. Robert Kennedy figured prominently in those chapters, too, and indeed wrote several books himself.

Surprisingly, Robert Kennedy's mission against organized crime as attorney general has been described incompletely. Indeed, more is known about his formative experiences as counsel to the highly publicized McClellan Rackets Committee and its congressional efforts to expose racketeering in labor unions than is known about the nationwide program he mounted thereafter at the Department of Justice. This gap is especially surprising in view of the fact that as attorney general Kennedy's campaign against organized crime was his chief and abiding interest. As a matter of fact, this subject involved the only area of legal expertise he brought with him to Justice after he was appointed the nation's chief law enforcement official on December 16, 1960.

It is curious. Major, informative books about him, such as Arthur M. Schlesinger, Jr.'s *Robert Kennedy and His Times,* and important books about the Department of Justice, such as Victor Navasky's early and extensive analysis *Kennedy Justice,* could pay relatively limited attention to the organized crime program. Unlike this book, which focuses exclusively on it, those two covered broader subjects, an extraordinary personal career, and a diverse departmental history. The plethora of recent Robert Kennedy books focus on his personal life, his presidential campaign, his speeches; but again little has been written about this special and precedent-setting program, which everyone who knew him well concedes was his long-term, special interest.

Kennedy's vision was unique and it was heartfelt. His was a personally directed program, not one he inherited from the existing federal bureaucracy; indeed the chief law enforcement official in the country at that time, J. Edgar Hoover, disagreed with Kennedy's conclusions and resisted his plan. Kennedy devised the program, used every opportunity to push and publicize it, generated press interest in it, created a legislative package to provide his staff with the weapons they would need to prevail, and set up a special corps of prosecutors. He armed and encouraged us and personally oversaw all our work.

Our young but powerful leader was not the Robert Kennedy who, as described by some politicians and authors today, has taken on almost mythic saintly features. Then, he was very human—avid, intense, witty, interested in people and in results, an activist, growing before our eyes. The Robert Kennedy of his Senate years was chastened by the assassination of his brother. He read seriously and quoted poetry and the Greek classics. He was adopted by needy constituents who eventually saw in him a believable savior and awakened in him a religious-like commitment to their causes. After his death, his charismatic persona grew as the public and his fellow politicians came to realize that a unique political figure was gone.

Nor was he the demagogic demon portrayed by his many critics. The Robert Kennedy of the time before and during his Justice

Department tenure was distrusted by the left, criticized for his earlier work as counsel to two Senate committees as a man blind to civil liberties and, in the early days at Justice, for his lack of commitment to civil rights. Understandably then, he was widely viewed as a ruthless, insensitive chip off the old block of family despot Joseph Kennedy. His appointment to the cabinet was seen cynically at the time to be nothing more than nepotism. Wherever I traveled in the early 1960s, I found myself defending my boss and our work from the onslaughts of the liberal community.

In fact, the Robert Kennedy who led the Department of Justice was a young man—thirty-four at the start, thirty-seven when he resigned on September 3, 1964—who was maturing exponentially; who surrounded himself with estimable legal talent and relied on these aides; who was curious about issues, comfortable with the use of his extraordinary powers, and action-oriented to a fault. All these skills, attitudes, and resources he applied with single-mindedness to stand up to what he saw as the pernicious, widespread, evil influences of organized crime in the United States, to strike at the roots of evil (to adapt Henry David Thoreau's phrase) rather than hacking at the branches, though we cut off more than a few of those. Before his appointment, few law enforcement officials had tackled this problem on a national scale, and most had ignored it.

This book is about Kennedy's motives and vision and behind-the-scene activities fighting organized crime, about the politics of his stewardship. It is about the group he gathered to wage his war, and about our most interesting battles, including one major case history, which was seen by some observers, including Kennedy himself, as a metaphor for what all of us in this program were doing during those exciting years.

I believe now that our experiences were part of a special time, an important and unique endeavor. The passage of time has provided the distance and details to tell this story, to take a measure of the man who inspired us, and to reflect on the actions we generated. All the participants are older now and more experienced; a few are deceased. Each person I talked to spoke of our adventure and our leader with nostalgia, affection, admiration. Such a time has not come again for any of us, I believe, although most veterans of that group have gone on to notable accomplishments.

Facts—revealed in the burgeoning assassination literature and in books and interviews by or about bit players and notorious characters—complicate, but I do not believe change, the final measure of our work. Rather, like so much we have learned about the Kennedy family, they reflect both the family's extraordinary vigor and their inspirational leadership while raising questions about the steadfastness of the moral compass that guided them. This new information is relevant and interesting and I will report it. It does not alter my judgment of the success of our program; but it demands reflection.

Now it is clear that our team wreaked havoc with the powerful forces of organized crime in our country; our success as a small but powerful band of government lawyers battling an elusive enemy was effectual. But, along with the lamentable likelihood that such an exciting and purposeful time will not come again soon, we are also left with the speculation that the Kennedy family and this country paid a horrific price for this moment in history.

PERFECT VILLAINS,
IMPERFECT HEROES

Chapter 1

THE FATHER WITHIN

For a Christmas present in 1960, John F. Kennedy, then president-elect of the United States, and his wife, Jaqueline, gave Robert Kennedy a leather-bound copy of Robert's recently published book, *The Enemy Within*. It was inscribed by his sister-in-law, "To Bobby—who made the impossible possible and changed all our lives. With love, Jackie." A second inscription followed: "For Bobby—The Brother Within—who made the easy difficult. Merry Christmas, Jack."

The private family incident was typical of the Kennedy style: rough-and-tumble good humor, close family kinship, and a keen sense of the risks and rights that came with the use of power. The words used were warm, witty, and personal, but the message—at least in hindsight—had a touch of the prophetic, or at least an intriguing ambiguity.

The elder Kennedy's clever reference was to the title of his younger brother's book, which was about his experiences between 1957 and 1960 as chief counsel to the Senate Select Committee on Improper Activities in the Labor or Management Field, known as the McClellan Committee after its chairman, Arkansas senator John L. McClellan. As committee counsel, Robert Kennedy's work helped to highlight labor union corruption, and in the course of it, he had often encountered hoodlums and racketeers who had infiltrated and perverted the American union movement with the aid, and sometimes at the instigation, of corrupt union leaders. Kennedy's clashes with the contentious Teamsters leader, James Riddle Hoffa, were the most notorious of these run-ins, though not the only ones, and it left both combatants bitterly antagonistic. Senator John F. Kennedy had been an active member of that select committee and profited from the national exposure it provided him when he later launched the presidential campaign that his brother managed.

Robert Kennedy was truly John Kennedy's "brother within." The seventh of nine children, the third son, he was a scrapper and, however energetic and privileged, an underachiever. By his own account, he was not a sociable youngster, with classmates or the girls. He followed his siblings to Harvard. He left college at eighteen and enlisted in the Navy, where he served as a seaman aboard the U.S.S. *Joseph P. Kennedy, Jr.,* for two years. Later, he barely made the Harvard football team and edged into the University of Virginia law school, where he had a lackluster academic career.

One of his professors, Mortimer Caplin, later to be IRS commissioner in the Kennedy administration, remembers: "He didn't volunteer much in class. He was a good, strong student . . . when you called upon him, he gave very good, sensible answers. He was a toughminded sort of fellow, taciturn, and he didn't really sparkle very much." His one achievement was presiding over the student legal forum, where he was able to bring such notable speakers to the school as Congressman John Kennedy, Ambassador Joseph Kennedy, Kennedy family lawyer James Landis, and Wisconsin senator Joseph McCarthy.

After graduating in the middle of his class at Virginia, he'd drifted from a job in the Justice Department's Criminal Division investigating loyalty and security cases, to managing Congressman John Kennedy's Senate campaign, to a job working for the infamous McCarthy, with whom the Kennedy family was friendly and with whom they held common views. Kennedy's brief career as assistant counsel to the McCarthy investigating committee was short-lived, not for ideological reasons. He told a reporter years later, "At that time, I thought there was a serious internal security threat to the United States; I felt at that time that Joe McCarthy seemed to be the only one who was doing anything about it. I was wrong." But in 1961, he didn't think he was wrong.

Kennedy left the committee because he found it impossible to be an underling to McCarthy's distasteful aide, Roy Cohn. Their antipathy was well known. As a young reporter covering those hearings, Anthony Lewis watched the two lawyers almost come to blows arguing publicly about some difference of approach. After a brief stint working as an assistant to his father on a federal body evaluating government efficiency, the Hoover Commission, Robert Kennedy returned to the same Senate investigating committee, this time as minority counsel to the Democratic members.

With the eclipse of Joseph McCarthy, Kennedy moved to the McClellan Committee, where he learned about the spread and impact of racketeering in the United States and began his campaign against the rackets and corrupt labor leaders, including his Ahab-like pursuit of Jimmy Hoffa. While Senator Kennedy had sat as a visible, thoughtful member of the Rackets Committee, his aggressive younger brother actually ran it, and he did so in a brusque, no-nonsense fashion, as its staff director and chief counsel.

Robert Kennedy's introduction to the national legal scene then was through his derivative access as son and brother of Joseph and Jack Kennedy. It was as a hard-line, conservative aristocrat whose loyalties first and foremost were to the family and to its use of power that Robert Kennedy entered public life near the top. Insofar as Kennedy family politics were concerned, he was very much the inside brother.

Later, Robert Kennedy made a hard-driving campaign manager. That he masterminded the tough campaigns that defeated Adlai Stevenson and Hubert Humphrey—two darlings of the Democratic Party, especially its liberal wing—confirmed to many observers that this young man was ruthless—the word would recur—and insensitive. One reporter at the 1960 convention told Murray Kempton, "Whenever you see Bobby Kennedy in public with his brother, he looks as though he showed up for a rumble."

In both roles, Robert Kennedy had gained a national reputation as a fierce and feisty fighter, relentless in his single-minded investigatory and political quests, the underling pushy kid who was not himself a major figure. As a friend, newspaper editor John Seigenthaler, later noted, in the service of his brother Jack, Robert Kennedy had been willing to be the villain. Some folks would not forget that role. As Robert Kennedy was said to be callous about the constitutional rights of the committee's witnesses, the floated idea that he might be appointed attorney general was viewed widely as unacceptable nepotism.

Using family connections to jump-start a legal career was one thing; using them to appoint a young, relatively inexperienced lawyer to the top legal post in the country was quite another. When rumors of the possibility that Robert Kennedy might become attorney general began to leak, reactions were predictably negative. A *New York Times* editorial complained that the political nature of such a prestigious appointment would be a bad precedent. The *Baltimore Sun* feared he might not be a crusader, "but an overcrusader." *The Washington Post* speculated that the president was already looking forward to the 1964 campaign for reelection.

Robert Kennedy himself had displayed uncharacteristic diffidence about taking this job. "I was never dying to be attorney general," he confided to friends. He was concerned that at Justice he would become a lightning rod in the civil rights storms that already were building. He was aware that the president would have enough problems as the first Catholic president, in addition to coming to office so young (at the age of forty-three), and as only the second member of the Senate to be elected. JFK did not need nepotism and family dynasty charges on top of those concerns. Furthermore, Robert Kennedy, never having done anything except government lawyering, was interested in pursuing other experiences. He was aware, too, that his presence in departments such as State and Defense, where he did have interests, would be awkward and troublesome to the two new secretaries. Kennedy said he was "tired of chasing people," wanted something different to do. He had options most other young men at his age and career stage did not have. He considered buying a newspaper, running a college, campaigning for elective office in Massachusetts, taking a sabbatical to travel, write, and study. He sought advice from friends and mentors. His friend Ed Guthman advised that assuming the attorney general's post was a bad idea. Others advising the president—except his father—spoke against the appointment.

According to insiders, the president first offered the attorney generalship to Connecticut senator Abraham Ribicoff, who turned it down, preferring a less controversial cabinet post, and then to Adlai Stevenson, who was not interested. But Joseph Kennedy, to many an odious character, who had stayed out of public view during the campaign, was much interested in the careers of all his sons, and he clearly favored the idea of his second oldest son becoming the fourth-ranking member of the cabinet.

Veteran Washington insider Clark Clifford was asked by the president-elect to approach the elder Kennedy and persuade him that Robert Kennedy's appointment as attorney general would be a bad idea. Clifford visited Joseph Kennedy in New York City and carefully presented all the reasons why his middle son should not be appointed attorney general, among them that he'd never practiced law and didn't want the job. The father listened politely, complimented Clifford for making a reasonable case, and announced, "Bobby is going to be attorney general." Making it clear who was privately calling the shots in the Kennedy family, regardless of such public diversions as the election, Kennedy told Clifford, "All of us have worked our tails off for Jack, and now that we have succeeded I am going to see to it that Bobby gets the same chance that we gave to Jack."

Charles Bartlett, a reporter who knew the Kennedys and had worked with Robert Kennedy on an investigation, spoke to JFK and RFK about the latter's prospective role in the new administration. John Kennedy wanted his brother in the administration. Robert Kennedy was apprehensive. Joseph Kennedy wanted his son Robert in Justice. When Bartlett told Robert Kennedy he'd have problems at Justice, the young man replied, "Well, maybe you'd like to call Dad." Then, Bartlett got a call from John Kennedy saying he should "Lay off. It's all settled." As one journalist observed, "Joseph Kennedy had an effective affirmative action program for the family."

For the president-elect, choosing his younger brother was easy, even if problematic; family pressure aside, Robert Kennedy was his brother's perfect counterpoint and confidant. For several years, on the McClellan Committee and during the political campaigns, the two brothers had successfully played the roles of good cop and bad cop, and it was the younger man who was the heavy. The president-elect wanted an attorney general he could trust completely, and more than anyone else that was his brother Robert.

When one reporter questioned John Kennedy about why he'd

appoint an attorney general who'd never been in a courtroom, the president-elect replied: "Well, an attorney general doesn't have to be a lawyer, he doesn't have to ever be in a court. An attorney general is supposed to run a department of some thirty thousand people, and it needs a hell of a manager, and my brother is the best manager I've ever had and the best one that I know of—and *that's* why he's going to be the attorney general."

Press leaks fed charges of dynasty building. Victor Navasky reported that when the negative reactions to these trial balloons "were loud but not deafening," the president-elect decided to follow his father's wishes and his own general predilection. He would, he said in response to the negative responses he'd heard, "open the front door of the Georgetown house some morning around 2 A.M., look up and down the street and if there's no one there, I'll whisper, 'It's Bobby!' "

Late one snowy day toward the end of the year—between Thanksgiving and Christmas—as the rumors were swirling about his prospective appointment, Robert Kennedy spent the day with his close friend and colleague from McClellan Committee and campaign days, John Seigenthaler, on leave from the *Nashville Tennessean,* where he had been a reporter. Seigenthaler had helped Kennedy write *The Enemy Within* and had been living with him and his family at their Virginia home, Hickory Hill, for months. They had become close friends during that time, and Seigenthaler was trusted as part of the Hickory Hill family. He remembers, with a smile, that Joseph Kennedy's feelings were more arm's length. The elder Kennedy worried that his son Robert would suffer the same cynicism about his authorship of *The Enemy Within* as John Kennedy had over the question of whether *Profiles in Courage* was written by him or his close aide, Theodore Sorensen. After hearing his father's admonitions repeatedly, Kennedy and Seigenthaler played a prank. Joseph Kennedy took them to dinner at a fine French restaurant in New York City to celebrate the completion of their work. Robert Kennedy brought him a copy of the finished manuscript, but he added a false cover page listing himself and Seigenthaler as the authors. Joseph Kennedy flew into a rage, pounded the table, and warned that the story would be in all the gossip columns the next day—while his young dinner guests enjoyed a long laugh.

Seigenthaler drove Kennedy around Washington to call on an eclectic group of knowledgeable insiders whose opinions on his future Kennedy solicited. Senator McClellan, his former boss, suggested that Kennedy become a law school dean, or write and practice law. Supreme Court justice William O. Douglas told Kennedy to go walking to clear his head of all the excitement and then teach. Attorney General William Rogers, the lame-duck Eisenhower appointee at Justice, told Kennedy the job was a big honor and a bigger headache. It was no fun dealing with the Senate, appointing judges, and doing all the drudgery required of an attorney general.

Only J. Edgar Hoover told Kennedy to take the job. But Kennedy told Seigenthaler and his wife, Ethel, as they discussed his day's consultations over a late dinner at Hickory Hill that he doubted Hoover's sincerity. Hoover probably presumed the president-elect was going to appoint his brother, and thus Hoover was playing smart politics by endorsing the inevitable. Ethel was braced for and supportive of his idea to leave government service, and Seigenthaler was ready to return to Nashville. Robert Kennedy called his brother at his home in Washington to let him know his decision. It was negative. "This will kill my father," Kennedy told his friend.

John Kennedy had a dinner guest and couldn't talk. He invited his younger brother to breakfast in Georgetown the following morning, asking him to hold off any decision until then, when they could "get this resolved."

Seigenthaler drove to Georgetown with his grim-faced, silent friend early the next morning. When they arrived at his brother's house, the president-elect was upstairs, but he soon joined them in the dining room downstairs, where the three men stood, drinking orange juice, making small talk. Then they sat at the dining table, and as their breakfast was served, John Kennedy looked directly at Seigenthaler and said, "Here's my position," as if he was arguing his case to Seigenthaler, rather than to his brother Robert. He described how Dean Rusk had persuaded Adlai Stevenson to become U.S. ambassador to the United Nations, with cabinet rank, despite Stevenson's displeasure over not being made secretary of state. He repeated Rusk's words to Stevenson: "I've signed on for this man's army and he's commander in chief and this's the job he's chosen for me and for you."

Seigenthaler realized the president-elect was doing a selling job on his still-silent younger brother. John Kennedy reported the sacrifices other cabinet appointees were making: McNamara gave up a huge corporate salary; Rusk gave up a foundation presidency. He commented about all the new appointees. Udall was terrific; he hardly knew Postmaster General Day; Abe Ribicoff was at HEW because they feared a Jewish attorney general would exacerbate the civil rights battles they predicted were coming.

Eventually, Robert interrupted: "Johnny, could we talk about my situation?" Finally, Jack Kennedy spoke directly to his brother. "You know, Bobby, there are people in my cabinet I don't know. They'll help, but they don't know my point of view. A relative is different. None of them can do for me what you can do for me. I need someone who, in difficult times, will tell me the absolute truth. You're the best person to deal with organized crime. You've got the courage to take on businessmen under the antitrust laws. When things are tough and the administration is in trouble, I'll need you more than anyone else. The president needs someone to tell the unvarnished truth not hedged by anyone else's self-interests. With you, there's no need to have job insurance. I can't be sure with anyone else. If I have the right to ask the other cabinet members to make sacrifices, I can tell you I want you to be attorney general."

His coffee finished, the younger brother attempted to reply: "I've got some points I'd like to make." But he never got to make his case. The president-elect already had risen from the table, and smilingly concluded: "OK, General, let's grab our balls and go out and tell them."

But the press had to wait one more day for the official announcement. Robert Kennedy and Seigenthaler drove home quietly, told Ethel what had happened, said little; there was little left to be said. The following morning, December 16, 1960, at 11 A.M., John F. Kennedy stepped outside in front of his Georgetown house on N Street in Washington, D.C., to greet a throng of reporters and cameramen who had gathered. That same day, the announcement of the appointments of four other top officials had been made on those steps. Now the handsome president-elect was accompanied by his younger brother, who looked a bit sheepish, shy, showing a slight, uncertain grin. "Comb your hair, Bobby," he'd told his kid brother as they walked outside. "You're going to be the next attorney general of the United States."

"Don't smile too much," the droll president added in a whisper, "or they'll think we are happy about the appointment." Robert Kennedy would be the next attorney general, he told the waiting news people, then said impishly that his brother needed some solid legal experience and this job surely would provide it.

To observers in the general public, it was a questionable appointment. The extraordinarily powerful J. Edgar Hoover was cynical about the official who in the department hierarchy would be his new "boss." He remarked to one of his aides, William Sullivan, that Kennedy had the perfect qualifications for this cabinet job: He had managed the campaign, never practiced law, and never tried a case in court.

All but Kennedy's closest friends and aides predicted he would be over his head as an important cabinet member, in charge of Justice no less. The Justice Department is not an agency with a constituency—like Agriculture or Commerce—but rather one with broad jurisdiction, and a special need to be nonpolitical. The attorney general acts as the nation's chief law enforcement officer as well as the principal legal advisor to the president. Recent history has demonstrated that, inevitable as it is for presidents to operate under that presumption in making their appointments to this cabinet post, such a combination of roles is often untenable, and not in the public interest. Robert Kennedy's appointment provided the quintessential example of built-in conflict. Indeed, years later, Congress passed a law forbidding a president's family members from serving in the Cabinet.

While it is quite understandable why John Kennedy wanted his trusted brother at his side, perhaps an appointment as White House counsel or as a special assistant with roving responsibilities would have made more sense.

The president has the constitutional duty to see that the laws are "faithfully executed." He does so through an attorney general who oversees a department that came into existence in 1870 and in 1961 had a $400 million budget and more than 30,000 employees (currently there are more than 100,000 employees, of whom more than 7,000 are lawyers, and the annual budget is over $13 billion.) The attorney general has vast and varied responsibilities: investigating and prosecuting federal crimes; representing the government in all its civil litigation and in all its Supreme Court cases, advising the president and cabinet on legal questions; managing a burgeoning collection of bureaus and agencies as disparate as the Bureau of Prisons, the Immigration and Naturalization Service, and the Federal Bureau of Investigation; supervising the country's U.S. attorneys and U.S. marshals; assisting with the department's and the administration's legislative programs; and screening and evaluating federal judges. The attorney general has more patronage at his or her disposal—appointing judges and U.S. attorneys, as well as others in the department—than any other cabinet member.

John Kennedy was not the first president to want a devoted attorney general. Presidents traditionally have used attorneys general as private counselors in troubled times. President Andrew Jackson told his attorney general, Roger Taney, to solve a problem in the way he wanted "or I will find an Attorney General who will." One book on the federal legal system, in noting that "the flavor of politics hangs about the opinions of the Attorney General," quotes Henry Clay's prescient comment that "the pestilential atmosphere of Washington" can lead to the discrediting of an attorney general's opinions.

The ideal standard of the Justice Department, first enunciated by a former solicitor general, Simon Sobeloff, is that the department's goal is not victory (Robert Kennedy's reputed lodestone) but justice (not his reputation in 1960). Of course, defining and achieving that noble standard, especially in contentious situations, is highly subjective and subject to compromise.

Before and after Robert Kennedy's appointment, men who had served presidential candidates as campaign managers were subsequently appointed attorney general by their successful clients—Herbert Brownell by Eisenhower, and John Mitchell by Richard Nixon, for example. But Robert Kennedy's blood relationship with John Kennedy made his appointment the most controversial example of this disquieting phenomenon. As one serious analysis of the Department of Justice concluded: "The appointment of such a person is at odds with the kind of image which should accompany the office of the Attorney General; it is inconsistent with an atmosphere conducive to the Attorney General's functioning in an even-handed way, free from distorting influences."

There was the question of ideology and temperament, as well. Robert Kennedy had a reputation for being blind to constitutional protections. It wasn't that he was against civil liberties, one government source told Gore Vidal (who wrote about Kennedy in *Esquire* magazine); "it's just that he doesn't know what they are." His brief but notorious past was catching up with him.

The highly regarded Yale law professor Alexander M. Bickel made the critical case against RFK's appointment as attorney general in the January 9, 1961, *New Republic*. There, Bickel articulated the general distrust of Robert Kennedy that many others felt at that time. Kennedy abused his powers as Rackets Committee counsel, Bickel argued, by leading punitive expeditions and subverting the administration of justice by using his powers to damage and destroy witnesses. His questioning was not civil; it was a "purposeful punishment by publicity," Bickel wrote. However loathsome the witnesses might have been, Bickel argued, and many other respectable critics agreed, it was an abuse of investigating powers to accuse, judge, and condemn people. The congressional investigative power was "a kind of wild horse in the American constitutional system," Bickel said, and Kennedy abused it. Kennedy's campaign to cleanse unions of their corruption took on the glow of demagoguery that harkened back to his earlier work for Senator Joseph McCarthy and confirmed fears that Kennedy, too, could turn out to be an abusive official.

"The sum of it all," Bickel stated, "is that Mr. Kennedy appears to find congenial the role of prosecutor, judge, and jury, all consolidated in his one efficient person." His tunnel vision, his self-righteousness, his ends-over-means ardor, his public record to that date, rendered Kennedy unfit for the office of attorney general, Bickel concluded. He had put forth a troubling case that disturbed many Americans, including me, who were otherwise excited by the prospects of a vital "new frontier" in government as administrations were about to change.

It is interesting to reflect today, in a time when skepticism and harsh inquiry characterize the appointment process, how this appointment could have survived in 1960. There was a brief hearing on January 13, 1961, before the Senate Judiciary Committee. He was introduced, inaccurately, by the interim senator from Massachusetts, Ben Smith (who held the office briefly between John Kennedy and Ted Kennedy), as "Robert Fitzgerald Kennedy." The candidate was praised by his former boss, Senator McClellan. J. Edgar Hoover had reported to the committee that the FBI's investigation of the candidate disclosed "no information which reflects on his character, reputation, or integrity." Chairman Everett Dirksen had commented, in opening the hearing, that he considered young Kennedy a friend; he remembered "the excellent work you did on the McCarthy Committee."

Kennedy followed, describing his earlier Justice Department work on loyalty and espionage cases, endearing him to some observers but confirming the worst fears held by his liberal doubters. His comments sounded rather insipid: Politics should play no part in the attorney general's work; he had strong feelings against corruption and dishonesty; the Justice Department should set up a group to fight organized crime as it had in the past to combat Communism and subversion. Organized crime and internal security seemed to be his two sole frames of reference.

After only perfunctory questioning by the Senate Judiciary Committee, and lame answers to soft questions, Robert F. Kennedy was confirmed by a 99–1 vote. Only Senator Gordon Allott, a Republican from Colorado, voted against Kennedy's confirmation. Three hours after the senate vote, at the ripe old age of thirty-four, one day after his brother's inauguration, he was sworn in as the sixty-fourth attorney general, along with the rest of the new Cabinet.

The outgoing attorney general, William Rogers, provided Kennedy and his first few aides—Seigenthaler, Walter Sheridan, and his secretary, Angie Novello—a suite of rooms one floor below the capacious office Robert Kennedy would soon occupy, so they could begin their transition. As a wry reminder of their earlier conversation in November, Rogers left him a welcoming present: a large bottle of aspirin.

No one could have anticipated that, though his tenure would be precipitously cut short, Robert Kennedy would serve longer than most attorneys general in the history of the Department of Justice, in the most exciting and demanding of times, and that in this highly visible, unusually dramatic role he would grow from the consummate insider into a major public figure in his own right.

Chapter 2

RECRUITMENT OF A

ROOKIE PROSECUTOR

During that same period, shortly after the election of John F. Kennedy, I sat deep in conversation with a friend in a noisy, smoky tavern in Greenwich Village, a neighborhood drop-in place with sawdust on the floor and strong ale on tap. We were enjoying a mugful of the house brew on our way home. Formerly roommates at Yale Law School, Bruce Cohen had recently graduated, and I was at work counseling a civil rights group and writing a book. Bruce tried to persuade me to come with him to Washington to find a job with the recently elected New Frontier.

"Not me. I never could see living in Washington; too dull a town. You can't see the Knicks and Giants; you can't take the Sunday *Times* to bed on Saturday night. Besides, it's the South. I don't know anyone there. Nah!"

"But it's exciting now. Mike Purtschuk's gone to work as a legislative assistant for Senator Neuberger. Arthur Fleischer's working as Bill Carey's executive assistant at the SEC. Cliff Alexander is in the White House."

"Washington is not for me. Besides, what would I do there?"

"You've tried criminal cases in the Air Force. Your specialty is criminal justice. How about working for Bobby Kennedy?"

"Are you kidding? Look, I was for Adlai Stevenson. I'd have preferred Hubert Humphrey. And there's no way I'd be a good prosecutor. Especially working for someone who worked for Joe McCarthy. Bobby Kennedy frightens me."

"Come down on the train with me for the day. I've got a few interviews. What do you have to lose? Just give it a look."

"Forget it, Bruce. You go; I'm going to be a law professor."

I was resolute. Washington seemed too monochromatic. Government work was not in my frame of reference; it was for bureaucrats who couldn't get real jobs or make it on their own. The only person in my family who had worked for the government was an uncle, a scientist working on secret research in Los Alamos—so secret no one in the family had seen or heard much of him for decades. The curtain hadn't gone up yet on Camelot, and the whole Washington and Kennedy scene seemed remote.

———

As we rode the train home to New York from Washington several weeks later, Bruce smiled. "Resolute," he said. "You sure were so resolute about not coming with me to Washington." We laughed.

As I recall our conversation and the impromptu trip now, I think how innocent young people can be of the ultimate import in what seem to be no more than simple daily decisions.

"Now, aren't you glad you came?"

I *was* glad, and puzzled. I was pleased because I'd gone to see one of my legal heroes, Justice Hugo Black, who took me to lunch at the Supreme Court dining room. How could I be blasé about that? And I was puzzled because, though I had not come looking for a job, I just might have been offered one. I was bemused, still trying to sort out what exactly had happened.

A twenty-seven-year-old lawyer living in the Village, I viewed Washington, D.C., and the New Frontier team from a perspective that was distant and distorted. I had no contacts with either Kennedy, and had not worked in the presidential campaign. I had recently passed the New York and California bars, spent three years in the Air Force Judge Advocate General's Corps trying courts-martial, and returned to Yale Law School, where I finished my master's degree in law and was working on my doctoral dissertation.

But I was confused about exactly what I wanted to do at that moment. I had enjoyed the drama of trying cases during my Air Force experience, and I had been successful at it. As for teaching law, I was told by those in the profession that a true academic was supposed to be ready to go anywhere and teach any subject, for the sheer intellectual challenge and the joy of teaching. But I wanted to teach only criminal law and civil liberties, and only in interesting cities at top-notch law schools. And I wasn't the kind of genius who could write his own ticket, so it seemed unlikely that the perfect teaching job was going to fall into my lap.

What had come my way, however, was an offer of a fellowship at New York University Law School. The Arthur Garfield Hays Civil Liberties Program administrators had heard about my work at Yale on a book about the contempt power. They offered me a stipend and two assistants to continue my work at NYU, and helped me get a part-time job at a civil rights organization to complete my schedule and supplement my meager income. So there I had been in New York City, reading about the Kennedy election like everyone else and wondering what to do with my life.

When my ex-roommate persisted in urging me to join him on his quick trip to Washington, I decided to go. It was a lark, a chance to visit with an old pal, and possibly to persuade Justice Hugo Black to write a foreword to my nearly completed book. Columbia University Press had agreed to publish it, and Yale Law School had agreed to accept it to complete my doctoral degree. This lark evolved in more substantial ways that I never dreamed of at the time.

Lunch with Justice Black in the Supreme Court dining room had been a delight; he praised my book, though he declined to write the foreword. He thought doing so might create potential conflicts in cases that might come before the Court. Our farewells completed, he returned to work in his chambers and I went to join Bruce at the Justice Department, where we had agreed to meet for the trip home.

First, I dropped in on a Justice Department lawyer, one that a law school friend had referred me to, just to say hello, and kill time until Bruce was ready to return to New York. In her office we talked first about academic matters and eventually about what was going on at the Department of Justice. We discussed the recent appointment of a young, dynamic New York prosecutor to run the Organized Crime and Racketeering Section, reportedly Robert Kennedy's main interest in the new department. By chance, I had just read of him—Edwyn Silberling was his name—on the train ride from New York to Washington. She asked if I'd like to meet him. She picked up her phone, and suddenly I was in Silberling's office.

The New York Times that day had profiled Silberling, so I knew a little about him. A "dedicated foe of crime," he had come to Kennedy's attention as a special prosecutor in Suffolk County, Long Island, prosecuting political "skulduggery." During the campaign, he had been an active member of his local Citizens for Kennedy group, where he'd met its director, Byron White, and Robert Kennedy. After the election, Robert Kennedy offered Silberling the U.S. attorneyship in his area, but when local politicians objected, he invited him to Washington to become chief of the organized crime section. A former assistant in the office of New York City district attorney Frank Hogan, Silberling was committed to his antiracketeering mission. "This is the kind of job you take, not for the money," he had told the *Times,* "but for the challenge of the opportunity to do something that has to be done." Silberling, charismatic, energetic, open, and engaging, was just the man to head Kennedy's pet project.

We hit it off well: It turned out he too had been born in Jersey City, nine years before I had, and had served in the Air Force; he too enjoyed playing competitive, if small-stakes, poker. Surprisingly, he talked for a long time about what he wanted to do with this special band of prosecutors in the department's organized crime section. Silberling had no experience in federal law enforcement, but came from an active prosecutorial background in New York City where Thomas Dewey and Frank Hogan had conducted notably successful rackets bureaus. His fundamental plan was for his lawyers to coordinate major criminal investigations, spend time in the cities where the action was, and handle their own grand juries, trials, and appeals.

The crimes and criminals Silberling and Robert Kennedy had targeted were clearly defined, well organized, and well financed: gambling, prostitution, loan sharking, and narcotics activities. Silberling's staff of rackets lawyers would focus on the interstate and international aspect of organized crime. Violent crime was not the crime of choice for members of organized crime syndicates, not their specific business, though they used it widely as a tool of control and a means to move into legitimate businesses. They engaged in public corruption wherever they operated.

I found myself drawn by his new challenge, intrigued by his plans, and moved by his commitment—which was contagious. Silberling asked about my own legal background and plans. He asked if I'd ever tried criminal cases, and I told him about my three years in the Air Force judge advocate general's program prosecuting or defending many courts-martial. Nothing about being a lawyer provides the rush of excitement and intellectual focus that trying cases does, I admitted.

When I told Silberling that I intended to teach criminal law, he abruptly asked: "Why not *do it* for a while before going off and talking about it?" Not quite realizing the import of his question, I replied, neutrally, that his was an interesting idea.

"Come join us," he said. "We're doing something important and worthwhile, something that can make a real difference, with real people, in the real world."

"I'll think about it," I replied, backing off.

While struck by his zeal, I was not entirely serious, nor sure I was even being offered a job.

These guys are hot-shot activists, I thought. I remembered reading that when President Kennedy offered noted Harvard law professor Paul Freund the solicitor generalship, Freund turned it down because he wanted to continue editing a massive and authoritative history of the Supreme Court. "I'm sorry. I'd hoped you would prefer making history to writing it," the president had replied. There was something seductive about these Kennedys and their key team players, an ebullient optimism, plus an activism that suddenly seemed the opposite of the academic life.

Even so, over the next ten days I rather perfunctorily and not too seriously filled out the Department of Justice forms Silberling mailed to me. I felt no real commitment to the Kennedy administration nor any abiding interest in joining the Justice Department. *My* father wasn't pushing *me* there.

Then, out of the blue, I received the formal offer of a job with the organized crime section, for a vast sum, over $10,000 a year, more than I'd ever earned or was likely to earn teaching law.

I had to think about trying it. Perhaps, I should do it for a year, and then, with some experience under my belt and my first book published, I would teach. Still, I had two big hang-ups. I'd never seen myself as a hard-nosed district attorney type; my self-image was as a fiery defense lawyer—a modern Clarence Darrow, not a Bobby Kennedy–like prosecutor. I had enjoyed defending court-martial cases more than prosecuting them, and I was not at all sure I had the toughness, the fire in my belly that Kennedy and Silberling would be looking for.

The other problem was that while I thought Silberling was a nifty guy, dynamic and knowledgeable, I thought Robert Kennedy was a potential despot whose appointment as attorney general was outrageous. His father was influential and represented everything I disliked, and while his brother was a charming figure, the meaning of his presidency was questionable. If fascinated by Robert Kennedy's unique potential, I was frightened by his limited but flamboyant quasi-legal experiences and by his reputation for ruthlessness.

I probably would not have taken the Washington job if the right law school had called and asked me to teach. None did. It was time to move, and a surprising option had become available. Admittedly, there was a pull—others felt it more than I, but I was not immune to it—toward the presumptuousness and idealistic promise of the New Frontier. There is a recurring undertow when administrations change and public attention focuses on who will do what job in the new government.

My roommate never did go to Washington, opting instead to practice law in Connecticut. But, in an ironic twist, I did.

What the hell, I decided, it's only a short-term commitment. While I worked at my jobs and continued research for my book in New York, my wife, Joanne, drove to Washington and found us a pleasant place to rent in Alexandria, Virginia. We had trepidations about living in this small, sleepy Southern town, though for the same rent that we paid for a one-bedroom apartment, a third-floor walk-up, on West 11th Street in New York City, we were able to rent a whole townhouse with a garden in back and a flowering cherry tree in front on a charming quiet street, South Lee Street (could one live on *North* Lee Street in the old Confederacy? In the town that was Lee's boyhood home?) For one year I could endure the culture shock of living someplace where you couldn't buy a drink or a bagel, where segregation was still in place and the last-place Washington Senators were the home team. Drab, monolithic, governmental Washington would do for a year; I'd temporarily replace the Hudson River with the Potomac one street away; then I'd be off to some picture-book college town.

So it was that, filled with contradictory emotions about being a professional prosecutor and particularly a Bobby Kennedy cop, and with deep reservations about the strange place where we would be living and working, I showed up for work in the spring of that year, of my life, and of the new Kennedy administration.

Chapter 3

―――――――――

THE EMERGENCE OF

ROBERT KENNEDY

In the Eisenhower Republican years pre-1961, Washington, D.C., must still have been a quiet, small, conservative, mostly segregated, one-business town. The monuments are beautiful but the office architecture was bureaucrat boring, and life downtown stopped early as carpools and buses transported government workers home to the suburbs of Virginia and Maryland and the residential enclaves of Washington. But John F. Kennedy's election brought glamour, new brain power and young professionals, extraordinary media attention, and an excitable, optimistic generation of Democrats to the capital. Quickly, a newly energized bureaucracy seemed to become a place of can-do activism. The town itself began to come alive, socially and culturally, personified best by the elegant first lady, Jacqueline Kennedy, and the élan of White House parties peopled by artists, writers, musicians, and sports and entertainment figures. Robert Kennedy was the second most celebrated star in the new administration, and his daily diary was evidence of his constant contacts with top politicians, journalists, and Hollywood personalities. He hosted seminars on serious subjects at his home, and was seen at the "best" parties.

We younger recruits lived on the outskirts of what later would be called Camelot, but not so far from its center that we couldn't feel the glow.

To my surprise, I found that I enjoyed Washington and living in Alexandria. Law school friends were in town. The city that seemed drab and dull from afar was easy to enjoy and socially active.

In the beginning, I spent all day at the Department of Justice learning the prosecutorial ropes, and most nights at home completing my book. Soon, over lunches in Washington and at Yale Law School meetings, with old friends from school and new friends from faraway states who had come to work for Congress or on burgeoning new programs or at the White House, I was swapping stories and socializing at frequent dinner parties. Everybody was from someplace else, so friends replaced family in ways that made friendships grow fast.

I found myself catching Potomac fever. I went to the opening-day baseball game to see the Washington Senators, now defunct and not much better then, though they were the capital's home team. Life was full of work, and of promise. I began to feel connected to a center of action. My doubts about taking the job were evaporating. Before long, I was feeling gung ho.

The president, exhorting the nation in his inaugural address to ask not what the country could do for them but what they could do for their country, got a palpable response. Newton Minow, the chief of the Federal Communications Commission, sought to enliven the discussion and enrich the possibilities of television by characterizing the existing state of the art as "a vast wasteland." "Whiz kids" from industry were recruited to streamline and modernize the defense agencies. Activist academics such as John Kenneth Galbraith, Walt Whitman Rostow, Arthur Schlesinger, Jr., and Archibald Cox were recruited to major posts around government. Sargent Shriver, a dashing Kennedy brother-in-law, headed the new Peace Corps, which sent altruistic volunteers to exotic and faraway countries, offering American expertise—or at least an American hand. And the beat of the oncoming civil rights revolution could already be heard. My friends and I would soon march to the Lincoln Memorial and listen to Reverend King's emotional dream.

At Justice, it quickly became clear that Robert Kennedy wanted a quality team and would give them support and independence. RFK knew Byron White from his work with the Citizens for Kennedy.

After the election, John Kennedy had asked White to be part of the new administration and White was interested. Byron White was the first person Robert Kennedy called when he returned from his breakfast with the president-elect and John Seigenthaler.

As a Denver attorney with good ties to the American Bar Association, and an extraordinary record as an athlete and Rhodes Scholar, White seemed to be the perfect complement to the controversial choice of the young Robert Kennedy at the Justice Department. White told me he never doubted Robert Kennedy would be a good attorney general, despite his obvious lack of legal experience. "He knew Congress," White explained, "and I knew he would be good at running a department that would be involved in everything the new government did."

The night after the decision was made that he would be John Kennedy's attorney general, Robert Kennedy called White. In a five-way phone conversation between Hickory Hill and Colorado, Kennedy asked White to think about becoming his deputy, though other good job offers would surely come his way in the new administration. As Ethel Kennedy and John Seigenthaler listened in to White and his wife, White said: "Are you there Marion? Unless you disagree, I think Justice is where the action is going to be. That's where I want to be!"

Kennedy had his first acceptance immediately (his second actually, as Seigenthaler had already agreed to postpone his return to journalism and to stay on as Kennedy's administrative assistant). White's loyalty would be rewarded two years later when he became President Kennedy's first and only appointee to the U.S. Supreme Court.

During the pre-inaugural period, Robert Kennedy used a small office provided by the holdover attorney general to begin recruiting his team of top advisors and close assistants. His secretary at the McClellan Committee, Angie Novello, learned of Kennedy's appointment to attorney general while she was vacationing in Rome in December 1960, resting after the hectic election campaign. When she returned in January 1961, she called her former employer to offer congratulations. Kennedy asked her to meet him at the Justice Department the next day. "How nice," she thought, "he's going to show me around his new offices where the transition is taking place." When they arrived at Kennedy's temporary office, phones were ringing, and Kennedy said, "Answer that, Angie." Today she recalls, "I did and I never left." Angie was never officially asked to take a job. "I was just *there*. It was up to me to take care of him, not the other way around." So Angie never stopped working as Kennedy's personal executive secretary.

Ed Guthman, a Pulitzer Prize–winning reporter with the *Seattle Times,* had worked with Kennedy and his McClellan Committee staff. Leery of him at first because of Kennedy's days with McCarthy, Ed had come to trust and admire his commitment and seriousness. "He kept his word, protected sources, did thorough investigations, didn't look for headlines." Guthman never thought he'd be anyone's assistant, but "Bob was different." When Kennedy asked Ed to come to Washington and take charge of the department's public information office, Ed came and stayed.

Byron White was Kennedy's point man in running the department and recruiting most of the top-level assistants. At his suggestion, highly qualified lawyers—many, as he, were Yale Law School graduates—were brought over from big Washington law firms to run the department's divisions—men like Burke Marshall and John Douglas and Louis Oberdorfer. From the academic world, Archibald Cox was brought aboard as solicitor general, and Nicholas Katzenbach as an assistant attorney general, Office of Legal Counsel.

Bob Kennedy himself recruited a Republican lawyer, Herbert Miller, to run the Criminal Division. "Jack" Miller had little criminal-law experience, but had been a lawyer for the Teamsters' court-appointed monitors. Kennedy called Jack in February, out of the blue. "My wife said to me one day when I came home from work, smiling, 'Honey, the children and I will stay with you.' " Jack didn't know "what the heck she was talking about. 'Oh, my God, what have I done?' " he asked her. She told him, " 'The attorney general wants to talk to you.' I called him at his office that night, saw him there the next morning, and was hired on the spot. He gave me two weeks to wrap up my law practice and start at Justice."

The tone at the top of the department was lustrous; the management team Kennedy recruited was youthful and smart. And Kennedy recognized and encouraged talent already on board; regardless of their politics, he wanted first-class talent. Kennedy used good sense in creating a staff of able assistants. Theodore White said, "I wouldn't characterize Bobby as an intellectual. I'd characterize him as something more important: the guy who can use intellectuals."

Kennedy had sound managerial instincts. For example, he put Burke Marshall in charge of the Civil Rights Division, which had been a quiet group but was soon to be thrust into the limelight. Marshall was highly regarded by White. Despite a lackluster personal interview, Kennedy hired him rather than the better-known and politically proven activist Harris Wofford—for an interesting reason. Kennedy thought the job should be filled by someone who was able but without any identification with or deep emotional involvement in the civil rights field.

While he brought in his own new leadership team and used them all in major departmental decision making, Kennedy also respected department veterans, whose good services he rewarded in simple but meaningful ways—an invitation to a White House reception or to accompany him when he testified before Congress. His press aide, Ed Guthman, recalled a thank-you note from a veteran clerical worker, Bessie Greene, whom Kennedy invited to a congressional hearing. She'd served ten attorneys general before him, working in the mimeograph office, and none had ever acknowledged her work. "This is what sets you apart from other men," she'd written. "You have a heart and you use it."

Kennedy noticed there were few black faces at Justice (10 of 950 lawyers), and personally pushed all department heads and U.S. attorneys around the country to change that fact.

The pace was swift and demanding and informal. His office, one recruit noticed during his first visit, was like a busy hotel lobby. "His appetite for work and information was insatiable," Guthman reflected. But he had a self-deprecating wit that modified the uptempo charge permeating the department. He'd tell groups of department lawyers, "I started in the department in 1950 as a young man, worked hard, studied, applied myself." Then he'd pause and smile, "And then my brother was elected president of the United States." Byron White noted that Kennedy did not run the department, unlike others had before him, like a big law office. "He's given it the sense of the public man."

———

Robert F. Kennedy epitomized the administration's activism, the optimism of youth, the vitality, allure, and tempo of the times. And his chief interest was in making the Justice Department's organized crime section an elite corps in the New Frontier. We quickly came to know that we were in the spotlight, in the crucible.

At one of our first staff meetings in Kennedy's office (meetings that would become regular events for us), when a general problem about the corrupt use of union pension funds was discussed, one young lawyer in our group chimed in with a suggestion. He'd written about this question for his law review and had an idea. After he spelled it out, Kennedy turned to Criminal Division head Jack Miller and said, nodding toward the rookie volunteer, "He's in charge. See that he does that." The young lawyer returned to his office and drafted what turned out to be 18 U.S.C. 1954, the Welfare and Pension Funds Amendments Act. He later received a pen the president had used to sign the new law; but he knew right then and there, at that early meeting—we all did—that if he had something to offer, he was part of the first team.

Not only did the Kennedys' charisma draw talented lawyers to the Justice Department; there would also be action, and the sense of a mission, of slaying dragons, of fighting for a good cause. Robert Kennedy had recruited Silberling early, and Ed wasted no time energizing the organized crime section. Months before his family could join him, Silberling had moved to Washington.

Given free rein to recruit his staff, Silberling was inundated with candidates from across the country. They had read about this adventure and wanted to be part of it. No one was hired because he had a famous name or a political connection. Silberling wanted noncareerists with trial experience. Laughingly, he told us later that after hiring Goldfarb, Goldberg, Subin, and a few other obviously Jewish lawyers, then bringing Bill Lynch aboard, Robert Kennedy inquired: "Where did *he* come from?"

Silberling's section quickly absorbed a handful of experienced members of the Criminal Division and, through aggressive recruitment, expanded the section from a handful of attorneys to what eventually became a growing band of active litigators, based in Washington, traveling to wherever the action was, and with special permanent squads working in New York, Chicago, Los Angeles, and Miami.

Experienced prosecutors from the U.S. attorney's office in New

York City and from the highly regarded New York City district attorney's office—Tom McBride, Jay Goldberg, Bill Lynch—found jobs with Silberling's new group. Up-and-coming lawyers from established private law firms, such as Henry Ruth from Philadelphia, left their profitable private-sector jobs to be part of Kennedy's public-spirited team. Others, outstanding students on their way to academic and judicial careers, like John Sprizzo, Bob Blakey, and Earl Johnson, took detours (as I had) to be part of the action. Blakey moved to organized crime from another section in the department where he had recently been selected for its honors program. President Kennedy was "bright and young and Catholic and Irish, and I'm all those things. So he was literally my president," he recalled to me. Robert Kennedy came in and changed the department from "a Republican law factory with a staid hierarchy," Blakey added, to a direct, action-oriented, personal place.

We young recruits became absorbed in our new city, new job, new life as part of this hot spot in the new government. Kennedy's personal contacts with us proved to be regular and direct. It soon became clear we were his alter egos and we'd have his attention. Once, one of my colleagues mentioned during a meeting in Kennedy's office that the IRS chief in the city where he was working was not especially cooperative. Kennedy looked toward an aide and said, "Take care of that." The next time that lawyer returned to his assigned city, the recalcitrant IRS officer was gone, and everyone in the office—most were many years his senior—stood up and all but clicked their heels when our colleague entered. Thereafter, everyone was *very* cooperative with our man. We had respect, power, authority—and it all derived at first from Kennedy. We had direct access to Kennedy, and we threw his name around when we needed to, or called on him when we needed help. We always got it.

———

In the interval between making my commitment and moving to Washington, I read whatever I could find written about organized crime. After arriving at the Justice Department, I combed its fifth-floor library for books and articles on the subject.

I learned that around the turn of the twentieth century, with the richness of the mass immigration to the United States from Europe came some Italian immigrants who had exotic, underworld backgrounds in secret old-world criminal societies. These regional organizations were known as the Black Hand, the Honored Society, N'Drangheta, the Camorra, and the Mafia. They specialized in local crimes, which they imported to their new country, mostly vice crimes such as prostitution, and loansharking (which was rigidly enforced). By the 1930s, when older members were purged from gang leadership by younger Sicilian and other American-born Italian racketeers, their activities came to include hijacking and then narcotics. Though some, paradoxically, viewed drugs as somehow immoral, eventually the high profits made it irresistible. Eventually, they became still more sophisticated and expanded into labor racketeering, political corruption, and white-collar crimes deriving from their takeovers of legitimate businesses. Organized crime had become big business, Daniel Patrick Moynihan pointed out: It was no longer to be viewed as "picaresque tales of individual acts."

These organizations used violence to enforce the regulation of their own underworld and to terrorize society; they were widely tolerated by (or they corrupted) local law enforcement agencies and for the first half of the century were largely ignored by federal prosecutors. Mafia violence was brutal, but it was not random and was usually confined to their own members, competitors, or those who failed to pay up. Drive-by shootings of competitors and sealing up bodies of informants in deserted buildings were common tactics. Sometimes, traitors were dispatched under more gruesome circumstances. One Chicago loan shark, suspected of informing on his mafia mentors (incorrectly, it turned out), was tortured for three days; the coroner reported the hapless employee, "Action" Jackson, was found impaled on a meat hook, having been cattle-prodded in the rectum and genitals, his limbs punctured with an ice pick, his penis incinerated, his body burned by a blowtorch. Finally, he was shot. These criminals were emphatic.

As the stakes grew higher, the deterrents used by the mob grew more violent. Key witnesses disappeared, were intimidated, or even eliminated. Juries were fixed or intimidated. In one narcotics case, a defendant threw a chair at the jury; in another, a jury foreman "accidentally" fell down the stairs and was injured. Lawyers, judges, police, district attorneys were paid off. Nothing was unthinkable, little left undone.

Individual families controlled cities or regions, sometimes collaborating with other ethnic groups or individuals (Jewish racketeers and hoodlums, especially, to my chagrin). This development was a perverse offshoot of the otherwise enriching phenomenon of the melting pot of the first half of this century. Most of the people in these ethnic groups lived decent, conventional lives and many eventually struggled into the middle class. But crime has always been an enticement to some members of disadvantaged groups because it is a way to obtain rewards and power quickly and disproportionately, if antisocially. It is still so.

By mid-century, large, very active criminal cartels operated in dozens of American cities. Their monopolistic syndicates seemed to be beyond government control and were expanding their spheres of activities. Members operated exclusive franchises in geographical areas, but they cooperated with and assisted one another. Robert Kennedy told of one mobster who offered to sell a one-half interest in the mayor of his city to a second mobster, but the mayor was blown up in gang warfare before the deal could be completed.

By the second half of the century, some of this story was becoming better known. The Senate hearings in 1950 and 1951, conducted by Tennessee senator Estes Kefauver, highlighted the problem of syndicated crime (and made him a household name, as well, perhaps hinting to the Kennedy brothers several years later that there was political pay dirt in conducting such publicized hearings). The Kefauver Committee reported that: "There is a sinister criminal organization known as the Mafia operating throughout the country." But its alarming conclusions did not galvanize the world of law enforcement as might have been expected. Local law enforcement did not have the resources to fight organized, interstate crime, and they were often corrupted by manipulative crime figures. And, with some exceptions, the federal government accomplished little or ignored the problem.

Later generations would learn about this criminal culture from specialists and defectors, from our group's experiences, and, after that, from a growing "godfather" literature on this subject; but in 1961 the implications were not yet widely recognized.

In 1954, the first organized crime and racketeering section at the Department of Justice—small and ineffective—had grown out of the Kefauver hearings. But there was no master plan to coordinate federal law enforcement activities, nor adequate resources to institutionalize any national effort. And many people—including influential members of the federal law enforcement establishment, particularly the FBI's J. Edgar Hoover—scoffed at the idea that anything like a Mafia existed in this country.

The American public would get a glimpse of what was truly a subterranean world of organized crime. On November 14, 1957, about 100 major mob members from fifteen states and from Cuba and Italy met at the palatial, fifty-three-acre country estate of Joseph Barbara, Sr., in the remote small town of Apalachin, New York. They had convened, it was later learned, to deal with intramural mob problems: the recent murder of mobster Albert Anastasia, the move into drug trafficking, and gambling investments in Cuba. As the prosecutor who would soon investigate this criminal conclave later reported: "Never before had there been such a concentration of jailbirds, murderers free on technicalities, and big wheels in gambling and dope rackets."

A state trooper who noticed suspicious activity in this quiet rural town followed a hunch and discovered a caravan of out-of-state cars at the Barbara estate. When he was spotted the convention broke up, and some attendees fled while others (about fifty) were arrested.

The surprise spectacle of the mass arrests gave credence to the controversial claim that a far-flung national crime syndicate did exist. The FBI, denying the reality of organized crime, nonetheless soon started a "top hoodlum" information-gathering program. Hoover still remained skeptical about the existence of the Mafia and had been less than aggressive about pursuing its members than was the Bureau of Narcotics.

In April 1958, the deputy attorney general, Lawrence E. Walsh (years later he would become the independent counsel of the Iran-Contra scandal), set up an Attorney General's Special Group on Organized Crime to investigate and prosecute any criminal activity at Apalachin and to investigate the problem of organized crime generally. A small group of almost two dozen lawyers were recruited to coordinate a federal attack on this criminal empire. Its leaders soon found their task unenviable: Law enforcement bureaucrats felt threatened and provided reluctant cooperation; "the FBI gave us the cold shoulder," the deputy director of the group later reported; they found a dearth of intelligence and a lack of coordination of federal agencies;

and they were criticized by civil liberties groups for impinging on the constitutional right of peaceful assembly and for overreaching and prosecuting notorious characters on insubstantial charges.

What the special group did do was indict twenty of the attendees for conspiring with forty-three other nonindicted conspirators to thwart and obstruct the investigation of Apalachin by cooking up an incredible common story about what was going on at Barbara's estate. An eight-week trial, whose record ran to six thousand pages, and in which no defendants testified, resulted in a mass conviction. The convicts included such notorious characters as Santos Trafficante, Jr., Carmine Lombardozzi, Vito Genovese, Joseph Profaci, and Joseph Bonanno. Trial judge Irving Kaufman sentenced the defendants to from three to five years in prison. He commented that their probation reports "read like a tale of horrors," and that they had "attempted to corrupt and infiltrate the political mainstreams of our country."

The group's reward for its efforts was to be disbanded in April 1959, shortly before the trial, after which the trial team of prosecutors also departed. But Milton Wessel, the head of the special group, testified before Congress and spoke out publicly about the need for a permanent office on syndicated crime to coordinate all organized crime prosecution efforts nationally. Wessel disagreed with the McClellan Committee's (and Robert Kennedy's) view that the answer to the organized crime problem was the creation of a national investigative crime commission. A prosecutive agency with power to coordinate and *follow up* investigations was the answer, he urged, or the country would never match the power and ingenuity of organized crime syndicates. They had gone "big league," he warned, and become an extraordinarily wealthy, powerful, and elusive "monster."

A New York State investigation in 1958 had disclosed that the mob was also infiltrating legitimate businesses and perverting union operations. Eight hoodlums served sentences for refusing to testify before that New York commission, which offered them immunity from prosecution if they testified. No one did.

Wessel's trial success turned out to be "a first-act victory," and as so often had been the case, the mobsters walked away free men. In November 1960, the federal Court of Appeals reversed all the Apalachin convictions because there was insufficient evidence that any laws were being broken at the gathering, or that during the forty-minute period between 12:40 and 1:20 P.M., when they were spotted and dispersed, the defendants all mutually agreed to lie at subsequent potential investigations. The fact that bad people gather is not evidence that they do so for evil purposes, the court ruled. Likely as that presumption may be, it is not evidence of a crime. Collective culpability is not a legal basis for individual guilt in a court of law, the court ruled, and this case was too much like a shotgun conspiracy. "The administration of the criminal law is [not] in such dire straits that crash methods have become a necessity," one judge warned. What the special prosecutors thought was an ingenious stratagem the appeals court considered a civil liberties disaster. The mob's credo of *omerta* had served them well. Their silence was golden as they returned to their wicked work.

Federal surveillance soon disclosed Mafia meetings planned for other cities, New Orleans and Miami and New York. Robert Kennedy was working for the McClellan Committee at the time and was shocked to discover how little the Department of Justice knew about organized crime. He had seen evidence of what happens when corrupt unions clash with legitimate businesses and how public corruption naturally follows well-organized, high-stakes criminal activity. He was indignant, critical of the lack of federal action, and obviously impressed with Wessel's conclusions.

Many of these bits and pieces of information I was absorbing had been brought together and analyzed by Earl Johnson, one of my new colleagues. He had written his master's thesis and a series of articles on organized crime before coming to Justice in its honors program, which recruited outstanding law school graduates. Earl was working elsewhere in the department, but when his study of organized crime became known, he was recruited to our section.

Earl's academic study went beyond the popular folklore of organized crime, analyzing the national power structure of the crime syndicate and explaining its operations. He had described, on the basis of a vast amount of material, how this multibillion-dollar, carefully organized and brutally managed, national criminal organization operated. Its vast ill-gotten fortunes were infiltrating once-legitimate businesses such as the distribution of vending machines and juke boxes, liquor, and laundries. It was funded mostly from gambling profits and was enforced effectively by fear and violence.

We soon learned from our daily reports how violent and deadly was the world of organized crime. In April 1961, two rackets figures, who had been convicted of obstruction of justice for attempting to murder a witness, went on a radio talk show to complain about their judge and about Robert Kennedy and his "special" prosecutors who were prejudiced against citizens of Italian descent. A former U.S. attorney was kidnapped and pistol-whipped for problems arising out of a planned "fix" of an SEC investigation. In Canton, Ohio, a rackets figure was found in the trunk of his car so badly burned he could barely be identified. A suspect in the bombing killing of another racketeer was killed; he was being deported by the INS at the time. A New Jersey hoodlum and violent shylock was jailed for severely beating a Denver businessman. In a Chicago shootout, an escaping narcotics law violator shot and severely wounded a narcotics agent, who returned fire and killed him. In Detroit, a narcotics informant's head was blown off. When an FBI agent surveilled the funeral services of a member of the notorious Lombardozzi family, two nephews and a brother of the deceased beat him up. A witness in a narcotics case in New York was slain. Another witness in a labor case was killed and his wife wounded in a bowling alley parking lot. A Chicago ex-cop killed a Narcotics Bureau informant. In Florida, one witness in a stolen-bonds case shot and killed another. A West Virginia gambler was car-bombed and suffered a severed arm and leg. In Denver, after a convicted gambler offered to cooperate with the government and provide information about other gamblers, he was murdered. In New York, a government witness was shot and seriously wounded in his automobile from a passing car.

Earl Johnson's study endorsed the points Kennedy himself had made during and after his work on the McClellan Committee. In addition to the obvious legal and moral dimensions of organized crime, it had become a deadly and continuing economic monopoly. It could destroy the free enterprise system by perniciously affecting businessmen, labor, and private citizens having no relation to the criminal underworld. Perhaps worst of all, the syndicate's tentacles inevitably reached public officials who had to be co-opted from enforcing the laws in order for the criminal syndicates to operate flagrantly. The public, seeing this, became cynical and disillusioned and lost respect for the law. As a result, it was not hyperbolic to fear that the impact of organized crime, if unchecked, could do nothing less than undercut the very life of our democracy.

Earl Johnson's study was informative and frightening, and his findings stunning: "America has never lost a war. Nevertheless it has been put to plunder for half a century. At the hands of organized crime, America has endured the exaction of billions every year, the stifling of free competition in hundreds of markets, the maiming and murder of countless human beings, the systematic cultivation of human weaknesses in our population, the fostering of thousands of derivative crimes, the corruption of sports, the subversion of democratic institutions, and the crumbling of moral supports. This is a horrible price for American society to pay. And yet organized crime continues unquashed and largely unscathed."

In their writings, Johnson and others showed clearly how these criminal organizations functioned. They had common features. The organization was continuous. Members were easily and endlessly replaceable. Management insulated itself by seldom committing any overt acts, by using "fronts," by strong-armed enforcement of silence through fear and reprisal, by a social-welfare system of its own to support loyal members, by executives living in jurisdictions other than where their operations took place (partly to stymie local law enforcement), and by buying or coercing cooperation from local politicians who had the power to interfere with their profitable monopolies—and thus neutralizing genuine attempts at law enforcement.

As Robert Kennedy had urged in his speeches and writings (and experts on this subject agreed), public ignorance and apathy had to be ended for good; we had to go beyond the common but harmful misperception that systematic violations of laws of "social regulation" were not important or dangerous; it was naive for the public to think that there was no relation between vice and the other forms of criminal activity that were its subdivisions—assault, extortion, bribery, murder. There was a widespread but misguided attitude that vice was inherent in people and ought to be left alone, that the government couldn't legislate and shouldn't enforce morality, and that those who advocated doing so were overreaching moralists if not misguided hypocrites. This same liberal mantra is heard today by commentators who urge that the way to cut crime rates, for example, is to legalize drugs.

Kennedy's crusade would run head-first into these attitudes, and it could not succeed if it did not change the public perception through education as much as prosecution. The American public did not yet see the racketeers' power to do pervasive evil, but would be responsive when confronted directly with a clear look at their growing power and its harshly inhumane and ubiquitous consequences.

Kennedy, who meant to be a visible as well as avid attorney general, would use his office as a bully pulpit to get this story out to Americans. And he would prove to be good at this. He was soon testifying frequently before Congress. He gave speeches around the country. He cultivated the media, cajoling them to get his message about organized crime before the American public. It was not only indictments that were needed—we'd take care of that, he said—but an end to indifference. We needed everyone's help. He reminded businessmen, when they invited him to speak, "I can't think of a case where a union became corrupt by itself. Management always is involved, too." The majority of the press liked the Kennedys, and Robert Kennedy's favorites from the media were given special access to the department, and were included in the family's fun and games after work hours. They responded as he hoped, and from the start, we got good press. The story might get through to the public.

What I had read in libraries and journals was rather general and presented an essentially intellectual view of the subject. It filled in the blanks, in a general way, about what one intuitively speculated. To be against organized crime, after all, required no leap of faith; to be for motherhood and abhor the brotherhood were obvious choices. It wasn't until I began reading departmental reports about specific people and real events, and hearing from my new colleagues about their experiences in small towns and big cities, that I began to feel something personal about the fight I was about to join.

The idea that official corruption can contaminate a town is one that anyone can understand at a theoretical level. But to learn about what happens to real people when the law enforcement world is corrupt offered me a whole new perspective. Women molested in police stations in towns like Newport, Kentucky, where the police were crooked and no one stopped their lawlessness and complaints ended with new ordeals for the complainer—the actuality of episodes like this gave flesh and blood to the words "official corruption." Incidents where honest police attempting to enforce the law were ridiculed by their colleagues, viciously beaten, and driven from their jobs, drove home the realities. It doesn't take long in such places before the bad drives out the good and incidental corruption becomes complete. When reform-minded lawyers are rebuffed in their efforts to fight the system and decide to join the other side, there soon becomes only one side. These kinds of incidents occurred regularly in places where the law was corrupted; this would be the case in the town in which I would find myself.

Studying organized crime, I became convinced that Kennedy was pursuing an appropriate, if formidable, target. No doubt, Attorney General Kennedy's perception of what he was planning to do was colored by his Senate Rackets Committee hearings and his clashes there with crooked union bosses. Committee counsel Kennedy had his victories over pernicious labor leaders such as Dave Beck and his frustrations with other corrupt labor leaders like Jimmy Hoffa. He had come away from these experiences with the attitude that the disease in the workplaces of the nation struck at America's basic values. Because the problem was fundamental and growing more serious, Kennedy believed passionately that its solutions must be uncompromising and aggressively enforced.

On the McClellan Committee, Kennedy had pushed for and got reforms of existing labor laws. He exhorted his congressional committee staff, the press, and anyone or any group who would listen, his longtime press aide Ed Guthman recalls. "We have to be successful because it can't be any other way," RFK lectured them, turning up the rhetorical temperature. "Either we are going to be successful or they are going to have the country." The relationship among the mob, public corruption, and law enforcement was becoming his crusade; in Kennedy's mind it was the paramount domestic problem the country faced at the turn of the decade into the 1960s. In his book *The Enemy Within,* written after his McClellan Committee experiences and before he became attorney general, Kennedy had written, in words that seem dated but remain apt today:

It seems to me imperative that we reinstill in ourselves the toughness and idealism that guided the nation in the past. The paramount interest in self, in material wealth, in security must be replaced by an actual, not just a vocal, interest in our country, by a spirit of adventure, a will to fight what is evil, and a desire to serve. It is up to us as citizens to take the initiative as it has been taken before in our history, to reach out boldly but with honesty to do the things that need to be done.

His words sounded sensible to me, but not to everyone. His "ruthless" label clung to him, and his zealousness about Hoffa hovered over all our initial efforts. Whenever I mentioned where I was working, the cynical reaction invariably was "Oh, you're on the Get Hoffa Squad!" But, as I was learning, the Kennedy crusade against organized crime was to be much more than that. Labor racketeering may have been what Kennedy knew most about, and indeed that was one priority for our group; but much more than labor cases developed when our group got going.

A gradual revisionism began to develop in my outlook about, for instance, gambling. On its face gambling appeared to be a victimless offense, hypocritical to outlaw because "we all do it." Didn't our own organized crime group have a regular poker game? But, as noted, gambling had become the basis, the extraordinarily lucrative bankroll, for all the rackets, and for the public corruption that invariably succumbed to them.

Gambling financed the biggest business in the country. It was the mob's treasury, its banker. According to one survey, it grossed close to 10 percent of the national income. The gambling syndicates paid no taxes to the legitimate government, which all other citizens financed, but rather paid its own form of "tax" to corrupt officials who worked for these private masters and for their private gain. In effect, gambling financed an invisible, dirty subgovernment.

In places where large-scale gambling was rife, despite widespread laws against it, "bust-out" gambling was a regular result. Bust-out gambling, which I was soon to learn about firsthand, is crooked gambling enforced with strong-arm tactics. A businessman, staying in Cincinnati and out on the town for some sporting life in a Newport, Kentucky, casino one evening, might find himself losing more than he contemplated when he started or more than he even realized at the time. Then, after being cheated, he would be compromised, blackmailed, or beaten if he resisted a big payoff. When he returned home from the nightmare, he would find his bad dream was not over: Extortion, bribery, threats often followed. Complaints to condoning authorities in such places were, of course, fruitless. Lives could be ruined, including those of innocent families, and businesses and fortunes lost. Victimless crime?

Senate hearings around that time had disclosed both the lucrative proportions of the illegal gambling business and the pernicious aftermath of its sinking deep roots into a community. At that time, one expert estimated that 30 million Americans bet about $3.5 billion a year on horse racing at tracks and another $50 billion with bookies. This was more than the national defense budget at that time. Of these billions that gamblers paid their bookies (their "handle"), fortunes were used to corrupt law enforcement officials and others. Another expert estimated that "fully half of the syndicates' income from gambling is earmarked for protection money paid to police and politicians . . . in bribes." Gambling inevitably led not just to the influencing but to the nullification of government.

Nor were politicians the only citizens corrupted by the syndicate. The going rate for protected use of a telephone line (critical to organized gambling) in New York City, an expert told the McClellan Committee, was $1,000 a week; $750 a week in Chicago. There were at least 400,000 decks of marked cards in use around the country, he testified, and they were used in one out of every five poker games where the stakes were $10 or more.

The notion that gambling was a *local* problem that reflected local values, and should thus be controlled by local law enforcement, ignored what investigations were revealing. Most large-scale gambling involved interstate management and clientele, and included a national lay-off betting system whereby betting managers around the country spread their risks among themselves (as do legitimate insurance companies). Our intelligence reported—and our cases soon would prove—that most, if not all, gambling operations ran interstate, and thus defied the common thesis about local law enforcement. Soon our lawyers would be prosecuting gambling cases involving connections between West Virginia and Tennessee, Ohio and Kentucky, Rhode Island and Massachusetts, Indiana and Kentucky, Las Vegas and Hawaii, New Jersey and New York and Connecticut, the Carolinas and Georgia, Pennsylvania and New Jersey; even ventures that included Washington, D.C., Maryland, and Virginia, run out of the Pentagon.

There was then, as there is now, a debate about legalizing gambling. Some observers argued that puritanical prudery had spawned an underworld, that if gambling in itself was not immoral, why make it illegal? If you could not fight it, control it; and by doing so raise significant public revenues. The opposing argument was that legalization opens Pandora's box, that it was naive to presume there would be no cheating or corruption, and that an aftermath of related criminality and other abuses must inevitably flow from the fundamental concession. Also, legalization did not mean that illegal gambling would disappear. I was learning that my own views on this subject were naive and uninformed.

My cram course on organized crime was not limited to the chapter on gambling. The move from it to white-collar crime was frightening. Reading that mobsters used terror tactics was bad enough; but learning in detail about how a mobster takes over a legitimate business was horrific. First, a shylock might provide a loan ("juice") to an honest businessman with a temporary financial problem, running up a 700 percent–800 percent weekly compounded interest ("vigorish"). The collateral was the debtor's body. In twelve weeks, the hapless businessman might have solved his original problem, but he had a bigger debt than the one he started with. And to a deadly creditor. He'd been coerced into paying the equivalent of 2,000 percent a year to the mobster who, after the inevitable default, moved in—as his business "partner." The original businessman eventually was pushed out of his own business altogether, ending up with nothing at all. He might finally learn that his former business had been burned to the ground in an unprovable but arranged arson (fire-for-hire) for the insurance money or had been milked dry by the mobster and put into a fraudulent bankruptcy. To hear of such events—as I began to do at our regular staff meetings—provided quite a bleak perspective of the shylocking problem.

At our office meetings with Silberling and his staff, we were exhorted to use every law we could find to pursue the most powerful, pervasive, and elusive mobsters. What additional laws we needed, Kennedy would try to get passed. We decided to focus on big-scale gambling syndicates; on narcotics trafficking because its public and personal impact, even more so than gambling, was a scourge; on white-collar crime because this was the evolving trend and it was becoming as pervasive as it was difficult to prove; on labor racketeering, a subject Kennedy knew and cared about; and most particularly on political corruption because it was the final impact of organized crime on society, the end of law and the perversion of the social contract. It was the final coup of criminal organizations: taking over competitors, then legitimate business, then governments. As Kennedy said repeatedly in his public statements at the time, "The racketeer is at his most dangerous not with a machine gun in his hands but with public officials in his pocket."

What got me past my initial defense-minded predilections was the realization that ours would be no ordinary prosecutor's office. These special criminal targets were not Jean Valjean stealing a loaf of bread for his starving family; nor ghetto kids, many victimized by an unjust and unfair society; nor troubled individuals whose sins one could vicariously empathize with as isolated, even deviant, acts as much to be understood as to be deterred. No, these people were clever actors, hard to catch, well organized, motivated by benefits far in excess of the usual sanctions they faced. These were predators, often totally asocial animals, who preyed on society, had no socially redeeming ends, who used the vilest means to get their way, and whose actions, if unchecked, would lead to anarchy. They were massively rich and powerful, and operated outside the law. They were perfect villains. One could pursue them without feeling queasy. The spirit of Clarence Darrow wouldn't object.

In ways I had come to realize, the world of crime had changed. So, too, it became plain, would law enforcement have to change. Individual crimes—street robbery, home burglary, furtive rape, financial misdeeds, even the escapades of gangs—still occurred, always would, and should be prosecuted. But that was not what Kennedy, Silberling, and their growing cadre of recruits were to devote their main energies to. The local police could deal with isolated criminal acts on their cities' streets, and the FBI was good at solving bank robberies, kidnapping, auto thefts. The overarching crime problem was changing in ways law enforcement had not fully comprehended nor coped with adequately.

After Prohibition, the mobs were rich and were learning techniques for expanding their wealth, influence, and expertise. Bloated by black-market bounties during World War II, and joined by a growing contingent of mostly Sicilian mafiosi who had immigrated to the United States in search of their version of the American dream, the syndicates grew, expanded, and organized regionally and nationally. (Paradoxically, I noticed, some of the literature contained brief references to Joseph Kennedy and the bootlegging fortune he amassed during the Prohibition era, as well as his contacts with racketeers in his business dealings.) Senator Kefauver's Senate hearings showed that it was naive to view liquor, gambling, and drug crimes as victimless, predicated on outdated vice laws.

When Senator John McClellan and his young Rackets Committee counsel, Robert F. Kennedy, had attempted to look into the reasons for the 1957 Apalachin mob meeting, they could find out little. Even the correspondents and reporters who covered the department were not interested in organized crime. "When I became attorney general, I proceeded on the basis that there was such a thing as organized crime . . . crime as a business," Kennedy later reported.

The previous attorney general, William Rogers, had set up a small organized crime unit in the Criminal Division of the Department of Justice. But it lacked resources, intelligence data, and other techniques to cope with the elusive, complex national challenge. A young attorney from New York—Bill Hundley—was pulled over from the Internal Security Division, where he had been prosecuting Smith Act cases, to run the fledgling new section. Rogers was not about to challenge Hoover, who denied that there was a national crime syndicate, so the departmental move was essentially a ceremonial start. Justice Department lawyers reviewed cases that the U.S. attorneys tried and they screened investigations conducted by the FBI and other federal agencies. Their work was passive and reactive.

Now, in 1961, Kennedy was converting that small inactive office into the hottest spot in the department. He centralized control of organized crime cases from the almost one hundred U.S. attorneys' offices around the country into our one section. We didn't wait for cases to come to us; we were to go out into the field, work with investigators, and help to make cases where there was a basis to do so.

Kennedy and Silberling dramatically increased personnel and intensified our activities. In 1960, there were seventeen lawyers in the organized crime section; Silberling's charter was to get us to fifty quickly. During the first two-year period, days spent in the field by our lawyers jumped from 660 to 6,699, days before grand juries jumped from 100 to 677, days in court from 61 to 1,364, indictments secured rose from zero to 683, and the number of defendants convicted went from zero to 619.

If Robert Kennedy came to the Department of Justice with character flaws and a lack of experience, he did have two things going for him. First, he had a brother who was president. This fact provided him with much more power than any politically or intellectually superior or more experienced candidate ever would bring to the job. When, for example, he told the holdover commissioner of narcotics, "I told my brother I want you to be kept on," he gained not only an ally but a friend. And when agents in the field learned our orders had come directly from the attorney general and we reported directly to him, they paid attention.

Second, his experiences with Congress and personal sense of outrage provided him with extraordinary motivation. His impetus made his crusade against organized crime a priority of the Kennedy administration. From the beginning at the McClellan Committee and later at Justice, Walter Sheridan, Kennedy's key investigator, knew Kennedy "meant business," and found working for him "exhilarating."

> You grow up with idealistic ideas, but you realize more and more that you can never get them into action. All of a sudden the things you had thought should be done *were* being done, and *could* be done, because this man felt strongly enough to do something about them.

Carmine Bellino, another career government investigator Kennedy recruited and kept thereafter as part of his coterie, felt this same special commitment: "Bob is the only man I've met in government who is willing to go all the way, all the time."

Kennedy's inspirational leadership quality, Ed Guthman has reflected, was like the tough platoon sergeant whose men knew the strength of his commitment and were prepared to follow him into battle. One became quickly convinced that Kennedy knew what he was talking about, that he believed passionately in his convictions. His sense of mission would become contagious.

There was only one way to work for Kennedy, and that was 100 percent. He worked hard, and was a constant presence around the department; he set the tone and the standard. When one of my colleagues, John Diuguid, took his wife shopping one Saturday and parked his car in the department garage, he learned inadvertently about the new working style at Justice. Monday morning there was a note on his desk from Kennedy—thanking him for working on Saturday. The embarrassed lawyer did not respond, but he got the point.

Bob Blakey, a bright and hardworking lawyer who had recently joined our group, was alone in his office one Saturday reviewing a stack of files. The door opened, Kennedy walked in, sat down and asked what Blakey was doing and how he could help. "I'm Bob Kennedy," he advised.

"As if I didn't know!" Blakey remembers. He couldn't wait to get home to tell his wife. He too received a personal note a few days later thanking him for working on his day off.

John Sprizzo, who had started at Justice under the prior administration, remembers the difference in tone as palpable. "Washington was this sleepy small town with no snow equipment; so when it snowed everyone went home early. After Kennedy arrived, we had a storm and no one left. We figured he'd do a bed check. It took me four and a half hours to get home on the bus when I eventually left work."

Kennedy met regularly with department lawyers, often impromptu, and showed keen interest in what they were doing. At one meeting with lands division lawyers, he asked the group to let him know if they weren't busy enough. A young lawyer, Bill French, came forward saying he wanted more to do, more challenge. He was quickly moved to the growing group working on Hoffa's Teamsters.

A once-sleepy bureaucracy was coming alive, responding to an attorney general who seemed omnipresent and seemed to know and care about what was going on in his staff's lives. When Herb Bates, a department lawyer who had volunteered to join our section, told Kennedy he thought he'd have to leave Justice to take an administrative law judgeship that paid a higher salary, a GS 14, one notch more than the GS 13 he was at Justice, Kennedy said: "Stay." Next day, Bates was a GS 14: In those days a several-thousand-dollars promotion was important to an independent family man. Bates would be there for the duration.

Robert Kennedy's public luster was brightening the corridors of the whole department. Ramsey Clark, who was familiar with the department because his father Tom Clark had been attorney general, was brought in to run one division. He quickly noticed that what had been a lethargic, impersonal institution before had come alive, turned spirited, because of Kennedy's direct manner and personal presence.

Robert Kennedy would press Congress for legislation that would permit more effective, nationwide strikes at organized crimes' revenue sources and provide prosecutorial procedures to invigorate his law enforcement efforts. Putting together a package of proposed laws that included some revitalized proposals already pending, several fresh ideas put forth by our new brain trust, and a controversial wiretapping bill, he was ready to begin. At the heart of them all was the "interstateness" of organized crime, and thus the need for federal laws and federal law enforcement.

—

On May 17, 1961, Kennedy testified before the House of Representatives Judiciary Committee, Subcommittee No. 5, on behalf of his proposed new federal criminal laws to combat national organized crime and racketeering syndicates and to enable more effective law enforcement. His chief goal was to crack down on interstate gambling and "the huge profits in the traffic in liquor, narcotics, prostitution, as well as the use of these funds for corrupting local officials and for their use in racketeering in labor and management." He asked for laws prohibiting interstate travel and wire communications to promote gambling and racketeering, stopping the transportation of gambling paraphernalia, punishing the intimidation of witnesses, and permitting prosecutors to grant immunity to force incriminating testimony.

In words that would prove prophetic to this rookie prosecutor in a matter of days, Kennedy advised the committee:

There is wide-open gambling in Newport, Ky., adjacent to Cincinnati, Ohio, and Covington, Ky. A review of the financial statements of 4 Newport gambling casinos in 1957 revealed that 11 persons, who reside outside of Kentucky, participated in the casino profits. With this bill we would be able to move against interstate travel to distribute the profits of these casinos to the out-of-State owners.

Kennedy informed the committee that "gambling in the United States . . . involves about 70,000 persons and [its multibillion-dollar] operations are so completely intertwined with the Nation's communications systems that denial of their use to the gambling fraternity would be a mortal blow to their operations."

And the determined attorney general let the committee know that as the enemy was tough, so too would be his efforts to fight them.

The Department of Justice is going to be involved in large-scale combat with the forces which use interstate commerce to conduct their criminal activities. The persons who make up this element are tough and ruthless. They also are shrewd enough to be aware of the need of secrecy in the conduct of their activities . . . We expect attempts will be made to mislead us through intimidation of witnesses by threats or by violence.

Our opponents are ruthless, vicious, and resourceful. I cannot stress this too much. They will use every weapon at their command to prevent our discovery of incriminating information.

He advised the committee that this battle could not be left to traditional law enforcement powers in the states:

The face of organized crime has changed. While there still are crimes of violence, the modern criminal has become somewhat more sophisticated in the planning and perpetration of his activities in gambling, prostitution, narcotics, bribery, fraud, and larceny. He has moved into legitimate businesses and labor unions where he embezzles the funds and loots the treasury.

He asked for a broad immunity statute that would allow his prosecutors to call witnesses before grand juries and compel their testimony without being trumped by invocation of the Fifth Amendment. He had seen this happen too many times during his congressional hearings, and he did not want to be frustrated in his pursuits this time.

Kennedy repeated his calls for legislative help on June 6, 1961, in testimony before the Senate Judiciary Committee. Again using Newport, Kentucky, as an example of the interstate nature of crime, he repeated his call for help fighting "these hoodlums and racketeers who have become so rich and so powerful . . . If we could curtail their use of interstate communications and facilities, we could inflict a telling blow to their operations. We could cut them down to size."

On July 26, the attorney general sat in the Senate gallery watching that body adopt his recommended list of federal laws, laws we would use aggressively as we became locked in combat with the mob. RFK would be an active "general" in our war; he knew the battles would be hard fought; and he sent out all the signals he could that he was serious.

Kennedy met with the chiefs of the separate law enforcement agencies and told them that their world was changing; they could help or leave. The department was in charge, especially our band of special assistants, as we were labeled. No longer would the FBI, IRS, the Customs and Narcotics Bureaus, the Immigration Service, the Secret Service, and the twenty other law enforcement agencies of the federal government operate as isolated competitive fiefdoms; from now on it was to be a collaborative effort aimed at catching criminals, not garnering the best statistics to justify an agency's budget and existence. In addition, we sought help from agencies whose missions seemed remote to organized crime—the Coast Guard and the Social Security Administration—and even from private and state organizations with useful expertise—the Chicago and New Orleans Crime Commissions and the New York City district attorney's office.

Some years later, Kennedy told *New York Times* columnist Anthony Lewis that when he had asked the FBI for its files on the Apalachin attendees, they didn't have anything on most of them but some newspaper clips. The Bureau of Narcotics had files on all of them. "The FBI didn't know anything, really, about these people who were the major gangsters in the United States," Kennedy complained. Hoover eschewed long drawn-out organized crime investigations, preferring the better statistics his agency could publicize in pursuing easier cases. And, some speculated, he didn't want his agents exposed to the big money that major rackets figures used to corrupt law enforcement agents.

Kennedy overruled a Treasury Department memo stating it could not get into organized crime investigations, and enlisted the new secretary, Douglas Dillon, in his cooperative efforts. He recruited his former law professor from the University of Virginia, Mortimer Caplin, to be IRS commissioner, and Caplin promised to cooperate in collaborative efforts with the other investigative agencies in sharing intelligence. Prior IRS chiefs had focused their limited investigations on cases where the most revenue would be raised from fines and penalties. Kennedy got Caplin to emphasize investigations that would lead to organized crime convictions.

"He had me sit in when he had his U.S. attorneys in his office," Caplin recalls, "and I had Bobby come over, which was great for the IRS, and talk to our people." The agents in the field were stimulated by this prospect, feeling they were making an impact on society. On May 1, 1961, the president himself met with IRS directors to discuss organized crime. His appearance "had an electrifying effect on the meeting," Caplin's report to the attorney general noted; it had provided "a shot in the arm for the IRS."

No other attorney general could have done this on his own. Systems were entrenched, and Hoover in particular was too powerful to push into doing things he resisted. For example, Hoover had never allowed department lawyers to know what and who the sources were in FBI reports. They would use symbols—"T-1 alleges" or "T-5 states." Once, accidentally, a cover sheet explaining all the FBI symbols came to Silberling's attention, so we knew thereafter who our mysterious informants were—a bank, a phone company official, an undercover agent, or Dun and Bradstreet. Hoover insisted that only the FBI knew which individuals could be used in court and how to evaluate witnesses. Silberling didn't want his lawyers to sit in Washington and wait for cases to come to them; he wanted our lawyers to be in on some investigations, even the questioning of witnesses. He would win that departmental joust.

That perspective of action-oriented law enforcement led by prose-cutors was the model Silberling knew and followed. It would be a key to success in these cases, though a controversial technique to critics who disparaged "going after" defendants, even bad ones. But Silberling and Kennedy concluded that one could not expect bribes to be reported or narcotics shipments to be publicized or labor kickbacks to come to light. They'd have to be unearthed, and that would take action and unconventional efforts.

Having an impact is different when the president is your brother, and the attorney general took advantage of that relationship when, as here, he needed to. Later, Kennedy told interviewers, "There's no question that I could do it because of my relationship. They wouldn't have paid attention to me otherwise . . . gone over my head to the president . . . because a lot of them in the hierarchy were opposed to it . . . hated the idea. And of course, J. Edgar Hoover didn't want to get in."

The FBI was the most famous federal investigative agency in those days, and the one closest to the Justice Department—its main offices were housed in the same building. Attorneys general came and went, but Hoover was a permanent fixture who had assumed more power than those he served. Hoover had become director in 1924, a year before Kennedy was born. Their styles were in stark contrast; but for pragmatic reasons each needed the other, so a superficial association was forged.

It would take time before Kennedy truly took over any real control of the FBI (and that was incomplete). One weekend, when Kennedy, dressed in off-duty casual style, drove his convertible into the department garage, his huge dog Brumus perched on the seat beside him, a guard stopped him and asked for identification before he could enter. Smiling, Kennedy said, "I'm the attorney general." "I don't care if you're J. Edgar Hoover," the young guard responded, "you've got to show me your I.D."

Within a few months after his arrival at Justice, everyone knew who Kennedy was and who was the boss. A new system was operating. There was cooperation between government agencies. Centralization and coordination and depoliticization were critical to Silberling's philosophy for a rackets prosecution organization. This philosophy conflicted with traditional approaches of the FBI and U.S. attorneys, indeed with the historic work style of the Department of Justice itself.

When one of our attorneys first met with a large group of FBI agents he would be working with in one large midwestern city, an agent rose to ask, rhetorically, "What makes you think you'll make these strides, Mr. Bates?" Herb responded, "I suppose if I was the attorney general with a brother in the White House, I'd expect strides or heads would roll." Herb and his agents soon made strides.

At Justice, the work of career attorneys had been broken into areas of specialty—fraud, tax, antitrust, for example. Silberling wanted our group to have experts in all those areas, so we could follow all leads wherever they led. And he preferred noncareer lawyers who would not be worried about taking risks and pleasing everyone. The FBI's work was done city by city. If an investigation started in New York City but aspects of the case occurred in Miami, the FBI would send the New York file to its Florida office; its assumption was that one FBI agent was as good as another. Moreover, the FBI didn't trust Justice Department lawyers, fearing they'd end up in private practice knowing too much about FBI practices. Silberling thought the original investigator was better suited to follow his case wherever it led. And he insisted our lawyers be in on the big investigations.

Ed also thought U.S. attorneys were hampered in major organized crime cases because their jurisdiction was limited to their home state, and because they had limited staff and resources. More important, politics invariably affected organized crime cases and U.S. attorneys were political creatures who might be too worried about antagonizing the local power structure. Our experiences would prove the validity of Ed's wariness. When the U.S. attorney in Tucson failed to prosecute a case involving an important rackets figure in that area, one of our lawyers presented the case to the grand jury.

A list was made of the nation's forty major racketeers with intelligence supplied by all investigating agencies and coordinated by the organized crime section at Justice. Silberling had brought aboard Wyn Hayes, a veteran of the New York City Police (Narcotics) Department, to coordinate all organized crime data. Her top-forty list of racketeers soon would grow to over two thousand supporting players, and her expanding files included data concerning several hundred thousand individuals having collateral associations with organized crime. We would soon see what a profound difference this intelligence-gathering plan made.

These administrative changes seem simple, even obvious, now, but they were earthshaking at the time, and it would be months before the agents in the field offices around the country got the word and changed their ways. Whenever Kennedy was in a city on any business, he went out of his way to visit offices of the investigators in that area, to encourage and motivate them. Courtney Evans, the department's liaison with the FBI, said Kennedy did more of this than all his predecessors combined. As was the case with the attorneys in the department, this kind of personal encouragement was motivational, and the agents in the field responded to it. Kennedy's fundamental administrative changes would make a major difference to all of us in conducting our investigations and making our cases.

Each of us was assigned a city or region. We would meet with the local U.S. attorney, who ordinarily would assign one of his assistants to work with us. We would set priorities and embark on a plan of action aimed at targeted mob leaders. We'd coordinate the work of federal investigators (sometimes local officials would join in our efforts). IRS agents audited officials when there was evidence they were corrupt. We worked with labor investigators on union corruption cases. The INS was recruited when international questions arose. And we convened and ran investigative grand juries ourselves when the investigating agencies needed our assistance. Few attorneys general could have mediated the competition between these investigative agencies and assuaged the traditional independence of the nearly one hundred U.S. attorneys around the country as Kennedy did.

A year after Kennedy became attorney general, in January 1962, his dramatic changes were taking effect. A less reluctant but no less rhetorical J. Edgar Hoover would brag that his FBI had penetrated "the innermost sanctums of the criminal deity." In 1961, several high-visibility prosecutions quickly had taken place—Tony Accardo in Chicago for tax evasion; California boxing czar Frankie Carbo and his lieutenant Blinkey Palermo and several of their enforcers were convicted of extortion involving muscling in on the contract of the world welterweight boxing champion, Don Jordan, by threatening his manager and trainer; Mickey Cohen was convicted of tax evasion; the Lassoff-Decklebaum New Orleans–based interstate telephone gambling fraud investigation was instituted. In March 1961, we had convicted a well-known underworld figure in Minneapolis for a tax violation and attempting to bribe a juror. The day after his conviction, the INS had begun a proceeding to deport him as an undesirable alien.

But our work had just begun. The influential Miami crime figure

Meyer Lansky was boasting in those days that "organized crime is bigger than United States Steel."

The more I read and heard, the more informed I became, the more committed I was—and the more I began to understand Kennedy's strong antipathy toward what he had defined "the enemy." I could be comfortable fighting this campaign, energetically and imaginatively. One did not have to throw out all the rules, as civil libertarians feared, to fight this kind of enemy. The fight could be fought, I believed, within proper and civilized rules. One could be tough but fair.

And so, in those first months on the job, I gradually became an educated rookie prosecutor. I had been co-opted, my liberal friends would tease for years, by the Kennedy thing and inveigled into prosecutorial excess. And I became increasingly enthusiastic.

The "brother within" had combined with his "brother at the top" to continue the work they had started in the Senate, and to prove that RFK's appointment to Justice may have been as brilliant as it was nepotistic. The prizewinning veteran *Washington Star* reporter Miriam Ottenberg, an expert on law enforcement, described the scene at Justice: "With the election of President John F. Kennedy, the Justice Department got a new boss and a new approach to organized crime. Robert F. Kennedy brought to the job of attorney general this arsenal for his projected anti-crime crusade: a constructive anger, an intimate knowledge of the habits and habitats of some major criminals and their satellites, a capacity for attracting a cadre of dedicated young prosecutors and finally, a partner in the White House."

Chapter 4

LEARNING ON

THE JOB

My education through reading and research began to be supplemented at regular staff meetings. We would assemble in Silberling's spacious second-floor office down the hall from his growing crew of assistants. We also met periodically with Kennedy in his vast office on the fifth floor. Usually a few dozen of our lawyers were in town at any one time while as many were in the field working on cases. Silberling and his deputy, Henry Petersen, a career department lawyer, who was dogged, knowledgeable about all the department's systems, and gravel-voiced from smoking too many Camel cigarettes, would conduct our second-floor meetings assessing progress or problems with potential targets. Jim Misslbeck was also present. A trusted aide Silberling had brought with him from his prior prosecutorial life in New York, Jim had a crew cut, and was energetic, friendly, and easy to deal with.

The staff was composed of a mix of three groups. There was a cadre of career department lawyers who had been moved into this section from other places in the Department of Justice to add agency experience to our new group. They were mostly insiders who did the paperwork, reviewed files, and for the most part stayed in Washington; as careerists they were helpful, but some lacked the special zeal the newcomers brought to their work. These older lawyers came to work in carpools, had large families, and after work stayed in their own private worlds outside of Washington and politics. If the reigning government was concerned about loyalty cases, they would work on investigations in the internal security division; if the prevailing passion came to be organized crime, that subject would dominate their attentions. They were there before the Kennedy administration ("They've been here since Homer Cummings," one sarcastic Justice Department veteran told me), and they would remain after it.

The second group was made up of newcomers, just starting families (someone was always handing out cigars, arriving at work red-eyed after a long vigil in a maternity ward). Most came from good law schools and had outstanding academic credentials. They were highly motivated to get involved in this particular work at this particular time for this particular attorney general. The Criminal Division suddenly became the first choice for many of the best young recruits. They were full of ambition, brimming with self-confidence. Almost all of them would eventually leave for careers of their own. We all craved getting to court. After work we socialized with one another and friends who worked elsewhere in the Kennedy administration. A group of us played poker (Silberling included), and met at dinner parties at our homes.

A third subunit of our section was really a group unto itself. Theoretically, administratively, and physically located within the organized crime section, the labor racketeering group was under the supervision of Walter Sheridan, a nonlawyer, a former FBI agent who had worked as chief investigator for Robert Kennedy on the Senate Rackets Committee, had won his admiration, and had come with him to Justice to assemble a small group of fervent lawyers and investigators to "take a fresh look at labor racketeering . . . with particular emphasis on Hoffa and his empire." They would be labeled, as noted, pejoratively as the "Get Hoffa" group, not without some justification. They worked together, associating with, but working apart from, the rest of us, operating like a wholly owned subsidiary.

Several criminal cases and investigations arising from McClellan Committee investigations were pending during the transition to the Kennedy administration. They became the starting point for Sheridan's quick start. A loyal and dogged investigator, Walter recalled, "I was hired walking up the stairs at the old Senate office building . . . that's where half our conversations took place in the years that followed." Then Kennedy was off to the hospital where one of his children was being born. Sheridan would be a special assistant to Kennedy and one of his closest aides throughout his career before and after Justice.

Kennedy's passion about crooked unions, particularly Hoffa and the Teamsters, had begun with his work on the McClellan Committee. Steeped in labor lore through that experience, Kennedy was sure Hoffa was a thug who plundered and discredited a mighty union, cavorted with organized crime, and corrupted public officials. Senator John McClellan called Hoffa a "fountainhead" of union corruption who was faithless to the rank-and-file members and who used gangsters and racketeers to do his dirty business. In 1957, the AFL-CIO had thrown out the Teamsters, its largest constituent, for refusing to cooperate in an internal investigation. For decades thereafter, the Teamsters were monitored by court orders.

The man RFK chose to head the Criminal Division, Jack Miller, had been an energetic and devoted chief counsel to the Teamster monitors and thus knew the union's versions of hanky-panky. Miller, in turn, brought John Cassidy, a lawyer who had worked with him and the federal-court-appointed Teamster monitors, and John helped recruit a crew of talented lawyers to work with him and Sheridan. John Seigenthaler recommended Jim Neal, a tough Tennessean who was then a trial lawyer in Washington and who would try several of our important cases. They also recruited Charles Schaffer, a dynamic young New York trial lawyer, and Charles Z. Smith, the Seattle trial lawyer who had prosecuted Hoffa's predecessor, Dave Beck.

Smith's recruitment also was typical of RFK's style. When Dave Beck was called before the McClellan Committee in 1957, he took the Fifth Amendment in response to Kennedy's questions 164 times. The Washington State Bar Association called for a Superior Court grand jury. The Republican district attorney assigned the investigation to Smith. Smith was a smart, hardworking, gentlemanly young prosecutor who had been at this work for two years. Smith met Kennedy when he came to Seattle and provided Smith with a copy of the Senate committee's transcript. Carmine Bellino, one of Kennedy's key investigators, also came to assist Smith. Bellino, ex-FBI and a wizard with numbers, proved to be a brilliant researcher.

Eventually, Beck and his son were convicted of embezzling funds from the Western Conference of Teamsters. Though their conviction was affirmed all the way to the U.S. Supreme Court, the governor ultimately pardoned Beck. Charles Smith was frustrated, as Kennedy was, and he recently recalled: "My career was built on convicting two presidents of the Teamsters, neither of whom served one day of their sentences."

Kennedy remembered Smith's work, however, and called him shortly after he became attorney general. Smith didn't think he liked Kennedy, told him he was a Republican who had voted for Nixon. "I'm not looking for politicians," Kennedy replied, "I'm looking for lawyers." Smith was intrigued and said he'd think about it and call Kennedy back. When did he want him to come? "Tomorrow!"

The next week, Smith sold his house and moved to Washington. When Smith arrived, he was assigned to Sheridan's Teamsters crew and soon was part of the family of department insiders. "Kennedy emphasized the importance of family," Smith recalls. "He had us to parties at his house. We met with him in his office regularly. Once, soon after we arrived, when my wife was in the hospital, flowers arrived with a note signed 'Bob.' She wasn't even sure who the 'Bob' was. But my personal esteem and professional respect [for him] grew steadily. Kennedy was not the ruthless man portrayed in the Teamsters magazine images."

Courtney Evans, once FBI liaison to the McClellan Committee, continued to work with Kennedy and the organized crime group as the FBI representative. "Both sides believed in me," he said, as if the FBI and Justice were different sides.

Still, Sheridan's group was a small one: Along with carryovers from Kennedy's McClellan Committee staff and from Teamsters monitoring days, a few Criminal Division veterans were moved over from other parts of the department. It was hardly the big gang Hoffa supporters complained had been recruited to conduct a massive inquisition. Indeed, Hoffa had many lawyers working for him and, if not limitless resources, certainly adequate financial and research help. Sheridan's team eventually numbered thirteen lawyers. Hoffa was not flattered by all this attention, to be sure. Journalist Clark Mollenhoff later reported: "For the first time, Hoffa and his million-dollar stable of Teamster lawyers faced a superior force."

One of Sheridan's lawyers, usually John Cassidy, routinely came to Silberling's meetings to share information.

We were nearly all men, and all white for that matter, except for Charles Smith, the handsome Seattle prosecutor who was recruited by Sheridan at Ed Guthman's suggestion, and Harry Alexander, another black lawyer with good trial experience, recruited by Silberling from the D.C. U.S. attorney's office. But we had our wonderful big sister, Wyn Hayes, who was tall, muscular, tough-talking but bighearted to all of us—her "babes," she called us. Silberling had worked with her in New York. She collected and controlled the evolving data we were accumulating from every available source about every known crime figure; she coordinated it, and worked with all the attorneys to be sure we had every bit of available information about everyone under investigation. We all loved Wyn, partied and flirted with her platonically, and profited from her industry, savvy, and helpfulness. Every request we made was met with gusto, as she chain-smoked Lucky Strikes and helped us build our cases. Wyn was everyone's helper, advisor, confidante, pal.

At the informal assemblies in Silberling's office, each of the attorneys would describe the work he was doing. Silberling and his two deputies would note what else needed to be done to help us with our cases—a call to a regional Internal Revenue Service office to expedite an investigation; assigning an extra lawyer to an investigation that was gaining momentum; intervention with another federal agency by higher-ups, including RFK himself when it was necessary and important enough. These meetings would provide all attendees with an education in techniques—what investigatory gimmick or legal argument solved a particular quandary—as well as a panoramic view of the national battlefield. We would use old laws in new ways while developing new ones to add to our arsenal.

Earl Johnson, in his study of organized crime, had analyzed the available tools of enforcement that we should be using. The conspiracy laws were the obvious vehicle for nailing the behind-the-scenes managers of the criminal syndicates, who were rarely involved in hands-on criminal acts but who controlled decision making and exploited the profits. To prove the conspiracies, we would have to force reluctant witnesses to testify through grants of immunity backed by contempt convictions of those who were adamant. We would have to squeeze the underlings to extract the evidence needed to reach the bosses. Immunity laws would preclude their remaining silent by resorting to the Fifth Amendment. But that technique would not always work, so strong was the code of silence and so fearful were witnesses of the consequences of their cooperation, however coerced it might be. Some of the Apalachin attendees, for example, spent up to two years in prison for refusing to testify about what was scheduled for their aborted conclave. And in those days there was no general immunity law we could use, so we had to stretch to find federal laws that included immunity provisions in those limited situations. In fact, our research disclosed there were thirty-five immunity laws in the voluminous federal code, and we would use them when it could be rationalized, even in situations not envisioned when those laws were passed. Our favorite was the FCC law that permitted use of immunity where the phones were involved, which in interstate gambling and most other examples of organized crime was always.

We pressed responsible local and state officials to revoke licenses of businesses that operated illegally and of businessmen who failed to cooperate. We contacted bar associations when crooked lawyers were conspiring with their clients. We proposed stronger laws about intimidating witnesses and destroying evidence, and Kennedy took the proposals to Congress and pushed for their passage.

Criminalizing the making of false statements to law enforcement officials and increasing the use of the hard-to-prove perjury laws were tough cases to make, but we'd have to resort to them. Both laws provided opportunities to close investigatory circles and pressure witnesses to cooperate or incriminate themselves. The false statements statute, for example, S.1001 of the federal penal code, made it a crime to lie in certain documents. We would snag racketeers for doing so on home improvement loans, naturalization documents, FAA loans, FCC radio- and telephone-operator license applications, IRS tax documents, and Small Business Administration and Veterans Administration loans. These were not the laws we preferred to use, but they were the ones on the books at the time. The pinch was that if the records were filled out properly, the people might have incriminated themselves in more serious offenses.

The same was so with the perjury laws. Though they were difficult to convict under because of rigorous standards of proof, we nonetheless could question suspects or likely witnesses and force them to either testify or risk being indicted for perjury. Sometimes we'd defer prosecution for perjury if that reluctant witness chose to cooperate and testify. We did this in a Youngstown, Ohio, grand jury investigation of gambling; a Missouri inquiry into labor payoffs, and another in Philadelphia; a Boston grand jury investigation into race-wire operations in Massachusetts; and a tax inquiry concerning the two top racketeers in Wisconsin. We pressured underlings, girlfriends, associates, in attempts to zero in on our targeted, leading rackets bosses.

We used bribery and obstruction of justice laws to counterattack our adversaries' attempts to ward off our attacks. When a New York organized crime figure forced a government witness to recant his testimony, we prosecuted him for obstruction of justice. When grand jurors or jurors in criminal trials were approached for fixes, we moved quickly under these statutes.

Our adversaries left us no doubt they would not abide by Marquis of Queensberry rules of decorum, though their lawyers would hold us to the highest constitutional standards.

We wrestled with rationales to persuade Congress to expand the wiretap laws to permit eavesdropping and phone taps, where appropriate, under adequate judicial supervision. This would be a ticklish proposal because there was widespread and understandable public reluctance to these techniques because they were viewed as incursions upon personal freedom and conflicted with the strongly held American aversion to any invasions of privacy.

One of our wisest lawyers became our resident expert on the Fourth Amendment and advised us on questions about warrants, searches, and seizures. I had my own queasiness about the potential for abuses in these cases, as I sensed there had been in internal security cases in prior administrations. Yet, it was logical and necessary to seek telephonic evidence in some cases, for example in proving lay-off betting—a nationwide gambling network that used private phones as an illegal utility. In fact, my colleagues asked, why not deny outright the use of interstate wire facilities to criminal organizations that used them for illegal purposes?

One of our colleagues, John Sprizzo, told us about a pending investigation that highlighted this problem. John was a young honors-program New York lawyer who had been recruited by the prior administration to work on the Apalachin appeal. Silberling kept John on. Recently, John recalled for me his first contact with Robert Kennedy. Everyone at Justice was aware of the change of atmosphere after Kennedy took office. For awhile, there were office practical jokes: "You got a call—see the attorney general," when there had been no call. Then one day, John got a real call and went upstairs with Silberling and Petersen. RFK wanted to know about pending cases, including the Apalachin appeal, and why things weren't moving faster and more efficiently. Petersen told Kennedy, "Don't blame the staff, we are encountering a lack of cooperation." Kennedy made a note, and we would soon see a quick change in the way investigative agencies worked with us. John Sprizzo remembers Kennedy as "tough, activist, curious to know everything, involved in our work." John was working then on a new and potentially important case.

Fast-talking, and faster-thinking, John's interest was centered in New Orleans; it involved nine lay-off bettors from Cincinnati, Florida, Mississippi, New York City, and New Orleans. Intelligence that came to us from several cities where interstate gambling was big business indicated a common pattern. Gamblers paid off phone company employees to get free lines and other unauthorized services, which saved them money and eliminated incriminating phone company records. We met with IRS and FBI investigators and representatives of the phone company's Long Lines Division to discuss cracking this scheme. The case John was working on might be our first chance to do so.

A phone company monitoring its lines discovered an employee in Winnipeg, Manitoba, Canada, who had given lay-off bettors free open lines to conduct their business in exchange for wagering tips. He did what is called past posting—by being given hot results he could bet fast and be guaranteed winning. The phone company told the Internal Revenue Service, which tapped the lines and gathered evidence that John and his colleagues thought might constitute wire fraud and conspiracy to defraud the IRS, which had a right to collect wagering taxes from the gamblers. Two other lawyers from our section, a rookie, Mike Fawer, and a veteran, Ed Molinoff, were sent to New Orleans to work with John on developing this case. Four phone company employees had been caught and agreed to testify. The case looked promising.

After John's report, the conversation moved around Silberling's large office. Through existing governmental regulations of commerce, business, and labor record-keeping requirements, we learned, we could close down or at least slow down criminal enterprises. The chief example of this technique was the excise tax requirement, which obliged gamblers to buy a wagering tax stamp, keep certain records, and pay taxes on their profits. If they did not comply, they violated federal laws; if they did comply, they confessed, in effect, to committing crimes, which we could press local authorities to prosecute. (That requirement was subsequently ruled to be an unconstitutional violation of the Fifth Amendment's self-incrimination provision; but the ruling came after our extensive use of this technique.) We pressed for expanded record-keeping requirements in other areas, particularly for labor union funds where organized crime had gained influence.

We dusted off and applied existing laws to our cases. The deportation laws came into play since so many members of the Mafia were recent citizens who had come from Sicily with criminal records in Italy. This could become a basis for denaturalization if they had misrepresented their past histories, as many had. Confiscation and forfeiture laws could take the profit out of criminal activities, too, if they were applied sweepingly to illegal operations.

In May 1961, an interesting situation came to light in Chicago. Three hundred automobiles had disappeared from an automobile agency that later went into bankruptcy. Chicago rackets figures with an interest in the company sold 125, at very low prices, to friends and relatives out of state. We opened a Bankruptcy Act fraud investigation.

We looked for crimes that were on the books but which only the most flexible mind might have considered applying to racketeers. We asked the FBI to conduct an investigation under the federal mutiny statutes (18 U.S.C. 2192,3) when a National Maritime Union strike might have involved disobedient sailors who were not members of the crew.

It became a joke among us to come up with bizarre crimes from Title 18, the federal penal code, to use against our elusive quarry. During our meetings in Silberling's office, at silly moments we played can-you-top-this with scenarios for charges: impersonating a 4-H girl, interstate transportation of unregistered dentures, misuse of the

Smokey the Bear symbol. Sometimes such ingenuity bore fruit. One of our attorneys put two investigations together to make a case the local U.S. attorney had scoffed at. A racketeer under scrutiny had told the IRS he was unemployed. But he had applied to the FHA for a home loan and provided the required job data to the FHA. He was indicted for making a false statement, and pleaded guilty. A second example arose out of a search of the home of Joey Aiuppa, a middle-level Chicago rackets figure. The investigators did not find what they were looking for, but one of them noticed a freezer full of game—563 mourning doves, to be exact. The hapless racketeer was charged under the Migratory Bird Act for possessing too many birds out of season (24 per person is allowed, everyone knows).

Of course, what we considered ingenious pursuit of evildoers others saw as proof of their worst fears about Kennedy. Just as they'd warned, Kennedy had unleashed a group of powerful prosecutors whose avid pursuit of certain targeted citizens would soon snare everyone. Ours was a fascistic, despotic, personalized vendetta, not a department of justice. The charge of selective prosecution was leveled at Kennedy throughout his tenure at Justice, and at those of us who prosecuted these cases (especially by those we prosecuted), sometimes with justification. Most of our cases were not as exotic as the one that snagged Mr. Aiuppa; certainly not our major convictions. Aiuppa's conviction was reversed on appeal because the search was improper.

If local law enforcement officials, traditionally the main line in the battle against crime, did not do their jobs, then the federal government had to move in. Many of the specialties of organized crime already were subject to federal laws—narcotics, interstate prostitution, mail or wire fraud, and illegal immigration. These laws were already in place and only needed to be invigorated and implemented. Soon we did just that, prosecuting major federal narcotics offenses in Chicago, Texas, and New York; million-dollar liquor-law violations in Minnesota, Maine, and Florida; and of course, income and excise tax evasion cases all over the country.

New laws would help, and would soon be passed and available to us. We would be allies of the honest law enforcement officials around the country who wanted help, and we would usurp cases when corrupt officials failed to do their jobs.

Silberling and Petersen were meeting with state and federal officials to coordinate a fresh and well-organized effort at collaborative law enforcement. Ed met with FCC officials to discuss that agency's promulgating rules prohibiting some and controlling other broadcasting of horse-racing information. He set up a liaison with the Royal Canadian Mounted Police to share information about subjects of mutual interest and to design procedures to expedite assistance between our organizations.

We met with cooperative state officials to set up liaisons for effective joint law enforcement work. In Jacksonville, Florida, one of our young attorneys, Mike Fawer, discovered a massive system of case fixing. Four thousand witnesses had told state officials of paying bonding companies to fix their minor cases by paying off police and a municipal court judge. IRS officials advised Fawer of a possible whitewash by state officials, and we took the investigation to a federal grand jury. Our lawyers met with Youngstown, Ohio, law enforcement officials who were concerned about that city's crime problems and intelligence reports indicating there had been payoffs to police and politicians by local rackets figures. They would work in collaboration with FBI agents we were using in that area to develop cases. The Hammond, Indiana, city council was indicted with other officials there for taking illegal payoffs, including a local district attorney who had been president of the National Association of District Attorneys.

We assisted aggressive and cooperative prosecutors in Wisconsin, Ohio, Minnesota, North Carolina, and New York who were interested in working with us toward common objectives.

Regional coordinators of the IRS's Intelligence Service met with Ed to develop methods of working together more effectively and coordinating organized crime intelligence, particularly but not exclusively between the IRS and FBI, through our attorneys. The INS also met with Ed to plan ways to coordinate special efforts in its jurisdiction. If we couldn't convict them, perhaps we could deport some racketeers to their country of origin—push them out if we couldn't pull them in. Most of them had lied about their past criminal records and thus were eligible to be deported, as the government does with former Nazis discovered in this country.

Ed met with state and local crime commission heads in Indiana, Illinois, and New Orleans to develop ways to share information and work together in particular cases. In the months and years that followed, we would see these liaisons and plans bear fruit.

In sum, I was learning: If there was a national emergency created by organized crime—and there was—there must be a national response by organized law enforcement, equally aggressive, inventive, and inspired.

We discussed new organized crime legislation being written by the department's legislative draftsmen. Two of our lawyers—a veteran, Ed Joyce, and a rookie, Harry Subin—described their struggle to capture in legislative prose our special need to deal with the interstate features of organized crime and racketeering. We were working on a law that would make it a crime to transport gambling paraphernalia between states, and another one making it a crime to travel or to use interstate facilities (such as the phones and national highways) for racketeering purposes. The idea was to fashion particular laws geared to the precise problems that had frustrated local law enforcement agencies, which would give the federal government a premise for moving in to fill this void. Well-briefed newcomers like Earl Johnson and savvy veterans like Henry Petersen led the discussions about these proposed new laws.

At one of our group meetings, Ed Joyce told us about a session he and Subin had with the attorney general, who was impatient to have new laws to propose to Congress. "Can't we make it a crime to be a *member* of the Mafia?" the impatient general asked at one point. The scholars among us squirmed at his suggestion. Joyce had to adroitly explain the difficulty of drafting such a catchall law that would survive judicial review. While we were impressed by our leader's commitment and involvement, we were surprised by his legislative naivete. "How about that Mafia conspiracy idea?" Joyce remarked. "We could call it the Interstate Cousins Act," Subin suggested, and we all had an anxious laugh.

In the first months, these meetings were especially interesting to me and the other rookies in our program. Socially, as I've said, we were getting to know our colleagues; more important, from their reports we were gaining a view of our enemies and their tactics, preparing us for what we would soon personally encounter. We listened and learned.

———

"What's the situation with Giancana?" someone asked at one of these first meetings in Silberling's office.

Sam "Mooney" Giancana was born in 1908 in a Chicago tenement. His immigrant parents named him Gilormo Giangona, a name he dropped as he grew into Momo Giancana, a street-smart hoodlum, stealing, fighting, "banging" girls, looking up to affluent gangsters, learning how to fix crooked cops, and gradually moving into high-stakes crime and up the rungs of the local gangs. He was audacious, vicious, and lucky, usually avoiding arrest or conviction for his escalating criminal escapades.

Giancana had become a part of the Capone gang as a driver for Paul "The Waiter" Ricca, Capone's successor, and later for Anthony Accardo. Brief stays in Joliet and Leavenworth prisons followed as Giancana rose through the Chicago underworld, getting deeply involved in the vast lottery games and bootlegging that were in vogue, managing profitable casinos in the Chicago suburbs. He was married to a traditional conservative Italian woman from the neighborhood, had three daughters, and eventually became widowed. He became an avid ladies man, a charismatic gangster with ties to show business stars such as Frank Sinatra and his crowd, and a lover of singer Phyllis McGuire.

Eventually he replaced Accardo, developed a ruthless coterie of aides, and by the time our program began, Giancana was one of the nation's Mafia chieftains, still based in Chicago but with interests that extended beyond and abroad. As one writer said after studying Giancana's power, "He personified organized crime in Chicago, and anywhere else for that matter . . . as operating boss he had his finger in every pie, cutting a percentage of deals, deciding on new concessions, okaying hit contracts, exacting discipline, smoothing out disagreements, interacting between the older dons and the young hustlers."

He had attended (and escaped) the Apalachin meeting, traveled to Cuba and Las Vegas, and now was high on our attorney general's list of top racketeers in the country. Earlier, he'd been subpoenaed by the McClellan Committee, where he took the Fifth Amendment while being hassled by its brash young counsel, Robert Kennedy. "Are you going to tell us anything or just giggle?" Kennedy pressed the witness. "I thought only little girls giggled." Later, Giancana complained to a reporter, "What's wrong with the syndicate? Two or three of us get together on some deal and everybody says it's a bad thing. But those businessmen do it all the time and nobody squawks."

Silberling filled us in on the data available to us. Starting on July 19, 1959 (it would continue, later records showed, until July 11, 1965), William F. Roemer and his FBI colleagues in Chicago had begun something new for the FBI: a top-hoodlum program. They regularly monitored Giancana electronically with a pineapple-shaped mike secreted in a tailor shop where he met regularly with his cohorts. The FBI nicknamed their tell-all device "Little Al." Used for "intelligence" purposes only, any evidence they got could not be used against Giancana or others because it was obtained without a warrant. But it told agents (and the attorneys assigned to relevant cases) what they could do to *prevent* some crimes from happening, led to developing informants, kept the FBI apprised of the mob's activities, and permitted tactical leaking of information that put the public spotlight on mob figures and their "business." They had overheard the deal under which Tony Accardo retired and was succeeded by Giancana in September 1959. It told of the national crime commission that managed Mafia affairs. Later, one hidden mike went into the Armory Lounge in Forest Park, an old speakeasy that Giancana used as his headquarters; the agents referred to it as "Mo." "After Mo went in, Giancana had few secrets," Roemer reported.

Secrets or not, we had no cases developing on Giancana.

Nor did we have anything promising on Santos Trafficante, Jr., another notorious Apalachin guest based in Tampa.

For Mafia purposes, Florida was divided into two parts: the west coast, centered in Tampa, the east coast in Miami. Meyer Lansky was the major figure in Miami. A financial wizard, Lansky was the fiscal brains of the various Mafia organizations, and while he was never nabbed despite persistent investigations and surveillance, he was dubbed treasurer of the mob's vast illicit financial empire. Santos Trafficante—first the father, later the son—ran Tampa. The older Trafficante came from Sicily in 1904 and gradually took over illegal gambling in Tampa. His holdings grew, as did his power within the reigning circle of the Mafia in the United States. When he died in 1954, his son, Santos junior, took over control of the numbers business in central Florida and ownership of the San Souci gambling casino in Havana. Trafficante had a deal with the Cuban dictator, Batista, and for many years profited from control of the gambling and nightlife on that island. When Castro took over in Cuba, Trafficante was imprisoned and eventually deported, losing his golden sinecure to Communist reforms.

Santos Trafficante, Jr., had contacts through his father with the New York Mafia families, particularly that of Joe Profaci. His influence in the Mafia grew through the years. He was in the hotel in New York (registered under an alias) when Albert Anastasia was killed in a nearby barbershop, raising the speculation that, for intramural underworld reasons, he had fingered Anastasia. When major Mafia meetings took place, Trafficante was there. He was in Apalachin, as well as at the infamous dinner for thirteen in September 1966 in Forest Hills, New York, at the La Stella restaurant, along with Carlos Marcello, Frank Ragano, and other top mafiosi.

Intelligence reports of an IRS raid turned up *bolita* records of a $500,000-a-week operation that might be tied to Trafficante. Our Florida contacts would follow up.

"Herb, what's happening in Detroit, any progress on your bankruptcy fraud investigation?" Silberling asked.

Herb Bates, son of a cab driver, graduated night school while working for the FBI on fingerprints, was a middle-aged career lawyer, dapper dresser, with a rich New York accent; he always had a thorough, well-documented, often colorful report.

"We're close to indicting three top level Teamster business agents for 'labor peace' payoffs by Interstate Motor Freight. Tom McBride and I have worked with our contact in the U.S. attorney's office, Paul Komives, in the grand jury in Detroit and we're about to indict Teamsters from Toledo, Detroit, and Chicago. We had great audits done on the records and used the immunity section of the Interstate Commerce Act to force some of the details onto the record. As you know, we're going to turn the trials over to the labor unit. They should be ready to go soon."

Herb recently had had an interesting communication from Kennedy; he interrupted his report to tell us about it. Bates had been approached by a social acquaintance who had contacts with the Teamsters. He'd been invited to lunch, where he was asked if he could help get information about an ongoing grand jury investigation in Chicago concerning Teamsters affairs. If so, his host would pass it on to Hoffa. "Everyone has their price," he told Bates. But Bates did not; he was abashed, and immediately notified his superiors at Justice, who advised Kennedy. Bates worried how Kennedy would view this approach, whether he'd suspect Bates, a twenty-three-year veteran government employee. He was relieved to receive a note from Kennedy several days later, remarking: "Herb, Relax—you should have done it and split with Walter Sheridan."

"We plan to work with the IRS on a crackdown on the local numbers operations; they're doing saturation work on records; then they'll have a raid and they even got a safecracker to open the dozens of safes the syndicate uses to store their money. We intend to give this a lot of local press—which they hate," Bates continued.

"We're looking into Joseph Zerilli, Detroit's top mafioso and a member of the national commission, and his . . . elder statesmen, John Priziola, Angelo Meli, and William Tocco, who run things and mediate disputes among three local groups under their jurisdiction. About two hundred and fifty members worked for these three families; but when we put on the heat, they were moving from gambling, hijacking, and traditional criminal enterprises into 'legitimate' businesses such as bars, restaurants, barbering, waste removal, dry cleaning. Often they got into these businesses via shylocking, extortion, and other aggressive techniques not taught at the Harvard Business School. We don't have anything yet, Ed, but we know who their associates are and what respectable facades they are pushing in on."

Bates told us how one recent scam worked. The idea had started in Chicago, and Herb's investigation showed that it was thriving in Detroit. Typically, a hoodlum would take over or start a company, develop credit, buy enormous amounts of merchandise from factories or wholesalers on credit, and then unload it at discount rates in cash to fences or to friends (one a law enforcement official) usually at one-third of cost. Or sometimes they would hide the goods in warehouses and disappear. The suppliers either could not find the scam artist because he would have changed names, cities, lives; or he might go into bankruptcy and "lose" his business records. Everything he made was profit for the con man, and everything was lost by the honest suppliers. Of course, few suppliers wanted to run after these criminals, so they wrote off their losses for tax purposes, and the government and everyone else shared these losses.

"We had a case like that in the Bronx, Herb," Henry Petersen said. His recall of cases monitored over his many years in the department was encyclopedic. "A meat-packing company needed cash to keep up its credit for meat and poultry purchases. An ex-con, Joe Pagano, with Mafia ties and a background in narcotics, posing as a meat salesman, offered to get the company an $80,000 loan. In return for getting and protecting the loan, he became a company official. He connected the company with a crony, Peter Castellana, who was a moneylender. Then Pagano bought hundreds of thousands of pounds of poultry from suppliers all over the country, sold it to Castellana for 'bargain' prices below what he'd paid for it—over a million dollars' worth in one month. Castellana wrote Pagano $745,000 worth of checks. Pagano deposited, then withdrew it all, split it with Castellana, and the firm Pagano joined as financial savior went bankrupt. The suppliers lost over a million dollars."

"We had a version of that in Miami," another lawyer added. "Only they didn't go through bankruptcy, so we indicted the scam artists on the basis of mail and wire fraud based on their use of checks on out-of-state banks. One of the defendants I was hoping to turn and testify for the government was found in a canal, face down. My name was in his wallet."

"I'm sending one of our guys, probably Allen Krause, to prosecute a bankruptcy fraud in Florida, because the guy involved is a *bolita* operator associated with Trafficante," Silberling reported.

This scam was apparently in fashion nationally. We made notes to look for signs that this technique might have spread to "our" cities. Other bankruptcy frauds would later be uncovered in Chicago, Iowa, and New York.

Herb Bates described another twist. The mob opens a new business. They use a front man with no criminal record and an assumed name. The mob puts up money to open an account and establish credit. The racketeer's "nut" is used to make purchases that are quickly paid for. The company's credit goes up; so does the size of its orders. They particularly look for items that can be sold fast and that leave few traces. Soon, huge orders are pouring in the front door and sliding out the back, to be stored, peddled, or bootlegged. By the time the creditors realize something is amiss, the "bust-out" has occurred. The company bank account is emptied out, so is the store, and the "entrepreneurs" are gone. Sometimes there is a fire at the store for good measure and all the business records are destroyed (if they ever existed). A local "torch" man loved his work: He'd leave home early in the morning with balloons filled with gasoline, and later that day watch the evening news story about a local fire that totally destroyed an office building. In other situations, like the one where a terrorized legitimate partner was removed, insurance money was siphoned, as well, to pay off the original owner's extortionist debt and to complete the mobster's financial rampage.

"What's happening with your investigation of Mike Rubino?" Silberling inquired. Rubino, an active Mafia bigwig from Detroit, was someone we had focused on from the beginning.

"Rubino has a deal working with Samuel Giordano and Gene Ayotte, Ed; they supposedly decided to plan some bankruptcies 'like the Jewish guys'—sorry you guys," Bates laughed amiably, quoting his quarry and taking polite note of the reactions of those of us "Jewish guys" sitting in the room. "He wanted to move his syndicate into merchandise. They started three businesses: two furniture places, one jewelry store. They got credit, sold their stuff, and disappeared, leaving the creditors holding the bag—just like the case Henry talked about. They filed for involuntary bankruptcy under their aliases. Meantime, they've moved into another store, which we're watching; we expect them to fold soon. In each case, the modus operandi has been the same: register a new business under a false name with phony credit information, request catalogs and price lists from wholesalers all over the country, order small amounts and pay all bills immediately to improve the credit rating, use warehouse and trucking controlled by the outfit, make bigger and bigger follow-up orders of merchandize on growing credit, pitch the stuff as fast as it comes in for whatever it may bring in cash, and on bust-out day, usually a quiet Sunday, strip the store naked, lay low, or leave town, with the creditors holding the bag.

"We're going to indict on this one soon, Ed, for conspiracy and bankruptcy fraud for concealing and transferring assets, valued in the hundreds of thousands. When we do, the U.S. attorney wants to give it a lot of press so the word goes out to the mob that we're onto this scam," Bates finished.

"Good work, Herb."

Others continued to brief the group about the developing state of our art. "Tell them about Lombardozzi, Ed," Jim Misslbeck said, and added, "It's one approach our guys should keep in mind." Carmine Lombardozzi was an Apalachin attendee and was on our Top 40 Hit Parade. Silberling filled us in. "Well, our dear and devoted leader here, Jack Miller, went bonkers when he read that a federal judge in Connecticut put Lombardozzi on probation in his home area in Brooklyn after he'd pleaded guilty to a million-dollar worthless stock conspiracy. We kept hearing, but couldn't prove, he was still pushing stolen securities, counterfeiting, doing strong-arm loan sharking, not your model probationer. He had a record an arm long including some questionable labor enforcement on the waterfront. He's got a whole bunch of legitimate businesses, jukeboxes, real estate, an ice-cream company, trucking and construction—and he manages to keep the police, congressional committees, Waterfront Commission, and us at bay.

"Jack Miller can't understand—frankly, I agree—why he isn't violating the terms of his probation, which always includes catchall general language about leading a clean, honest, temperate life and keeping good company and staying away from undesirable places. Gerry Shur was bird-dogging Lombardozzi's case at Miller's request, but the Brooklyn probation officer refused to find that he violated his probation by habitually associating with known criminals. He wants proof of an actual crime being committed. Thanks a lot, judge! If we had that, we wouldn't need him." Silberling nodded to Shur, who completed the story.

Shur's report sounded as if it were written as farce. "It turned out our quarry had gotten picked up by a New York trooper for driving with a phony Florida license, which he'd technically perjured himself procuring. But the understanding probation officer in Brooklyn didn't think that was enough. Lombardozzi had a questionable excuse and the probation officer bought it. Our lawyers tried to get the Florida state attorney to prosecute, but the statute of limitations had run out there. Once an FBI agent got beaten up by five thugs at Lombardozzi's father's funeral, but we couldn't tie the assailants to Lombardozzi.

"Finally, after two and a half years, we got our break. We were able to get the U.S. attorney in Connecticut to go before the sentencing judge there and ask him to rethink the probation violation questions—he'd been deferring to the officer in Brooklyn who was on the case. We persuaded him to revoke probation on grounds of Lombardozzi's being intoxicated and hanging around with known criminals, which our investigators could document."

Our crowd clapped raucously. "We're not done; it gets better," Silberling added. "We send the FBI to arrest Lombardozzi and he outsmarts himself. Lombardozzi tells the agent he wants to get a check to pay his attorney and bondsman, goes to a drawer in his desk to get his checkbook, and one of the agents sees a tablet with names, dates, and amounts of money—clearly loan shark records—and clearly not covered by our arrest warrant. 'You're not getting these records!' Lombardozzi tells the agents.

"Well, take them with you if you want to keep them safe, says our special agent. So Lombardozzi goes to jail with these hot records, which we couldn't legally take on the scene, but which he had to turn over with all his personal property when he arrived at the jail to await being transported to Connecticut. At the hearing, in addition to our FBI surveillance showing Lombardozzi drunk about fifty times, running around with a woman not his wife, and cavorting with twenty-one known hoodlums in the New York area, we were able to introduce the shylock records in his jail personal property locker, which the judge admitted into evidence. Now Lombardozzi is trapped: If he admits what they are, he incriminates himself; if he takes the Fifth Amendment, he kills his chance for probation. So, Lombardozzi admitted violating his probation by consorting with known criminals. The judge gave him back a year of his stock fraud sentence. Meantime, we're getting a tax case ready for him."

"The point I want to make to you guys," Misslbeck said, "is that something simple like probation revocation sometimes can do what we cannot do in a criminal trial, given the uncertainties and difficulties of trials."

"Revocation of parole, too," someone chimed in, mentioning a case in Texas where a bookmaker was sent back to prison for a year because his gambling activities violated a condition of his parole. Another mobster in Florida was imprisoned for gun smuggling by revoking his earlier probation, another lawyer reported. We all made a note to remember to ask that future probation and parole orders and suspended sentences be conditioned on limitations that we could enforce if the defendants continued any contact with organized crime. One California mobster was given a suspended sentence on the condition that he leave the country in thirty days!

"The up side," Misslbeck concluded this part of the discussion, "is we can push parole for convicts who *do* cooperate. We plan to try this in one case and hope it has a salutary effect on other inmates who may want to change sides."

"Another technique to keep in mind, you guys who are new and might not know about it," Silberling added, "is the immunity statutes. We don't have a general criminal immunity statute yet, but Bob Kennedy is formulating a proposal for one to send to Congress. Until then, there are some specific statutes—the ICC and FCC laws are examples—which do have immunity provisions. If you can find a legitimate basis to add those statutes to your investigations of potential crimes—labor cases, use of interstate wires or transportation—you can take advantage of their immunity provisions. That can be very useful. When we have a small potato who won't talk and we know he can lead us to whoever is the power behind the scene, we can give the witness immunity from being prosecuted himself and force him to testify. If he has immunity he cannot use the Fifth Amendment, so he talks or goes to prison for contempt for refusing.

"A contempt conviction can loosen some clamped jaws," Silberling ended, looking in my direction. He knew I was finishing my book on contempt. I was getting a good look at a not quite academic use of the contempt power, a set of laws I would be called upon to apply in some of our trickier cases. We would soon combine grants of immunity and contempt actions in Delaware in bookmaking cases, in New York in narcotics cases, and even against a Detroit mobster's mistress in an IRS investigation.

Next, we all were treated to another less than theoretical story about aggressive law enforcement, and equally aggressive challenges to law enforcement. Ed turned to the lawyer who was working in Louisiana. "John, clue us in on Marcello," Silberling asked.

John Diuguid had learned the ropes as a neophyte prosecutor in the U.S. attorney's office in Connecticut, and was assigned to coordinate our work in a group of Southeastern states, including Louisiana. At one of our first Saturday morning meetings in Kennedy's office, Kennedy had questioned John about the status of the investigation into Carlos Marcello, reportedly a top syndicate member, if not *the* top Mafia boss. It was clear that Kennedy was especially interested in Marcello, and a deportation case against him had been hastily revived. We had already heard the background earlier from Diuguid at a meeting in Kennedy's office. Now John brought us up to date.

Carlos Marcello was born Calogers Minacore in Tunis, North Africa, of Italian parents in 1910. They brought him to the United States when he was a baby but he never obtained U.S. citizenship. For years—since 1952—the government had attempted to deport him as an undesirable alien based on a 1938 conviction for a drug violation. Marcello's immigration lawyers had tried to have that narcotics conviction set aside. Meanwhile, the U.S. government persuaded the Italian government to accept our undesirable alien, and Italy agreed to his being sent back there. To avoid that action by the Italian government, Marcello arranged to get phony proof of citizenship in another country. A Marcello intermediary, Carl Noll, a longtime underworld figure, went to Guatemala on his behalf, negotiated a deal with a local fixer and go-between with government connections. They found a small village, San Jose Pinula, where the public birth entry ledger had a blank on the page of the date of Marcello's birth. They paid the clerk to handwrite the birth entry in the handwriting of other entries and with the same yellow ink; it was authenticated later by unknowing Guatemalan and American officials, and a photostat was flown home to Marcello.

The FBI had refused—all the way up to Hoover—to pursue leads about these activities in Guatemala, so Silberling said, "OK, if they won't do it, we'll do it." He sent John to Guatemala looking for witnesses to prove that Marcello had fraudulently doctored his citizenship papers. While there, John said he felt like James Bond; his room was searched, he was followed by David Ferrie, a Marcello minion. While John was taken around in a long black car provided by our embassy, he was followed by other big black cars with unknown people in them. John found Marcello's birth certificate in Guatemala along with a witness who said he'd created it at Marcello's request. The FBI was able to lift the ink and test it for age, proving it was a forgery. Apparently, along with frustrating the attempt to deport him to Italy, Marcello wanted to be able to escape someplace if he needed to, and decided Guatemala would be a safe sanctuary.

The head of the Immigration and Naturalization Service, General Joseph M. Swing, asked Kennedy, since there were two valid birth certificates, "Where do you want to deport him to?" Kennedy decided in April 1961 to deport Marcello as an alien to Guatemala; if he was going to play games, so would we. But the game was being played in a highly questionable manner, however provocative Marcello's machinations had been.

Without notice or hearing, Swing had ordered Marcello arrested; he was whisked away to the airport in a government car with blinds, taken to a government plane that was waiting on the runway in New Orleans, and flown to Guatemala City. He had been shanghaied. Within three months, Marcello finagled his way back to the United States through several Central American countries. Marcello said it cost him more in Guatemalan payoffs than he ever paid in the United States, according to one federal agent. Then, in an act of high chutzpah, the INS brought an illegal entry case against him. After pending for a long time, that case was eventually dropped.

Marcello was in hiding while all this was going on. A copy of the Guatemalan papers was sent to Italian government authorities. He had filed a law suit in the Italian courts in 1956 to establish that he was not an Italian citizen, and as a result of these new papers, the authorization for his being deported there was not renewed.

Marcello had first claimed—then later denied—that he was a Guatemalan citizen. His immigration lawyer filed a suit in the District of Columbia asking to enjoin his deportation to Guatemala on the basis of this forged Guatemalan birth certificate of whose origins Marcello claimed to know nothing. Guatemala was a country, Marcello now said, whose language and customs were strange to him; the United States government *knew* he wasn't a Guatemalan citizen— *it* must have forged his birth certificate. The appeals court held that the question of enjoining Marcello's deportation was moot since he was back in the country.

In effect, Marcello had defrauded three governments—Italy, Guatemala, and the United States—by creating the phony document and then relying on it and disclaiming it to suit his purposes in different courts at different times. To the Italians, he claimed to be Guatemalan and thus not deportable to Italy. To the Guatemalans, and to the U.S. government, he claimed to be Italian-born and shocked by any claim that he was Guatemalan. Marcello had more than matched the chutzpah of the government by doing a number on the United States and two of our cooperating foreign allies. He could be as resourceful as this brash attorney general; and if this sordid cat-

and-mouse game didn't prove it, the next chapter in our adventures with Mr. Marcello surely did.

When Marcello reentered the United States, he and his brother Joseph were indicted in the federal court in Louisiana for perjury and for conspiring to defraud the INS. The cases against him were that his counterfeit Guatemalan birth certificate defrauded the government in its legitimate efforts to deport him, and that he'd lied about being a Guatemalan national. In exchange for a reduced sentence in another case pending against him, the government had gotten Noll to testify about his work for Marcello obtaining the false birth certificate. The case seemed airtight.

Marcello had no visible means of support. Despite an extensive arrest record, a New Orleans crime commission report that he was a multimillionaire and a major Mafia don, and Fifth Amendment appearances before congressional committees investigating crime, Marcello claimed to be a $1,600-a-month tomato salesman. The FBI had no records of his criminal activities. According to Bureau of Narcotics investigators, he operated in a room in the Town and Country Motel in Jefferson Parish, outside New Orleans. John Diuguid told us of listening to a tape surreptitiously made after someone in a pending case told government agents that Marcello had hired him to kill a witness in our defrauding case. The narcotics investigators sent the witness (now immunized from prosecution) back to the motel room after bugging it and wiring the witness, hoping to hear, and thus be able to prove, an obstruction of justice. The overheard conversation between Marcello and other supplicants who came to see him and seek his favors sounded like a scene from *The Godfather*. But the government listeners did overhear conversations that there was a "contract" out on one of their witnesses—Noll. A trial was scheduled and soon John would return to New Orleans to continue the Marcello saga.

I was getting a sense of the dilemma of law enforcement in organized crime cases. We were held to high standards of constitutional conduct, and properly so; but our adversaries played by no rules except survival at any cost. Without condoning use of questionable law enforcement procedures, one certainly could rationalize taking legitimate extra measures if we were ever to catch and convict these characters.

Ed turned next to our "affair" with Hoffa. Sheridan's group officially worked with us, though they actually had a straight line through Walter Sheridan and Jack Miller to Robert Kennedy. "What's happening down the hall?" Ed asked.

"Ed, we're moving," a Sheridan aide reported. "At the end of last year, just before Bob became attorney general, the department reported three indictments of Teamster officials and two convictions. By June of '61, we'll have eleven indictments. By the end of our first year, we expect thirty-four indictments. And we've got thirty grand-jury Teamsters investigations going on in twenty-six different judicial districts including Detroit, New York City, Chicago, Los Angeles, San Francisco, D.C., Ohio, and Missouri."

"What kinds of cases?"

"Taft-Hartley Act violations, obstruction of justice, interstate theft, embezzlement, mail and wire fraud, and Labor Management Reporting and Disclosure Act cases. We've got cases going against international officers, local union presidents and vice presidents, union business agents and organizers, reps and stewards. We're starting to make the impact the attorney general is looking for. We make enough of these satellite cases and we expect we'll be led to Hoffa." Sheridan's group at Justice was creating a pincer movement aimed at getting to Hoffa through his crooked appointees and abettors.

Civil libertarians—and, it seemed, most people outside Justice I knew—all thought Hoffa was being stalked unfairly. Sheridan and Cassidy and those who knew the details about Hoffa's questionable career were certain that a violent, crooked, and corrupting hoodlum was hiding behind his underdog's facade, and that we'd soon prove it.

When Sheridan's group report was finished, we turned to an interesting long-term plan, developing a strategy to penetrate the mob's huge financial bonanza—the Las Vegas casinos. If gambling was the multibillion-dollar bank for organized crime, Las Vegas must have been its federal reserve. And we knew that despite superficial proclamations by Nevada state officials that appropriate measures were in place to ensure the legitimacy of gambling there, the mob had infiltrated. The stakes were too high for it to be otherwise. And we knew from all other instances, whenever there is organized, large-scale gambling, there is cheating, and other criminal activities as well. The built-in odds in all gambling ventures assured that the house—i.e., management and ownership—must win. Yet, the temptations were such that this guaranteed profit never was enough to satisfy. Sporting events had to be fixed, lotteries clandestinely rigged, strong-arm tactics, drugs, and sexual enticements used, to push the already house-favored percentages. If that was the case everywhere else, we guessed it would be so in the biggest-stakes gambling center in the country. Since the gambling operations at all the casinos were monitored carefully, it was likely the mob was taking its extra share some other way. The educated guess was that it came from skimming.

Gambling—and skimming—had been big business in Las Vegas for a long time. In 1934, the state legalized gambling, and by 1946 the mob discovered this Nevada oasis. Bugsy Siegel arrived in 1946 as their emissary. With financial backing from the syndicate he built the Flamingo. Other places, similarly funded, quickly opened—the Tropicana (Frank Costello and Phil Kastel), the Thunderbird (Meyer Lansky), the Dunes (the New England family), the Desert Inn (the Cleveland gang), the Sands (Doc Stacher), the Sahara (Al Winter, a horse-race gambler), the Riviera and Caesars Palace (Chicago, Giancana)—and others followed. Many of these blowsy palaces were funded with sizable Teamsters pension fund loans, like the $10 million that went into Caesars Palace, and the $5.5 million that helped finance the Landmark Hotel. According to one report, over $50 million in Teamsters funds went into "hoodlum-connected downtown business property" and other Vegas "Temples of Mammon." Reporter Ed Reid wrote in *The Grim Reapers* that the lines were clearly drawn "between Hoffa and his union, the mobsters who fawn upon him, and the people who figure that Las Vegas should be contained."

The final result was, in Reid's words, "a gawdy-bawdy . . . cowtown that made the big time with the help of a few thousand flocks of sheep in men's clothing." It was inevitable the mob would find such a place irresistible. So with its muscle, its Teamsters loans, its political power, its show-biz attraction, its "management" experience, it found a special home. Las Vegas was considered an open territory, not the exclusive province of any territorial Mafia family. Representatives of most of the major regional Mafia chiefs were plugged into the casinos.

"Skimming" is diverting cash off the top of proceeds from any business. It occurs where there is a heavy cash flow—vending machines, ticket agencies, and gambling casinos. Any amount skimmed before it is entered into accounting records is not subject to being taxed, and thus is pure profit that can be used for payoffs and luxuries. Skimming is, in one expert's words, "steady, unseen, incalculable cash as clean and unfettered as any money hoods can take." Exactly how the process works was explained by a veteran FBI investigator:

In each casino there is a counting room. It is under twenty-four-hour camera surveillance. Periodically, the drop box under each table is picked up by security guards and taken to the counting room. There it sits until the next day when its contents are officially counted and the day's tabulation is entered on the books. The proceeds of the slot machines are handled similarly, although the coins are weighed rather than counted.

The principal method of skimming money from the casinos is by intercepting it between the tables and the counting room or in the counting room before the daily tally is taken, using pit bosses and other casino employees who are under control of the mob. It can be accomplished by shielding security cameras or in the "eye in the sky" (the peepholes in the ceiling of the casino where security employees peer down on the tables). Carol Thomas, who worked for the acknowledged master of skim, Joe Agosto, was overheard by the FBI . . . to say that there were "twenty-one holes in the bucket," meaning there were at least that many foolproof methods of skimming. However the money from the tables and slots can be waylaid, this money never gets counted; it's never officially tabulated and recorded for income tax purposes; and it's never divided with the ostensible owners. It becomes pure gravy for the mob.

Our section planned to work with a special group of IRS agents to coordinate a long investigation into skimming. Then, by following the skimmed funds to their ultimate recipients around the country through various intricate schemes, major tax fraud cases could be made against top-echelon racketeers. It would be a classic example of what Kennedy told Congress was the interstate commerce of organized crime, whereby the big shots insulated themselves from on-the-scene criminal activities while plundering legitimate businesses to fill their criminal war chests. Our lawyers would work closely with the IRS, and eventually we'd send someone to Las Vegas to coordinate activities on the scene and then try the cases.

Las Vegas demonstrated dramatically the kind of situations where federal involvement in local affairs—usurpation of local law enforcement, our less enthusiastic critics would call it—was necessary to deal with major, complex investigations. In the early 1960s, Las Vegas had a population of about 200,000, many of whom were recent arrivals employed in the gambling industry. But there also was a core community of roughly 10,000, most of whom had lived there for decades and were employed in the typical jobs any town of 10,000 might have— in retail stores, as teachers, government workers, and lawyers. An unusually high percentage of this core community were Mormons or Roman Catholics. Overall it was a tight, law-abiding community. Most of these people seldom, if ever, gambled at the casinos. But they also knew where and how their bread was buttered—the legalized gambling industry.

The department did not feel it could sell the Las Vegas U.S. attorney's office on an independent organized crime field office. Nor did we feel we could impose one. And we certainly didn't trust any office that was under local control. The federal courthouse and prosecutor's offices were firmly in the hands of members of that core community, which for all its civic and personal virtues, our sources explained, was very protective of the area's main industry.

Our opportunity opened up unexpectedly. The U.S. attorney, William Bonner, had not practiced in federal court before his appointment and was unable to recruit anyone for one of his two assistants' slots. The assistant he did have on board had never tried a criminal case and was overburdened with civil cases. So Bonner attempted to try a couple of criminal cases himself, with disastrous results.

After two embarrassing losses, Bonner was only too happy to accept the Justice Department's offer of an "experienced" federal trial lawyer to handle all the district's criminal cases. That was Earl Johnson, who was appointed as a special assistant U.S. attorney for the district of Nevada and sent to Las Vegas with a dual mission. He was to try all the regular criminal cases and thus, ideally, make himself indispensable to the U.S. attorney's office. But he also was to work with the FBI and IRS officers on their organized crime investigations. If all worked out as planned, at some point Earl would spin out of the U.S. attorney's office and start or become our separate field office. (Later, that office would be dubbed "strike force.") The Las Vegas skimming investigation he managed was a cops-and-robbers scenario that would play out during the ensuing years.

We ended our section meeting that day on a lighter note, an update on Jay Goldberg's latest escapade. "What's with Jay, Ed?" one of the staff lawyers asked as we began gathering our papers and getting ready to leave. Ed, smiling, brought us up to date.

Jay Goldberg, tall, balding, extremely funny, loved criminal trial work and reveled in this unique chance to do it big time. His Jackie Mason–style delivery belied a very clever, hard-driving prosecutor who was unorthodox in the ways he developed his cases. He'd been sent to Gary, Indiana, to look into corruption charges there, and had caused a revolution with his rough and eccentric style. The latest brouhaha was caused by a claim one grand jury witness made that Jay said he would be run over if he didn't cooperate and testify the way Jay wanted. The witness had complained to his attorney, an influential Democratic party member from that area, who had gotten word of Jay's threat back to Robert Kennedy. Jay was called back from Indiana and put on the carpet to explain.

"Bob had him in his office with Whizzer White, Jack Miller, and me one morning last week," Silberling continued. " 'What's this about your running over a witness, Jay?' they asked. Jay was shocked. 'General,' he said, 'I had this penny-ante guy before the grand jury. I knew he was lying and I didn't want to waste my time trying him for perjury. I needed his testimony and the information we knew he had. So I warned him. Listen, I said, you're in trouble! I want you to get out of trouble by not lying to this grand jury under oath! Do you understand? Then I told him: "You are standing on a U.S. highway, mister, right in the middle of the road and a big truck marked U.S. government is coming at you a hundred miles an hour. You gotta move out of the way or you're going to get run over by it." Jay added, in some exasperation, 'General, these guys in Indiana don't know from a metaphor.' "

Everybody broke into laughter, and we left Silberling's office and headed back to our own offices down the hall, edified, motivated, and in my case anxious to get my own cases going, to hit the road out of Washington in search of my own dragons to slay—or at least annoy.

Chapter 5

MY TURN, IN

NEWPORT, KENTUCKY

Whatever the glamorous appeal or liveliness of our meetings in Washington, that clearly was not where the drama was. Reviewing files in Justice Department offices from nine to six may have satisfied some of the career lawyers in our group, but it soon became clear to others of us that the real action would come when we were sent to some distant city to conduct investigations and try cases. There, we could shed our Clark Kent suits for the capes of superlawyers.

I didn't have to wait long for my chance. On the bus ride from Alexandria to Washington one morning that spring, I read an article in *The Washington Post* about an arrest the night before of George Ratterman, a former football star, currently a reform candidate for sheriff in Newport, Kentucky. He had been found in a gambling joint, upstairs in bed with a stripper named, nicely enough, April Flowers. His pants were off, police reported, when, acting on an anonymous tip, they broke into the room and arrested Ratterman.

When I arrived at the Justice Department, I went to a meeting with Silberling—arranged the day before—to ask to be sent into the fray, someplace where there might be some action. To my surprise, Silberling referred instantly to the Ratterman incident. "OK," Silberling said, "there's a case breaking in Kentucky. You can go there and use it to start a broadscale grand jury investigation into payoffs to public officials in Newport. Newport's a notorious sin city the attorney general would like to see cleaned up."

"Kentucky," I groaned. I expected Chicago, or Miami, or New York—not a backwoods place like Kentucky.

"Somebody's got to look into the arrest last night," Silberling said. "The reformers there are calling the attorney general to look into Ratterman's claim that he was framed."

"What's the federal offense?"

"If Ratterman was framed by a phony arrest by local policemen, there could be a federal civil rights claim, S.242. The attorney general's got someone from the Civil Rights Division ready to go, but he wants the organized crime section in on the grand jury investigation. Whichever way the Ratterman investigation goes, we can get our foot into the door in Newport."

As soon as I left his office, I gathered all the material I could find at the Department of Justice about Newport: press clippings about the case, FBI and other available intelligence files. Newport was an interesting sociological case history, and I could see why Robert Kennedy would target it.

Of all the wide-open, corrupt cities in the country, Newport competed to be the worst. A town of about thirty thousand, surrounded by the Licking River on the west and the Ohio River on the north and east, it was connected to adjacent Cincinnati by several bridges and the lure of vice. An army military post had been built there in 1803. During the Civil War, when troops were garrisoned in Cincinnati, prostitutes were available across the river in Newport.

A century later, Cincinnati, self-advertised as the Queen City of the Midwest, a clean-cut, religious, wholesome, business-oriented town, would disgorge its conventioneers and some of its own citizens into wide-open, nearby Newport. The famous Louisville racetrack also was not far away. One local history book reported that Newport had too many "brothels, saloons, and bust-out gambling points" to count. Technologically advanced, Newport had also become a center for national betting syndicates, handling, over the wires, extraordinary sums of money bet around the country. All this went on under the noses of and with the aid and comfort of the local "law enforcement" establishment. The town was, one clergyman complained, the

"Gomorrah of America," leaving unspecified the identity of our Sodom.

It was inevitable that the underworld would eventually find Newport and capitalize on its opportunities. When the celebrated Elliot Ness had left Chicago after heading the law enforcement campaign against Al Capone, he was made public safety commissioner of Cleveland and promptly closed its casinos. Ohio governor Frank Lausche kept up the pressure, so the Cleveland syndicate moved into northern Kentucky, Havana, Florida, and Las Vegas. After bloody warfare over control, the syndicate took over in Newport, conducting all the action through a local board of directors. Now, as the nation's biggest lay-off betting site, where bookies from around the country could spread some of their heavier bets, the action was flourishing. As I had heard, bookies, to insure against the possibility of their own banks being broken, would "lay off" a portion of their big bets among other bookies, who in turn received reciprocal rights. One key to operating such a network was an amenable local political structure, particularly a cooperative sheriff and chief of police.

Kennedy had told Congress how alluring the stakes were. One national magazine estimated that $30 million was gambled in Newport one year. The IRS estimated, conservatively, that in 1961 numbers and horse bets alone in Newport totaled $6 million.

Most of the money generated went to the out-of-state syndicate bosses who controlled Newport, except about a million dollars, which went to pay off the local officials to keep the roulette wheels turning.

In the midst of such prosperity for the few, Newport, Kentucky, would never rival its sister city in Rhode Island. There was no downtown shopping district, no newspaper; the streets were worn and dreary. In every respect except vice, the city of red brick buildings and old streets was stagnant. While gambling had become Newport's number one industry, only about five hundred jobs for ordinary working people were created by gambling—as waitresses, bartenders, parking attendants. The majority of the city's laborers traveled to Cincinnati for work. While the population of Newport was 30,000 in 1920, and the U.S. population has grown substantially since then, the 1960 census reported the population of Newport at a stagnant

30,115. Newport was a depressing town "captive of its dark reputation," in the words of Hank Messick, a veteran investigative reporter for *The Louisville Courier-Journal.*

But the population exploded between 6 P.M. and 6 A.M. People poured into Newport most nights from all over the country looking for fun and excitement. One of the perennial places for their diversions was the Glenn Hotel, the scene of Ratterman's arrest. The term "hotel" was generous. Visitors who tried to register were told the rooms were for "customers," not guests. Eventually, the HOTEL sign on the building was removed, replaced by life-size neon nudes. Indeed, the telephone numbers of the hotel were identified as the phone numbers used by bookies around the United States to call in lay-off bets. There were forty-five phone lines running into the Glenn's Tropicana Club to handle these transactions.

The Tropicana Club, previously known as the Glenn Rendezvous, was on the first floor and the Sapphire Room for gambling was on the second floor. When the club first opened in the summer of 1941, a local nightclub reporter wrote, in pure boosterism-understatement: "A brilliant sparkle was added to greater Cincinnati's entertainment constellation." But during the twenty years before I first saw it, the club's luster tarnished and it became a notorious bust-out gambling joint, a "supermarket of vice" in Hank Messick's words, "where second-rate exotic dancers stripped and B-girls vied with prostitutes for the suckers' dollar."

In 1956, the Glenn had reopened with fan dancer Sally Rand as its headliner in the floor show. The new manager promised, "There positively will be no gambling at the Glenn. We shall endeavor to attract the convention patronage from Cincinnati and to provide clean, wholesome, continuous entertainment for the entire family." When reporter Messick visited the Glenn, he observed such family fun in progress as blackjack, craps, roulette, and razzle-dazzle, a multiple dice game in the casino, and a bookies' lay-off betting center on the third floor.

From time to time, the Glenn would be raided and closed down, and its expensive gambling equipment confiscated, but the magnetism of money repeatedly brought it back to life. There would be arrests, followed by trials and jury acquittals. The lawyers loved their gambling clients, and many of the citizens on the juries were "liberals" sympathetic to the casinos. One veteran trial lawyer explained to *Time* magazine in May 1961, "Everybody expects a little gambling, a little vice. Everybody's liberal around here." Any reformers caught hell from the merchants.

A block from the police station, whorehouses ran day and night. For a southern state, life could get fast-paced. At Newport's biggest brothel, it was said, eleven girls averaged a new customer every seven minutes from noon Saturday until 6 A.M. Monday.

News of the fun and excitement was really clever promotion to draw folks to places like Newport, where they often fell into holes of desperation, awful Alices in a wonderland that turned nightmarish. "The publicity mills . . . churn out puffs about stage shows, the high-priced entertainers, the romance and the gaudy trappings," Fred L. Cook wrote in his exposé *A Two-Dollar Bet Means Murder.* "But there is no publicity mill to deal with another and more important story—the story of the misery, destitution, and despair that are the inevitable legacy of unrestricted gambling." Occasional killings usually were written off as self-defense, including one case where the victim who was shot in self-defense was asleep.

The Ratterman incident seemed of a piece with the past. It would not be the first time a reformer was smeared by vested interests in Newport, the regional press reminded its readers. Reform movements in places like Newport were scoffed at. Reformers did not last long. A young policeman who tried to raid a gambling casino was beaten by thugs who warned they'd break his legs next time he tried such a stunt. The casino boss challenged the rookie: "What do you think I'm paying for?" Questioned about wide-open gambling, one veteran police officer responded, "I don't know nothin' about it."

Organized crime would do whatever it took to protect its multimillion-dollar-a-year vested interest in Newport. Payoffs, frame-ups, violence, all were merely methods of protecting those interests. For, as muckraker Messick remarked about Newport (and indeed as Robert Kennedy had recently told Congress): "Modern crime is big business, and modern hoods, however vicious and ruthless, are first of all good businessmen."

———

All my reading and all the briefings in Washington as a fledgling prosecutor did not completely prepare me for my first plunge into the realities of our work. A quick meeting with Robert Kennedy had been arranged before I left for Lexington, where the grand jury would be sitting. It was the first time I had met him on a case of mine, and he was then, as in all our subsequent meetings, informal, quietly intense, friendly, informed about unfolding events, questioning, decisive. He was slight of stature but strong-looking, wiry of body, with a burst of sandy-colored hair, steely-eyed but with a soft smile. There was an atmosphere of high energy in his presence.

Kennedy had been called by reformers led by Henry Cook, a former U.S. attorney in Kentucky, and pressed to jump into the investigation of the Ratterman arrest. The reformers wanted federal aid in cleaning up the area. Kennedy was concerned that our involvement in a local arrest might be seen as a usurpation by Washington. Already, the state attorney general had come and called, worried that state officials would be subjects of a federal grand jury. Kennedy knew Newport, as a center of crime and corruption, was ripe for our group's attention, but he was understandably chary about taking sides in a local case he knew little about.

"I don't want to get involved in local politics," he told those of us who had hurriedly assembled to discuss using the Ratterman arrest as a possible way to begin a broad grand jury investigation into payoffs and corruption in Newport.

"You can't avoid getting involved in local politics, General," I brashly volunteered. "If we don't act, the other side will say Ratterman wasn't framed. Since they know that we've been asked to enter the case, not opening an investigation will speak as loudly on the local scene as our going there will."

Kennedy wasn't happy with all the unknowns in this strange case involving a local sheriff's campaign in a place we did not know well, working with a new and unpredictable U.S. attorney about to be sworn in. But he agreed to seize the opportunity to at least start the official machinery; Ratterman's arrest opened the door for our investigation. Kennedy signed papers authorizing me as a special assistant to the attorney general with the power to conduct a grand jury investigation into potential federal crimes in Kentucky.

I didn't say so, but I had one problem: I had never been in a grand jury before.

From the FBI files I knew something of the "sociology" of Newport. I would have the hands-on guidance of A. B. Caldwell and his colleagues in the Civil Rights Division. But the politics of a criminal case, I was quick to discover, often eclipses the law, especially when a case threatened to be a celebrity event like this one.

On the plane to Kentucky, A.B. eased me into the situation we were about to face. He was a grandfatherly, seasoned government attorney with a mellifluous voice and generous manner. It would be my show when we got there, but he'd be my anchor in experience and a good counsel. We got along fine, and I was pleased to be teamed up with him. He reminded me about the thrust of the venerable Civil Rights Act, heightening my sense of what we'd need to establish in order to make a case under its ambit.

Originally passed in the Civil War reconstruction period, the civil rights statutes were aimed at bringing a federal presence against lawless law enforcers themselves. Used at first in lynching cases in the South, their application had been broadened to include various situations in which the law itself had been used wrongfully *against* citizens. If the perpetrators could not be prosecuted locally for the offenses they had committed, the theory was, the federal government should prosecute them for misusing their law enforcement powers and thus depriving citizens of their constitutional rights to equal protection and due process of the law.

A panel of citizens sits periodically for eighteen months in the federal court system to hear potential cases presented by the district attorney. When they decide there is enough evidence to commence a case, they vote a bill of indictment and send it to the court for trial. Later, a trial jury—technically called the petit jury—determines guilt or innocence. Historically, the grand jury, an arm of the court, was to be a bulwark to protect innocent citizens against overreaching government: Only its judgment could commence a serious prosecution. In fact, most grand juries are handmaidens of the prosecutors, who are the only lawyers working with the jurors; defendants and their lawyers are not present. As a practical matter, the district attorney decides what witnesses, which evidence, and what cases come before the grand jury. Our lawyers used grand juries as powerful investigatory bodies. Occasionally, what is called a "runaway" grand jury goes off on a mission of its own. While that is a rare phenomenon, I'd learn firsthand it was not an extinct one.

In Lexington, we were met by the local FBI agent assigned to the

Ratterman investigation. Frank Staab was a mature, tall, square-shouldered, stentorian-voiced veteran who would work closely with us in the ensuing years. Staab was smart and solid, knowledgeable about Newport and about how to get things done the FBI way (recently being fine-tuned to combine with the new RFK way). On the drive to our courthouse offices, Frank filled us in on the whirl of activity in Newport since Ratterman's arrest.

At the U.S. attorney's office, we encountered our first surprise. My introduction to bizarre legal politics followed, demonstrating the eccentricities awaiting Kennedy's hotshots when we stepped into areas outside the New Frontier. The U.S. attorney, appointed to office by John F. Kennedy, was waiting at the courthouse to be sworn in. But the holdover U.S. attorney, an Eisenhower appointee, would not leave, complaining to us, "The president of the United States appointed me, and I will leave when the president of the United States tells me to go!"

I called the Justice Department for guidance. The problem was shunted up to Nicholas Katzenbach, head of the Office of Legal Counsel. A few hours later, he called to advise me that an old Supreme Court case stated what should have been obvious to all concerned. As a practical matter, there was no way that a president would personally call every appointee of his predecessor to ask them to leave; his very appointment of a successor implicitly did that.

This was a reasonable approach. But the sitting U.S. attorney wasn't of a mind to be reasonable. I had the awkward task of telling the cantankerous, lame-duck U.S. attorney to get out of his office. I wasn't too effective: He simply refused. More calls to Washington.

"He says he won't go."

"Go to the District Court judge and tell him to swear in the new U.S. attorney."

I scooped up the new U.S. attorney, his wife, and family, who were all dressed up to witness his swearing in, and we went downstairs to the judge's chambers to ask him to swear in our man. The judge, well on in years and set in his own idiosyncratic ways, refused to evict the ex–U.S. attorney.

Another call to D.C. "Mr. Katzenbach, the judge says he won't swear him in."

"Well, Ronnie, the law states that anyone can swear in the U.S.

attorney. So you go down to the local drugstore, find a notary public, and get our goddamn U.S. attorney sworn in!"

I went back to the judge and told him what my instructions were and implored him to reconsider. We could eventually get our way, but I didn't want to affront a judge I'd be arguing cases before, or publicly insult the now former U.S. attorney, or demean both by traipsing down to the apothecary and spoiling a touching family moment observing the ceremonial swearing-in of the new U.S. attorney.

Reason won out. At the last moment, the recalcitrant judge capitulated. A hurried swearing-in took place in his chamber. Informed of this, the former federal prosecutor reluctantly left. It was dawning on me that I was embarking upon what was not an entirely cerebral adventure.

When opening day for our grand jury finally arrived, I decided to fake it. Until I could see what one looked like and how the prosecutors behaved and operated with the grand jurors, my silence might be viewed as wisdom. We agreed en route to Lexington that A.B. and the assistant U.S. attorney assigned to our case from the local federal office—N. Mitchell Meade—would start things off; I would be there observing and could pipe in when I felt comfortable with the scene— if ever.

The ex–U.S. attorney had subpoenaed several Newport witnesses whose names appeared in the news stories about the incident, and he was quoted as speculating there might have been kidnapping or Mann Act (interstate prostitution) violations. We decided to use them but to begin the grand jury inquiry with a synopsis of the events in the Ratterman episode and an overview of the criminal scene in Newport. Frank Staab was our introductory witness, and he set the scene and the tone. Frank's competent, fatherly way impressed the jurors, and the atmosphere was friendly and collaborative. Mitch Meade, the assistant U.S. attorney, was there to assure them, with Frank, that this investigation was the Kentuckians' affair. The Justice Department guests, so to speak, were present to show the flag of collaboration with Washington.

When Frank finished that first day, the grand jurors requested that certain witnesses, identified in the news stories and described by Staab, be called for our next session, a week hence. We also subpoenaed a long list of madams, procurers, and other Newport characters to flesh out the cast, so to speak. Our aim was to find out who was being paid off for wide-open prostitution to flourish, and to show how Newport's underworld system actually worked.

Then it was time to see the sights and meet the players. Frank Staab drove us to northern Kentucky, where we had arranged to see Henry Cook, lawyer for Ratterman and for the reform group supporting his campaign to clean up Newport. A lanky, craggy-faced man, Cook was a lifelong area resident who knew everyone and everything that happened in Newport. Cook saw the Ratterman affair and our arrival on the scene as the best chance the reformers had of making a serious change in the life of their community.

We met Henry Cook early in the evening at a pleasant roadside steakhouse overlooking the Ohio river. We sat outside viewing the river, and had drinks. (Henry followed my order of a martini with his own request for "Old Furrestor and some branch water besides of it.") Then, over sizzling platters of steaks and potatoes and cup after cup of coffee, we talked for hours.

Cook's story of the local—now national—cause célèbre was fascinating. The motive to frame Ratterman was clear: embarrass the paragon of virtue and demean his cause. Such seamy smears had happened before. But the motive applied citywide, and we federal prosecutors would have to charge specific individuals based on specific evidence if we were to prove our civil rights case. Cook's information provided some of the pieces to our puzzle, though important ones were missing.

Three policemen had sworn that they responded to a tip and found Ratterman in bed with April Flowers. She corroborated their story, as did Glenn manager Tito Carinci, and both of them had been scooped up and arrested at the same time. The other person present that evening was Tom Paisley, an out-of-town businessman who was Ratterman's friend and had no reason to lead him astray.

Both Cook and Staab found it suspicious that a man named Charles Lester was the attorney representing both Tito Carinci and April Flowers. Lester was the brains behind much of the legal arrangements shielding illegal operations in Newport, they believed. Crafty and clever, Lester had tried to challenge the powers in Newport as a young lawyer starting out years before; but he had soon switched sides and now represented some of the casinos (including the Glenn) and their owners. The FBI had reports he was depositing Newport gambling syndicate money in Swiss banks on tours to Europe, and Customs agents were asked to search the car he was shipping to Europe on the *Cristoforo Colombo* that year (nothing turned up). Lester had shown up in the middle of the night, arranged bail for Tito and April, and then was seen meeting in the early morning hours with the three arresting officers and Tito and his partner at the Glenn, Marty Buccieri. Staab and Cook were certain Lester had masterminded the frame of George Ratterman.

Cook could have gotten Ratterman off without a trial. The arrest was legally improper, having been made without a warrant on the basis of an anonymous tip. But to do so would have left Ratterman looking guilty, released only on a legal technicality. After decades of tolerating the depravity of their hometown, a local citizens group called the Committee of Five Hundred had pledged to end "the invisible government that controls Campbell County." If reform was to succeed this time, Ratterman's innocence had to be proved; his release on technical grounds would not do.

The independent reformers' candidate for sheriff, the key office of local law enforcement, was an unlikely but interesting choice. George Ratterman was a well-known personality. He came from a large and respected family. One brother was a priest, another a lawyer. He had a beautiful wife and eight young children. He had spent a high-visibility athletic career quarterbacking at Notre Dame behind their star Johnny Lujak and with the Cleveland Browns under the legendary Otto Graham. An investment banker with a law degree, he also was a professional sportscaster, doing commentary on football games on a weekly network program. But he had no law enforcement experience.

On April 4, 1961, an overflow crowd of about 350 people had gathered in a second-floor meeting room in the Newport Public Library at Fourth and Monmouth streets. They were there to draft George W. Ratterman to run for sheriff. Police were assigned to patrol the streets outside the library. A few blocks away, Newport's gambling casinos were operating as usual.

To a standing ovation, the clean-cut candidate accepted the reformers' unanimous summons to serve: He pledged to end "the invisible government," to conquer "the forces of evil" that controlled Newport, a town where "syndicated gambling finds a home, where prostitution flourishes, where officials are known to be corrupt, where alcohol is sold to minors at all hours, and where the illegal narcotics industry has also found a home." With a rhetorical flourish, Ratterman concluded his speech by reminding his supporters of the profound stakes involved in their efforts: "This is not a political fight. This is a fight of morality against stealth, of right versus wrong. There can be but one victor of such a battle." As if he'd read Kennedy's briefing books, Ratterman had noted "that corruption cannot exist without dishonest officials . . . we cannot have vice thriving as it does here without the consent of at least some officials."

The prognosis for the reformer was not unanimously upbeat. On the fringes of the audience at the Newport library were several local gambling figures. One who was not applauding, Albert "Red" Masterson, known locally as "the Enforcer," was asked by a reporter covering the event if he thought Newport could be cleaned up. "I am still waiting to see it," Masterson said. An editorial page writer wished Ratterman luck, but warned that while a reformer sheriff could make a big difference, other officials could not just watch him and develop "Newport eye, a rare disease that makes public officials unable to see" law breaking in their midst.

The Newport Ministerial Association called on Governor Bert T. Combs to oust Campbell County officials, including the incumbent sheriff, for failing to enforce antivice laws. But the governor said he did not think the Newport situation was so bad as to warrant his intervention. The current sheriff had been indicted the year before for nonfeasance but was acquitted. The Democratic candidate opposing Ratterman's independent race for sheriff was quoted as saying: "Is there any vice around? I've never seen any." He sounded like the police inspector Claude Rains played in *Casablanca*. ("I'm shocked to discover there is gambling going on at Rick's Place.") The gamblers were lying low until "the heat was off."

Ratterman's campaign showed signs of catching on. His group of followers was growing. The Committee of Five Hundred now had over 23,000 members. Ratterman was speaking often and warming to his candidate's role.

Then, on May 9, came the arrest. Released from the Newport jail on $500 bond at 3:50 A.M., Ratterman claimed he was framed, the "victim of a malicious plot." The Ministerial Association claimed the plot was hatched "by members of the local underworld who are seeking to defame [Ratterman's] reputation and discredit the movement to clean up Newport." They urged all good citizens to rally to Ratterman's support.

Several hours after arriving home that morning, Ratterman went to a Cincinnati hospital and was tested for drugs by a pathologist from Kettering Laboratories. Dr. Frank Cleveland found that Ratterman had been given a dose of chloral hydrate, known as knockout drops or, in the old-fashioned phrase, a Mickey Finn. That conclusion confirmed Ratterman's explanation of the night before. Ratterman made a formal statement later that morning that accounted, as best he could under the circumstances, for his activities that night.

I was drugged last night and awakened in the bedroom of the apartment of Tito Carinci at the Glenn Hotel in Newport . . . I was so groggy and weak I could hardly lift my arms. I was pushed to the floor several times. I recall seeing a woman with the men in the room when I was awakened. I have no idea who she was and had never seen her before. The officers refused several requests to return my trousers and I was taken to the police station wrapped in bed covering . . .

I have known Tito Carinci for a long time, from the days when we were both playing football . . . Since I announced my candidacy for sheriff he has approached a mutual friend on several occasions and has mentioned the fact that he would like to talk to me . . . Yesterday our mutual friend mentioned to me once again that Tito was very anxious to talk to me. I said that I did not believe Tito's place of business was a good meeting ground but would consent to talk to him in Cincinnati [where we met] yesterday evening in the Terrace Hilton Hotel . . . Carinci suggested that we come to his place of business and be his guests for dinner.

I mentioned again that I did not believe his place of business was a proper one in which I should be seen. He said that he lived over his place of business and suggested that we could get to his room unnoticed through a back door and eat in complete privacy.

This was obviously the wrong place to go as I should have

realized. Nevertheless the three of us did go to his suite . . .
Shortly thereafter I suddenly became quite groggy and stretched
out on a bed in the bedroom. I recall nothing more until I was
awakened by the commotion.

The local trials followed quickly. Cook's narration expanded on the
news clips we'd read and the trial transcripts we'd studied. An overflow crowd of more than three hundred people jammed the seventy-
five-seat circuit courtroom in Newport on Tuesday, May 16, to attend
the three notorious trials of Carinci, April, and Ratterman. There
were more national media representatives in attendance than any time
in the court's history. Reporters sat on the floor and in the jury box.
Time magazine, *The New York Times*, radio and television
reporters—all were there. Coverage was live during each break. As in
later cases, the very coverage was a story in itself. The onlookers were
raucous and partisan. Outbursts followed sensational testimony. One
man in the audience fainted. Some people brought their lunch and
thermoses. Some, including Tito Carinci, blew bubble-gum bubbles
that popped like small-caliber weapons. There was a bomb scare.

Members of the crowd were cynical, outraged, or even amused
about the unfolding story. The local newspaper dramatically
reported, "A city is on trial in a stuffy little courtroom rocking with
sin and shame." The mayor, who sat at the prosecution table each
day, said the case "is a ten-dollar police court case blown up out of
proportion."

Henry Cook had asked that Ratterman's case be tried first. The
judge decided to try April Flowers—whose actual name was Juanita
Jean Hodges—first because the charge of prostitution was the most
serious of the three cases. Tito Carinci was charged with breach of the
peace, for allegedly attempting to disrupt the arresting officers. Cook
was certain that Charles Lester orchestrated all the events, and that
Lester wanted the other cases to go first so all the lurid, perjured testimony of his clients, April and Tito, would be publicly aired to further
smear Ratterman.

Lester, like Cook, could have moved to dismiss the cases against his
clients, Tito and April, because the arrests were made without a
warrant, but that would not have served his ulterior purposes.
Ironically, neither lawyer—Lester or Cook—took advantage of the

short, sure route of having their clients' cases dismissed on technical grounds. Cook had to show that Ratterman was innocent; Lester wanted his clients to testify so they could make Ratterman look bad—or worse.

Mr. Lester's clients put on a show for the crowd. Tito Carinci took the stand and gratuitously offered to take a lie detector test to confirm his version of the disputed night's events. Then he reported that he'd gone to a Jesuit priest and knelt before an altar and sworn what he said was true, adding, "George, could you do that?" Carinci said he didn't want to embarrass his friend Ratterman, that he had warned Ratterman not to come to Newport, but Tom Paisley kept pushing him to make the trip, demanding of Carinci, "Where are the dancing girls? When do we get the broads? When are we going over the pond?" Carinci elaborated on his Good Samaritan role. He had asked Ratterman if it was all right if he got a couple of dancing girls. Ratterman said, "I guess so . . . You won't let anything happen? You'll protect me, won't you? Will you shake my hand on it?" But alas, when he later ran into his room because the police were there, April was, rather than dancing, nude from the waist up, and Ratterman was holding her in "sort of a Valentino grip and kissing her." Lester showed what a classy fellow he was after eliciting Tito's testimony. He had faith in his client's story, Lester told the press: "Why would Tito stink up his place like that?"

April put on a good performance, too. The twenty-six-year-old exotic dancer from Houston said Tito had stopped her act, to her artistic dismay, and asked her to come to his room on the third floor to meet some good friends for a drink. She took off her costume—a G-string and bra with glass sequins—because the hard surfaces of her costume were uncomfortable, and put on her leopard-skin "slave" robe. Removing her clothes meant nothing to her, she explained: "I'm a stripteaser. That's just like sitting down and typing out a letter to me." Ratterman was on the bed with his pants off, she testified, adding demurely that "his shirt was pretty long, so it wasn't too embarrassing." When the police barged into the room, she and Ratterman were embracing on the bed.

April offered a touch of pseudo-verisimilitude to her testimony: Ratterman had given her a ballpoint pen advertising his investment counseling business as a souvenir, telling her to call him sometime.

The pen was put in evidence. (Cook told us that the pen story had to be contrived: Ratterman was no longer in the investment business; the address and phone number listed on the pen were obsolete.)

April's story on the witness stand was confirmed by Bonnie Green, a twenty-two-year-old stripper who worked as Rita Desmond. (The strippers had imaginative names: My favorite was Tequila Mockingbird.) Rita testified that neither Ratterman nor Paisley seemed hazy, both were bashful, and that Paisley paid her $50 to go to his room in a Cincinnati hotel "when he couldn't move me by talk." He told her, allegedly, that "Ratterman and April wanted to be alone."

The police officers testified they'd received an anonymous tip with shocking news—one saying that "prostitution was going on at the Glenn and Ratterman is there." They thought Ratterman was on a crusade leading a citizen's raid at the Glenn and that they'd better be responsive to the call for police intervention. Officer Patrick Ciafardini had been at the Glenn earlier, at 10 P.M., he testified, after returning to Newport from a police meeting in Bowling Green. He'd gone from the Glenn to the police station, where he later got the phone call and the tip. A second detective, Upshire White, stated he heard Ratterman tell a sobbing Tito Carinci in the car on the way to the police station, "Don't cry, Tito. It's just one of these things that happen. We just got nailed. That's all."

They were laying the smear on with a trowel.

The sub rosa case against Ratterman was made; whatever the verdict in court, the slander was working. Local wise guys quipped that "Ratterman went to bed in May and woke up in April." It looked bad for the reformers.

When the first day's proceedings ended, the head of the reform committee told the attending press, "We ain't had our bats yet." He was alluding to Henry Cook's secret weapon, a bombshell that he hoped would explode the next day. While all this excitement preoccupied local observers, that same day, May 17, 1961, Robert Kennedy was testifying before the United States Congress about the need for new legislation that his staff could use to fight organized crime. He cited Newport, Kentucky, as a prime example of a city with wide-open, unchecked violations of the law.

Ratterman's defense opened with the testimony of four doctors about the blood and urine samples they took and tested the morning of the arrest. Dr. Frank Cleveland, a pathologist, concluded that there was half a gram of chloral hydrate in Ratterman's blood at about 9:15 A.M.—almost seven hours after the arrest.

He described how the drug dissolves quickly in liquid and said its taste would not be detected in the scotch and soda Ratterman had that night. Alcohol would intensify the effect of the chloral hydrate, the doctor testified, and the result would be mental confusion and physical incoordination. The drug takes effect in about fifteen minutes and could induce sleep in an hour. The doctors who took the sample from Ratterman around 8:15 A.M. the next day testified he seemed under the influence of drugs then. But, the doctors admitted, when questioned whether the drug could have been administered after Ratterman's release from jail, the time of ingestion could not be calibrated exactly.

Ratterman himself testified that he must have been drugged, because his memory of that night was so hazy. He had speculated that Carinci might have wanted to bribe him to drop out of his race for sheriff. Such offers, Ratterman had heard, are often made through good friends, as Paisley was to him.

Ratterman was a clever, articulate witness who could become testy when prodded. At one point, the prosecutor pushed Ratterman, about why had he—"the paragon of moral virtue"—not done anything about the notorious gambling he supposedly deplored? Good citizens were helpless, Ratterman replied, because they got no help from the police. When the prosecutor continued this line of cross-examination of Ratterman, the witness took him on. "I've done the same as you or anybody else to improve conditions," he shot back. "How do you know I haven't done anything?" the plodding prosecutor snapped. "Because they still exist," Ratterman replied, to an outburst of laughter from the spectators.

The trial continued into an extraordinary fourth-day Saturday session. It was then that Cook pulled his surprise. Thomas Withrow, a thirty-six-year-old local freelance photographer, took the stand for the defense. He testified that on April 14 he was asked by Charles Lester to take a picture of a man and woman at an unspecified future date. Lester told Withrow to go to the Glenn Hotel and see a man named Marty, adding, "You'll be well paid for doing this job."

"Don't worry, we'll protect you," Marty told Withrow when they met at the Glenn. "They'll be in a room. We'll open the door, you take the picture, and we'll jump out." He didn't like the sound of it, Withrow testified, and he decided he wanted out. At one point the witness and the cross-examining prosecutor seemed to be speaking two different languages.

"Did you feel indignation about the offer to you?" the lawyer asked.

"Indignation? What's that?"

"Did you remonstrate with this man about the offer to take pictures?"

"What's remonstrate? I don't understand that word," the candid cameraman replied. "I wanted to wash my hands of the whole cotton-pickin' works," he said. He told his wife that if a man named Marty called, "tell him I'm not here!"

The night of Ratterman's arrest, at 1:35 A.M., Withrow's wife, Nancybelle, testified, her phone rang and a man asked for her husband. She said he wasn't there. "Tell him to call Marty at the Glenn Hotel," the caller told her. She and Withrow's sixty-eight-year-old grandmother, Nancy Hay, testified that after the first call their phone rang at close intervals until about 3 A.M.

After this shocking disclosure, the prosecutor—obviously surprised—moved to dismiss the charges against Ratterman.

He never would have brought the charges if he'd known this information, he stated. The courtroom exploded with cheers and excited congratulations by hordes of Ratterman well-wishers. Amid the pandemonium, Ratterman thanked them for their faith in him, for their prayers, and praised the Withrows and Mrs. Hay for their courage in testifying. Vindicated, he pledged to continue his political crusade with all the more conviction, but said he expected more harassment from his enemies. For now, those enemies were out of sight. The crowd of detractors who had been around during the trial to jeer and exult had quickly dispersed and disappeared. LENSMAN'S STORY BRINGS TRIAL TO SUDDEN CLIMAX, *The Cincinnati Enquirer* reported in banner headlines the next day.

Lester attempted to peddle a revisionist version of the Withrow story. Yes, he'd contacted the photographer. But not with prurient purposes in mind. The Glenn wanted a photographer to take pictures of patrons, he and Carinci told inquirers, but they wanted pictures in the dining room, not the bedroom. His clients, the owners of the Tropicana Club at the Glenn Hotel, had contacted him about the tax consequences of having a photographer on contract to the club. "Some lawyer got a hold of him and colored his story," Lester speculated. "I don't see how any of this has anything to do with this fellow Ratterman." But the prosecutor said he questioned Lester about Withrow's testimony at the recess before asking the court to dismiss charges, and Lester said, "I'll see you in several days. Don't do anything. We'll come up with something."

After the local trial of Ratterman, his campaign gained momentum. He asked the governor to send state police into Newport to enforce state laws. The county grand jury quickly indicted Carinci and Paisley for conspiring to falsely arrest Ratterman (perhaps an attempt to provide Tito with an innocent cover, perhaps a wrong jump to a wrong conclusion); it also charged nine others with permitting gambling in their establishments.

The governor ordered the commencement of ouster proceedings against four Newport police officials for neglect of their duties to enforce gambling, prostitution, and liquor laws. A Lexington attorney was appointed to conduct those proceedings along with the state attorney general. The Kentucky Methodist Conference lent its moral support to the local reform effort.

Other federal agencies had begun to look into Newport. The INS was investigating whether any prostitutes had been imported from other countries. The IRS checked nightspots to see if they displayed the required gambling stamps. In the past, IRS efforts had been finessed by local law enforcement authorities who could have indicted locals who did have stamps, while the feds could indict those who did not. Had they worked in tandem before, they could have closed the casinos and put Newport vice in a vise.

Back in Washington, Robert Kennedy testified to Congress again, this time before a Senate committee, and again cited Newport as an example of the dangers of organized gambling. He called gambling "the lifeblood of organized crime," not merely a gaming sport but an activity that provided "the kitty, the working capital for a wide range of criminal activities." Several of our lawyers, working with a federal grand jury in New Orleans, had indicted a ten-state network of interstate gamblers for a nationwide horse-betting scheme that included several notable Newport lay-off gambling figures. Their center of operations was the same Glenn Hotel.

The local conspiracy trial of Carinci and Paisley was thrown out of court by the judge, who found "not an iota" of evidence, though it provided Charles Lester with another opportunity to examine Ratterman under oath, as he was a witness for his friend and business associate Paisley. Lester suggested that Ratterman had drugged himself after being released from jail to provide a cover-up of his misconduct.

At the ouster proceedings, a parade of witnesses described historic lawlessness in Newport. They described visits to Newport gambling dens, which did not bother at all to disguise or be secretive about their operations. One CBS newsman told of one night—a Sunday—when he visited fifteen clubs and was solicited for prostitution and gambling. It is not that policemen were nowhere in evidence: They could be seen in the illegal clubs. Officials condoned the "liberal" policies prevailing in Newport. One witness told of complaining to a police official and being told to "go back home before I lock you up in jail."

A former madam testified that she regularly paid off officials in order to operate. Two of them were the policemen who had arrested Ratterman—Ciafardini and White. She was given a list of people to be paid weekly and she filled their envelopes regularly. If these officials were not paid, they'd come by "on the muscle" to find out why. Once, when she refused to pay an additional amount, her club was closed by the police for three weeks. All the house operators then met and agreed to the increase. When the payoffs went right, "we'd have to add more girls," she testified. At one time, she met a group of brothel operators in Charles Lester's office and he arranged to put her into business. When the grand jury was in session, they'd be tipped off and a show raid would be held. Nothing happened to those who played along, she testified, though then she had to have state police protective escorts because she received threatening and obscene phone calls from unidentified members of the Newport "establishment."

Another witness, a former Newport detective, told how as a young man on the force he had conducted raids on his own. In one episode, he and his deputies were disarmed and manhandled by his own colleagues; later he was thrown off the police force. He said Charles Lester was the moving force behind the corruption of officials. A local racketeer, Frank "Screw" Andrews, told the detective to leave town or he'd be thrown out. A former marshal spoke of regularly paying off officials to permit his clubs to operate, including the Glenn Tropicana, while he was a law enforcement officer. Another witness testified the Newport police "were scared to death of gambling kings."

The state attorney general promised to help, as did the state public service commission. The Kentucky Bar Association began an investigation into conduct by attorneys in Newport to determine if disbarment was appropriate. The state attorney general disclosed that impeachment proceedings were being considered by the Kentucky House of Representatives against Newport officials. The state ABC Board closed the Tropicana at the Glenn Hotel for gambling. The FBI was stepping up its activities.

The power of coordinated law enforcement was plain. In the ensuing months, over one hundred local indictments—many against local officials—were issued. The mayor, one of those indicted, complained. This was "an example of what can happen when witch-hunting and politics take over in place of reason and rule by law." One man's reform was another's witch-hunt.

New U.S. Senate hearings into multibillion-dollar national gambling syndicates were begun. Ratterman promised, if elected, to deputize special citizen police deputies to help him control events in Newport. The word was out that the "Boys were leaving in droves," and that at least there was a suspension of activities—a gambling "holiday"—until the November election.

One knowledgeable observer predicted Newport's days as a sin city were numbered. Now the full court press was on for our section's accelerated role in Newport. Bill Lynch, the former assistant U.S. attorney from New York who had joined our group, was assigned to our investigation. He had trial experience; indeed, he had handled the Apalachin grand jury investigation years earlier. He and I teamed up and worked together for years, sharing cramped quarters at Justice, living down the street from each other in Alexandria, and becoming fast friends on planes, in motels, grand juries, and courtrooms.

In Lexington, our federal grand jury continued hearing an array of new witnesses. Indictments and convictions of relatively minor characters flowed from our investigation. The problem was that there was not enough solid evidence to indict anyone for framing Ratterman. Too much about the key facts was in conflict. It was a classic circumstantial case of conspiracy, but every eyewitness would testify against our theory of the case except Ratterman and Paisley; and, by their own hazy testimony, they were unsure of precisely what happened. They also had a motive to lie, to explain away an embarrassing incident.

We had to be sure Ratterman was telling the truth. The aborted local trial left many questions unanswered. Though we had good reason to believe him, everyone else present at the time of the arrest had told the same story, and their versions were totally different from Ratterman's. He had offered to take a lie detector test and we decided to take him up on his offer. Lie detectors were used commonly in law enforcements even though as a general rule the results of these tests were not admitted as evidence in courts. They were deemed to be insufficiently exact by scientists, too dependent on extrinsics such as the skill of the administrator and the evasions of the test taker, and likely to be overly relied on by juries. "The jury is the lie detector in the court room," one pragmatic court had ruled.

Through the FBI, we found the best lie detector technician in the area. The lie detector apparatus records blood pressure and pulse rate, muscular reflexes of the arms and legs, and respiration. Lying and consciousness of guilt usually is accompanied by emotion and excitement that is expressed in bodily changes—a sweaty palm, a dry mouth, a blush, or a pounding heart. A person tested will have different reactions to control questions than to the relevant questions at issue.

The lie detector can help an innocent suspect demonstrate his innocence. That was what we set out to do with Ratterman. But it turned out not to be so easy. After running a round of tests, our expert reported to us that his findings were inconclusive. Our hearts sank. Lie detectors do not determine that the suspect is telling the truth or lying; only that the results are consistent (or not) with truth telling. Our expert could not say that about Ratterman; fortunately, he couldn't say the opposite either. It turned out Ratterman had a genius IQ and was a bad subject for lie detector testing because he talked too much. "Ask him what time it is, and he tells you how to make a watch," one investigator complained after hours of interrogation.

We were worried. We talked to Ratterman and stressed the importance of his giving the yes-no answers his interrogators required, not the essays he was providing. He took the test again, and this time the experts found sufficient documentation of truth telling to conclude we could believe him. That helped us to accept the bumps we had found in the road of Ratterman's story. Why *did* he go to the Tropicana with Carinci in the first place? What was our Robin Hood reformer doing out on a drinking spree from late afternoon until early morning, consuming, as we learned, eleven scotch and sodas? Was this the conduct of a "do-good" candidate for sheriff? Of the father of eight young children? No criminal case was perfect, experienced prosecutors advised me. I was finding that to be a glorious understatement in my first major trial.

Of course, Ratterman would have been truly victimized and the frame-up would have worked if we didn't believe him because his enemies had managed to discredit him. There were strong circumstances pointing to a frame-up. The Withrows would put Lester and Marty Buccieri (Carinci's partner at the Glenn) into the scheme. The doctors would show Ratterman was drugged, but we couldn't prove when he had ingested the choral hydrate, leaving our adversaries to argue that it was self-administered *after* the arrest. And there was no proof at all that Paisley was drugged; his haziness about the night's events might well have resulted from all the drinking he did and been a convenient way to assuage his guilt the morning after.

The three arresting officers could make or break the case, especially since we were considering indicting under the Civil Rights Act, which required acts by police officials acting "under color of law." Of the three, the guiltiest-looking was policeman Patrick Ciafardini. We'd heard he was on the take. Though married, he regularly visited a girlfriend who worked at the Glenn, was at the Glenn earlier on the evening in question, and had to have known what was going on there. His story was suspect. He had lied about his whereabouts. One of his police colleagues told the FBI that Pat asked him to say they arrived in town later than they did. In the middle of the night he just happened to go to the police station for no reason, just about the time

Ratterman arrived at the Glenn, coincidentally the time when the photographer could not be reached. He had lied to the desk sergeant, too, about the time he arrived back in town from his meeting in Bowling Green. Even the anonymous tip he described—"if you want to get Ratterman, he's at the Glenn"—sounded like a Freudian slip.

But there was no evidence against the other two arresting policemen, Joseph Quitter and Upshire White. White had been made chief of detectives since the arrest, despite testimony during the ouster proceeding that he was on the take—or, perhaps, given Newport, because of it. Quitter appeared to be a good witness for the defense; he seemed honest and composed and did not have a long history of questionable conduct, other than being a veteran on a corrupt police force. But our questioning of the three led us straight to a stone wall. The local FBI agents (all but Staab) not only were not helpful, but some were also reluctant to do what we asked of them. I learned the facts of life: The agents' bread and butter was stolen-car cases, and the local police helped make their jobs easy. Beacause this was how FBI agents accumulated their case statistics, they weren't happy about our going after their sources.

I tried to get Officer Ciafardini to be a witness for the prosecution one night in a long conversation at the federal courthouse in Lexington. After making my strong and, I thought, movingly persuasive speech, he looked me in the eye and said, "Mr. Goldfarb, I'd like to help you. But I've got this expensive lawyer, see, and he says to me, 'Pat, don't talk to Goldfarb.' What am I going to do?"

Despite the impasse with the civil rights investigation, we continued to run witnesses through the grand jury, pursuing our agenda of tying payoffs to officials. In doing so, the grand jury and I got a further education. Madams and pimps told us how the system worked. There was what they called a day line and a night line in the prostitution business. The former was smaller and its volume was modest: it kept the flow going for the busier houses that ran all night. The proprietors—the cooperative ones who would tell the truth— told of regular payoffs to intermediaries who then distributed the graft to the privileged officialdom, which sanctioned that which they were sworn to police and prosecute. Some madams kept precise records of all payments, labeling the payoffs "Laundry" and "Ice" on their business spreadsheets.

We had clashes with lawyers, and indicted and convicted one for obstruction of justice for destroying records subpoenaed by our grand jury. We encountered recalcitrant witnesses and brought contempt proceedings against another lawyer. We indicted a Tampa gang for traveling to Newport to set up a gambling enterprise at one Newport club, staffed by B-girls, steerers, and shills; the World Series in Cincinnati had tempted them to come north. But it was "hotter" in Newport than in Florida as a result of our clean-up activities, so they packed and returned home—under indictment for interstate travel for racketeering. Three brothers who managed renowned houses of prostitution denied conducting prostitution on their premises, and despite our warning that we knew otherwise and only wanted to know who they paid off, they persisted in their denials. I prosecuted one of them for perjury and he was convicted (the jury deliberated for fifteen minutes) and sent to prison for a year. Later, his brothers pleaded guilty and were sentenced to prison, too. (Years later, when I was trying another case in Lexington, I noticed one, James Bridewell, in the hallway outside one of the courtrooms. I tried to avoid him, but he spotted me and ran up to talk. I politely asked how he was, and he surprised me by replying in a friendly fashion: "I'm great, Mr. Goldfarb, I did my time, had my teeth fixed and my piles removed, and feel fine." It's always nice to be appreciated.)

While we raced between federal grand juries in Lexington and Covington, Kentucky, pursuing the civil rights investigation and other evolving Newport cases, we simultaneously worked with the IRS in nearby Cincinnati on breaking up a major citywide numbers operation run by one of the area's most notorious local rackets figures. The IRS in Cincinnati had planted undercover agents in the biggest numbers operation in the Newport-Cincinnati region. It was run out of the Sportsmen's Club, a huge building on the outskirts of Newport, by Frank "Screw" Andrews, his brother "Spider" Andrews, his nephew, "Junior" Andrews, and a gang of their underworld associates. Our agents were building an excise-tax evasion case, and we were planning a big raid with the coordination of the men undercover, including one informant in a case in Washington state who was so effective there we put him on the IRS payroll and infiltrated him into the Andrews operation.

Those lower-level numbers operators who refused to cooperate with the IRS agents voluntarily were given "forthwith" subpoenas by the FBI and were brought into the special grand jury Lynch and I were conducting. Because the federal grand jury in Cincinnati sat regularly (unlike the one in nearby Covington), we conducted our investigation there.

The squeeze was starting to work. Some of the numbers runners (locals who took the bets and passed them on to the operators) gave us proof that there was one huge areawide operation. Some of the higher-level clerical workers inside the operation, who were identified by our undercover agents, were given immunity when they refused to testify on Fifth Amendment grounds, and ultimately were forced to testify. One clerical worker lied to the grand jury and we indicted her for perjury; another was charged with making false statements to the IRS. Both turned, made deals, and promised to testify. The case was building.

We were getting plenty of publicity for our work in Newport and Cincinnati, as well as our interim courtroom successes, but some zings as well for the protracted—and so far inconclusive—investigation into Ratterman's uncanny arrest. Some of the members of the Cincinnati press had started referring to Bill Lynch and me as Sunshine and Moonglow, a reference picked up from one disgruntled hooker we had questioned in the grand jury. As she was leaving the grand jury room, a newspaperman asked her how things had gone inside. Sarcastically, she replied: "Sunshine treated me like a piece of evidence, but Moonglow looked at me like I was a woman." Lynch's fair complexion and blond hair led to his being nicknamed "Sunshine"; my darker aspect got me dubbed "Moonglow."

Eventually, there was a commando-like IRS raid. The agent we had placed inside Screw's operation met with his IRS colleagues to plan the raid with military-like precision. Any mistakes and he was a dead man. At one point, he pleaded to his fellow agents, "When I open that door, I want to see a lot of friendly faces flyin' by me." At the planned time and place, our planted agent pulled the switch and a posse of dozens of IRS agents charged through the electrically controlled entry to the vast building housing the very active gambling center and major numbers operation. The startled operators scurried, but could not destroy all the evidence or hide their paraphernalia and loot. The hard-charging revenue agents gathered up extensive numbers records, equipment, and cash (over $50,000), and arrested a horde of the

Andrewses' crooked operators. We filed an action to condemn the seized property.

We closed down the whole massive operation. We found extensive evidence all over the premises and in secret rooms, which enabled us to prove an areawide, multimillion-dollar numbers operation. Federal agents had long known there was *a* numbers operation. The raid and the records recovered demonstrated there actually were *two* separate day and night operations, conducted by the same "entrepreneurs." One was never reported; the other was, but was vastly underreported, seized records showed, and that permitted IRS auditors to prove the gambling tax evasion, traditionally an especially difficult kind of case to develop.

To our amazement, we also found evidence that the whole operation was rigged. The poor folks—and it was often the poor who played the numbers—who thought they were gambling were being fleeced. They not only fought the odds, but also the manipulations of the operators. The winning numbers were chosen each night from a glassed machine that blew Ping-Pong balls bearing numbers into the air. At an appointed time, the winning numbered balls were picked before an assembled crowd of onlookers. We were able to prove that the numbered balls chosen were preselected to make the winning numbers those that had minimal play that day, thus cutting the impresario's daily payoffs. We made certain that fact became public: With no honor among these thieves, we wanted the players in the community to know their games of sport and chance were virtually hopeless dreams.

Our specialists analyzed the records that the raiding agents had confiscated to determine the likely annual dimensions of the operation. Based on their calculations and the observations of our undercover agents (who had led a very precarious life inside the operation for as long as they went undetected), we were able to ask the grand jury to return multiple indictments for what was the biggest excise tax evasion case in history, almost $4 million. Screw and his crew were indicted for conspiracy, thirty-one counts of excise-tax evasion, and our old standby, one count under the Federal Communications Act. That trial was set for the following summer.

But in the civil rights investigation, we were frustrated. So were some members of the grand jury who could not understand why we did not just go ahead and take our best shot at everyone in sight. Legalistic explanations did not satisfy the foreman, who finally threatened to indict *me* for obstructing justice if I didn't take some action soon. He even called Robert Kennedy to complain about the attorney general's lackluster, overly hesitant assistant on the case. Just what a young prosecutor wants to happen—being portrayed to his hard-driving boss as afraid to take decisive action and unable even to control his own grand jury. On my next trip home, I explained to Kennedy what the problems were with proceeding with the evidence we had, and he was very understanding. "Go with it when you're ready. Just keep me informed. Good luck."

Stalemated in Lexington, we were very busy in Cincinnati and in Covington with other cases that arose out of our investigations. Lynch and I were becoming well-known denizens of the federal courthouse. However, many months passed with no new action on the Ratterman investigation. Then, when we were home in Washington, preparing other cases, hobnobbing with our colleagues, catching up with our families and friends, out of the blue we got an unexpected jumpstart.

In my office in Washington one quiet afternoon, a call came in from Staab. A Cincinnati television reporter had been called by April Flowers. She told him she had some important disclosures about the Ratterman affair. She refused the TV man's offer to pay her to come to Cincinnati for an exclusive interview. She would only talk to the FBI agent in the case, Frank Staab. He got word to a fellow agent in northern Michigan where April was performing at a small club in Port Huron (she was billed as "Red Hot from Newport"), and he brought her back to Lexington. There she met with Staab, Lynch, and me—we were on a plane to Kentucky almost before Staab hung up—and told us what happened that racy night in Newport.

Throughout a long night's meeting in a cramped room in the bowels of the Covington, Kentucky, federal courthouse, April chain-smoked and talked; Lynch and I listened and prodded her with occasional questions; and Staab took extensive notes. With April's new testimony, we had our case.

Our talk lasted four hours. We believed April, but again wanted to be sure. She agreed to take a lie detector test. We set it up and waited for news of the results like expectant fathers. When the polygraph operator finally reported to us that April had come through perfectly, we were exultant. "I got a strong reading on her. That girl is telling the truth," he reported. Paradoxically, her simple, straightforward manner had worked better on the lie detector than Ratterman's genius IQ and the involuted thinking that derived from it.

The case we pieced together fell into place with April's testimony. Ratterman was having a drink with a friend, Tom Paisley, at a hotel in Cincinnati. Tito Carinci, one of the Tropicana proprietors, convinced Paisley to help get him together with Ratterman. Carinci arranged to bump into Ratterman and Paisley at the bar, where he surreptitiously dropped chloral hydrate into Ratterman's drink. Paisley offered to take Ratterman home. When Ratterman passed out on the way, Carinci and another person, possibly his partner, Marty Buccieri, dragged Ratterman to Carinci's room in the Tropicana and put him in the bed with April. Paisley was waylaid with Rita Desmond. When the photographer was unavailable, they called the police, who had been alerted to this unfolding event and were ready to pounce. They arrived on schedule to arrest Ratterman and throw him in jail.

We wanted one more turn of the screw. We asked Staab to locate Rita Desmond and see if she would now confirm the story Ratterman and April told. The FBI found her in Alabama. Then twenty and divorced, she admitted that Ratterman was dressed all the time she saw him. More important, Rita reported that she was in Charlie Lester's office and heard him tell April to lie about Ratterman's pen. That did it.

We went back to Washington with the outlines of our case clearly in mind. There was barely time to unpack and repack our bags, however. Things happened quickly now. We met with Civil Rights Division lawyers who went over the proposed indictment Bill and I prepared. They, and all our bosses in the section and the division, all the way up to Kennedy, signed off on this one. Meade arranged for the grand jury to be called back into session on October 26, 1961. Bill and I flew to Lexington on the Sunday evening before the grand jury was scheduled to meet.

Frank Staab met us at the airport and drove to our motel on the outskirts of town. We were to meet April there and review her testimony and prepare her for her appearance before the grand jury the following morning. We arrived at the motel early that Sunday evening. The red message light on the phone in my room was blinking. April wanted to see us right away in her room. We dropped our bags and hurried there and stepped into a scene for which I had not been trained at law school, the Justice Department, or anyplace else.

The room was a mess. Liquor bottles were scattered everywhere. April was in an imitation leopard-skin kimono, her hair was up in curlers, and cold cream was on her face. Her two poodles were yipping, scrambling over the bed. Her boyfriend, Charlie Polizzi, a gun strapped across his chest Pancho Villa–style, pulled us into the room. "There's a contract out on April," he reported, "they want to get her before she testifies tomorrow. If they lay a hand on her, this town is going to have a bloodbath," Polizzi warned.

My mind was racing; my heart was pounding through my shirt; it took every ounce of physical strength to keep my bladder under control. Polizzi repeated in a very agitated state that the word was out that April was going to testify, and some of the prospective defendants had checked into a hotel in Lexington. "There's gonna be a hit on April tonight," he warned.

I took Staab aside, hoping to be reassured that he had his weapon with him. He did not. Here we were in a tiny glass-walled hotel room at the edge of town on a dark night, waiting for a bloodbath; and he wasn't carrying a weapon! Of all the macho FBI agents in the country, we had the luck to draw one who didn't carry his gun. "Someone could grab it and shoot me," Frank joked. But his wry humor and self-possession were unappreciated at that moment. I tried to remember by what logic I had chosen my profession, and wondered how quickly I could engineer a change.

We left April in the "professional" hands of Charlie Polizzi while Frank made a call. Other federal agents were quickly sent to guard April's room. The three of us devised a scheme to sneak her into the courthouse alive the next morning. That night, I slept very little.

There is a postscript to that eventful Sunday night scare. Years later, I bumped into April's boyfriend, Charlie Polizzi, at the federal court house in Cincinnati. I was trying a case and he was being prosecuted in another courtroom. He greeted me, and confessed in an aside that in all his experiences with the law enforcement world, he'd never met a "tougher guy" than me. He was awed that I could have been so cool that night the "hit" was out on April.

I smiled, and looked away as the marshals led the shackled prisoner to his detention cell. Bad characters make bad judges of character.

April testified. Rita Desmond followed her. Indictments followed them. We indicted the new chief of detectives, the two other arresting officers, the notorious trial lawyer who had long been reported to be the behind-the-scenes power in Newport, and the two proprietors of the Tropicana Club, for conspiring to drug, frame, and arrest George Ratterman.

We brought our freshly typed indictments and presented them, with a special smile, to the impatient foreman. This red-hot grand jury foreman was going to indict some folks, and I was pleased it was not going to turn out to be me.

At 4:10 P.M., the indictments were filed by the grand jury with the federal court. The grand jury said there was evidence that Lester, Carinci, Buccieri, Ciafardini, Quitter, and White all had conspired to violate Ratterman's civil rights while the policemen acted under color of law. If the trial jury agreed, Ratterman's constitutional rights to not be deprived of liberty without due process of law, to be free from arrest without legal cause, and to equal protection of the laws, were all taken illegally from him when he was arrested on trumped-up charges.

The grand jury added a report of its own about conditions in Newport generally. "The foul odors of vice, corruption, and bribery cover Campbell County officialdom like a pall," it charged. The press gave extensive coverage to the grand jury's report. The media quoted some of the major players when they heard about the indictment. Upshire White stated: "I'm glad." Carinci: "I'm bitter." Quitter: "I'd rather not comment." Ciafardini slammed the phone and said nothing, and Ratterman was quoted as saying, "I'm relieved." Following Justice Department injunctions against pretrial publicity by our prosecutors, Goldfarb and Lynch had "no comment." Our words would come soon enough.

———

The early auditions of the players' performances in the local courts, and our private rehearsals for the federal case we prepared in the grand jury, were now completed. Our opening night was upon us.

Our trial—formally titled *U.S.* v. *Lester et al.* but widely referred to as the Ratterman case—began on June 5, 1962, in the big, old-fashioned federal courthouse in Covington, Kentucky, before the Honorable Mac Swinford. Judge Swinford was a ramrod-straight, clear-faced, white-haired, wise judge, who had been appointed by FDR and could have been sent from central casting to preside at our celebrated trial. He lived in rural Cynthiana, and traveled to several cities in Kentucky to conduct the federal government's judicial business. Kindly, with a country twang, courtly and always in control, he was consistently fair and proper. He'd never permit the kind of travesty that had taken place in the local court involving these same characters. Bill and I were pleased he was in charge, and ready to finally get to trial.

Most of our investigation had been conducted in the federal court in Lexington, which was far from the action involved in our case but was the main center for federal legal affairs in the eastern part of Kentucky. But the Covington court was next door to Newport and was the natural site for the trial. The courtroom was crowded; the press was present and pressing for interviews. Four well-known members of the local bar—each experienced trial advocates—represented the defendants. It was going to be a long, hard tussle. The ten of them huddled around several tables looked like a mob, and we liked that image. Lynch and I enjoyed the look of being outnumbered by this gang of notorious defendants and their stellar defense team. We intentionally excluded all our other assistants from our side of the courtroom, except for Frank Staab, who sat at the counsel table with us. He coordinated all our administrative efforts and projected the solid, wholesome, fatherly, local look we wanted to show the jury.

We spent the first day picking a jury. Considering all the pretrial publicity, it was not as difficult as we feared. Over a year had passed since the event itself and the local trial, and while our every move was given front-page, top-of-the-news coverage, the jurors in this rural area might have tended to be less attentive about the details of the case than urban jurors are with celebrated cases. "They are not here because they want to be," Judge Swinford noted; they'd rather be "plowing and setting tobacco." Swinford decided not to sequester the jury because it is an imposition and he had faith they'd follow his daily instructions given at every recess not to discuss the case with anyone or expose themselves to any news coverage. This made us very anxious.

Bill and I had prepared our case with punctilious care. Each of us had a loose-leaf book with a list of witnesses we'd be responsible for presenting, documents we'd need to get into evidence, and information about defendants and defense witnesses we'd be responsible for cross-examining. My zeal to take over more of the case vanished that first morning as I stood, heart pounding, to make the opening argument for the government. The affair had become a national cause célèbre, and was being watched carefully back in Washington because it provided a clear example of what Kennedy's program intended to accomplish. It was more than one criminal case; it had become a showcase for our program.

Our trial strategy was logical and conservative. Our case was circumstantial, and we worried that it would be hard for the jury to follow the bits and pieces of the mosaic we would be presenting, especially as we expected there would be a fight over the admission of most of the pieces. I read the indictment to the jurors and highlighted the evidence we would be presenting over the ensuing weeks so they could follow the course of the trial as it evolved. I cautiously promised only what I was certain would be delivered so the jury would have faith in our case when it ultimately retired to make its decision.

Tom Steuve opened next on behalf of Carinci and Buccieri. Steuve was younger than his colleagues, more tailored than the others, with a gray crew cut; he was smart, and as a former U.S. attorney in Cincinnati, experienced in the courtroom. His clients did not conspire with anybody, he told the jury. Rather, the evidence would show that Ratterman sought out Carinci on the night in question, and they returned to the Glenn, despite Carinci's protests, in search of entertainment.

Leonard Walker, an elderly man from Louisville, was chosen by Lester for his reputation as a successful and respected trial lawyer. Walker told the jury that the few acts they'd hear about Lester concerned no more than the acts of a good lawyer acting for his clients. Lester tried to help his clients find a photographer to be a concessionaire at the nightclub, not to take furtive pictures. He was roused from sleep by clients who had been arrested, bailed them out, and subsequently defended them in the Newport court.

Morris Weintraub, Ciafardini's lawyer, was wiry, shrill, loquacious to the point of distraction; a former speaker of the Kentucky state legislature. He told the jurors they'd learn that Pat Ciafardini was part of no conspiracy, and only performed his duties as a policeman on the night in question. Pat just happened to go to the police station at around 1 A.M. to discuss recent events at a police convention. A policeman is never off duty, he advised the jurors. The desk sergeant had directed Ciafardini to accompany Quitter and White to the Glenn, and he left thinking Ratterman had reported criminal activity there, not that he was involved in it himself. How could Officer Pat have conspired with Carinci, when he had arrested him? His client knew nothing of any setup, and was right to arrest Ratterman, who had misbehaved and resisted arrest.

Dan Davies, the lawyer for Quitter and White, opened last. He was savvy in the courtroom, clever and concise in his questioning, ingratiating in style. He was extremely knowledgeable, with an effective common touch. In an engaging, soft-spoken manner, Davies described his clients: veteran police officers, ex-Marines, close to retirement, innocently sent on an investigation initiated by an anonymous call, a common event in police business. The arrests they had made were quite proper under the circumstances, and they knew nothing about any conspiracy. Ratterman was not drugged, and rather than being deprived of a fair trial, he was fairly treated, and indeed was acquitted. What a paradox to be accused now of misusing the law to deprive Ratterman of his constitutional rights.

We were off and running. Lynch and I had decided that to make it easy for the jury to follow the meaning of each of the pieces to our circumstantial puzzle, we'd start with Ratterman laying out the basic story, with its holes and ambiguities. Then, specific witnesses would testify to the particular parts they knew about. Ratterman would be a strong witness because he was not one to be rattled; but by his own testimony, he could not explain many of the critical events of the evening of May 8 or the early morning hours of May 9, because he was drugged. And some parts of his story were weak and implausible—he had been out on a drinking spree, meeting late at night with a disreputable character while in the middle of a reformer's political campaign.

Everyone's attention was rapt as Lynch examined Ratterman, who told all the details—those he could recall—of his now well-aired story. Ratterman testified that his recollections of the rest of the evening were episodic. But he outlined the case in broad strokes. His contentious cross-examination by the four defense lawyers lasted two full days. Ratterman was composed and handled the hard questions as effectively as possible, we thought, but we were relieved when he was excused. We followed his testimony with Henry Cook, who was straight-arrow, comfortable in the court room, quite unimpeachable, and able to fill in one of the missing parts of Ratterman's story—the part after the arrest.

We shifted next from defense to offense. If Ratterman was innocent, who was guilty? We began by pointing a finger at Pat Ciafardini. I called his pals on the force who had accompanied him to the police meeting the day before our events; they testified that Ciafardini had asked them to lie and provide him with a cover-up of some "awkward" facts.

An FBI agent, Royal Blasingame, had drawn a picture of Room 314 at the Glenn and had it enlarged. We put his drawing into evidence so the jury could follow the witnesses' descriptions of what had gone on in Tito's room.

Next I put on Tom Withrow and his wife and her grandmother. From the night we first met Henry Cook and learned about the case, I had sensed the Withrows would be terrific witnesses. In most cases, there is one witness or incident or piece of evidence that has a decisive impact on the jury's and the public's perception of a case. Sometimes it is a small piece of the puzzle; often it is a disproportionately telling one. I knew the Withrows and Granny Hay would have such an impact. They did not disappoint.

Then the court adjourned for the weekend, and Judge Swinford told the jurors to be particularly careful not to violate his instructions, as they were not sequestered. One juror asked if he could play in his dance band, the Basin Street Four, which was scheduled to appear on Saturday evening at the Glenn. He was a teetotaler, he said. The judge preferred he get a replacement. We all were ready for a rest.

We couldn't go home because there was more preparation for the following week's work. And Bill and I were to begin the big Screw Andrews trial as soon as this one ended. Barbara Lynch had just given birth to their first child, but it would be weeks before Bill saw little

Kevin. I had been awarded a doctorate degree for my dissertation (now a book) about the contempt power. But an appearance in New Haven to receive this honor was out of the question. We took Friday night off for a long and pleasant dinner, then worked with the witnesses and the federal agents the rest of the weekend.

We opened the second week of trial with the testimony of a phone company representative that the number of the Glenn Rendezvous was Axtel 1-4800, the number Ms. Withrow stated Tom was told to call the early morning of May 9. Buccieri was the responsible party listed for that number in the phone company records. Then we returned quickly from the mundane to the exciting. When the bailiff called out the next name—Juanita Jean Hodges—all eyes in the courtroom turned to April Flowers, our critical and notorious star witness.

We had prepped April in attire, attitude, style, the works. She appeared in demure dress—as the press described it—conservative but not jarringly out of character. Her demeanor was light and restrained. Bill took her through the whole story as the jury, judge, public audience, and press paid rapt attention.

First, April explained why now, long after the event, she had recanted. Her mother was dying of cancer, she told the jury, and she felt terrible about her life and wanted to do something honorable. She felt bad for Ratterman and couldn't live with herself for what she'd been pushed to do. Sordid as her life was, there was a note of sadness about her and a touch of dignity—odd as that word might sound in describing a stripper who had participated in a frame-up that had caused a national scandal.

She knew nothing in advance of the arrest, and truly had been surprised and annoyed when Tito Carinci, her boss at the nightclub, suddenly stopped her act. Her show started at 1:30 A.M. Hers was the last act, usually running twelve to fifteen minutes. About five minutes into her act, the band played her offstage, to her and the crowd's displeasure. She was hustled up to Tito's room after she changed from the G-string and bra to the slave robe with the leopard-skin design. Tito had never done this before. She saw Marty hurrying gamblers and shills out of the Sapphire Room where gambling went on usually until 5 or 6 A.M. When she got to Tito's room, Ratterman was there asleep, fully dressed, on the bed. He seemed in a stupor, grunting and blinking when she touched his shoulder. Rita and Paisley were on the couch but soon left for Rita's room.

Within minutes, the door blew open and three policemen rushed in. She knew Ciafardini because he dated one of the waitresses there and had been on the premises visiting her earlier. When she asked Pat what was going on, he winked at her, indicating it was a phony arrest. There were the sounds of commotion in the other room, and soon they brought out Ratterman with his pants off, wrapped in a bedspread. He had been dressed when she left him moments before, she was certain. And she was clothed, too, but lied about their state of dress at the police court trial.

She had gone to Charlie Lester's office twice with Tito and his partner at the club, Marty Buccieri, never having hired the lawyer, paid him, or even given him her view of the events. Lester told her to just listen to what Tito and the police officers said and agree with them about what happened, and to make her story as dirty as possible. She went along with the phony story, testifying that Ratterman's pants were off; that her robe was off and her bosom, legs, and thighs were showing; and that they were embracing. All that was untrue.

The story about Ratterman's pen was a Lester concoction, too. He showed it to her in his office and told her to say at the local trial when it was produced that Ratterman gave it to her and asked her to call him sometime at the number listed on it. None of that was true.

"Why did you lie at that trial?"

"I was told to keep my mouth shut and nothing would happen. They'd say things like: People who talk wind up in the river. I was afraid."

We were ecstatic about April's testimony and bullish about how our case was going. We had anguished about whether to call Tom Paisley. We did not want to tip our hand, so we had subpoenaed Paisley, who was waiting in the witness room. During a brief recess, we made a critical decision: not to use him. Paisley would not help, and he might hurt our case. His conduct the night in question was suspect, and it clouded Ratterman's story and made it more suspect. And he was likely to be a weak, nervous witness who would not be credible.

April and Ratterman had been excellent witnesses, and the shaky part of our case had been presented without any serious damage. We didn't want to jeopardize the case by injecting some of the side issues raised by Paisley. We lapsed into bravado by telling the press that the case was going in so strong that we didn't need him.

Ann Ratterman, George's wife, testified to the before and after facts of the May 8 and 9 events. Our trilogy of medical experts described their blood and urine tests of Ratterman on May 9 and the discovery of chloral hydrate in his system.

Frank Staab completed the presentation of our case; he was the person who knew most about the case and would be a solid witness. A twenty-one-year veteran of the FBI, he was fatherly, yet John Wayne–like, reeking of rectitude, the very personification of credibility and competent law enforcement. We wanted to conclude our presentation to the court and jury with such a strong, believable witness. In the course of his investigation, Staab had interviewed about five hundred people.

When Bill Lynch said the magic words "The government rests," I felt as though a phase of my life was over. Of course, we hadn't even completed our trial.

But the burden had shifted. The defense rested its case after all the defendants took the stand and denied any wrongdoing. Had they not testified, the jury inevitably would have wondered why innocent people did not take the stand to proclaim their innocence. We called a few rebuttal witnesses. All issues were joined and the final question would be: Who would the jury believe?

Legal maneuvering followed—motions by the defense, requests by both sides for instructions to the jury, summations—and we were done. The defendants' motions for an acquittal by the court were denied. All of a sudden, I could relax. Bill and the defendants' lawyers would sum up; I was now an interested spectator.

Summations lasted a full day. Each of the attorneys finished his work in character. Bill was earnest, methodical, and completely prepared. He highlighted the inconsistencies and incredibilities in the defendants' stories. His rectitude shone brightly as he described and explored the sordid story of Newport vice and deplored Ratterman's frame-up. Occasionally, Sunshine's face turned a fiery red as he pummeled at the misconduct of each of the defendants and the incredible stories they concocted. The jury followed his plain-talking sermon intently, though displaying no signs of their own views.

Each defense lawyer picked at the parts of the government's case that pertained to their clients. As they had been throughout the trial, Davies was cordial and engaging, Weintraub overly wordy and shrill, Steuve precise, lawyerly, analytic, and Walker strangely obtuse and rather unimpressive.

One sums up as if everything in a case depends on that presentation, though at this stage the real surprise would be if the jurors had not reached their own conclusions. Lawyers, as partisans, become so certain of their own positions they can not imagine how a jury could not agree. But approximately half of us in every case discover how wrong we are.

Neither of the usual alternatives happened in our case. The jury did not share our view of the evidence we presented to it, nor did it agree with the defendants' views. After several days of their private deliberations, our continuous and increasingly anxious speculations, and the obvious tensions of everyone involved, the jury advised Judge Swinford it was hopelessly deadlocked.

"Hung" is the word used to describe this no-one-wins phenomenon. When he accepted its conclusion that more time deliberating would not get them past their impasse, Swinford thanked the jury, showing no signs of his personal feelings, neither surprise nor remorse, and dismissed them.

—

Bill and I were stunned. A hung jury is not quite a no-one-wins verdict. For the defendants, while it does not exonerate them, it is the close equivalent, because the government often does not go through the time and expense of another trial, where its case usually lacks the surprises and freshness of the original trial. Bill and I were bereft, shocked that what seemed to us a strong case had not persuaded the jury, and worried that Washington would not authorize a second try. We were unlikely to come up with new, stronger evidence; we thought the case we'd presented was strong, despite a few rulings on the admissibility of evidence that went against us. The prosecutorial line on retrying cases was that it was like kissing your sister. Our long, hot trial had been expensive, in many ways, and it was by no means clear to us that we'd be given the go-ahead to retry *U.S.* v. *Lester et al.*

The defendants' lawyers immediately clamored for a mistrial. Judge Swinford denied it. Bill told the judge we were prepared to retry the case as soon as feasible (betraying none of our doubts that we would be authorized to do so). The case remained on the docket. Publicly, the defendants put their spin on the verdict; they thought they had dodged the big bullet from Washington.

Bill and I didn't have time to sulk; the following Monday morning we were set to start the Screw Andrews case in the same courtroom. I thought it ironic to be prosecuting this complex, major tax case when I could not understand my own 1040. But trial lawyers, especially when they are exhaustively briefed by experts, can focus on a specific situation of any kind, learn everything about it, and manage what in other contexts might baffle them, as the world of tax law ordinarily baffled me.

On one of our earlier trips home, I was pleased to report to my colleagues at the Justice Department that we were about to prosecute someone on the attorney general's list of the top forty racketeers in the country, and that we had landed the only one on that list who was not Italian—Frank Andrews. No one could accuse us of cultural prejudice, even in that time when political correctness had not sensitized most people. Silberling let the air out of my puffy announcement, however, advising me that Andrews's real name was Andriola.

Lynch and I prosecuted Screw and the seven other major numbers operators we had indicted. We won the Andrews case after a month-long, hard-fought jury trial, again before Judge Swinford. We were able to present a thorough case, sometimes boring as IRS agents analyzed reams of documents captured during the raid, alternately dramatic as out-of-town undercover agents described their capers inside the Sportsmen's Club. We used immunity (bets were called in by phone, so we used the Communications Act's immunity provision) to force several inside clerks to put our key defendants into the operation and management of the club, and the threat of a perjury indictment to force one key insider to testify against her employers. We made a circumstantial case against Screw and his top aides.

The IRS auditors were able to extrapolate a year's income from the one month's records we seized and the undercover agent's impressionistic reports of activities over a longer period. Notebooks recorded the proprietors' shares of all proceeds. Their records were vastly different from the reports some of them had made to the IRS on the required business and personal returns.

None of the defendants testified, a constitutionally permissible but tactically questionable strategy in criminal cases. The threat of perjury if they lied, or of cross-examination about their other criminal exploits if they took the stand and put their veracity in issue, kept them mute, which probably didn't help their case with the jury. After long weeks of trial that included the presentation and analysis of hundreds of documents and an extensive line of government witnesses, after a several-days-long deliberation by the jury that had us prosecutors panicked about another hung jury, we finally got our verdict: All defendants, guilty. Judge Swinford sentenced the defendants to serve serious time—five years in prison for most of them. We had a big victory, at last.

Our successful investigation and prosecution in the Andrews case effectively closed the citywide numbers operation in that area, sent away for a serious time a group of the area's major gambling impresarios, and won the eternal devotion of the IRS, which was warming to the Kennedy war on organized crime and the encomiums that followed major, successful efforts at law enforcement. Exhausted but exhilarated, Lynch and I returned to Washington, he to see his son, I to pick up my degree and the rest of my life. We were veterans now, and our program was in full swing. We enjoyed the plaudits of our colleagues and bosses. For days, it was fun to walk the halls at Justice and tell our war stories to the new cadre of rookies and our colleagues who were home from their own wars.

With the law enforcement successes that followed our investigations and trials in Newport and Cincinnati, the area was changing dramatically. Events were going our way. On November 6, 1961, Ratterman was elected sheriff, getting twice as many votes as both the Democratic and Republican candidates. Rackets figures who had not been tried and convicted left the area for more hospitable climes. Newport was becoming a quiet, small town. The Glenn burned down, probably the result of what one of my law professors called a "friction fire"—what happens when you rub the mortgage against the insurance policy. But alas, April Flowers's honorary Kentucky

Colonelcy, awarded her during her few months of celebrity, was rescinded by the state.

It would be months before we could officially raise the question of retrying the Lester case and completing the Newport saga. But my rookie days were past.

Chapter 6

A RESPITE

IN WASHINGTON

We filed into the attorney general's office, about thirty-five of us. We were seated in rows of chairs set up before RFK's huge desk. The wood-paneled walls were decorated with his children's drawings, and the ubiquitous family photos made his lineage clear. The expected formality—we were brought coffee in china cups and saucers—was relaxed as the attorney general sat jacketless, sleeves rolled up. As we were to learn, his tie was often askew, his feet sometimes on his desk; sometimes his huge black lab dog was on the floor beside him. As his wife, Ethel, admitted, "You'd never confuse him with Dean Acheson."

Often, Kennedy would be chatting with his close aides as we arrived, but he always stopped and stood up to greet us individually with a handshake, direct eye contact, and some personal comment indicating—to my amazement, as he had so much else on his agenda both at Justice and, increasingly, all over the New Frontier—he knew us and what we were doing. He clearly cared, and we as clearly appreciated it.

Kennedy received a daily report from our section, usually a few pages long, noting that day's significant action. The daily reports were matter-of-fact, succinct highlights of our special news of the day. They provided a way of keeping Kennedy apprised of what was going on by noting our political activities ("Ed Silberling will meet in Oklahoma City with the fifty-member Council of Judges of the National Council on Crime and Delinquency"), our court action, ("Jack Yetman pleaded guilty today in Hartford to a count of perjury . . ."), and our organized crime scorecard ("In the first case under the new gambling statutes Menieri was sentenced to eighteen months and two of his six conspirators to nine and six months respectively") Occasionally, some convoluted English slipped in: "The killers, three men in a dark-colored Cadillac, fired three shots which entered Donato's head and then sped from the scene." A touch of droll humor sometimes found its way into these otherwise dry reports: "Customs and treasury agents had a tip that he was carrying a million dollars out of the country in an old suitcase. Although they swarmed all over Doc at the airport, not only was there no million dollars—there was no old suitcase."

Kennedy was always on top of our activities; but these regular meetings in his office gave him the opportunity to find out in depth what we were doing. And they gave us the opportunity to ask him to take steps we needed from him. He always delivered. Our meetings were focused but unofficious, in the special Kennedy style. Once, while we discussed serious matters of prosecutorial policy, Kennedy and Whizzer White, seated and listening, tossed a football back and forth. Occasionally, Kennedy would interrupt one of us to take a call from the president while we exchanged wondering glances. Was there a world crisis? Or were two brothers simply exchanging family stories? At one meeting, the special red phone near his desk rang. It was set apart from the white one he used regularly, and we all presumed it rang only at times of genuine emergency. A hush came over our group as we watched him listen quietly and respond with brief muffled remarks. We all wondered—another missile confrontation? Is the world about to blow up? When he hung up, he looked around the room at our anxious faces, and said—deadpan—"Wrong number."

Another time, in the middle of a meeting, the door to his office swung open and in walked two tourists wearing shorts, carrying cameras. Obviously lost, they had mistakenly wandered onto the wrong floor and into the wrong office. How open life and government was in those days. No security guards monitored visitors or screened guests, as they do now. Our embarrassed interlopers exclaimed an embarrassed "Oops, excuse us," turned, and walked out.

Lynch and I were tired of living in Covington motels and Cincinnati hotels and were glad to be back in D.C. to catch our breaths. It was interesting to get a panoramic picture of what was going on around the country from the reports of our colleagues. We had not seen much of them for months. And, of course, it was always an extra excitement to work directly with the boss. We had come to know RFK gradually through personal experiences with him, our observations of his standards and style at Justice, the endless anecdotes about him at the department and, as with everyone else, our growing understanding of his wider influence in the government and in his brother's councils. My impression of the man surely had changed dramatically as a result of this knowledge; my earlier doubts were assuaged, my estimation of him was rising steadily.

There was usually some preliminary banter between Kennedy and one of our section's leaders. He turned his wry humor, for example, on Henry Petersen, Silberling's deputy, who had shared a small office with Kennedy in 1952 when both were starting their careers. Kennedy looked around his massive office, looked at the retinue of aides surrounding him, and asked: "How come we started out in the same office, Henry, and here I am the attorney general of the United States, and you're just a deputy section chief?" We laughed, remembering Henry's story about the young Kennedy in those earlier days. Henry had risen through the ranks as an FBI clerk, worked his way through night school, and eventually became a criminal division lawyer living on his civil service salary. An administrator at the Justice personnel office came to Kennedy and Henry's office to inquire why none of Kennedy's recent salary checks had ever been cashed. Kennedy opened his desk drawer and pulled out a handful of them. Henry shook his head as he noted Kennedy's seeming indifference to his accumulated salary checks.

Silberling, and later Hundley, started the business with brief introductory remarks. Early on, he said that this had been a busy period, momentum was building, our lawyers were all over the country starting, trying, and in a few instances, concluding cases. He was certain the attorney general would be pleased to hear our status reports.

First, there were comments by Jack Miller, Silberling, Petersen, or Hundley about their own news. Miller mentioned meeting with the mayor of Youngstown, Ohio, who was worried about corrupt officials in his area; he felt powerless to move against the rackets, and wanted to. We were sending in two section attorneys and a score of IRS and FBI agents. We promised to turn over any local cases we developed that weren't federal crimes. Miller sent a lawyer to Toronto to work with our consul general there and Canadian authorities to extradite four narcotics heavies we indicted in New York—Albert and Vito Ageuci, John Papalia and Rocco Scopellitti. He was being kept apprised of a CBS investigative report—"Biography of a Bookie Joint"—about a Boston key shop that was fronting for a big gambling operation. The IRS and FBI were being brought in, and the IRS was planning a raid.

Bill Hundley had met with Pennsylvania's attorney general and its chief of the state police to establish a liaison with our organized crime efforts.

Henry Petersen had met with New Hampshire's deputy attorney general to discuss that state's new sweepstakes law, to be sure it didn't violate our new federal interstate gambling paraphernalia laws. They assured us there would be no use of the mails; we'd coordinate with postal inspectors to be sure the mails were not used. Traveling interstate with the tickets could pose a problem. Henry had also met with Senator Everett Dirksen to work out problems in a pending slot machine bill, particularly an immunity provision we wanted but the legislators didn't.

Our focus on political corruption was working, too, our bosses' reports demonstrated: Investigations and cases were pending on a state parole board member in Detroit who took payoffs; a county sheriff in Tennessee who was on the take; a former Texas chief of police now in the drug smuggling business; a Michigan court clerk who was furnishing information in criminal cases to racketeers; Clifton County, New Jersey, city councilmen for bribery and corruption; a South Carolina sheriff and four of his deputies who were paid off to assist moonshiners carry on their business and were protecting them from arrest; Wichita, Kansas, vice squad officers indicted for taking payoffs for permitting gambling; twenty-two Indianapolis police officials who took bribes for protecting the multimillion-dollar numbers operation there (an IRS raid had unearthed records of who was paid what amounts); Jacksonville, Florida, detectives who took payoffs from gamblers; an Illinois mayor who extorted money from a contractor who did business in his city; a Georgia sheriff and state legislator for tax evasion based on an illegal liquor operation.

Wherever we found organized crime flourishing, we were finding officials cooperating, and we were going after them.

As our meeting continued, Silberling or Hundley introduced each of us, gave each of us an introductory nod, and, one by one, we told our stories. Kennedy would ask questions, give a smile, a nod, thanks, or encouragement (however perfunctory, it would make our day and make it possible to casually report to friends over dinner, "I was talking to Bob Kennedy today and . . .").

Ed Joyce, a veteran department hand, had been working on the new statutes Kennedy had gotten passed and reported some of the repercussions with national gambling wire services that were affected. Ed had worked with McClellan Committee counsel Jerry Adlerman on designing a statute specifically dealing with race wire services. Meanwhile, we were managing with the laws already on the books.

A major wire service in New Orleans that serviced gambling operations in Mississippi; Hot Springs, Arkansas; and Newport, Kentucky had gone out of business. We'd won a court victory requiring the telephone company to remove Telephone News Systems telephones that they used to transmit gambling information. We were about to indict a key gambling figure in Pottsville, Pennsylvania, for using Western Union sports tickers and phones in a large bookmaking operation. We'd negotiated with three large manufacturers of punch boards, tip boards, and similar gambling paraphernalia to cease selling and distributing these items. We'd prevailed in litigation in Illinois to enjoin AT&T and Western Union from offering their facilities to Telephone News Systems and Illinois Sport News for disseminating gambling information. The court upheld the constitutionality of our new statute. Ed also met with proprietors of the Caliente racetrack and their lawyers to discuss the impact of the new crime laws, sections 1952 and 1953, on tickets distributed in California for bets at the track in Mexico.

The FBI was compiling and analyzing telephone toll traffic involving sixty-one top gamblers in twelve cities to clue us in to the best sources that could lead to choking off the major flows of gambling action. If we could stop the key sources of fast information, we could frustrate the business of gambling: Joyce's report indicated our strategy was netting good results.

The Las Vegas skimming investigation being run by the IRS was being managed by Earl Johnson. He was eventually moved from Washington to the U.S. attorney's office in Las Vegas, and then into a small, nondescript office, far enough away from the federal law enforcement local premises to attract minimal attention. What Earl and his agents were learning confirmed early suspicions.

Earl spelled it out, and he had our rapt attention. "Every table in a gambling casino—craps, 21, roulette—has a locked 'drop box' suspended under a slot in the top of the table. If a player wants to buy chips at the table, the employee operating the table takes his money and inserts it through the slot into the drop box. At the end of each eight-hour shift (and sometimes more frequently) the drop boxes are collected and taken to the counting room. Regulations require the casinos to record the money removed from these drop boxes by table and by shift. Thus, the casino books contain a list of tables and the cash receipts from each table for each shift.

"The IRS assembled a large team of undercover agents. They posed as gamblers and placed bets in the casinos for several months. The agents moved from table to table, but always ensured that at least one of them was at a given table through an entire eight-hour shift. As customers purchased chips at the table the agents counted the money going into the drop box. By rotating among tables, the undercover IRS gamblers were able to keep track of the drop-box revenues at several tables each shift.

"After the casino filed its tax return for the year during which the agents had counted the take, the IRS opened an audit. The auditors compared the cash amounts the casino records said those tables received during the relevant shifts with the agents' count. The results showed the casinos were underreporting by an average of about one thousand dollars per table per shift. That, as you can imagine, soon adds up to big money. Ironically, most of these same casinos were claiming to be losing money or barely breaking even as far as their 'on the books' income."

"What do you do with the figures you come up with?" someone asked Earl.

"For civil purposes and possibly the criminal prosecutions, too," Earl explained, "we planned to use the sample undercounts at some tables during some shifts to project the total annual underreporting at the casinos we were investigating. When so projected, the tax evasion was massive, amounting to millions of dollars each year at each casino. So in addition to criminal penalties, the casinos and their secret owners faced millions of dollars in assessments for unpaid taxes, interest, and civil penalties."

"Furthermore, they couldn't be sure the IRS wasn't repeating the process during the current year. So it would be risky to continue the skimming from the table drop boxes in order to provide profits for the real owners, or to replenish the coffers the tax men were invading with their civil suits collecting taxes evaded in earlier years. Our investigation turned the casinos from money cows for the mob owners to money eaters."

Long, tedious surveillance and records analysis by the IRS was building toward a major series of prosecutions. This could be a major breakthrough for us.

But what we did not know at the time was that the FBI had begun, without our knowledge, a parallel investigation tracing the money skimmed in Las Vegas to racketeers around the country. As we suspected, Mafia leaders from all over the United States held secret interests in most of the casinos through fronts. Their interests were supervised by trusted, designated men on the scene. Each mobster's hidden share in the casino was priced at $52,500 and their ratio of return generally was a monthly dividend of $2,000, a 45 percent annual return, off the top and untaxed. The early 1960s were lush, and New Jersey gang leader, Gerardo Catena, received $50,000 a month; Cleveland gangster John Scalish received $52,000 a month; Meyer Lansky and Vincent Alo received $80,000 a month; and Giancana received over $65,000 a month (eventually escalating to $300,000 a month, according to his brother).

The bounteous skimming proceeds were brought each month in satchels of cash by bagmen—and women—to mob accountant Meyer Lansky in Miami. The couriers, traveling by plane, train, or car, were met en route by intermediaries; they carried cash usually amounting to around $100,000 each. After Lansky took his cut for overseeing the financial management of the mob's money, couriers then delivered to each absentee owner of these secret shares his dividend, or deposited his shares in numbered bank accounts. First, the money would be laundered through the Bank of World Commerce and the Atlas Bank in the Bahamas, and then sent to the International Credit Bank in Switzerland. The mob had representatives on the boards of directors of these banks to ensure that the cash carefully traveled its circuitous route and got to its proper proprietor.

These two investigations were, in their lack of coordination, to cause us major problems eventually.

Next, Sheridan's lawyers updated their Hoffa investigations; it sounded as if they were near the culmination of two investigations that had gone on for years. In November and December 1962, James Hoffa, with a union associate, was tried in federal court in Nashville, Tennessee, for receiving payoffs from 1947 to 1958 from a company that employed Teamster members. That case only involved a misdemeanor, but Hoffa recognized the importance of not being convicted and approached the trial—as did the government—as if it were all-out war. Unlike the government, Hoffa was prepared to fight any way necessary to win. Soon our attorneys had received reports of attempts to fix the jury.

The trial judge then ordered a grand jury investigation into the government's allegations of jury tampering. Painstaking study of voluminous phone and travel records, along with persistent grand jury questioning and the critical testimony of a Teamsters member, Ed Partin, who had worked undercover for Sheridan while assisting the Hoffa defense team, resulted in a new and more serious indictment. On May 5, 1963, Hoffa and five others were indicted for a felony: jury tampering.

While this case was proceeding in Nashville, a long-pending investigation had finally resulted in another indictment in June 1963—this one in Chicago—of Hoffa and several others for mail fraud. These charges emanated from a series of fourteen loans from Teamsters pension funds totalling $20 million and the diversion of another $1 million for their personal benefit. These financial shenanigans had to do with a Florida land development project, a Teamsters retirement community—"Sun Valley."

Before either trial began, Hoffa's lawyer in Tennessee, Tommy Osborn, was discovered attempting to fix that jury and was disbarred. The tampering trial was moved to Chattanooga—fifteen months after the original trial in Nashville. The pressures and the stakes were building. We would hear more about these two major cases in later meetings.

Hoffa was not the only labor leader we pursued; nor were the Teamsters the only union, as the next report showed. "Jake Tanzer has had an interesting development in Toledo, Bob." An IRS investigation of filched documents had led to a major criminal investigation of Richard Gosser, the head of the United Auto Workers Union there—a big organization, twelve thousand members—and a real power in Ohio.

"Great!" Kennedy kidded. "But can't you guys come up with a steel company president once in a while?"

Jake's Toledo case was a good example of how our centralized and energized section was working. The IRS in Toledo had come to an impasse because its agents with whom we worked regularly, the Intelligence Service, had discovered wrongdoing by its own staff. They had to call in the Inspection Service, which historically took charge of investigating internal corruption. If the case had stopped with a staff member caught under suspicious circumstances, that standard procedure would have made sense; but in this case the insider wrongdoing led to a potential criminal case involving a big fish outside the IRS who turned out to be a very powerful local labor leader named Richard Gosser. When the agent in charge of the Toledo office called Tanzer, our lawyer coordinating cases with that office, Tanzer wasted little time jumping into the case. "I grabbed my TRs [travel request forms] and I was on my way."

Jake Tanzer told a story of sleuthing, as much police work as lawyering. "The IRS was running a very secret tax investigation on Gosser, General, and one day I got a call from Ken Cannon, the IRS agent in charge. One of the agents in their office spotted a secretary copying files when the office was deserted during lunch hour. The scene made him suspicious. When she left the office, he looked around her desk and discovered she had been copying the notebooks of other girls in the office, and they included our intelligence reports on Gosser. He had Intelligence Service officers follow her. She went to a bar in the Polish district and slipped these papers to her cousin, a mob-related numbers operator. Things clicked. The agents had been wondering how a big gambling operation could flourish at a Toledo auto plant without Richard Gosser knowing about it, in fact approving."

"How did they know what was on the papers she removed?" one Kennedy aide asked.

"The FBI labs raised the typing on the back-up pages she used instead of carbons," Tanzer replied, knowing the attorney general would love to learn about the cooperation between investigative agencies. "Then they monitored her calls to this guy who asked her for names in our open files. Interestingly, and suspiciously, each character was a business associate or friend of Gosser. When the agents finally confronted her, she confessed she'd been delivering intelligence reports to this character at a bar once a week, for fifty dollars a delivery, penny-ante stakes. But he'd told her, 'Stick with me, baby, and you'll be driving Cadillacs.' This guy told her he was turning her papers over to Donald Pinciotta, who is—ready?—Gosser's administrative assistant. She'd been regularly turning over our hot reports on Gosser and his cronies, including three public officials and one big-time gambler."

"How do we tie all this pilfering and payoffs to Gosser?"

"Well, the plot thickens, General," Tanzer continued. "We set up the secretary, who was now cooperating with us, with specially marked documents and spread them with fluorescent powder visible under ultraviolet light so we could positively identify them and anyone who touched them.

"We brought in thirty-five agents from Detroit, Indianapolis, and other cities so no one could be recognized. Some spoke Polish because in the bar where the meetings were taking place anybody who spoke English was suspect. I was in charge of the group so there would be no sensitivity between the agents from different offices. We held a 'sales convention' of all the agents at a local motel, and this's what we devised.

"Our undercover agents were positioned in the bar when she arrived and we had agents in cars outside, connected by radio to follow the papers when they left the bar. Those agents established that she departed the bar without the papers she brought and with fifty dollars she didn't start out with. She was told by her cousin at the bar that he was going to turn over her papers to Pinciotta Monday morning at a pancake house and that he would get it to Gosser.

"That Monday morning we had thirty-five agents and inspectors watching the only two pancake houses in town, with some agents eating at tables in both of them, while I was driving around town on the radio barking orders to our agents about the people we were following. We gave them all code names: Gosser was Papa Bear, Pinciotta was Mama Bear, and the undercover secretary's feckless cousin was Baby Bear. When the papers were passed from our co-operating secretary to Gosser's man, I headed to the judge's house to be ready with the warrant when I received word the marked papers had gotten to Gosser, the final destination. I sat outside the federal judge's house with papers drawn for a search warrant of Gosser's home once the agents radioed me that the connection was made."

This melodrama was better than a movie thriller, and Tanzer's gravelly voice added dramatic effect to the story he told.

"Well, our agents let us know when the marked cousin left home and where he was headed. Our guys surrounded the pancake house he was headed to; they were inside and out. Sure enough, they got a good view of him giving two envelopes to Pinciotta, who took them and headed straight for the Toledo Health and Retiree Center, where, coincidentally, our guys who were tailing Gosser reported he was heading.

"I retyped the warrant on a borrowed typewriter perched on my lap while we hurriedly drove to the judge's house. We had to change the information on the warrant from a request for a search of Gosser's house to a search of his office. Our agents waited for Pinciotta to come out of the center. The plan was to arrest and search him on the spot and, if he didn't have the papers, to go to the judge with the warrant and get the warrant to our agents who could catch Gosser with the papers.

"But things were getting clutchy. First, the judge left his house and our guys following lost him in traffic. It was getting late in the day, and we could have problems with the adequacy of our warrant after five o'clock because after sunset you have to be more certain where the items are; you can't just describe them generally; and we couldn't say for sure where in the building they were, even though we were sure they were someplace with Gosser.

"The problem was that Pinciotta didn't come out. And it was getting closer and closer to five. We decided we had to go in after him.

"Just before five o'clock the judge returned home. I got the judge to sign my before-sunset warrant. I sent out my coded signal to the agents. The agents poured into the center's offices. Pinciotta didn't have the papers. As expected, when we converged on Gosser—in the next office—he demanded a warrant. He got it! When I got there with the warrant, Gosser was with Neufio Scott, a.k.a. Rony Paul, formerly with the Licavoli mob in Detroit and one of the people mentioned in the purloined papers. We couldn't tell if Pinciotta's hands were ultraviolet, but we found the papers in Gosser's desk drawer.

"Under the ultraviolet light, they glowed."

Everyone in the room applauded. Our boss smiled. A lot of work and coordination had paid off.

"Jake and the U.S. attorney got an indictment from the grand jury in Toledo, Bob, for conspiring to defraud the government of the good and faithful services of its employee," Silberling said. "But it's not going to be an easy case. Gosser is *very* powerful and well liked in Toledo and the union is so big it's going to be impossible to find a juror at the trial without some connection to it."

"We're getting letters already saying we're the gestapo, that we're persecuting Gosser," Kennedy said.

Silberling shifted gears, from the new Gosser case to our old Ratterman case.

"I want to send Bill Lynch to work with Jake and the U.S. attorney on this one, Bob. Bill has the trial experience and Jake knows the case. Bill has just finished two big trials in Kentucky and Ron can take over the work there."

I had my lead in for a Ratterman retrial pitch; now I had to persuade the department to go to the expense. It was no certainty.

"What's the story in Newport, Ron?" Kennedy asked.

"I've got a perjury trial set to go, General, involving a brothel owner who lied to the grand jury about payoffs. We didn't want him, but the word has to get out we're serious if we're to get witnesses to testify about payoffs. I know the party line is that perjury cases are supposed to be hard to win, but I'm confident. We won our obstruction of justice case against a lawyer who destroyed documents we were after in another case."

Now I had to make my case for a retrial, and I felt the butterflies. "We told Judge Swinford we intended to retry the Ratterman case and I hope you'll let me do it." I was doing a "Give me the ball, coach" routine, hoping Kennedy would be moved. "The Screw Andrews case was more important in many ways, but this case is symbolic of our seriousness to close down the criminal scene in Newport. Everyone who knows about Newport thinks Charlie Lester, the lead defendant, is behind everything. The town is changing and Ratterman is keeping up the pressure. But, to walk away from this case and let these characters off is to admit we didn't have a case, and we do. Almost all our preparation is done. I want to finish this fight."

"What do you think, Ed, Jack?" Kennedy asked.

Miller and Silberling were in favor of going forward.

"Good luck," Bob said with a smile. That was it. Decisive. Go for it was the basic approach. I had my go-ahead. During the rest of the meeting, my mind was racing with ideas about how to energize the next trial.

A moment-of-truth report came next. Doug McMillan, a young Floridian, had joined us recently and was assigned to the West Coast. Reading reports about the movie industry, Doug had come across repeated references to Frank Sinatra's ties to organized crime figures, including Sam Giancana, who was on our list of top racketeers in the country. Sinatra was a legendary showbiz figure and a friend of another well-known figure, too: the president. The singer had been active in JFK's campaign as a fundraiser and celebrity sponsor, bringing money and visibility to the campaign. He had been the master of ceremonies at the inauguration festivity. Doug McMillan thought the president should know what the intelligence reports were telling him, but he could not be sure how the attorney general would react to his advice. After all, Doug would be telling his boss—and the boss of all of us—that his brother was, at best, in an indiscreet position.

Doug made his report. Bob Kennedy listened respectfully, and asked him to provide all the details in a memorandum. Doug did that, presenting the attorney general with a nineteen-page memorandum on August 3, 1962. Doug's memo included information from monitored telephone conversations and informants' reports describing Sinatra's historic and continuous dealings with many gangsters and Mafia elite throughout his career, including his ownership of a Las

Vegas casino with Giancana, his directorship of a Massachusetts race-track owned (secretly) by New England Mafia boss Raymond Patriarca and New York Mafia figure Thomas "Three Finger Brown" Luchese, as well as his involvements with New Jersey Mafia tough guy Angelo "Gyp" De Carlo.

Robert Kennedy also became aware of the fact that Sam Giancana expected Sinatra to soften our organized crime drive by persuading the Kennedys to take the heat off Giancana. One of the Chicago FBI tapes disclosed a conversation between Giancana and a Las Vegas crony, John Formosa. In it, Formosa informed his boss that Sinatra said to him: "I took Sam's name and wrote it down and told Bobby Kennedy, 'This is my buddy and this is what I want you to know, Bob.' Formosa then added, "Frank saw *Joe* Kennedy three different times—that's Joe Kennedy, the *father.*"

When the president got Doug's memo, he stopped seeing Sinatra. In fact, Sinatra reportedly had built a helicopter landing pad and extra rooms so the president could use his Palm Springs home on presidential vacation visits, as he had done during the campaign. After Doug's report, the president stayed with Bing Crosby. However disillusioned with Sinatra's influence-peddling powers Giancana may have become, the Chicago mobster continued to try to reach Robert Kennedy through Sinatra. Chicago FBI agent William Roemer later reported that in 1963 a Giancana emissary, Chuckie English, brought him the message that if Kennedy wanted to meet with Giancana, he knew who to contact—it was clear to Roemer the reference was to Sinatra.

Doug's touchy report finished, Kennedy asked for an update on Giancana. Our report was a mixed bag. Frustrated by the failure to establish any proof of crimes by Sam Giancana, who was reputed to be the Chicago mob's leading citizen, the FBI—warming to its accelerated role as pursuer of organized crime—had placed him under around-the-clock surveillance soon after Kennedy's program started. Giancana was steaming, as teams of FBI agents literally lived with him, kept him under constant surveillance, flashing their lights around his Oak Park home. Irritated by the constant presence of cars full of agents trailing him night and day, stalking him at his home, encountering him provocatively at airports, embarrassing him in front of his friends, even playing behind him on the golf course, Giancana eventually mounted a legal counterattack.

He sued Hoover in federal court in 1963, claiming the FBI's tactics amounted to an unconstitutional invasion of his privacy, an assault on his civil rights. He had movies of his FBI shadows constantly surveilling him in public while he partook of a suburban existence, and demeaning his relatives and harassing his employees. The government had "violated the sacred institution of the home," Giancana pleaded, as if any institution was sacred to him. He asked that the government be enjoined, and he sought our investigative records concerning his activities under scrutiny.

A federal trial court in Chicago granted Giancana's request for an injunction against the FBI, chastising the FBI for "ineptness" and fining the agent in charge $500 for civil contempt. However, the federal appellate court ruled in the summer of 1963 that, for procedural reasons, the trial court was powerless to act, and lifted the injunction. "Defendants . . . are a part of the executive department of the United States and they are not subject to supervision or direction by the courts as to how they shall perform the duties imposed by law upon them," the court ruled. "The courts will not assume to supervise and direct the manner in which members of the executive department . . . perform their responsibilities. That would be an unwarranted interference . . . upon the discretion vested . . . in the director of the Federal Bureau of Investigation."

William Roemer, the FBI agent in charge of the investigation, questioned the wisdom of the Justice Department's tactic to not question Giancana when he testified in this proceeding. Why not ask him about all the things we knew he had done or caused to happen to demonstrate that the surveillance was not capricious? If Giancana wanted to complain that he was a law-abiding citizen (he had sworn that he'd never broken any local, state, or federal laws), why not pull out all the intelligence information we had to negate his claim?

The Justice Department decided to rely on the jurisdictional point only, arguing legalistically that the courts cannot run the FBI. It turned out to be a successful tactic in preserving the right to watch Giancana closely; but it missed the opportunity to turn the tables on him and put him in the vulnerable position of having to deal publicly with his questionable past. Kennedy had sent a telegram to the judge pointing out that opening our records to suspected criminals would be a dangerous precedent, and the court agreed.

The tactic also played into the hands of our critics who argued that we were brave in harassing our targets but fainthearted in an open and fair confrontation. When the FBI officer in charge of the Chicago office took the stand, he refused to answer thirteen questions about their tactics, claiming he was instructed to refuse to answer by the attorney general. The judge found him in contempt, but that was reversed on appeal. Even though the Chicago racketeer ultimately lost his case, he made his point. Giancana had turned the spotlight on the department and subjected his detractors to indignities they had been accustomed to piling on their prey.

A year later, Giancana sued again, this time charging the agent in charge of the Chicago FBI office with violating his Fourth and Fifth Amendment rights to privacy, personal liberty, and freedom by constant surveillance. This time the trial judge issued an unprecedented order that showed how ludicrous our cat-and-mouse game had gotten. Thereafter, the judge ruled, at least one foursome of golfers must intervene between the pursuing FBI agents and Giancana's group, and only one car of agents would be allowed within one block of Giancana's home.

Again, the injunction ordered by the trial court was withdrawn by the appellate court, which ruled that the trial judge was powerless to act for jurisdictional reasons (the statutory requirement that $10,000 or more be at stake in the case could not be inferred from the invasion of the complainant's civil rights). We were working hard, but getting nowhere with Giancana.

We weren't doing much better with Trafficante, although a big narcotics case in Houston involved Joseph Stassi, a major rackets figure from the New York–New Jersey area who was associated with Trafficante. We were following developments in the Texas case, hoping it might lead to tie-ins in Florida with the elusive Mr. Trafficante.

Our reports moved on; we needed some better news. "Arnold Stone's got a hot one going; you'll find this case interesting," Silberling said, directing attention to a swashbuckling case that had been developed by a lawyer from our section who had been assigned to Texas.

"You know part of the story," Henry Petersen said, speaking about Stone's case in Texas. "Let me give you the rest. It began with a fortuitous discovery by a Customs guard and an agricultural inspector. They had followed a suspicion about a car crossing in early morning at the Mexican-American border at Laredo, Texas. The two federal guards found sixty-six bags of heroin totaling seventy-six pounds stuffed behind the front door panels and under the backseat of a Canadian car, which was driven by a married couple of French Canadians. They just seemed suspicious to the guard, whose intuition turned out right. On the street, this cache would go for thirty million dollars."

There were gasps and groans as Henry continued in his raspy voice.

"Well, it turned out the couple were amateurs. Canadian narcotics experts and Royal Mounties and our Customs agents got into the case. The Canadians clued us in that the couple—Caron is their name—had worked for Lucien Rivard, who we suspected was the biggest drug trafficker in Canada. He runs a legitimate business—a big resort near Montreal—but our Canadian law enforcement friends said he's Mafia-connected, brutal, and into everything—gold smuggling, counterfeiting, hijacking, bank robbery, extortion, murder, you name it.

"Rivard used associates and paid employees to drive cars abroad and bring them home loaded with narcotics. The Carons had been paid twelve hundred dollars to be Rivard's couriers on this trip. It had not been Caron's first trip, nor his biggest smuggled cache. He usually traveled with four young children as a cover. The kids were back in Canada and Caron was worried sick that Rivard would abduct them to ensure their silence, or punish their cooperation with law enforcement authorities.

"As you know, General, with your personal intervention, we got help from the Canadian Ministry of Justice for our INS to smuggle the kids out of Canada before Rivard's organization could learn we were on their trail and get hold of the kids before we did. A caravan of armed cars whisked them away in the middle of the night, with matrons calming the bewildered kids, who were two, four, eight, and nine. Customs agents' wives watched over the kids in city after city while we got them across the border and into a safe haven in the States. We arranged new names for the kids and put them up with a temporary foster family. We orchestrated the trip, and local and state police watched out for them along the way. Eventually, charges were dropped against Mrs. Caron and she joined her children in a southern city where their welcome had been arranged. Our lawyer delivered them to the safe haven, then returned to his investigation.

"The Carons had talked. The Canadian police followed every one of their leads, investigating a hundred suspects. It turned out that Rivard was importing millions of dollars worth of heroin with schemes like this one. He'd hire people to take cars abroad, and leave them along the way temporarily with someone who would be identified by codes and gimmicks. The contacts would return the cars unloaded, or loaded with the stuff, and the innocent, or not so innocent, drivers would drive the cars home to Rivard, often unaware of what they'd done. Agents uncovered ship manifests, hotel registers, passport records, and telephone toll charges that bolstered Caron's story.

"Pumping the Carons, we came up with the identity of an American he'd contacted twice, in Bridgeport, Connecticut, named Frank. Caron had delivered one hundred fifty pounds of heroin to him at Rivard's instruction. But our intelligence people, mostly Wyn Hayes and her Customs contact, speculated a big drug trafficker, Joe Stassi, might be involved and one of his contacts was a guy with a criminal record that made Wyn's files, named Frank Coppola. We took Caron from Texas to Bridgeport where, hidden in a panel truck with a one-way window, he fingered Coppola as our Frank. We were led to another Canadian courier through Caron's leads, and he talked and gave us Rivard."

The scheme was ingenious. Rivard's hirelings never knew the contact people they'd do their business with. They'd be given a tie and told to deal with someone having a matching tie, or they'd be given a torn $10 bill and told to deal with someone presenting the matching half. The couriers would drive cars abroad and leave them with their contacts there. When they were returned, either a load of heroin was added into the secret panels, or one already there was taken away. Once, Caron reported, a car that had been unloaded off a ship went up in smoke and the fire department—not realizing it held eighty pounds of heroin—put out the fire and unwittingly rescued Rivard's treasure.

The evidence gathered through all these leads disclosed a network run from Canada, crossing United States and Mexican boundaries, and including clandestine laboratories to process the heroin in southern France and passage through Dutch ports, ending on American streets and in American arms.

"We had a helluva time extraditing Rivard and his gang, General," Petersen went on. "We wanted to try them all in Texas. Rivard was threatening our witnesses, and his allies even tried to bribe and blackmail and solicit help from highly placed Canadian officials to snag his extradition to the United States." (There would eventually be a national inquiry into political interventions on Rivard's behalf, accompanied by hurried resignations, and public condemnations of the sinister influences of organized crime upon government.)

"Then, Rivard escaped from the Canadian prison where he was detained, and for four months he eluded a national manhunt. Reportedly, he overpowered six guards, went through three steel doors and scaled a high prison wall. More likely, he'd had help. Eluding Canadian and American authorities, as well as Interpol and the French Sûreté, the Canadian press was calling him 'the Gallic Pimpernel.' Radio programs would sign off, 'Good night, Lucien, wherever you are.' His wife publicized love letters she received from him from distant places.

"Finally, the Mounties found him hiding in a lakeside cottage not far from his home in Montreal. He was arrested and whisked out of the country in a U.S. Coast Guard plane."

"Great case!" Kennedy had enjoyed the story as much as we all had. "I should write a letter of commendation to the different agencies who helped us. Henry, would you draft something for me?"

(We tried Rivard and his gang in Laredo, Texas, the next year amid vast security to protect our witnesses. Arnold Stone worked with the U.S. attorney's office, which had an expert on drug trials. Rivard and his gang members were convicted after a ten-day trial, and received two concurrent twenty-year terms; his associates got twelve- and fifteen-year terms; Mr. Caron's ten-year sentence was commuted after he testified against all of them.)

Silberling looked around the room. "Bob, you'll recall Bill Kehoe's earlier reports of our long investigation into the Mannarino brothers." Sam and Kelly Mannarino ran a multimillion-dollar gambling operation in New Kensington, Pennsylvania. Gabriel "Kelly" Mannarino had attended the notorious 1957 Apalachin meeting, and had taken the Fifth before the McClellan Committee in 1958. The brothers owned the town for years and operated the biggest gambling joint in western Pennsylvania, Ohio, and West Virginia, with links to the national mob. They had much of the city on their payroll for years. Police gambled there, delivered messages in and out, and cruised the area to protect it.

Bill Kehoe had led the IRS undercover investigation and the raid on the Mannarinos' building. Kehoe's team found a lay-off betting operation, along with dice, horses, barbotte, and blackjack, that ran day and night for gamblers from all over the state and from other states. All this went on with the knowledge of everyone in town.

Ed reported now about our investigation. "Two IRS undercover agents from the Pittsburgh office staked out for observation and eventually penetrated the operation for about four months before one of them was spotted and the raid had to be set up immediately. A truckload of IRS agents, deputized as marshals so they could make arrests—sixty-five of them to be specific—entered through a series of bolted doors and one-way-glassed screening stages. They used cameras, sledgehammers, axes, and crowbars to expedite their sudden arrival. The agents arrested a houseful of about a hundred people including some policemen. Naturally, nobody talked. Our tax experts analyzed the paper and money we rounded up and estimated we could prove a $175,000 wagering excise tax evasion. We indicted seventeen members of the Mannarino mob in Pittsburgh for tax evasion and conspiracy. But no one—neither the gamblers, the employees, nor the businessmen they had to deal with—would talk and connect the operation to the Mannarinos.

"When Bill Kehoe left the department, his younger sidekick, John Mullaney, took over the investigation and moved to Pittsburgh to work on it full-time. He became the Department of Justice pest of the year pushing his thing," Silberling joked.

"We've been pushing for a year to try a case we've had in the Tax Division for a long time to get at the Mannarinos. Tax felt we needed more evidence. We knew the Mannarinos and another guy we had just indicted, Willie Sams, owned a citywide pinball machine company. An ace IRS investigator on our team uncovered a scam they used all over town. When the company rep came to the numerous stores, clubs, restaurants, and taverns where the machines were, they'd empty the machines of all the money but only record half. They'd tell the owners to report half of their take on their tax returns, using year-end forms the company would provide them. Everyone went along. They weren't about to expose the Mannarinos or argue with them. And everyone likes to pay less taxes anyway. But, John couldn't corroborate the fact that the collectors turned the money over to the Mannarinos, though we knew they must have.

"We got one break. Our lead IRS agent spotted one ex–newsstand and luncheonette owner who had dealt with the pinball company. He was a former ally of Carlos Marcello in New Orleans, and he was serving a sentence in Lewisburg penitentiary. The agent visited the prisoner there, discovered he had a personal grudge against Sam Mannarino, and brought him here to Washington the day he was released from prison. Sure enough, he put Sam Mannarino into the whole payoff operation. John wanted to go ahead and prosecute, but the Tax Division wanted more witnesses than our one ex-convict to bolster this case.

"So, Mullaney spent months talking to every merchant in town trying to persuade them to open up to him. He let each of them think we had proved our case and they'd better join in and cooperate with us now.

"You want to cooperate or lie to us?" John had asked each of the frightened businessmen he interviewed. "If you lie, we'll be free to prove you lied. If you cooperate, you'll be one of many helping us." Eventually, and it took a *long* time and a *lot* of talk, John got over fifteen of them to corroborate the ex-con and admit how the system worked.

"After our being a pest," Ed smiled in the direction of the representative from the Tax Division, who had given him a hard time with his conspiracy case, "we got folks here to agree to add a conspiracy-to-defraud count to the sixteen filing-false-returns counts the Tax Division had approved. The U.S. attorney got a conviction on the conspiracy count," he concluded, subtly rubbing it in to the Tax Division, whose added charges did not result in guilty verdicts.

"We also took in about $675,000 in fines, taxes, and penalties, Bob," Henry Petersen added, "so the Mannarinos more than paid for our years of investigation. One Mannarino was convicted, one was acquitted. The pols in power who had been on the take, all are out of office. And the town is free of the mob."

"Terrific, that's all terrific. Especially congratulations to John," Kennedy said as he rose to stretch and signal a recess. We sipped coffee, stood and stretched, and talked among ourselves as the attorney general returned some pressing calls. Then he returned and we resumed.

John Diuguid had been sent to Wheeling, West Virginia, between his battles with Carlos Marcello; there, he wound up prosecuting the case that would eventually test the question of the constitutionality of the new antiracketeering legislation Kennedy had persuaded Congress to pass. It was directed at interstate travel for gambling, and it was one of the several new prosecutorial tools Kennedy had asked Congress to provide us.

The case was one against Anthony Zambito, who ran a numbers operation between Ohio and West Virginia. Zambito was not a particularly big shot—he just happened to get caught in a raid involving an operation that went between two states. It was time to try out our new weapon, the interstate travel statute.

John reported his adventure in West Virginia that resulted in his stumbling onto a test case. Zambito and five confederates were charged under our new statute, convicted, and sentenced to four years in prison. They argued that they ran a bar where there had been some numbers betting, but there was no way they could have known the traffic of their bettors was interstate. The jury and the court ruled that from the evidence presented, it was a rational conclusion for the jury to draw that the proprietors knew exactly what was happening.

The government proved that, after twenty years running the numbers business in that area, two numbers operators decided to get out of the business in September 1961, when the new law was passed. They had operated out of Martin's Ferry, Ohio, but did interstate business in the nearby northern panhandle of West Virginia as well as in eastern Ohio, as is often the case with these operations. When they pulled up stakes, Zambito temporarily took over, running the same operation on a special line from his Jolly Bar in Wheeling. He bought the machinery and "sundry tools of the trade," as the court labeled it, and functioned as the operations banker for three months. Each day, he received bets from writers and runners who were paid on a commission basis, and whose customers were in both states. The cars regularly parked in the bar's lot bore out-of-state licenses. His phone records confirmed the interstate business between the two states. In

December 1961, government agents raided the Jolly and confiscated money and gambling paraphernalia they found on its premises.

The appellate court, too, ruled that the uninterrupted pattern of interstate activity justified the circumstantial conclusion that Zambito knew what was going on. The facts were plain, the court ruled, noting wryly that "the law does not forbid a jury to reach the conclusion, which rational men would reach in the circumstances." That case was appealed all the way to the U.S. Supreme Court on the ground that our statute was unconstitutionally vague. The Court denied cert and upheld the conviction in May 1963.

The new law looked as if it would be a major tool for Justice. Another positive fallout of that conviction was that the FBI, observing the IRS make that case, decided to get into the business—their competitive juices got running—and Silberling arranged a Memorandum of Understanding between the IRS and FBI setting out territories and circumstances where one or the other agency would be in charge in these cases. Within months, the FBI had opened 2,700 cases under the new statute. Zambito may have been a small fish in the organized crime world, but his conviction was an important one, and everyone, especially the attorney general, was pleased.

John finished by catching us up on his pursuit of Carlos Marcello. Carlos and his brother, Joseph Marcello, had been acquitted for fraudulent use of a phony Guatemalan birth certificate. The jury "deliberated" for an hour and a half. John was heading south soon to work with the federal prosecutors in New Orleans to prosecute Marcello for the jury fixing that flowed from that case and his early deportation maneuvers. If Marcello wouldn't go quietly to Italy, or noisily to Guatemala, we would oblige and send him to an American prison. Kennedy had been clear on this one: We'd not quit until Marcello was stopped. And Marcello was just as adamant, and he and his lawyers seemed to be working full time defending our charges and making their own. The latest was a request that a lunacy commission be appointed to examine our star witness against him, Carl Noll, who'd had mental problems in 1930. For years, the daily reports from our section to Kennedy tracked the persistent maneuvering, incessant legal machinations, and constant surveillance that locked us to Marcello.

John's story had become more and more fantastic. "When we tried

Marcello for jury fixing, we [his colleagues from the Justice Department and the U.S. attorney's office] were worried that that jury might also be gotten to. We went to the federal trial court judge and asked that he switch the panel of three hundred prospective jurors for their case at the last minute to cut the risk of their being reached. The judge refused. We prosecuted the case, and despite our strong evidence, lost." John was devastated.

(David Ferrie was in the courtroom for weeks each day of that trial—the same David Ferrie who, the House Assassination Committee noted years later, was in the courtroom with Marcello the day of the JFK assassination and then drove to Texas. Ferrie's death during the Garrison investigation was explored decades later in Oliver Stone's controversial movie *JFK*.)

Before long, John and his government team started to receive reports that several jurors in that case had been fixed. They could prove that four members of the jury had received fixes, and they could tie the payoffs to Marcello, right down to having pictures of jurors, including the foreman, cashing checks that were traceable to Marcello. One juror's favorite charity, a local YMCA, received a check for $10,000 from a Marcello aide. When John asked him before the grand jury why he gave such a big sum to the Y—he'd never in his life given anything to charity—he replied: "It just seemed the right thing to do." The four fixed jurors were given immunity and testified, admitting they were bribed.

Again, the trial judge refused to take extra precautions to protect the next round of trial jurors from being fixed—now a third time—in the jury-fixing case that was set to be tried in November 1963.

While all this was going on, we ended up with a case against Marcello that did stick. After the grossly illegal deportation, and two good cases against him where he was able to fix the juries, Marcello fell in the flukiest way. An FBI agent who spoke Italian with a Sicilian dialect said something that angered Marcello, who took a swing at him. He was indicted for assaulting a federal officer.

John decided to mousetrap Marcello. He knew from prior cases that Marcello's lawyer always made pretrial motions complaining that his client could not receive a fair trial. This time, instead of arguing with him, they would accede and urge the court to move the venue—to Laredo, Texas. Laredo was a small town with an 80 percent Spanish-speaking population, a town that John knew about from his days there in the Air Force, and where, presumably, Marcello's influence would not be as potent as in New Orleans. Marcello was tried in Laredo and sentenced to five years in prison. That conviction was being appealed, as John closed his latest chapter of the Marcello story to our dazzled group. Marcello demonstrated both the elusiveness and power of our quarry, and Kennedy's commitment to fight back as hard as it took to put them out of business.

The difficulty of trying cases in New Orleans was not confined to Marcello. John Sprizzo's case against the nine lay-off gamblers (including one who operated out of the Glenn Hotel in Newport and who would peripherally become involved in my case there) had gone to trial early in 1963. Frank Cunningham was lead trial counsel after Ed Molinoff got sick. The theory of the case that our lawyers had developed and John had supported with an extensive legal analysis was that the gamblers' gimmick amounted to a conspiracy to conceal large-scale gambling activities through the use of the free long-distance privileges the corrupt employees provided. Long-line repairmen from the phone company placed free calls for the gamblers, which amounted to stealing services from the company and money from the government by avoiding gambling and excise tax payments on the long-distance calls. Five former phone company employees testified they'd placed thousands of these calls for the defendants. Three defendants pleaded guilty; one was too ill to be tried; nine lay-off gamblers went to trial after the government refused a deal they offered whereby they all would plead guilty to misdemeanors in exchange for the government not recommending any sentences, or assuring them of no more than six-month sentences.

In May, after presenting what our lawyers thought had been a strong case that lasted fourteen weeks, the jury deliberated for four days and acquitted all nine defendants of all twenty counts. John and his colleagues had worked hard to develop our successful legal position that skirted the defense motions to suppress our wiretap evidence. Their theory was that the phone company had the right to monitor its own lines, and it had tipped off the Internal Revenue Service, having sought its help in nabbing its crooked employees. But, as John noted later in frustration, what matters most is what happens at the trial and "I guess gambling and stealing from the phone company is OK in New Orleans." One defense lawyer called the government witnesses "wiretappers, listeners, and peeping toms," and the jury apparently bought his argument.

All our work had been for naught. When he reported the New Orleans results to Kennedy, who'd had daily reports about how well the case was going, the attorney general's reply was a terse "Pity." In June 1963, Sprizzo returned to New York to the U.S. attorney's office. (He is now a federal trial judge there.)

We were treated next to a preview of an extraordinary story, which the country would soon see televised before the Senate Rackets Committee. Bill Hundley, who eventually replaced Silberling as head of the organized crime section, was an affable, experienced veteran Justice Department trial lawyer, who was well liked by the old timers as he was by us newer members of the group, despite our feeling that Silberling was being mysteriously and unpleasantly pushed out of office. Bill had been meeting regularly for months with a Mafia character, Joe Valachi, who was talking, providing the FBI with inside stories about the inner workings of what he called *cosa nostra* ("our thing," as it is literally translated).

Valachi's testimony would provide the opportunity once and for all to explain the Mafia (also known as the Black Hand and the *Unione Siciliano*) to the American public and dispel the cynical view that it was a figment of our overly imaginative gangbuster minds. Robert Kennedy would call it "the biggest intelligence breakthrough yet in combating organized crime and racketeering in the U.S."

Bill laid it out for all of us, though Kennedy and the higher-ups had known the outlines all along, and a few of us knew that something secret and exciting was going on. Until then we didn't know the whole extraordinary story. As it evolved, one tip from a small fry New York dope peddler was converted into the discovery of a $150-million international narcotics conspiracy by a combination of five countries' special police. The same tip led as well to the first public exposure of *cosa nostra*.

Bill had a squeaky, singsong voice, with a distinct New York accent; but he told a captivating story. "It began in the summer of 1960. Joe Valachi, a fifty-eight-year-old professional hoodlum, was arrested for jumping bond on a dope trafficking charge. Hoping for a light sentence, Valachi provided a narcotics agent with a telephone number that happened to tie into a suspect in a case that agent was investigating—Salvatore Rinaldo. Suspected of narcotics trafficking, Rinaldo was being watched. The surveillance led narcotics agents to Pier 84 in Manhattan, where the Italian Line's *Saturnia* had docked. More federal agents were summoned. Rinaldo met another person, named Matteo Palmeri, and the two of them greeted an immigrant family. They all went through Customs with the couple's baggage, leaving at the loading dock a coffinlike gray wooden chest that Rinaldo later stashed in a waiting truck marked PALMERI'S BABY.

"The truck headed off and was followed, surreptitiously, by a growing caravan of federal agents. They overtook the truck on the New York State Thruway and, guns drawn, arrested Palmeri and Rinaldo. On examination, the agents discovered the chest had a false bottom that hid ten kilos of heroin worth five million dollars on the street. Other agents were alerted and they found the immigrant couple at Penn Station about to embark for California. They were visiting relatives, it turned out, and when their travel agent in Trapani, Sicily, asked them to deliver the chest to friends in New York, they obliged. The chest was filled—except for the secret compartment—with innocent objects, dolls and a blanket. After the investigation, it turned out the fisherman and his wife were innocent, and they were released.

"A search of Rinaldo's house disclosed a secret cache of a quarter million dollars worth of heroin and over twenty thousand dollars cash, along with marked bills that had been put into traffic by agents acting as dope addicts. Rinaldo decided to talk. He wanted to lighten his inevitable sentence, and federal agents, now joined by two of our people at Justice, Frank Cunningham and Robert Bailey, were pumping him long and hard. Rinaldo provided us with good leads. One tied our friend Joe Valachi to international drug smuggling, and the Italian police were brought into the investigation. One lead provided by Rinaldo led to the capture of a fugitive named Caruso who the INS connected to a smuggling operation between the United States and Italy.

"Dogged investigation by the federal agents assigned to the case continued, and Palmeri started to talk and corroborate some of Rinaldo's story. Next, the Royal Canadian Mounted Police and the French joined the Italian police in the hunt to pursue our clues.

Canadian drug suppliers were identified. A laboratory in Southern France where heroin was manufactured for sale in the United States was discovered.

"Slowly, indefatigably, the information our lawyers were squeezing out of Palmeri and Rinaldo was being corroborated by exhaustive document searches—airline records, long-distance phone toll calls, passport records, passenger manifests. The plot was thickening and we decided to provide protection for Palmeri and Rinaldo and their families. Somehow the word got out they had been cooperating, and we decided we had to move fast, despite knowing we were midstream in our investigation.

"We would have preferred to keep going longer. The U.S. attorney's office had a good staff and an impressive leader, Robert Morgenthau, and they were given the case to present to the grand jury. We started rounding up defendants, arraigning them, and getting high bail set. But their attorneys were getting the federal judges to reduce the bail to fractions of what had been set originally by the U.S. commissioners, despite pleas by the assistant U.S. attorney that these characters would flee if freed on bail. But judges were compromised by the bail laws, which required that bail must be an amount the defendants can afford and that bail could not be used as a form of preventive detention.

"Our State Department cooperated with Canada to extradite the Canadians involved, but most of them were freed on bail. Defendants started to disappear, as we expected. One potential witness was found dead on a Bronx street. The FBI was brought in to search for fugitives. Interpol joined in. One of the Canadian defendants was discovered dead in a field in upstate New York by hunters. His charred corpse was smoldering, his hands were bound behind his back, and he had been choked. You can't be too emphatic teaching lessons to would-be informants.

"To arouse public interest in the search for the missing defendants, the Canadian press was given their pictures. Sure enough, a Toronto woman reported seeing two of them—in Montague Beach, Nassau. Our persistent investigators were led to Jamaica where they missed the fugitives by two months. They were traced next to a hotel in Nice, France, then to a meeting in Rome with the deported Mafia kingpin Lucky Luciano, then to a swanky hotel suite in Barcelona. There, with American intelligence agents arriving from around the globe and the help of Spanish law enforcement officials and a dancer named *La Frivolidad* [Miss Frivolity], investigators closed in. The three elusive fugitive defendants were arrested and extradited by Spanish authorities and returned by our narcotics agents to New York. They eventually pleaded guilty and got fifteen-year prison sentences. Eleven other defendants already have been convicted by a jury, which was obviously impressed by Rinaldo's testimony.

"While all this fugitive hunting was going on, the agents on the case had gotten word that Joe Valachi was having troubles serving his long sentence in the federal penitentiary in Atlanta. He'd killed someone there recently, thinking he was going to be killed as an informant on orders from fellow inmate Vito Genovese, allegedly the Mafia's boss of all bosses. Genovese had heard from the prison grapevine that Valachi was informing—at that point he wasn't—and planted the kiss of death on Joe. Valachi was put into solitary confinement at his request because he feared he would be killed.

"The Narcotics Bureau persuaded the Bureau of Prisons to put Valachi back into the prison population. They hoped he would be frightened enough to start cooperating with the government. The gambit worked. A frightened Valachi got word to agents in New York who he'd refused to talk to in the past that he was ready to talk now. And we were ready to listen."

Hundley's story sounded like the most colorful cops-and-robbers adventure of all. It got more colorful as he focused on Valachi.

"Valachi was brought north, first to Westchester, where Rinaldo and Palmeri had been converted into important government witnesses [both were released for providing major testimony in major trials], then secretly to the stockade at Fort Monmouth in New Jersey for his better protection. It soon became clear he was talking and had a very long and very interesting story to tell. Security was intense. That's when I got personally involved and the FBI came into the case with the OK of the Bureau of Narcotics, which had been primarily responsible for developing this whole case."

Hundley and FBI agent Jim Flynn worked on Valachi after narcotics investigators passed on the now-talkative witness. It was one of the best examples of the kind of cooperation between investigative agencies that Kennedy had insisted on, and it really paid off.

Valachi had a lifetime of details and stories that provided missing links in countless cases, but astonishingly, Hundley told us, "We made no major cases based on Valachi's testimony, and he never was a witness in any of the cases we made." However, more usefully, during over eight months of intensive interrogation, he spelled out to Hundley and Flynn in colorful detail the inner workings of the Mafia, in which he had long been an active member. Everything he revealed was checked and double-checked with our own sources. The existence and power of the Mafia could no longer be denied, nor could its highly structured system. Valachi had a prodigious memory and "described in intricate detail the structure, power bases, membership requirements, codes, and identities of many members of the mob. . . . He described crime after crime committed by the mob, providing names, dates, and places," a top FBI official later reported.

Valachi told federal agents which characters would never cooperate with the government and who might, and how to get to them, all of which was invaluable. He was a colorful character and full of graphic and at times very funny tales, despite their gruesome implications. Once, asked when he had joined the Mafia, he replied.

"It was during the war."

"Which war? World War I or World War II?"

"No, I mean the war with Chicago."

Valachi's whole world was the mob and its crime wars. Valachi named someone as the killer in an unsolved slaying and the agent asked how he knew if he wasn't there at the time.

"Because I told him to," Valachi explained.

Valachi's testimony would open the inner workings of the Mafia in this country to public attention. On September 27, 1963, Valachi, disguised and surrounded by a phalanx of federal marshals, told his story to a vast American public over national television before the McClellan Committee in the Senate caucus room. Even in this intense hearing, the cagey witness maintained his morbid sense of humor. Hundley had told Valachi before his committee appearance not to lie about anything. "Remember," Hundley told him, "if you are asked if you were a killer, you're just as guilty legally if you drove the getaway car." Sure enough, Valachi was asked by one senator if he had ever participated in any killings. Valachi leaned forward and earnestly told his interrogator: "I know, Senator, that the guy who drives the getaway car is just as guilty as the killer—so I'd have to say yes." When Senator Curtis asked Valachi if there was any tie-in between the Mafia and the Teamsters, he replied, coyly: "Senator, I'll tell you that in private."

During his celebrated stay in Washington, Valachi was kept under special guard in the D.C. jail, in its safest accommodation—the execution room. There, he jokingly relaxed by sitting in the old-fashioned electric chair.

For days, Valachi tore away the Mafia's veil of secrecy and publicly exposed its hierarchal chain of command. For the first time the American public heard about *omerta,* and blood oaths, and bosses, and soldiers, and buttons, and capos, and consiglieri, and all the exotic appellations of a vast and organized criminal syndicate.

Valachi told names and places, described major crimes and murders, and supplied the lingo and the exotic operating procedures of the mobsters, most of whom he knew personally. At the public hearings, he vowed: "I'm going to destroy them." The cold, calculating, revengeful, and frightened killer had provided Kennedy's organized crime team with more intelligence than we had ever had.

—

No one could top Bill's story, and our morning with the boss ended when we broke for lunch. Now I could turn to preparing my case and trying to do what my more experienced colleague couldn't do in a trial that had gone in strong and come out wrong the first time. I had asked for it; now the final act in Newport was mine.

Chapter 7

POLITICS IN JUSTICE

There are two obvious truths about politics and justice: The former should not affect the latter; and it is impossible to keep the two totally separate. Between these two competing values lurk the pitfalls and perplexities. It is precisely this kind of delicate decision making, however, that defines the quality of a prosecutor's office. Surely that would be so with a high-stakes, high-visibility office such as Kennedy's Organized Crime and Racketeering Section.

We knew that each of us had to behave like Caesar's wife. Everything we did would be pitilessly examined by the media and viciously fought by our opponents. We could not give our enemies reasonable grounds to attack. We, the troops, could be single-minded. The attorney general, however, by unleashing us, was opening himself to excruciating pressures.

The Department of Justice, to understate, does not operate in a political vacuum. The winning party in an election picks the chiefs of its agencies, and the chiefs pick the staff, for the most part. All the U.S. attorneys around the country are political appointees, as are all federal judges. In addition, the department's priorities are set by the victors (though sometimes determined by circumstances). So it would be naive to pretend that political elements are not ever-present in the justice system.

Nonetheless, a constant effort to be evenhanded is essential in the administration of justice, as is the public perception that the system *is* evenhanded. Politics as usual may have its place, former attorney general Elliot Richardson once noted, "but not in the Department of Justice." He noted the important distinction between "the proper role of the political process in the shaping of legal policies and the perversion of the legal process by political pressure." Former solicitor general Archibald Cox also drew a similar distinction between appropriate philosophical and policy considerations about economic and social issues—how to interpret a law, which legal theory to advance, etc.—and outright party politics that, as he well knew from his later Watergate experiences, should have nothing to do with the running of the Department of Justice.

Looking back, I think it is clear we frequently faced two types of political pressures, as all prosecutors inevitably must. There are politics and there are politics. First, there are problems relating to the incursion of party politics into the justice process. Second, there are issues of choice, emphasis, and policy—little "p" politics, one might call them. Party politics add partisanship to a process that must abhor the intrusion; on the other hand, politics involving prosecutorial discretion and internal priority setting is an acceptable aspect of real-life jurisprudence.

Nevertheless, politics of both kinds frustrate the administrators of justice, as former attorney general William Rogers had warned Bob Kennedy. Some kinds of politics are inherent and necessary and acceptable; some are extrinsic, avoidable, and condemnable. Great attorneys general are renowned both for the values reflected in their choices of priorities and for their minimizing of political influence peddling.

Each new attorney general focuses on problems he and his administration think warrant particular attention. Another official sees a different range of problems and pursues those. These questions do not involve issues of right and wrong, but of social agendas. Priority setting is the proper form of "politics" of justice.

The other, and unacceptable, form of politics concerns tipping the scales of justice by giving weight to political considerations, favoring individuals in the dispensation of justice. Some party politics is traditional—choosing U.S. attorneys in consultation with senators from the state in question, for example. Other political influences on the administration of justice are pernicious—being influenced by the political clout of a prospective defendant is the classic example.

Robert Kennedy's Justice Department dealt with all types of political pressures. The big "P" political cases—situations where influential people attempted to alter the course of a criminal investigation—were, while contentious, more obvious in their implications and solutions. The more elusive little "p" politics involved those situations where the question was not whether we pulled our punches, but rather whether we had gone too far. For example, we were constantly criticized by civil libertarians who thought it improper for our section to target individuals as criminal suspects and to zero in on them with extraordinary resources and intensity. No one could elude such a prosecutorial vendetta, they argued. Noble ends did not justify such worrisome means.

It was the jump from mere emphasis to special intervention that was troublesome to our critics, and it was a subject I pondered often. When Kennedy became attorney general, it was no surprise that he gave subjects he knew and cared about his serious attention. Nor should that have been viewed as idiosyncratic. An election had been held. Both he and the president had been publicly identified with opposition to organized crime and labor corruption, and they could be expected to follow through on assuming office. Had they not acted, their earlier views could be seen as hypocritical, irresponsible headline hunting. No surprise, then, that Robert Kennedy had immediately sought the kind of department changes that he had called for earlier, as a critic of sluggish prosecution.

Kennedy demonstrated ultimately in his Justice Department career that he also could grow intellectually and work just as hard in other areas of evolving concerns. Civil rights was not his priority when he arrived at Justice, but it became one because events drew the department in that direction. When they did, Kennedy acted, as vigorously and as passionately as he had against organized crime from the beginning. This is how the Justice Department should operate: Begin with certain priorities and develop others to meet new challenges.

In those days, the Lands Division was a backwater, lackluster part of the department because little evidence of wide public concern was shown on issues under its jurisdiction. In later years, with the deepening interest in environmental law, that division would become more active and its work more visible. For the same reason, the Internal Security Division had been big and active in pre-Kennedy decades when J. Edgar Hoover's influence was greater and the country was obsessed with the Communist threat. During the Kennedy years, it was minimized and almost dismantled.

The ebb and flow of emphases are proper institutional responses. It was in this historic tradition, then, that Kennedy took a token, flagging section—organized crime—energized and expanded it, and emphasized its mission. Some of us were always conscious of whether we were overdoing it and crossing borders of zeal into taboos of prosecutorial excess.

Were we out to "get" Hoffa, as some civil libertarians argued? Was it right to compile dossiers on individuals—even Mafia mobsters—and to conduct coordinated, concentrated investigations into all aspects of their lives, and the lives of their friends, family, and business associates? Could anyone survive this kind of scrutiny? Was all this attention fair?

I wrestled with this question, especially with respect to the Hoffa investigations, and decided that with a few exceptions, we were fighting hard but not crossing the lines of fairness and justice. There was no way to catch and convict the organized criminals without being organized, focused, and relentless in our efforts. These were no casual criminals. Our subjects were capable of intimidating and killing witnesses, destroying evidence, corrupting public officials, fixing juries—most of our top targets had long histories of this kind. This still didn't mean we could cross lines ourselves or become lawless—but it did justify the kind of heat we brought to bear. We were not indicting the Hoffas or the mafiosi for spitting on the street.

When I met with the federal investigating agents, I made it clear that we would be playing by the rules. I didn't want to lose any case on appeal because we'd not done so. Whether for reasons of pragmatism or for reasons of ethics, we would play it hard and tough, but straight. And we did.

Tom McBride recalls a revealing experience that occurred when he investigated corrupt trial judges in Philadelphia. "I had a very strong ethical mission with regard to political corruption," McBride said, because "that is really far more dangerous and damaging than simple racketeering." After his investigation began, McBride encountered the facts of political life: The FBI special agent in charge told the U.S. attorney what was happening in McBride's touchy investigation; the U.S. attorney told Bill Green (the congressman and local political leader); Bill Green in turn told President Kennedy; the president told Robert Kennedy, who told Henry Petersen, and Henry Petersen called McBride to say that "some people were upset."

What impressed McBride, however, was that "Bob Kennedy's message was not 'Don't do it,' but 'for Chrissake tell me next time what you're doing.' I've always held that reaction much to his credit. He easily could have told me to cut it out." Kennedy needed to know about political cases, not to avoid them, but to be forewarned to expect repercussions.

Harry Alexander had a similar experience. He was sent to Puerto Rico to investigate union racketeering there. When he was about to indict officials of the International Union of Electrical Workers on racketeering charges, he was called to a meeting at the White House with the attorney general, the president, and James Carey, the president of the Electrical Workers' Union, who had supported Kennedy's presidential campaign and who did not believe his union officials could be thieves. Carey claimed his union was clean, had adopted a Code of Ethical Practices, and he cried out publicly against presuming guilt before trial. He told the press he was filled "with shock and resentment" over our vindictive prosecutorial tactics concerning arrest and bail. Union lawyers refused to cooperate with FBI accountants regarding union records.

Alexander would not go to the White House meeting Carey had requested.

"I am the prosecutor," he told the attorney general, "and when Mr. Carey meets me for the first time it will be on the witness stand where I don't want him to recall having met with me and the attorney general and the president."

Robert Kennedy deferred to Alexander's judgment, and a good thing, because what Harry suspected is exactly what happened. Carey met with the president and the attorney general, but "nobody ever put any pressure on me at all," Alexander recalls. Politics went on, but the case went forward; Carey testified as a defense witness, and Alexander's prosecutorial position was not prejudiced.

When Charles Smith was in Los Angeles working with the organized crime strike force in the U.S. attorney's office there, an FBI agent questioned him about the possible ramifications of subpoenaing Frank Sinatra in an ongoing investigation. Sinatra's social relationship with the Kennedys at that time was well known and the agents were not sure how the attorney general would react. Smith said, "Let's find out," and called Robert Kennedy in front of the agents. Kennedy's response to Smith's questions was: "If the bastard has done anything criminal, indict him!" Smith noticed that thereafter the agents were gung ho in their work, true believers in Kennedy's rectitude.

Years later, Smith harkened back to that incident when a major contributor to the Kennedy campaign complained about his brother being subpoenaed in a grand jury investigation into improper Teamsters pension fund loans. The contributor called the White House, which referred the call to the Department of Justice. Kennedy's secretary, Angie Novello, referred the call to Smith with the admonition: "Handle it the way he wants it handled." Remembering Kennedy's earlier remarks about the Sinatra inquiry, Smith told the caller to "get lost." His brother subsequently was indicted. Smith knew what we all came to rely on: When we made our cases legitimately, we had our boss's support regardless of outside political pressures.

There were other telling examples. The top political animals in the Kennedy administration watched helplessly as Robert Kennedy's organized crime drive knocked off politician after politician around the country, most of them Democrats. In one of our regular meetings in Kennedy's office, as the lawyers described their cases, one after another reported the corruption scalps he was gathering. Robert Kennedy—sleeves rolled up, tie loosened, fingers together in front of his face, swiveling in his chair behind his immense desk, listened, asking questions here and there, including inevitably, "Was he Republican or Democrat?"

One after another, the lawyers reported: "Democrat."

After three or four such exchanges he commented, with a smile, "If you guys keep this up my brother is going to have to take me out of here and send me to the Supreme Court, where I can't cause him any more trouble."

It was for us a matter of levity that we were convicting so many Democrats; and if it wasn't a laughing matter to Kennedy, he never imposed his political problems on us. The president remarked to a friendly journalist, Charles Bartlett, after his brother had committed an act of prosecutorial independence: "What this administration needs more than anything is an attorney general we can *fix*."

The point is that the fairest, most detached attorney general—in the most apolitical Justice Department—cannot avoid the presence of political factors. In fact, Robert Kennedy was a very political attorney general; he was related to the president, roaming into other areas of public affairs, extraordinarily influential, and acutely aware of his brother's interests, including reelection. The questions to be asked are how he dealt with politics, not whether, and to what extent and in what ways politics were handled in the national prosecutor's office. My colleagues all agreed that our overriding sense of mission was to do the right thing—that very phase was often used.

My current case raised the question of emphasis and degree. Was it unethical or excessive to indict Ratterman's conspirators under the Civil Rights Act, even though that act was designed generally for other kinds of cases? Was it abusive to indict a Mafia chief for tax evasion if our real aim was to end his murders, extortions, or briberies? I think not. A prosecutor has to prosecute the cases he can prove. And prosecutors have to use the witnesses and evidence available, and that often means witnesses with questionable pasts and evidence with questionable provenance. Crimes aren't committed in Yankee Stadium, and usually they are not witnessed by clergy or model citizens.

In time, we would convict a remarkable number of powerful syndicate mobsters, union leaders, and politicians because we went after them. Any other effort would have been a waste of time and resources.

Into the mix of small "p" politics must be figured the influence of J. Edgar Hoover and the FBI. For decades before the Kennedy administration, Hoover was more powerful than most if not all the attorneys general he "served." As a result, the FBI had its own politics, which often were distinct from those of the Justice Department. The FBI is under the administrational jurisdiction of the Justice Department, but Hoover ran his organization like a private agency, and few political figures took him on.

There were rumors after the election that President Kennedy had wanted to retire the independent director. But recent reports have shown that Hoover had compromising information about the young president's peccadillos and after the two finished a private luncheon meeting in the early days of the new administration, the president announced his reappointment. Thereafter, Hoover and Robert Kennedy had a testy and tense relationship, which RFK controlled, but which Hoover resisted whenever he could, throughout the almost four years when the two powerful, totally different men worked together.

One change was remarkable because it put the two into administrative contest. Hoover had made a career fighting Communism and keeping the FBI as the patriotic champion of democracy. For decades, with Hoover's full cooperation, the department's Internal Security Division conducted investigations and prosecuted cases on loyalty and security. Under Kennedy, as I've mentioned, that division waned and almost disappeared, though Hoover might have predicted otherwise given Kennedy's own history. It was revived by the Nixon administration, which used it to prosecute draft evasion cases arising out of the Vietnam War protests.

What I presumed at the time was simply a matter of opposing priorities between two strong-willed men has been described differently in a recent book. It asserts that Hoover was compromised by crime figures and purposely pulled his punches. Anthony Summers's disclosures that major racketeers had embarrassing evidence that Hoover had social ties with and was expensively entertained by known racketeers could explain his reticence at the time to join our crusade. Certainly they placed the director—self-proclaimed as a model of rectitude—in a potentially compromised position.

———

Less subtle than questions of emphasis and policy, and more testy than making appointments or dealing with Hoover, were the questions raised by the inevitable instances of potentially true political influence (the capital "P" variety). Two cases illustrate. One involved a midwestern mayor whom had been influential in the recent presidential campaign and whom the president had rewarded by designating him U.S. ambassador to Greece; the other involved a New York

State Supreme Court judge who happened also to be the brother of a congressman.

CACHERIS

Of all the hotshots Silberling brought to the Justice Department, Jay Goldberg was perhaps the hottest. With a Phi Beta Kappa key and a Harvard law degree, Jay was an experienced prosecutor, having learned the ropes in Manhattan in the well-regarded office of Frank Hogan, then the preeminent big city district attorney in the country. As had happened with Bill Lynch when he left the U.S. attorney's office in Manhattan for a stint in private practice and hated it, Jay too craved the life of the aggressive prosecutor and was happily recruited by Silberling. In addition to being smart, Goldberg was flamboyant, brash, dramatic, histrionic, very funny, and very tough. He was a wonderful ham, whose prosecutorial style was unconventional but remarkably effective. He had a penchant for the spotlight and for drama.

Goldberg got both in Gary, Indiana, where he was sent to look into allegations of racketeering and political payoffs. But, while his efforts resulted in major convictions, his style caused him serious personal problems in the department.

When Robert Kennedy was counsel to the McClellan Committee in 1959, he had unearthed information about corruption in Lake County, Indiana. His efforts then inspired the formation of a privately financed Northwest Indiana Crime Commission, headed by a former FBI agent, Francis Lynch. The Lake County district attorney, Metro Holovachka, was suspected of involvement in payoffs for protection. The reformers could not work with him. Francis Lynch went to Kennedy after he took over at Justice and asked for help. When his plea got to our office, Silberling sent the recently recruited Goldberg to look into the situation. It did not take long before there were fireworks, smoke, and flames over Gary, not caused by the steel mills.

Goldberg found there was no U.S. attorney in Gary—somehow, no one had been found to fill this important office. When Jay got there in September 1961, he was told by the FBI in Gary that they had no evidence of payoffs. But the Indiana resident IRS agent had another clue: The professional gamblers in Indiana were paying more money for federal wagering taxes than any other place in the country.

For there to be such open and extensive gambling, public officials had to be taking payoffs.

In Goldberg's view, the focus changed from "all those potential defendants whose names ended in vowels"—Frank Zizzo was supposed to be *the* local mobster—to the officials who countenanced this sham. "I wanted to take down the people from the top who permitted this system to function," Goldberg said. Jay persuaded Silberling that the ones to go after first were the politicians, not the hoods who ran the gambling and prostitution operations in Gary. The investigation led down unexpected paths to defendants who were not sons of Italy—and not all gamblers.

Goldberg worked with the crime commission's Lynch and the IRS agent in charge, Oral Cole, and eventually took the results of their investigation before a grand jury. They had detected a complicated system of payoffs, but needed to corroborate some of their suppositions before they could bring formal charges. With the pressure of a grand jury, Goldberg was certain he could gain the corroboration needed to make his cases.

The flamboyant Goldberg worked closely with his meticulous IRS agents, who collected and analyzed reams of business records. His premise (based on prior experiences as a prosecutor) was that all contractors paid bribes, but they, as good businessmen, paid by check in order to claim a tax deduction for a "business expense." It was a fact of life: Being a contractor on an Indiana highway meant that bribes *were* one of the costs of doing business. For Goldberg, it was just a question of converting the businessmen into witnesses.

Goldberg's tales weren't exactly out of the law school evidence books. "These guys were not as tough in Indiana as what I had been used to in New York," Jay reported. "They'd be brought into the grand jury room and I'd be sitting in a high-backed chair with my back to them so they wouldn't see me. They'd just hear my voice. I'd tell them in stentorian tones that they were in hot water because the government had evidence they'd paid off public officials. Did they want the water temperature turned up so they would be burned; or did they want to tell the truth—which we already knew—and come clean? We had subpoenaed all their books and records, so they knew we had mined them dry. They knew from the heavy press coverage of our investigation and from their own grapevine that just about everyone doing business on the highway was coming into our grand jury. They were afraid.

"Invariably, they collapsed and talked. Every one of them confessed that they'd paid off every city council member. Tribute to all of them went into one account."

Still, there were legal problems, and political ones, as well. Legally, there was a problem with tracing the conduit from the payers of these bribes to the ultimate recipients. Politically, while Jay was turning up the heat on the Indiana public officials, they were turning up the heat on him in Washington. For a while, the whole investigation was thrown into jeopardy.

What Jay had found was a community so corrupt that no businessman could transport his products on the streets of Gary without paying a fee to the councilman whose district he had to pass through. For example, one man in the trucking business told Jay that for his trucks to carry sand through the city, he had to pay off three councilmen whose districts his trucks traversed. Before long, Jay had evidence that the sheriff, each councilman, and the mayor—George Cacheris—were all on the take.

Goldberg and his IRS aides discovered one ingenious scam. All the turnpike contractors' checks were made out to a "George Combs." Someone tipped off Goldberg that Combs in Greek is *Cacheris*. Sure enough, the payoff checks were traced via conduits who fronted for him to Cacheris's bank account and to dummy accounts he controlled. The corporation counsel admitted he'd been a conduit for Cacheris on a payoff from a sewer firm (an appropriate source); so did an investigator for the state liquor authority, and soon many others.

The problem—as Goldberg would soon discover—is that to reward Cacheris for his notable help in the recent presidential election, President Kennedy had nominated him to be our next ambassador to Greece. He was supposed to be untouchable.

Cacheris hired a former Indiana U.S. attorney, Alexander Campbell, then a Democratic National Committeeman, to represent him, and he went directly to the White House and to Robert Kennedy to complain about Goldberg's unorthodox tactics. The FBI was asked to investigate whether Goldberg—who was a popular hero now, locally, because of extensive press coverage—was responsible for a huge billboard sign that read: GOLDBERG: LEAD ME TO YOUR TAKER. Jay swears he was not the instigator, that his visibility was not the result of self-promotion but rather a grateful press and public that saw him as a champion fighting a corrupt system no one had challenged before. There was no U.S. attorney; the local district attorney was under indictment; the crime commission was riding the wave of Kennedy's reform; and the people were responding.

Of course, Jay's theatrical style did play into the hands of his critics. For example, when he told witnesses that they were in a vat of hot water, and that by cooperating they could lower the temperature to a livable level, but by lying they'd get badly burned, it was merely a Goldberg metaphor, like the U.S. truck bearing down on the witness, which we'd heard about. In addition, every time someone with seemingly acceptable credentials and with connections was recommended by Indiana congressmen for the vacant post of U.S. attorney in Gary, Goldberg came up with information to veto the choice. One nominee claimed Goldberg abused him by saying he was so corrupt he was not fit to serve. (After an FBI investigation, his name was withdrawn. Years later, that same nominee, then a county judge, was convicted of participating in a racketeering scheme.) But while Jay was winning a great reputation with the people and the press in Gary, he was gaining vehement enemies in high places.

Indiana congressman Ray Madden, a member of the House Rules Committee, told White House officials that if they wanted his vote to get their farm bill out of committee, they'd better get Goldberg out of Indiana. Goldberg was called back to Washington to account for his stylistic excesses, and to assure Justice Department officials that he had a solid case. At one point, the day before the grand jury was to convene, after Goldberg had subpoenaed fifty-six witnesses, he was called by Robert Kennedy. Goldberg says Kennedy asked him to delay his grand jury investigation until Cacheris's lawyer, who was out of the country, returned to discuss his case with them. Cacheris asked who the witnesses were who testified against him, what they said, and what documentary evidence of his wrongdoing we had. Goldberg refused to discuss the evidence with Cacheris and his lawyers, advising Kennedy this would imperil his investigation. Kennedy ordered

Goldberg home to Washington because Cacheris—present in Kennedy's office at the time—had told Kennedy that Goldberg had threatened to "crucify" him and his lawyer.

Goldberg flew back to Washington, met with Criminal Division head Jack Miller early the next morning, and was told the meeting with Kennedy was off. In Kennedy's office, Cacheris had broken down in tears and confessed that he had lied about Goldberg's threats. A face-off was no longer necessary. Still, Goldberg was outraged that he'd been pulled off the investigation and told Miller: "Doesn't the attorney general appreciate how important this investigation is, the kind of work we're doing in Indiana?" Miller's response stunned Goldberg: "How would you feel if someone was trying to lock up your friends?"

John Seigenthaler recalls Robert Kennedy's treatment of Cacheris. Ray Madden, a Democratic congressman, had called, and Seigenthaler spoke to him at Kennedy's request. Madden came to Justice with Cacheris to meet with Kennedy and Seigenthaler, pleading: "You can't do this to him. You'd be doing what Eisenhower didn't do." Kennedy had agreed to see Cacheris who pulled out all the stops, reminding Kennedy, "Some of that money [his bribes] was for Jack." Seigenthaler remembers Kennedy's attitude: "Bob regretted that he was corrupt, and had no sympathy for what he had done. But he felt he had to be able to look Cacheris in the eye and hear what he said, just as he'd done in the campaign when he needed his help."

Seigenthaler and Kennedy were beginning to understand the agony of the job William Rogers had described to them late in 1960. Kennedy told Cacheris that the evidence against him was very strong, that it was his job as attorney general to enforce the law, and that he hoped Cacheris had a good lawyer. Cacheris dropped his head on Kennedy's desk and wept.

Silberling had recommended to Kennedy that we indict one of the city councilmen first; he was a bartender with the weakest defense. We should go after him first and in that way influence the others to roll over.

"What's wrong with being a bartender?" Kennedy asked ruefully, "My grandfather was a bartender."

Goldberg returned to Indiana, only to be pulled back to Washington again for more administrative questions. There were rumors that there would be no indictments. Then—Goldberg swears he had nothing to do with the stunt—one hundred coconuts were sent to the White House from Gary with the word HELP carved on each, a reference to President Kennedy's PT boat rescue story. The note (Jay thinks it came from a local citizens group) accompanying the coconuts asked for Goldberg to be sent back to Gary.

The ploy worked. Goldberg was sent back, and the indictments he proposed were issued by the grand jury. Indicted for extortion were the mayor of Gary, the Lake County sheriff, the entire Hammond city council, the police chief, traffic commissioner, and other lesser public officials—twelve in all. Cacheris's lawyer told a press conference that Kennedy "was out to get Lake County Democrats," and that his clients were victims of "a grotesque investigation." Testimonials of support were organized to raise defense funds for these beleaguered politicians. Contractors doing local business were told to buy tickets or "their trucks would be taken off the roads." No local prosecutions followed Goldberg's broad disclosures of graft. We were charged with committing "baseless character assassinations."

Deputy Attorney General Byron White announced the indictments in Washington, D.C. When he next came back to Washington and was called to Kennedy's office, Goldberg found out that he was not going to be the one to prosecute the cases he'd made. He was told he had become too controversial, too personally involved in the cross fire of accusations, and was to be replaced by a veteran tax lawyer. The case he developed, however, was so strong that all the defendants eventually pleaded guilty to tax evasion charges. They had not reported and paid taxes on their graft.

While our group ended up with more scalps, the successes cost us dearly. Goldberg read the writing on the wall that his work, for which he was honored for his courage and skills with a testimonial dinner by the Indiana Crime Commission and accolades in the press, was not appreciated by the top officials in his own department. He had spent too much time defending his own conduct to be comfortable contin- uing to work there. Goldberg was sent to other cities, but when Silberling and Petersen told Jay he was "dead" in the department and "there was no point in his staying" because he had become too controversial, Jay returned to New York.

Not long after, Silberling and Misslbeck left as well. There had been conflicts between Silberling and Criminal Division chief Jack Miller, it was rumored, and Silberling had rubbed RFK wrong as well. Silberling had been appointed by Kennedy soon after he became attorney general; strangely, Miller's appointment came later. As our section became the tail that wagged the division's dog, resentments built. When he arrived, Ed hadn't known the difference between a section chief and a division head. He thought he had a line and staff job, and would report directly to Kennedy. When Miller arrived, a problem was inevitable. Kennedy wanted Silberling's independence; but Miller had to endure the complaints of U.S. attorneys and the FBI when Ed crossed institutional lines. Kennedy wanted the results Ed was getting, but he also had to deal with the bureaucrats and politicians we antagonized.

His staff all liked Silberling, who was consistently supportive and inspiring. He should have been made a player-coach, as his celebrated trial skills never were tapped at Justice. It was the Peter Principle that did him in. The rumor was that he was not as good with those above him as he was with those he hired and supervised. He, along with Jay Goldberg, fell on the slippery rocks less because of what they did than how they did it. The departures of Silberling and Goldberg were the unhappy fallout of otherwise imaginative and aggressive investigations, and part of our group's growing pains.

Jay Goldberg remembers a postscript to his experiences in Gary. Years later, when Jay was practicing law in New York City and RFK was a senator, both were invited to a swank Central Park West celebrity fundraiser for Richard Hatcher, who was running for mayor of Gary. Hatcher thanked Kennedy in his remarks for ridding Gary of corruption. Lifting his glass and nodding in Jay's direction, Kennedy told the crowd: "The credit does not belong to me, it belongs to Jay Goldberg for the work he did while on my staff."

There are two ways to interpret that postscript. Both are probably correct. The cynical view is that Kennedy had no choice but to acknowledge Goldberg's success after the fact, though he was begrudging at the time, and that it was Goldberg's avid commitment in the face of hostile allies that preserved Kennedy's reputation for crusading law enforcement. The other is that Kennedy set something in motion that Goldberg capitalized on, and that despite whatever reluctance Kennedy may have felt in the face of political pressures at the time, the cases went forward and were successfully prosecuted after all. Kennedy had provided the cudgel of law enforcement and Goldberg used it.

KEOGH

Those experiences in Gary led to other changes in our group. Bill Hundley was promoted back to his former job to replace Silberling. Much as we who liked Silberling and Goldberg were dismayed by their being pushed out, it was hard to fault the appointment of Hundley. Ironically, Hundley remembered being pushed out of this same job by Kennedy and was not anxious to return to it. He did not want to administer the now large and active organization, and he was ready to leave Justice for private law practice. Kennedy pressured him to stay. Having gained wide respect, including Kennedy's, for his prosecution of a major (not organized crime) case, and being popular among department lawyers, Hundley was a natural choice. Experienced, affable, equally strong in backing his staff, the transition was easy even if our sympathies were with the recently departed. There was immediate evidence that our work was to go on without other changes. Indeed, it was Hundley himself who was sent into the second political minefield we were to traverse.

Eugene Keogh, whose name is immortalized for most Americans as the author of the tax deduction for pension investments, was a powerful New York congressman. The ever loyal Kennedys felt a strong political debt to Keogh for his crucial help with the New York delegation during the presidential nominating convention in 1960. He was a friend of Joseph Kennedy and a Kennedy loyalist in the House of Representatives.

What an irony, then, that Representative Keogh went to the 1962 Army-Navy game with President Kennedy four days before his brother, J. Vincent Keogh, a New York State Supreme Court judge, was indicted in a case brought by the organized crime section, a case over which Robert Kennedy had agonized before authorizing the indictment.

William Shannon, in his book *The Heir Apparent,* called the case an example of Robert Kennedy's incorruptibility. Ed Guthman

Joseph Kennedy and three of his young sons, 1939. Joseph Kennedy was not satisfied when his son John (right) was elected president. He pushed the candidacy of his next-in-line son, Robert (second from right), for attorney general. Eldest son Joseph junior (left) was killed in World War II.

Robert Kennedy's brief work for Senator Joseph McCarthy early in his career marked him in many critics' minds as insensitive to civil liberties.

Robert Kennedy, as counsel to the McClellan Committee (Senator McClellan is to the right of Kennedy), questions Jimmy Hoffa of the Teamsters Union about labor racketeering in sensational hearings that catapulted JFK and RFK into the national limelight.

Robert Kennedy interrogates witnesses before the McClellan Committee. Senator John McClellan is on the far left; investigator Carmine Bellino is between McClellan and RFK; Senator John Kennedy is at right.

In a lighter moment, Robert Kennedy seems determined to look into and under everything connected with the Teamsters.

James Riddle Hoffa, Teamsters boss, the subject of what some
saw as Robert Kennedy's Ahab-like pursuit of organized crime
that began with the McClellan Committee hearings and continued
when RFK moved into the Justice Department.

Campaigning: Robert Kennedy speaks with West Virginia coal miners during his brother's run for the presidency. His image as a ruthless campaigner was difficult to change.

Robert Kennedy, "tired of running after people," did not want to become attorney general, but his brother, and especially their father, felt otherwise.

As attorney general, Robert Kennedy brought the IRS into partnership with the FBI in the war against organized crime. Here, with Treasury Secretary Douglas Dillon (center), he attends the swearing-in of his former law professor Mortimer M. Caplin (left) as IRS commissioner.

Robert Kennedy recruited New York City prosecutor Edwyn Silberling (right) to run the organized crime section of the Justice Department, and Silberling in turn recruited the author.

John F. Kennedy signs into law the new organized crime bill proposed
by Robert Kennedy, as J. Edgar Hoover (behind right shoulder of
Robert Kennedy), Lyndon Johnson (far right), members of the Judiciary
Committee, and others look on.

Robert Kennedy was intense, involved, and sometimes introspective, though usually informal, as he ran the activist Department of Justice.

Kennedy brought an informal, shirtsleeves style to running Justice, often lunching simply at his desk—and with an outgoing demeanor.

Robert Kennedy's direct, often high-spirited management made meetings of his Organized Crime and Racketeering Section great fun—and the reports of cases in progress offered story after story. Here he meets with part of that section, Walter Sheridan's Teamsters prosecutors, and other interested staff members.

George Ratterman (left), football hero and reform candidate for sheriff, with the author during the federal trial of conspirators who plotted to defeat Ratterman. A staged episode caught him in bed with a striptease dancer, though it was later shown he was drugged and framed.

Charles Lester was the number one catch of the Newport, Kentucky, investigation; he was convicted of conspiring to deprive Ratterman of his civil rights.

Ratterman's wife supported him despite the scandalous mess he found himself in when he was arrested with a stripper and charged by local police.

April Flowers, who turned out to be the star witness, and her boss at the Glenn, Tito Carinci, in court after they were arrested with Ratterman.

During the Ratterman investigation, the author confers with his prosecutorial partner, Bill "Sunshine" Lynch (right), and the FBI agent in charge of the case, Frank Staab (left).

Robert Kennedy's wide-ranging interests included the welfare of children. To demonstrate his concern, he involved celebrities from the sports and entertainment worlds, including Cary Grant, pictured here.

Carlos Marcello: "You, Jim, and me are in for hard times as long as Bobby Kennedy is in office. Someone ought to kill that son-of-a-bitch." (Marcello to Santos Trafficante, Jr.)

Santos Trafficante, Jr.: "We shouldn't have killed John. We should've killed Bobby." (Trafficante to Frank Ragano)

Sam Giancana: "We took care of Kennedy. . . . The hit in Dallas was just like any other operation we'd worked on in the past." (Giancana to his brother)

Johnny Rosselli: Contact
man between the CIA and
the mob. Rosselli was found
hacked to death, floating in
Biscayne Bay.

Joe Valachi: Called by some
cynics "the Italian Canary,"
Valachi put the Mafia on
prime-time TV for the
first time.

Moldea Collection

Hoffa shooting craps: "Something has
got to be done. The time has come for
your friend and Carlos to get rid of
him. . . . This has got to be done. Be
sure to tell them what I said." (Hoffa
telling Ragano to give a message to
Marcello and Trafficante)

reported that Kennedy considered it "the most difficult decision" he faced as attorney general—and he had many. It was a telling test of Kennedy's approach to politically sensitive cases. It seemed so for all of us there at the time. The case presented a moment of truth that no one shied away from, and which defined Kennedy's let-the-chips fall integrity.

Like many of our cases, it started unpredictably. As Victor Navasky concluded in his 1971 book, *Kennedy Justice,* "nothing about the Keogh case was routine." But, coming in the early days, it was a defining case that told the world, and certainly told us in the organized crime section, that politics might heighten the drama of a case and force a higher standard of rigor, but it would not lead to pulled punches. It proved the gung ho atmosphere was not just histrionics; our work was for real.

The case began when John Lally and Charles Schaffer heard about a talkative criminal who was complaining about his recent sentence in a bankruptcy fraud case. Silberling had sent Lally, a reserved, white-haired Justice Department veteran to New York to interview the criminal, Sandy Moore, about his connection to Tony "Ducks" Corallo, a rackets figure we had an interest in. Moore wasn't talking, at first, but on Lally's third visit to Moore's detention cell, Robert Kennedy happened to come walking through the jail accompanied by a local U.S. attorney, Elliott Kahaner. Kennedy was known to stop in on prosecutors and investigators for informal visits during his frequent travels, and this was one such unplanned sojourn.

When Sandy Moore saw them, he told Lally he had "a story you won't believe." Moore told Lally and his colleague, Shaffer, a handsome, aggressive young assistant to Walter Sheridan with a special interest in labor racketeering cases, about a payoff to chief assistant U.S. attorney Kahaner and a New York State Supreme Court judge to fix a sentence in a criminal case.

When word of this sensational charge reached Washington, everyone in the department's higher echelons sat straight up. Lally and Shaffer believed their informer, and over a five-month period, they presented their developing case to the grand jury. There were rumors in the press of a "fix" by the department, and anxious meetings with Kennedy and his top staff assistants and our lawyers on the case. Eventually, Shaffer was replaced by Bill Hundley, who Kennedy viewed as more experienced (he was also a Republican holdover from the last administration). But despite all the rumors and tremors, all the special meetings with Kennedy, the case proceeded.

Sandy Moore's story to our inquisitive colleagues was, as he had promised, hard to believe at first, and for a while hard to prove. After Moore's conviction, his cousin had introduced him to a successful orthopedic surgeon, Robert Erdman, who apparently had friends in the right places. Erdman would act as an intermediary with Elliott Kahaner, the chief assistant U.S. attorney in the Brooklyn office handling Moore's case, and the very same person Moore fortuitously had seen walking through the jail with Kennedy. Dr. Erdman said he'd worked a deal with Kahaner: If Moore and his co-defendants would pay $35,000 and plead guilty, they'd get suspended sentences. At a later meeting, "Ducks" Corallo joined Moore and Erdman to discuss the fix.

The plot got thicker when Kahaner reported he could not work the fix because the U.S. attorney in charge of the case would not cooperate. Then Dr. Erdman contacted another friend, New York State Supreme Court judge Keogh—the influential congressman's brother—and himself a veteran of New York politics, a former U.S. attorney, and a man with many connections and friends.

The evidence developed by Lally and Schaffer showed that some of Moore's fix money had gone to Kahaner and that Erdman had given some of it to Judge Keogh, who then contacted Judge Leo Rayfiel, the sentencing judge, about Moore's sentence. Keogh also arranged a later meeting between Rayfiel and Erdman to discuss Rayfiel's sentencing of Moore. Kahaner and Keogh also intervened in the bankruptcy proceeding, attempting, with Erdman, to see if settling the bankruptcy fraud might induce Rayfiel to reduce the sentence. Rayfiel refused.

Judge Keogh categorically denied attempting to fix the case, and testified before the grand jury that his contacts with the case were innocent, though he admitted receiving significant gifts from Dr. Erdman through the years—cash, a car, work on his house, free medical services. He voluntarily took a lie detector test, but the results were inconclusive. Erdman was the direct link to Keogh, but his testimony could be questioned. There was anxiety about bringing the case without greater certainty of getting a conviction. The judge's lawyer had cooperated with our lawyers by turning over financial records, but they, too, were not conclusive.

To add to the inevitable concerns felt by everyone involved, the grand jury was becoming cynical about the department's reticence to charge Keogh, and a New York newspaper ran a story that our investigation of the fix included a congressman as one of the targets. Ed Guthman, Kennedy's press secretary and close advisor, was able to get the newspaper to issue a retraction (without disclosing what the grand jury *was* doing, because its proceedings are required by law to be secret), but the incident added to the building tension.

Hundley recalled to me: "I knew I had to try this sucker," but it was going to be tricky. It was essentially a one-witness case [Erdman] with "a lot of circumstantial evidence." Kennedy conferred regularly with Hundley and Lally, with Silberling and Jack Miller, and with his closest advisors and aides, Deputy Attorney General Byron White, John Seigenthaler, Nicholas Katzenbach, Burke Marshall, Louis Oberdorfer, assistants whose wisdom Kennedy respected, along with top FBI officials involved in the case. His anguish was apparent; his wry sense of humor rarely flashed. Once, when the vise on Keogh was clearly closing, while the political pressures outside Justice built, he mock-moaned to Silberling, "I *told* my brother I didn't want this job." But his evenhandedness was constant.

Hundley was instructed to be dispassionate and objective when he took over the investigation and was assured he'd have a free hand in the case. He said that there was never any pressure put on him by RFK, "never, never, never." Silberling remembered, "There was a much greater pressure to proceed because of the danger of not proceeding."

When all Hundley's work was done, Kennedy was advised we had a triable case, albeit one without the clear and decisive evidence against the judge that would have made the decision obvious. His criminal division advisors recommended indicting Keogh, along with Kahaner and the others involved. But others, elsewhere, were apparently putting pressure on Kennedy. One top White House aide urged RFK to let Keogh resign. Again, John Seigenthaler would be the alter ego for Kennedy, who felt a special obligation to Congressman Keogh, whose help with the New York delegation had been important to Kennedy's wresting the nomination from Lyndon Johnson. After months of agonizing over the preparation of the case, Kennedy's decision to go ahead and indict still had not been made. Seigenthaler and Hundley remember a group of key Justice Department aides gathering around Kennedy, who sat on the stairs at a White House reception honoring the justices of the Supreme Court. Kennedy feared the evidence was not strong enough. He didn't want to indict a judge if he could be acquitted; that would destroy him, and Kennedy didn't want "to have that on my conscience."

"The weight of the evidence is for the jury to decide," one go-get-'em prosecutor replied.

"I want to be sure we can convict," Kennedy argued, "We can't indict him and lose."

Another pushed Kennedy further, "Are you giving us a tougher test than other cases?"

Kennedy snapped, "In this case, the test is—Can we convict him!"

While the reception continued nearby, Kennedy and his aides debated the decision with Byron White, Miller, and Hundley. "I'm tired of one lawyer saying we should indict and another lawyer later on saying we shouldn't," an exasperated Kennedy said. Hundley wanted to try the case, the others concurred. Eventually Kennedy agreed. He neither recused himself from making this tough call nor sought an excuse not to indict.

But the indictment was delayed for several weeks. Before action was taken, Kennedy asked Seigenthaler to call Congressman Keogh and tell him he'd like to come to see him. "Tell him the evidence looks very grim, but no final decision has been made, yet." To his credit, the congressman told Seigenthaler to tell Kennedy he didn't need to see him. "I understand that if my brother committed a crime, he'll be indicted . . . I accept that you are doing everything you can."

The night before our lawyers asked the grand jury to indict, Seigenthaler called the anguished legislator to let him know what was going to happen and how painful the whole episode was for the attorney general. The congressman wept, told Seigenthaler he had dreaded this day, and told him to tell RFK he thanked him for his solicitousness. Seigenthaler told Keogh that Kennedy would call him, but the congressman—elegant to the end—said no, he insisted on calling Kennedy himself, and he did. No one knows what the two said to each other.

On the eve of trial, Erdman's attorney called Hundley demanding his client get immunity if, as had been agreed, he was to testify for the government. Hundley saw his one-witness case going out the window, but wouldn't be finessed. He gambled.

"Go back and tell your client there will be no trial of Keogh on Monday; but we'll be prosecuting *him*." So advised, Erdman backed off. Hundley breathed a sigh of relief: He would not have to call Kennedy to report losing this contentious case before it began. The trial began Monday, as scheduled. The veteran John Lally, and one of our young attorneys, Henry Ruth, assisted.

Of five defendants, two pleaded guilty and three were tried and convicted. Keogh and Kahaner and Corallo got two-year prison sentences; Erdman's sentence was suspended because he had cooperated; Sandy Moore finally did get his original three-year sentence in the bankruptcy fraud case reduced—to one year.

Kennedy's intense dislike of corruption had met head-on with his strong sense of political loyalty. When the choice between the two values became necessary, he sided with the fair administration of justice, which his critics feared he was blind to. Long after the case was over, Congressman Keogh told Ed Guthman he "knew that a call from me or any intercession on my part would only make matters worse. Besides, I know that everything that could be done would be done and that if there was nothing that could be done, nothing would be done."

What Keogh alluded to was the elusive line between prosecution and Politics. Influence peddling cannot be tolerated, and it was not. Political debts could be paid in certain currencies—a prudent appointment, particularly delicate treatment—but not in others, not in the currency of the fixed case or the pulled punch. The politics of the Kennedy Justice Department gave priority to prosecuting public corruption, and that meant, inevitably, because there are essentially two major political parties in this nation, that many Democrats would be indicted and imprisoned. As leaders of the Democratic Party at that time, the Kennedys were knocking off many of the very people who got them where they were. I know and have learned of no case where Robert Kennedy did not approve an indictment of a political crony or because of a political debt.

Like thwarting labor racketeering, unearthing and condemning political corruption was a key part of Kennedy's organized crime program. We often bargained away cases against the bri*bers* to get at the bri*bees,* dealt with the fix*ers* to get the fi*xed.* While it takes two to tango, Kennedy pushed us to go after and not compromise with crooked politicians. He truly thought them to be the backbone of organized crime, and the most morally reprehensible of all our targeted villains.

Wherever our lawyers went to investigate organized crime, we found crooked politicians. Wherever we found them, we acted.

Chapter 8

LABOR AND THE

RACKETS

When Robert Kennedy came to his attorney generalship steeped in the story of labor racketeering learned from his McClellan Committee experiences, he truly believed that unions-gone-wrong were doing nothing less than perverting the free enterprise system. That system was the backbone of American capitalism—and crooked union officials were its cancer. He had learned from his own investigations of the common and large-scale misuse of union pension and welfare funds, of violence and terrorism frustrating the democratic processes of union elections, and of alliances among some union officials with tainted employers and corrupt politicians. This sector of criminal activity became a major component of his prosecutorial game plan.

Because he knew about the Teamsters and thought they were a special case, Kennedy took special interest in their officials, especially Jimmy Hoffa. But by no means did our section's efforts ignore other unions. We went after union corruption vigorously wherever we found it. And we did find it; two major examples involved the United Auto Workers in Ohio and the Bakery and Confectionery Workers Union in our own backyard.

GOSSER

In Toledo, seemingly everyone had a connection to the United Auto Workers union, whose local chapter, UAW 12, had sixteen thousand members. Its longtime leader, Richard Gosser, was an up-from-the-ranks veteran union man who, over three decades, had accumulated political power, influential friends, and a public image as a community benefactor. Locals knew about the union's summer camp for kids and its health and retirement center. Fewer people knew that Gosser and his friends sold the land for the camp to the union.

That deal wasn't the sum of Gosser's less visible activities. Not long after we fanned out around the country, the IRS reported to Jake Tanzer, our man in Ohio, that it was conducting an investigation into broadscale gambling by workers at a Toledo auto plant. In the course of routine investigation, Jake had reported, the IRS discovered that one of its own secretaries was regularly pilfering confidential intelligence records and turning them over to a relative of hers, a local racketeer, who turned them over to a Gosser aide. Once on to her, they set a trap that eventually led to and incriminated Gosser, along with a local gambling figure and several public officials. Gosser's interest in the stolen documents was to find out the identity of the informant who drew the IRS into the case in the first place.

Our lawyers coordinated the intricate trap, which was engineered by thirty-five IRS agents, and which led to Gosser's arrest on Veterans Day, 1962. This was the cops-and-robbers story of sleuth and ingenious law enforcement that was told to our group by Tanzer at one of our meetings. But, however adroit our investigation had been, convicting Gosser in Toledo would not be easy. We charged Gosser with conspiring to defraud the government by corrupting the IRS secretary. Gosser claimed he was framed, and argued that we had employed gestapo tactics and engaged in a political prosecution—all our adversaries did! Using Gosser's considerable influence, union officials started a citizens' letter-writing campaign; all of those letters were cleared "for accuracy" at a central coordinating point in Ohio. A Gosser aide had gone to Washington to try to stop the case and met (futilely) with IRS commissioner Mortimer Caplin at the suggestion of someone in the White House.

The Gosser prosecution ended my prosecutorial partnership with Sunshine Lynch. He was assigned to work with Tanzer on this tough case, leaving me in charge of the Ratterman case retrial.

On the freezing (17 below zero) first day of trial in January, our prosecutors faced a more chilling prospect: finding a jury of people unconnected to the union. The jury finally selected included seven members with present or past ties to the union. Gosser supporters filled the courtroom. The local newspaper ran a long special supplement just before the trial describing Gosser's civic contributions to the community. Indeed, one county commissioner had tried to replace the fountain in front of the courthouse with a statue of Gosser. The commissioner was one of the officials mentioned in the purloined IRS papers that had ignited the investigation.

Gosser, a feisty and contentious witness, denied any wrongdoing. Lynch fought him feverishly. The prosecution's case proved airtight. At the trial, as one agent after another told of sitting at tables overhearing and observing Pinciotta at the pancake house, Gosser glared at his hapless colleague. There was no way to get out of the steel trap Tanzer and his IRS band had set.

The press was unfavorable. We were unable to keep UAW-related jurors off the panel. Indeed, no sooner did the case go to the jury than the FBI informed our trial team that an anonymous caller reported that the jury had been approached and Gosser was going to be acquitted. However, after nine tense days of a hard-fought trial, and over five hours of deliberations, the jury returned a verdict of guilty, and the judge sentenced Gosser and his co-defendants to three years in prison.

The trial judge, Frank L. Kloeb, a distinguished twenty-five-year veteran of that bench, commented that he thought the verdict was correct. Had it been otherwise, he added, "it would have seriously shaken the faith of the court in the jury system. It seems to me that all thinking people in northwestern Ohio who followed the case in any detail must have breathed some fresh air when the verdict was returned."

After the trial, a new Gosser lawyer—a former state official who had recently been retained by the union—filed affidavits from three jurors suggesting prejudice and misconduct. When the jurors denied the affidavits, we began an investigation of subornation of perjury. The battles never end, it seemed.

Gosser's case arose fortuitously from our general probes into large-scale gambling in Ohio. But once we discovered the tie-in to this major and influential labor leader, we spared no effort or resource to win.

Years later, reminiscing about this case, Jake Tanzer (who had returned to his home state of Oregon to a stellar public and private career, including a period on the State Supreme Court) recalled a part of the story I'd not known. When he had first left Washington to begin his work with the IRS agents on Gosser, Herb Bates, one of our veteran colleagues, said to Tanzer, then a green rookie like myself, "Gosser, I remember that name; he was in *The Enemy Within*." As Tanzer left Washington for Toledo, he thought, "Wow, this one is important."

Tanzer plunged into his case. Months later, when Jake was returning home to Washington, he stopped at an airport book rack and purchased a copy of *The Enemy Within*. Settling into his seat, Jake opened the book to the index and sure enough, there was *Gosser*. Jake read the chapter on the flight home, presuming he'd just snagged one of his boss's old nemeses. "It turned out," Jake told me, "that while the Senate Investigating Committee was investigating corruption within the Teamsters, the Republicans (Senators Goldwater, Mundt, and Curtis) wanted to embarrass the Democrats by putting some of their supporters in the limelight. When Barry Goldwater insisted that they investigate dated and peripheral incidents affecting Gosser, the junior senator from Massachusetts and his brother actively resisted them on the basis that it was a Teamster investigation, that the UAW was a fine union, and their suggestion was just a retaliatory witch-hunt against two fine labor leaders, Walter Reuther and Richard T. Gosser.

"My heart sank to my stomach. I started thinking about getting a job back home. It turns out that Gosser organized northeastern Ohio for Kennedy in 1960. We'd essentially destroyed the Democratic organization in that area.

"The gratifying thing was, however, that Henry, Ed Silberling, and Jack Miller, all of whom must have been conscious of Gosser's identity and role, never caused me to pull back. My instructions were if Gosser did it, I was to do my job and see that he was fairly convicted. There was never the slightest hint or suggestion of political considerations communicated to me or as far as I know to Bill Lynch, who was lead counsel in the trial. I've always been very proud of the integrity that Kennedy brought to Justice."

CROSS

Bob Kennedy knew about James G. Cross and the Bakery and Confectionery Workers Union from the McClellan Committee, too. The relatively small but long-established union—almost sixty years old then and consisting of 319 locals composed of 150,000 members—had been criticized by dissidents who deplored Cross's high-handed, autocratic management.

Under Cross, one of the dissident leaders told committee counsel Kennedy, democratic procedures were perverted and union funds regularly misused by Cross and his cronies. Cross controlled union affairs dictatorially and peremptorily: "Parliamentary procedure was made for senators," he once said, "not for bakers."

Kennedy had questioned Cross before the McClellan Committee in July 1957 about strong-arm tactics at the union's convention in October 1956 in San Francisco. He denied knowledge of a series of physical assaults and intimidations of union officials who proposed changes in the union's constitution at that time. When witnesses before the committee later testified that Cross and others had roved through hotel rooms one night beating officials (and one official's wife), Kennedy called Cross back to the committee and asked about those events. Cross stated that he was asleep when those assaults took place.

Cross was charged with perjury for lying to the committee. His case was dismissed by the trial judge on technical grounds (not on the weight of the evidence, but because when he was requestioned it was to trap him and not for a proper legislative purpose). Two of our colleagues, Phil White and Bill Hundley, had been involved in that appeal and, for them as for Kennedy, frustrations over Cross's elusiveness remained. The Cross file at Justice was thick, and it was natural that our group would take another look at his full record.

Kennedy's congressional staff investigation had also shown that Cross had grown "closer to the executives and officials of the companies that employed his union men than he was to his own membership." As a result, Cross prospered personally, in one situation receiving a large personal loan from the owner of a company that did business with his union. Cross said the executive had a "paternal fondness" for him; coincidentally that executive received contractual concessions from the union.

Cross "developed rich tastes," Kennedy found, living high on union funds, traveling to Palm Beach and Europe, and keeping a girlfriend whose services were questionable on the payroll of a local union in California. Cross and his coterie of crooked colleagues used strong-arm tactics on dissidents to keep control over their union powers. When questioned about such actions, when Cross wasn't lying, he and his friends took the Fifth Amendment before the McClellan Committee.

Cross was convicted in Chicago of embezzlement. Nonetheless, his hold over the union remained strong. The AFL-CIO ousted Cross in 1959 and chartered a new union, but Cross's faction remained composed of over half of the original group and stayed under Cross's control.

By July 1961 huge FBI and Department of Labor files had been reviewed and analyzed, and Kennedy was regularly briefed about our section's prosecutorial game plan. The decision was made to empanel an investigative grand jury, and to tempt some co-conspirators to cooperate by offering them immunity.

Kennedy had recruited Harry Alexander from the U.S. attorney's office in Washington, D.C., because he had a good reputation as a prosecutor and because he wanted our lily-white group integrated. Eventually we were to have several more black lawyers; but Alexander was the first, and he was a tough and very competent trial lawyer. When the recently appointed U.S. attorney David Acheson heard that Kennedy had recruited Alexander, he offered him a raise and a better assignment to stay. But Alexander accepted Kennedy's offer, and soon after joining us was given the bakers' union investigative files.

Years earlier, Alexander had been the junior member of the U.S. attorney's office team that prosecuted Hoffa for attempting to bribe a McClellan Committee staff member, Sy Cheasty. Hoffa's lawyer, Edward Bennett Williams, outgunned and outmaneuvered the government attorneys (this was the notorious case in which Joe Louis greeted Hoffa warmly in front of the jury) and Hoffa was acquitted. Now fate would provide Alexander with another chance to prosecute a major labor case.

This time, Alexander would be in charge. Alexander sensed the investigation he inherited might lead to a prosecutable case, but he needed time and the additional investigatory power he would have if he could pursue his cold leads before a grand jury. Bob Blakey was assigned to work with Alexander. They made a terrific twosome: one, an experienced trial lawyer with considerable know-how about the District of Columbia court system; the other, a brilliant scholar and ingenious legal theorist. It took them eighteen months working before the D.C. grand jury to make a case, but they made one. John Mullaney would assist Alexander at the later trials that resulted from the investigation.

Blakey pointed out that we did not have to seek ingenious theories in this case. Because any criminal offenses had taken place in the District of Columbia, we had only to check the local penal code. Blakey and Alexander found information in Cross's files compiled by the Labor Department suggesting a larceny-by-trick and embezzlement of union funds.

Their theory was that when Cross faced his perjury trial (the one that had been thrown out), he and his colleagues stole $35,000 of union funds, gave it to a New York lawyer, Milton Levin, who said he'd use $25,000 of it to bribe the judge and jury. Blakey and Alexander swallowed hard; the judge had thrown out the perjury case. But there was appropriate legal authority for him to do so. "We didn't think he had taken a bribe, but since the allegation had been made, he had to know about it, and we had to have his response," Blakey recalled. Investigating a sitting federal trial judge is, at best, touchy. "You could feel the electricity in the room when we discussed the case with the judge."

They concluded that the judge was honest; that lawyer Levin had pocketed the money in a classic scam. If the case was won, it would look like the bribe was made; if not, the con man–lawyer could say, "The son of a bitch took our money and split on us. Here's my $10,000 back," keeping the $25,000 earmarked for the judge. What could they do, complain to the Better Business Bureau or the Bar Association?

All Blakey and Alexander had to do was prove this theory. They decided to use the grand jury to squeeze the union officials who had to have participated in the original embezzlement of the $35,000 bribe money. The break came when they subpoenaed the union's accountant and his work sheets. His notes about expenditures he questioned provided Blakey and Alexander with a road map. With that map, they could in turn question union officials about these questionable disbursements.

One by one the union men were called; one by one they capitulated, cut deals, and testified. One by one they told the grand jury that Cross and some close aides pressed for phony loans and organizing money, not following normal union procedures, and traceable to Cross's misuse of the money.

First, Blakey and Alexander indicted the secretary-treasurer of the union, a Minnesotan named Peter Olson, on twenty-three separate counts of criminal misconduct. Olson eventually implicated all eight of the union vice presidents for issuing a series of seven $5,000 checks, totaling $35,000, for the purpose of bribing the Washington, D.C., judge. The strategy had worked.

The testimony Alexander and Blakey developed in the grand jury showed that the $35,000 taken from Local 3 of the union in New York City for a strike fund was a hoax. Not only was the $35,000 not for a strike fund, but the union vice presidents talked openly at their meetings about the real use for the funds—helping Cross with the "fix." The fix was never attempted or made, however, so the grand jury indicted Cross for embezzlement, for stealing funds from his union for one reason and labeling it as a strike fund. This was the very thing crooked union officials invariably did: plunder their members' funds for their own purposes.

Union officials from the New York local testified that the "Dirty Bakers" or "Bad Bakers," as they referred to the fixers, had perpetrated a fraud with their union funds to reimburse the earlier embezzlement Cross intended to use to fix his case. When Olson and four of the indicted union vice presidents caved in before the grand jury, testified, pleaded guilty, and implicated Cross in the embezzlement, we indicted Cross for obstruction of justice and embezzlement.

Several other vice presidents decided not to cooperate; they committed perjury before the grand jury and were indicted for that.

After they testified and helped convict the chief wrongdoers, Olson and several other cooperative defendants were given probation, fines, and suspended sentences. Cross was sentenced to one to three years in the Lewisburg Penitentiary. The sentencing judge noted that Cross had violated his trust, engaged in nefarious schemes, committed perjury, and attempted to corrupt the judge and jury.

The union lawyer, Milton Levin, was supposed to use the money to fix the case, but he absconded with it instead (proving again that there is no honor among thieves). He had received the money in two installments in a park near union headquarters at 1001 16th Street and then taken off. Levin was indicted for larceny "by trick" and obtaining money under false pretenses. The lawyer's defenses were that his signatures on the checks were facsimiles printed by a machine, and that he couldn't have taken these payoffs in Washington after sundown on a Friday, as claimed, because he was an orthodox Jew who always was home in New York on Saturdays observing the Sabbath. The all-black D.C. jury didn't believe him—or thought him highly unorthodox. After deliberating for two hours, the jury convicted Levin of grand larceny "by trick" and conspiring to fix Cross's perjury trial. He was sentenced to six months to two years in prison for his crimes. Later, the New York City Bar Association would initiate disciplinary proceedings against Levin.

Harry Alexander vividly recalls the kudos he received from Kennedy after the trial. "I remember he called me to his office to congratulate me, saying 'I want you to know my brother is very pleased with what you've done.' I knew quite well who his brother was!" Alexander reminisced a quarter-century later. He and his young colleague had culminated the earlier work of both the then-senator and the counsel of the Rackets Committee.

HOFFA

Better than anyone, Kennedy knew the Teamsters union was growing extraordinarily powerful at the same time as it was being pervaded by corruption of extraordinary magnitude. In 1958, he told his legislative staff that Hoffa's cynical attitude that everyone had his price had resulted in corruption spreading "to the leading citizens of the towns across the United States, the leading bankers, the leading business-men, officials, judges, congressmen." Genuinely outraged, Kennedy moralized, "If he can buy them, then you can see what it means to the country."

In 1960 in *The Enemy Within,* Kennedy had emphasized the pernicious effect of labor corruption and stated the moral premise of his crusade.

> The tyrant, the bully, the corrupter and corrupted are figures of shame. The labor leaders who became thieves, who cheated those whose trust they had accepted, brought dishonor on a vital and largely honest labor movement. The businessmen who succumbed to the temptation to make a deal in order to gain an advantage over their competitors perverted the moral concepts of a free American economic system.

Robert Kennedy's book, based on what Pulitzer Prize–winning labor reporter Clark Mollenhoff called "The Great Investigation," was written between his stints as congressional committee counsel and attorney general. Written with the help of John Seigenthaler, *The Enemy Within* was a critical success and made it to the best-seller lists. It almost made it to the movies. Why it didn't is an interesting story.

In the early 1960s, fresh from the success of the classic *On the Waterfront,* screenwriter Budd Schulberg came to Washington to meet Robert Kennedy and to discuss making a movie based on *The Enemy Within.* Schulberg was briefed by Kennedy and Sheridan, and immersed himself in the fifty-nine volumes of the McClellan Committee hearings. Schulberg later described what he saw in the committee's record: "testimony of thousands of witnesses who talked (or balked) about pension funds looted of millions of dollars, with a majority of those six- and seven-figure loans going to notorious Mafioso [sic], of 'sweetheart' contracts arranged between greedy company executives and union officials on the take (including Hoffa), of once respectable industries and unions infiltrated by a blatant array of extortionists and enforcers, terrorizing the would-be honest into silence or connivance."

Schulberg decided he would make a movie about "the increasingly effective alliance of big money, labor racketeers, the mob, and dishonest . . . government officials." As part of his research, Schulberg interviewed investigators and union officials, including one honest Teamsters officer who had become disgusted by the "wholesale looting of union funds, the terrorizing of union members who protested, the Mafia leaders allowed to pass themselves off as union leaders."

Schulberg wrote his script for the film producer Jerry Wald. But Wald died suddenly and their deal with Twentieth Century–Fox did too, Schulberg wrote, when "a labor tough walked right into the office of the new head of the studio to warn him that if the picture was ever made, drivers would refuse to deliver the prints to the theaters. And, if they got there by any other means, stink bombs would drive out the audiences."

Schulberg tried to produce the movie himself. One film star came to his home drunk to say he loved the script but was afraid he'd be killed if he did it. Ties between the mob and other studios led to the movie being rejected by the major studios, despite Schulberg's exceptional reputation. Columbia, which had released *On the Waterfront*, expressed interest; but on the eve of Schulberg's meeting with studio executives, they each got a letter from Hoffa's lawyer stating that Fox had wisely abandoned the project when "all the possible eventualities had been pointed out to them" and urging that Columbia do the same. The meeting was canceled and the Jimmy Hoffa–*Enemy Within* movie was not made.

If Schulberg was frustrated, Kennedy was undaunted. His liaison with the Justice Department in the McClellan Committee days convinced him that inadequate resources and personnel were being directed at what he saw as a major national problem. Hoffa had managed to elude convictions in several criminal cases brought against him while he rose to the top of the Teamsters union management. By 1961, Hoffa's bitter battle with Kennedy was notorious; their acrimonious contempt for each other was extraordinary; and they both were at the top of their powers. An elevated Robert Kennedy was attorney general of the United States and an undaunted Jimmy Hoffa was reelected Teamsters president for a five-year term.

The Senate committee investigating Teamsters corruption had information about crimes by 141 Teamsters officials. Of those subpoenaed, 73 refused to testify, on constitutional self-incrimination grounds, to over 3,000 questions by the committee.

Hoffa's name had become a household word as a result of the McClellan Committee hearings. Presidential candidate John Kennedy had said in his debate with Richard Nixon, "I'm not satisfied when I see men like Jimmy Hoffa in charge of the largest union in the United States still free." Responding, Hoffa had swung the Teamsters vote to Nixon, complaining, "I don't think an American ever lived who was so thoroughly investigated as I have been for three years."

Hoffa, the cagey union leader, cultivated an image as a folksy victim of the Kennedys' political machinations and gained vocal support from civil libertarians who traditionally supported labor and who distrusted Robert Kennedy as a child of a rich father and ruthless demagogue.

Hoffa played the little guy representing the working stiff, which he accented by purporting to do battle with wealthy political dilettantes. Referring to Robert Kennedy as a "spoiled rich kid," he portrayed himself as a rough-hewn David standing off a silk-stocking Goliath. He told his rabid supporters, "All this hocus-pocus about racketeers is a smoke screen to carry you back to the days they could drop you in the scrap heap," arguing that when rich employers used hoodlums as strikebreakers it was OK, but "now we've got a few and everybody's screaming."

Hoffa and the Teamsters became the personification of the Kennedys' sustained clash with crooked unions. John Kennedy had made Hoffa a campaign issue, complaining that Hoffa ran the nation's largest union, one which controlled Americans from birth to death, from hospital ambulances to hearse drivers, and everything in between. Robert Kennedy had called Hoffa's control of the Teamsters "a conspiracy of evil." Hoffa replied that the Kennedys wanted a police state.

Jimmy Hoffa's battles with the law enforcement world generally and with Robert Kennedy in particular were epic, and would turn out to be tragic. They had begun long before Robert Kennedy learned about labor racketeering during his work with the McClellan Committee. But the two fierce competitors' backgrounds brought them, inexorably it seems in retrospect, toward their inevitable clash. Again, ironically, Joseph Kennedy reportedly had historic connections with powerful union leaders and with racketeers during his swashbuckling days in business, where he earned the vast fortune that permitted his children to devote themselves to public life. It was an odd choice, then, for John and Robert Kennedy to have seized on the mob and the unions as a vehicle for gaining national prominence, rather than, say, the Cold War, civil rights, or health reform.

They did go after the rackets, however, and in Robert Kennedy's case with characteristic single-mindedness. It wasn't only Hoffa and the Teamsters. During the McClellan Committee days, there were investigations and subsequent criminal proceedings involving top officials of the bakery workers, carpenters, operating engineers, textile workers, and meatcutters unions. But in this contest, Hoffa and the Teamsters were the main event.

Hoffa had risen from the ranks of the growing Teamsters union— The International Brotherhood of Teamsters, Chauffeurs, Warehouse-men, Stablemen, and Helpers of America, known in shorthand as the I.B.T.—to the point where he was a contender for its presidency. When his predecessor Dave Beck was convicted of tax evasion and sent to prison, RFK had, in a perverse sense, brought Hoffa into greater prominence, and each became a foil for the other in their subsequent high-stakes battles for power.

It is a paradox that the McClellan Committee's success in toppling Beck created the opening for a more dangerous labor leader, Hoffa. As one close observer of that scene wrote:

> Though Beck commanded considerable influence and power, he turned out to be a paper lion, a feudal lord with courtiers but no army. His sin was avarice. Hoffa did not covet money solely to enrich himself, as Beck did; he used it, rather, to consolidate and expand his power. He believed with the utmost cynicism that every man could be bought. In grabbing power and in using it boldly and in forming open alliances with some of the toughest, most unsavory racketeers alive, the ever-defiant, muscular little giant from Detroit made Beck . . . look . . . smalltime.

Hoffa seemed during these years to be able to beat the odds in a union career marked, as noted, by continuous evasions of the law. In 1937, charged with an assault, he was merely fined and released. The same result occurred in 1940 in a case charging conspiracy to restrain trade. The same again in 1947 for an attempted extortion. In 1957, he was acquitted of bribing a Senate investigator. In another case where he was charged with illegally tapping a subordinate's phone, first the jury hung (eleven to one for conviction); but on retrial, Hoffa was acquitted. A case of perjury had to be dropped because of an illegal government wiretap.

By 1957, the AFL-CIO had thrown out the Teamsters, its largest constituent union, for refusing to cooperate in an internal corruption investigation. Senator McClellan charged that the record showed that Hoffa misused millions of dollars of union funds for himself, his cronies, and his racketeer connections; that he was faithless to the rank-and-file members; and that he used gangsters and thugs to do his dirty business. All the while Hoffa himself cavorted with the mob and complained of being picked on by law enforcement officials. Yet he'd survived two acquittals and one hung jury and defiantly challenged both the AFL-CIO and the U.S. Congress. His arrogance grew with his power as the highest paid union president of the world's largest union. "I may have faults," he admitted, "but being wrong ain't one of them."

In 1957, a group of New York Teamsters brought a suit in federal court in Washington, D.C., accusing Hoffa and Beck of rigging the Teamsters' convention, which would elect the new union leadership. Eventually, a court-controlled, three-man monitorship was created. Its charter was to supervise Hoffa's union management, safeguard the democratic rights of the membership, assure the financial integrity of the union's funds, advise the court regularly of Teamsters activities that violated the law, and make recommendations to Hoffa. The court provisionally approved Hoffa's presidency, but the union was to operate under the monitors' supervision.

In fact, Hoffa ignored the monitors, used every device to frustrate them, reviled its members, and repeatedly appealed every act they undertook that was designed to clean up the union. Hoffa's contentious lawyers filed an endless stream of appeals, petitions, and legal writs, and after three fractious, litigious years, the monitors represented to the court that no steps had been taken by Hoffa to clean up the union "and there is no indication that Mr. Hoffa has either the inclination or the ability to do so." There were so many harassment lawsuits and appeals by the Teamsters that Hoffa's litigating legions were facetiously labeled the Teamsters Bar Association, and the court case had a record 1,200 docket entries. As a diversionary tactic, Hoffa appointed his own union racket committee that—no surprise—found the Teamsters "free of corruption," despite the monitors' charges that racketeers, criminals, and extortionists held office with Hoffa's blessings, if not at his urging. Attempts to oust Hoffa seemed to be futile.

If some more sympathetic observers of the American labor movement saw Hoffa as a popular, if rough-cut, man of the people, Kennedy thought otherwise. Hoffa symbolized the corruption Kennedy was fighting against.

While the Teamsters union grew to become the biggest and surely one of the most influential unions in the world and, in the words of one of its closest allies, Hoffa "put more bread on the table than any man alive," there was mounting evidence that he did much union business under the same table, and put more bread on *his* table. Hoffa lived a luxurious life of travel and retained retinues of satraps and professional staff. Yet, he dealt only in cash, kept no bank accounts, used pay phones that could not be tapped, and systematically destroyed all his personal and union records.

Hoffa cultivated a reputation as a rehabilitator of ex-offenders, labor reporter Clark Mollenhoff commented, but he was really using thieves and thugs as high labor officials working for his own interests.

By 1961, the Teamsters pension fund had assets of $200 million. Hoffa was using it to help his friends make money, and to win the friendship of the mob, which was delighted (and indebted) to have this resource available for their investments. As one wry observer noted, the pension fund had become the mob's savings and loan.

Hoffa's media machinery, in portraying him as a champion of the working man and a heroic figure, showed him at war with powerful establishment forces. "The McClellan Committee, big business, and its political stooges in the federal government have gone all out to destroy us," he told Teamsters in their union magazine.

Hoffa suffered the delusion that "organized crime is a major force in the social contract," the inimitable social critic Murray Kempton has stated. Kempton has labeled a "disabling misapprehension" the suggestion that Hoffa made a Faustian bargain with the mob to help his worker constituents. Hoffa was not a social radical; he was an antisocial rebel. "His genuine hatreds were reserved not for those who owned the country but for those who wrote and enforced its laws." It should have come as no surprise that his "outsized reverence for the authority of organized crime"—Kempton's words again—led to his recruiting a new guard of faithful union officials "from the gangster cadres." Hoffa's alignment with the mob had the effect, one observer remarked, of "placing the underworld at the very jugular of the American economy."

That is precisely what he was doing, as volumes of Senate testimony and reams of supporting documents demonstrated. He used the mob as enforcers to beat off competitors for union power. In return, the mob, as noted, used the munificent Teamsters pension funds as a veritable private and preferential banking system. Copious court records show how Hoffa plundered and discredited his mighty organization. In 1994, one of his longtime lawyers, Frank Ragano, described how one scam worked. Another Hoffa lawyer had advised him not to send traditional monthly bills for legal services.

"Jimmy had a private system of liberally compensating his lawyers. Sitting me down, he told me the facts of life in the IBT. I must have clients back home who needed financing to construct office or residential buildings and other projects. Jimmy controlled the union's welfare and pension funds—about $1 billion—available for loans to builders and developers. It was up to me . . . to steer clients to Jimmy for loans. I could charge the contractors and developers 5 to 10 percent of the loans as a commission for obtaining the financing. Developers unable to get normal financing from banks or insurance companies were eager to borrow from the Teamsters. . . ."

"You'll make a hell of a lot more money that way than by sending him statements," Ragano was advised.

By early 1961, events had conspired toward the inevitable showdown. Kennedy had formed his organized crime section and his special Teamsters group; the frustrated federal court gave up on the Teamster monitorship; hoped-for reforms permitting insurgent union officials to ascend to positions of power faded; and in July 1961, against phantom opposition and claiming to have outlived a long list of persecutions, Hoffa was elected to a five-year term as Teamsters president. At the nineteenth national convention at the flashy Deauville Hotel in Miami Beach, Florida, Hoffa told his boisterous supporters, "Now the Kennedys ought to know the time and effort they've put in trying to destroy the Teamsters have completely failed. It was a waste of time."

When the question of readmission of the Teamsters came before the AFL-CIO executive council, it was defeated 24–3. President George Meany said that the Teamsters appeared to be even more dominated by criminal and corrupt elements than four years earlier when they had been expelled.

Following his congressional experiences, his book and aborted movie, Kennedy would try again, as head of the nation's law enforcement apparatus, to bring Hoffa down. No lesser result would suffice.

—

Two investigations that Walter Sheridan's group had taken over would result in two indictments of Hoffa. One case had started under the prior administration, but the indictment was delayed until after the election when Vice President Richard Nixon implored Attorney General Rogers not to indict the politically helpful Hoffa. The other case arose out of Hoffa's jury meddling.

In the first of these, Hoffa, with a union associate, was tried in federal court in Nashville, Tennessee, in November and December 1962, for receiving indirect payoffs from 1947 to 1958 from a company that employed Teamsters members.

Executives of a Detroit trucking firm set up a truck-leasing company in Nashville, Tennessee, giving interests in it to Hoffa's wife (in her maiden name) and another Detroit Teamsters official's wife. The company did business with the Teamsters union. If that obvious connection meant Hoffa received a benefit, it would have violated the Taft-Hartley law as a conflict of interest. It was hard to conclude otherwise, since over the years about a quarter-million dollars had flowed to Mrs. Hoffa.

The Test Fleet case, as it was referred to, while only a misdemeanor, joined a battle that had been brewing for about a decade. Sheridan's army moved to Tennessee, as if it were a civil war. Union flunkies from all over the country assembled in Hoffa's hotel suite, which was transformed into a war room. In court, his aides and lawyers attempted to provoke the judge, and to goad government officials— anything to upset the process and avoid a conviction.

Despite the government's attempts to deflect Hoffa's designs on the jury panel, including the exclusion of two jurors who had been approached and the eventual sequestration of the others, the jury hung, with seven of the twelve jurors voting for Hoffa's acquittal. But, as Hoffa's famous lawyer Edward Bennett Williams once said, Hoffa is "a jumper," someone who escalated all the dangers he faced. "He has a genius for improving a misdemeanor into a felony." That's exactly what he did in Nashville.

When Sheridan's lawyers brought information to him indicating that some jurors had been approached, the trial judge in the Test Fleet case ordered a grand jury investigation. Painstaking study of voluminous phone and travel records, along with persistent grand jury questioning and the critical testimony of a shadowy Teamsters character, Edward Grady Partin, who had worked undercover for Sheridan while assisting Hoffa during the trial preparation, resulted in a new and more serious indictment. On May 5, 1963, Hoffa and six others were indicted for jury tampering.

Partin's role was intriguing and controversial. Just as I had learned with April Flowers in Newport, even given all the hard work of investigation, most big criminal cases are made on the basis of happenstance events prosecutors cannot anticipate or control. The man who would prove so critical in bringing down the heretofore invincible Jimmy Hoffa turned out to be one of his own low-life union underlings.

On September 29, 1962, Ed Partin, an inmate in a Baton Rouge, Louisiana, jail had told the warden that he once was involved in a plot to assassinate Robert Kennedy. Hoffa had asked Partin at the Teamsters' headquarters building in Washington to get explosives to kill the attorney general. "Something has to be done to that little SOB, Bobby Kennedy. He'll be an easy target, always riding around Washington in that convertible with that big black dog," Hoffa had told Partin. "All we need is some plastic explosives tossed in with him, and that will finish him off." And, Hoffa had added, if they didn't get him in his car, they'd try his home.

The warden called the local district attorney, who called the U.S. attorney, who called the Justice Department, which sent one of Sheridan's attorneys—Frank Grimsley—who was working in Atlanta, to see Partin. The jailers sneaked Partin into a middle-of-the-night meeting with Grimsley at the FBI office in Baton Rouge. Partin's story sounded straight, if hard to believe, and he passed an FBI lie detector test. Though he had been indicted for misusing union funds, Partin was released. When he checked in with Hoffa, he was asked to come to Nashville to help out. Meanwhile, Kennedy was warned not to drive around in his convertible for a while. Partin stayed in touch with Sheridan, who told him to keep his eyes and ears open to any evidence of, among other things, jury tampering.

In Nashville, Partin was told to stand guard at the door to Hoffa's suite at the Andrew Jackson Hotel. He was not included in the trial strategy sessions with Hoffa and his lawyers. However, while the defense was being planned by Hoffa's attorneys, Partin was told by Hoffa and others that they had paid off one juror and were trying to reach several others. Hoffa's comment to Partin that "I have got the colored male juror in my hip pocket" would prove to be key testimony tying Hoffa personally to the jury fixing.

All the top Justice Department officials conferred with Robert Kennedy about this aspect of our case: Was our use of Partin a violation of Hoffa's Sixth Amendment right to counsel? Partin had guarded the door to Hoffa's hotel suite during the earlier, fixed trial and had been part of the Hoffa team of hangers-on and helpers—at Hoffa's request, not Sheridan's. He'd heard the jury-fixing talk, from Hoffa and others, and reported it to Sheridan. He did not participate in the planning of the legal defense or the strategy sessions between the lawyers and their clients.

Since all Sheridan's contact with Partin was concerned solely with the jury tampering and not their trial defense, most of Kennedy's top assistants agreed we should indict. Solicitor General Archibald Cox said he was comfortable arguing that the government had taken reasonable steps to protect the integrity of the jury if the case was appealed to the Supreme Court. Kennedy was not comforted by Cox's confidence: "How about keeping this out of the Supreme Court!" Bill Hundley was against going forward: "I wouldn't touch the case with a ten-foot pole," he advised. We couldn't afford another lost Hoffa case—we'd be scarred with vendetta claims forevermore, Hundley feared. Hoffa would deny all, and Partin would be discredited and so would we with him.

The decision was made to go forward. There was no such thing as a perfect case. To avoid seeming like carpetbagger prosecutors, a well-respected local attorney, John J. Hooker, was hired to try the case along with Jim Neal and John Reddy, the Tennessee U.S. attorney. Lawyers from Sheridan's group provided all the backup they needed for a major-league litigation.

While this case was proceeding in Nashville, the second prosecution was beginning. A long-pending investigation had finally resulted in another indictment in June 1963—this one in Chicago—of Hoffa and several others for mail fraud.

This case started with financial shenanigans and ended with a cover-up. As a trustee of union pension funds, Hoffa was barred by law from personal use of this growing fiduciary fortune. Hoffa had a major financial interest in Sun Valley, the Florida land development project designed to be a Teamsters retirement community. When the Orlando bank he was dealing with on this land deal required collateral as security for a $395,000 loan, Hoffa deposited $400,000 of local Teamsters pension funds in an interest-free deposit with the bank. To cover up this improper use of Teamsters money, Hoffa had a crony arrange financial deals with needy contractors and real estate developers for huge, questionable, high-risk loans from other Teamsters pension funds, for which Hoffa and his agent made 10-percent commissions—paid in cash coincidentally amounting to about $400,000. Eventually, there was a series of fourteen loans from Teamsters pension funds totaling $20 million and the diversion of another $1 million for their personal benefit.

Before either trial began, Hoffa's lawyer in Tennessee, Tommy Osborn, was discovered attempting to fix two members of that jury and was disbarred. The jury-tampering trial was moved 140 miles away, to Chattanooga—fifteen months after the original misdemeanor trial in Nashville. On January 20, 1964, our lawyers faced Hoffa and his Tennessee defense team in court.

Kennedy kept in daily contact with Sheridan, his defensive team, and his band of prosecutors. Once, when he called Sheridan's hotel room, he heard in the background the tinkling sound of end-of-the-day libation among the hard-working crew. He called Jack Miller immediately, jokingly, if worriedly, to report: "They're drinking in Chattanooga."

After a raucous and cantankerous trial, during which the jury was watched by seventeen federal marshals, Hoffa and three co-defendants were convicted on two counts of obstructing justice (fixing two jurors and one prospective juror) in his 1962 conspiracy case. The jury had deliberated about six hours. On March 12, Judge Frank Wilson sentenced Hoffa to eight years in prison and a $10,000 fine, remarking that in corrupting the jury system he had tampered with the very foundation of the administration of justice. Surly as ever, and snarling at onlookers, Hoffa claimed he'd been railroaded.

The trial judge ruled that Partin's deadly testimony was admissible, that he wasn't a government plant but rather had been "knowingly and voluntarily placed there by one of the defendants." Partin had testified that Hoffa said he'd pay $15,000 to $20,000—whatever it took—to get a few jurors on their side. Despite his long criminal record, the jury believed Partin's devastating testimony. The department did too, after the lie detector test, noting that Hoffa had earlier sought his help in assassinating Robert Kennedy. Again there were attempts to bribe jurors, to corrupt witnesses, to tamper with evidence, anything to cause a mistrial.

Our highest-visibility effort to rid the labor movement of corruption had worked. Hoffa was *not* invincible. Soon thereafter, on April 27, 1964, Hoffa and his seven co-defendants went on trial in Chicago for defrauding the Teamsters pension fund.

The Chicago case was not the brawl that characterized the Tennessee case. Charles Smith and a veteran Justice Department trial lawyer, Abe Poretz, were assigned the case, and both were quiet, low-key lawyers. Smith was the researcher, master of the evidence, encyclopedia of Teamsters information; Poretz was the savvy trial man. The ten Teamsters trial lawyers were among Chicago's best, men who Smith respects to this day. They were rough in the way of big city lawyers, Smith recalls, but not unethical or personally offensive. Frank Ragano was the only one present whom Smith deplored and would not deal with; he was a *Guys and Dolls*–like hanger-on, not part of the trial team that tried the case. The trial judge was courteous, efficient, smart, fair, and always in control.

But if the trial was to be less bizarre than the earlier one in Tennessee, it got off to an unsettling start. The day before the trial was to begin, Charles Smith learned that Poretz could not try the case with him for sudden health reasons. The judge denied the government's request for a delay to recruit another trial lawyer, threatening to dismiss the charges if the government did not proceed. Smith knew the case cold, but did not feel he was the courtroom litigator to handle so important a case. Smith resisted recruiting any of the young department lawyers working on the case and turned instead to a thirty-two-year-old assistant U.S. attorney in Chicago, Bill Bittner.

Over the weekend, Bittner was educated through total immersion by Sheridan's staff while Smith began the trial alone. Amazingly, Bittner was soon a critical part of the prosecution team and eventually took over the complicated, fiercely fought trial. Smith helped Bittner organize material from the ten file cabinets full of records and documents accumulated in the course of the investigation, and put into evidence the FBI charts and graphs prepared to aid the jury in following the technical, paper-heavy case against Hoffa. Bittner was brilliant in his cross-examination of Hoffa and in his summation of the complicated case. Because he was part of the Chicago trial bar culture, as Smith was not, he turned out to be the perfect partner in what was a complex ninety-day trial.

The essence of the Chicago case was that $20 million of loans were made from the Central States Pension Fund so that high finder's fees could be diverted to Sun Valley creditors—all to get Hoffa, a 45-percent owner, out from under debts to those creditors. Hoffa fought furiously again, planting articles in the press, calling on sympathetic politicians to support his claims that the government had acted improperly. Over $1 million in Teamsters funds were spent in Hoffa's aggressive defense.

After a thirteen-week trial that included 114 witnesses and 15,000 government documents, Hoffa and the others indicted with him were convicted on several counts of conspiracy and mail and wire fraud. The trial had started in the spring and ended near the end of summer. Hoffa was sentenced to five years in prison, to run consecutively with his prior eight-year sentence for jury tampering.

For years, Hoffa fought to save his job and freedom, pushing and pulling every political lever available, clamoring to get a new trial, making outrageous charges of government misconduct—none of which were ever proved—and using every pressure to get witnesses who had testified against him to recant or change their testimony. After over three years of appeals, both convictions were affirmed by numerous appellate courts and finally by the U.S. Supreme Court.

Justice Potter Stewart decided Partin's role had been as a result of "misplaced confidence" by Hoffa, not misconduct by the government. "Courts have countenanced the use of informers from time immemorial." Only Chief Justice Earl Warren dissented, arguing that Partin's reports amounted to an infiltration of the Hoffa defense; as such, it was excessive government zeal that violated Hoffa's constitutional right to a confidential criminal defense.

On March 7, 1967, bearing prison number 33-298NE, Hoffa entered the sprawling, overcrowded, dreary federal penitentiary in Lewisburg, Pennsylvania. Robert Kennedy would be killed fifteen months later, and Hoffa would not be released until four years, nine months later, on December 23, 1971, when President Nixon commuted his sentence on condition that he not engage in any union business.

Those were the most notorious two Teamsters cases, but far from the total picture. By the end of Kennedy's four-year tenure at Justice, Sheridan and his staff had gotten indictments against 201 Teamsters officials and associates and won 126 convictions.

Hoffa continued to fight the government, appealing the restriction that prevented his return to union affairs, until his own disappearance and presumed murder in July 1975. There are various unproven theories about who killed Hoffa and why. The most feasible theory is that mob members—the names Giacalone and Provenzano are prominently mentioned—had him kidnapped by a hit team after luring him to the Machus Red Fox restaurant outside Detroit, murdered, and his remains ingeniously destroyed. The mob decides when it wants a body discovered and when not. The latter course is followed when it wants to add shame and disgrace to a murder by embarrassing the victim's family who are left with no body or funeral, no final end. Hoffa posed a threat to Frank Fitzsimmons (Hoffa's chosen successor, who was under mob control—much more so than Hoffa, who was intent on being reelected and ending Fitzsimmon's reign) and the mob's comfortable situation.

"Deep down, he really was a hood," one former Hoffa associate said, and ultimately he was killed "because he became one of them." As his sympathetic biographer, Arthur A. Sloane, noted, "The world of violence was never very far from Jimmy Hoffa." Hoffa's life and death and his own vendetta against Kennedy were truly tragic dramas of Shakespearean fury and violent sweep.

—

Did we conduct a concerted, persistent, and pervasive investigation of Hoffa's activities? Yes. Would such an investigative effort lead, inevitably, to prosecutions against anyone, as the critics suggested? No; not for the offenses Hoffa and his criminal colleagues were convicted of—jury tampering and serious financial frauds. Hints of these cases were available to the earlier administration and investigations of the charges had begun. It's not as if we dreamed up these cases.

Moreover, these crimes were not contrived, nor were they the inevitable lapses that any citizen might be shown to have committed after inquisitorial investigations into every corner of their personal lives.

Was it obsessive to focus such intensive and costly federal investigations on one man and one institution? Was it a pernicious form of selective prosecution, or a proper setting of priorities? The government did no less in its investigations and prosecutions of civil rights violations, which Kennedy's liberal detractors applauded. As Kennedy himself asked about the use of Partin to convict Hoffa: "Should we have told Partin we didn't want to hear about jury tampering? And once we heard about it, should we have done nothing about it?"

Whether it is broadscale scandals or preeminent emergencies or necessary institutional reforms, this is what the Justice Department does: It establishes priorities, and deals forcefully with the most pressing and precedential problems that call for national prosecutorial responsibility.

Kennedy made no apologies to his critics. He had "an underlying distaste for the kind of people his father used to buy," columnist Murray Kempton said; he "recognized the devil in Hoffa" and saw his nemesis as "insatiable and wildly vindictive," one whose "fanaticism for evil could be thought of as the opposite of his own fanaticism for good."

There have been few, if any, combatants in this century who fought so public, so long, and so dramatic a battle as Kennedy and Hoffa.

Walter Sheridan, who was in the middle of this fight for decades, said to me in 1994, shortly before he died: "The two people who I thought were indestructible now are dead."

———

Though it was perceived by skeptics as a vendetta against Hoffa, the organized crime section's emphasis on attacking union corruption wherever we found it was a major theme of Kennedy's program. The McClellan hearings had led to new laws combating misconduct by union managers, and many of the committee's investigations continued when Kennedy came to the Justice Department and led to early indictments.

A few months into Kennedy's regime, a United Mine Workers official was sentenced for receiving kickbacks from a coal company whose employees he represented. Three more UMW officials were convicted under the Taft-Hartley laws of receiving illicit payoffs from coal operators to prevent labor trouble in their mines. Another UMW official, in Scranton, was convicted of thirty-four counts of embezzlement from a bank whose board of directors he chaired. An investigation was initiated into Taft-Hartley law violations and Hobbs Act violations by an iron workers union official who reportedly demanded money from an Illinois iron workers company as a condition for labor peace. A high official of the American Guild of Variety Artists was investigated to determine whether he had received kickbacks from resort hotels that hired AGVA entertainers. Officials of the International Union of Electrical, Radio, and Machine Workers in Puerto Rico were investigated and indicted for filing false records required by the Labor Management Reporting and Disclosure Act regarding documentation of union travel and entertainment expenses, and for embezzlement of IUE funds. Officials of the Plumbing and Pipefitting Union were indicted in New York City, along with officials of five companies they dealt with, for rigging bids to fix prices. An international organizer of the International Longshoremen's Association was indicted for embezzlement of a local's funds. The secretary-treasurer of an Independent Brotherhood of Production, Maintenance and Operating Employees Union local was indicted for embezzling $16,500 from its welfare fund. At the end of our prosecution of his trial, the secretary-treasurer of the Amalgamated

Workers Union pleaded guilty to Taft-Hartley violations. In Duluth, two officials of the Seafarers' International Union were convicted for conspiracy to obstruct justice by interfering with witnesses testifying before the National Labor Relations Board. In New Jersey, a Plumbers Union business agent was charged with receiving money from a contractor for ending work stoppages and mass sick leaves. In Illinois, we presented a seventy-two-count indictment charging four officials of the Industrial Workers of America with embezzling their local's funds. Organizers and officials of the Building Service Employees Union in Chicago were indicted for receiving payoffs. In New York, we had cases against carpenters union officials for kickbacks and textile workers union officials for embezzlement.

This panoramic survey of some of our labor cases ought to make it clear that Robert Kennedy stated very valid premises in *The Enemy Within* and set smart priorities for the organized crime section when he became attorney general. Our efforts in weeding out labor corruption were successful, broad-based, and necessary.

Chapter 9

ROUND TWO

IN NEWPORT

From the moment the attorney general approved our retrying the Ratterman case, we went into high gear. Everyone who mattered at Justice knew about the case. Enthusiasm for any retrial is low, and Lynch was no longer there, so I was out on a limb. The second time around, I had to do better than another draw, but I had no new ammunition. Worse yet, the defense now had our game plan; after the first trial, one of the defendants' lawyers said, "We played this one by ear, but now we know their case." The press would continue to cover the trial prominently; whatever I did, good or bad, would be very public. My father said he was coming to watch this trial he'd heard and read so much about. There would be no place to hide. Henry Cook's hauntingly apt words to Ratterman the night of his arrest came back: "This will either make or break you!"

Two men were assigned to work with me in place of Sunshine Lynch. Joe Corey was an older lawyer, low-key, experienced, short and rotund, with a jolly face and kindly, calm demeanor. Harry Subin was inexperienced, bright, and eager to be helpful, a recent Yale Law school graduate and a friend of mine. I had wanted to be in charge, and this time—twenty-nine and growing up fast—I was.

We went right to work in Washington, I devising a new, fresher strategy, and Corey and Subin researching several legal points that we hoped might enable us to get into evidence testimony that had been precluded the first time.

My key tactic was to present our case, however circumstantial, differently.

"Time," I told Harry and Joe. "Time is what makes this conspiracy comprehensible."

"What the hell are you talking about?" they asked.

"If we present the evidence in a new sequence, one which highlights the time each event took place," I explained, "the conspiratorial nature of otherwise ambiguous acts becomes clear."

I had reached a fundamental conclusion: I'd tell the jury that they might disbelieve any individual witness, but they couldn't argue with time.

I made a list of critical events: Listed in sequence, they composed a pattern that gave coherency to assorted facts that were in contention and that might be construed differently than we would ask the jury to do. First, we would change the order of witnesses to enable us to create this timeline, and I would have a chart made to use in my summation. By listing these times and the related facts in an order that painted the picture by the numbers, our theory would be easier to follow, if not irresistible to accept.

My wife designed the timeline. I asked FBI artists to make a blowup of the chart to use at the trial. Juries love pictures, I had discovered, and we would give this jury a picture drawn by time.

Showing my new partners the chart, we went down each point on it, and I gave each of them stacks of FBI reports, trial transcripts, and legal memoranda related to our case. "Inhale this, know every detail like the palm of your hand, and let's talk again soon," I said. "Give me any ideas you may have as you look at all this. Let me know if I've missed anything. You have one advantage over me: distance."

We brainstormed daily about how to strengthen our case, deal with problems that arose at the first trial, and keep our opponents off balance. We'd meet at the beginning of each day, split up to do what had been agreed, and then meet again at day's end to discuss what we'd come up with.

The riskiest decision I made was to put Ratterman's friend Paisley on the stand. Whatever weaknesses he would create by testifying about his own past misbehavior would not be as troubling as his failure to tesify. The defense lawyers had killed us for this failure at the first trial, leaving the jurors wondering why the government did not bring forward someone who should have been a friendly witness. We had to put Paisley on the stand . . . and do the best we could at damage control.

Subin researched how far the defense lawyers could delve into Paisley's running after showgirls to discredit him as a witness. We'd have a memorandum of law to present to Judge Swinford supporting our position that these inquiries would be collateral, prejudicial, and therefore improper. We could not allow the jury to accept the defense's syllogism that a) Paisley whored around generally, and specifically on the night in question with Rita Desmond, and b) Ratterman and Paisley were always together, as they were on the night in question, thus c) the circumstance that Ratterman was in bed with April that night pointed to the conclusion that he, too, was whoring and was not entrapped.

We also wanted to dispel the phony arguments Leonard Walker made at the first trial that Charles Lester was a reputable lawyer who should not be judged wrongly in this latter part of his honorable career. I asked Corey to find legal authority to allow us to bring into evidence the fact that Lester had been disbarred many years earlier. He came barging into my office at Justice one afternoon, clearly excited. He had struck oil.

"I found a recent law review article discussing a new federal case in Kansas that allowed evidence of disbarment to be used to impeach a witness's credibility."

"Work it up in a short memo to Swinford, Joe; we don't want Lester to get away with his bullshit about being a man of honor this time. It makes me sick."

Any witness's credibility is automatically at issue if he takes the stand and testifies, as Lester had done at the first trial and could be expected to do again. Credibility evidence is different from character evidence; it only bears on the witness's truthfulness—the very question our jury must grapple with in deciding whose version of the story it should believe.

We prepared a memorandum of law concerning the admissibility of experts' testimony. I had to be able to get into evidence Dr.

Cleveland's opinion that Ratterman was drugged between 11:30 P.M., May 8, and 12:30 A.M., May 9. That would explain Ratterman's going to the Glenn as an involuntary act and preclude the suggestion that he drugged himself after the arrest. At the first trial, Judge Swinford refused to allow Dr. Cleveland to give his expert opinion on this point because he thought it would usurp the jury's function and prejudice the defendants. But experts are always offered to, in effect, usurp a jury's role where questions are too complex or beyond the knowledge of ordinary people. And all incriminating evidence is prejudicial.

We had to get Cleveland's conclusion in this time, and I prepared a brief supporting our position and a five-page hypothetical question I'd put to Dr. Cleveland, meticulously crafted on the basis of the hard evidence I knew would be in the record. I might lose, but not for being unprepared.

Also, we had to have a verdict this time. Courtroom veterans were gossiping that no twelve people were going to agree about what had happened in this bizarre case. And this time a hung jury would be equivalent to an acquittal, because neither the department nor the court would be likely to approve a third weeks-long trial for a misdemeanor, no matter how extraordinary the misdemeanor.

I prepared a legal memorandum—just in case the jury showed signs of hanging—asking Swinford to use what prosecutors referred to as the Allen charge. Widely accepted by the courts in situations where juries say they cannot reach a decision, the Allen charge is an instruction by the judge that urges the jury to go back and try one more time to reach a verdict. It pushed them to do their "duty to decide the case, if you can conscientiously do so," and to "listen to each other's arguments with a disposition to be convinced." I was ready to press Judge Swinford, who was reluctant to press his juries, to get these folks to make a decision this time. I'd rather throw the dice with a chance of losing than have a jury hang again.

I prepared another brief supporting our right to use statements to Staab by the three policemen defendants early in his investigation, to the effect that it looked as if there had been a frame-up and they'd been "used" at the last minute when the photographer couldn't be recruited. There is no question that statements by co-conspirators can be offered by the government against all conspirators once the conspiracy is proved. Swinford had not allowed us to offer these statements last time because they were deemed too "prejudicial." Of course all good evidence against defendants is prejudicial. The judge was probably being overly cautious because he expected a guilty verdict and wanted a record on appeal that was protective of the defendants. But we needed that evidence this time or we'd never get to an appeal. I would be prepared to offer him plenty of legal authority to allow it.

One night, I invited Joe and Harry to my home for dinner and a long evening of plotting and planning. They'd been through all the records and the trial transcripts. After a long, vinous dinner, we pulled out our files and spread them over the dining table, converting our pleasant place into a war room. I went down a list I'd made of all the circumstantial evidence that I thought cut our way, and all the facts that cut against our case. We analyzed how best to highlight the positive and downplay the negative points.

"First, let's list the key evidence against Lester," I said. "He's the person behind this case and, Staab says, the brains behind all that's wrong in Newport. Besides, I hate crooked lawyers and I want to nail this one." Corey and Subin smiled; they knew I'd already prosecuted and convicted two other Newport lawyers in other cases, and that this kind of crook produced my flash point.

I ran down my Lester list of circumstantial evidence: the Withrows' testimony making Ratterman's arrest seem scurrilous; Lester's revisionist story about giving Buccieri tax advice about being a concessionaire versus being an independent contractor, which was such crap, I hoped they'd try it again; his comment to the prosecutor, "Give me time. We'll come up with something."

I moved down the time chart. Lester said he was out all evening with his wife and her friend, went to sleep around 12:30 A.M., got a call from Tito at the jail, made some calls to be sure it wasn't a prank, called a bondsman, dressed and drove to the jail, and bailed out Tito and April. But, as the time chart demonstrated, police records showed that Tito called Lester at about 3 A.M. and that Lester arrived at the jail at 3:15 A.M. No way he could have done all he said happened in that time. "What probably happened," I speculated, "is that he was waiting at the Glenn, probably with Ciafardini, both of them in on the deal all along. His wife and her friend retired at 12:30 A.M., early enough for Lester to have established his alibi and left. He was at the Glenn after the defendants were released, meeting in the middle of the night to be sure everyone's story was straight."

"I'm beginning to see what you mean about the importance of time," Harry noted. "That point comes out at you off the chart, but it wouldn't have occurred to me just reading Lester's testimony at the last trial."

"Voilà," I said, and made a mock bow. "Next, look at Lester's handling of the local trial. He says he never discussed the case with his clients after the arrest. Some preparation! He relied on Tito to prep April. He provides evidence to the prosecutor—Ratterman's pen— that in fact incriminates April as much as it does Ratterman. If there *was* prostitution, she's as guilty as he. But all Lester cares about is smearing Ratterman. Clearly!" I was nearly screaming. My colleagues grinned and exchanged glances.

"Not only does he not prepare his defense," I continued, "but he never moved to dismiss charges against April when Ratterman's case was thrown out. Why would he leave these charges pending against his client?" I asked. "To keep the case alive and to keep April in line, of course."

I added, "I'm going to call Judge Rolf this time. We didn't last time. But I've had Staab question him and he'll testify that Lester could have made a motion for an acquittal of April and he'd have granted it. If I put him on the stand, he'll state that Lester—the hotshot lawyer—never made such a motion." He would be a new witness, something to freshen our case, and a judge at that.

"What else do we have against Lester?"

"We have two of his remarks after the event. He told an IRS agent the next day, May 9, what the case against Ratterman would be. *How would he know? Why would he say it?* Because he cooked it up, and because he couldn't resist smearing Ratterman."

"And," I added, "we have Lester telling another IRS agent scurrilous things about Ratterman's sex life in a later conversation about another case having nothing to do with ours. His comments were so scummy the agent never forgot it; he came forward during our investigation to tell us about it."

"What has that got to do with our case?" Corey asked.

"It shows Lester's hate for Ratterman. And it dispels his self-serving comment about having nothing against Ratterman," I replied. "In the police court trial, Lester would ask Ratterman creepy questions solely to suggest questionable things about him. Ratterman could deny, but the public would hear Lester's disgusting accusation."

"You're going to have fun with Mr. Lester on the stand," Joe remarked.

"No, you are," I replied to my stunned trial partner, who looked at me, not understanding. "I'll take the big witnesses—Ratterman and April—and the tough ones like Paisley," I added. "But I'm so involved with Lester, I feel too much in the gut about him, that I don't think I should cross-examine. I don't want my animosity to come through to the jury, or to get in the way of clear-headed, careful questioning. I want to jump the guy, so I better not question him."

"Well, think about it," Joe said, "You may not be able to resist when we get to court."

"No, you prepare for Charlie Lester," I insisted. "I'm not going to chance screwing this one up because I'm too riled. We'll plan it together. And you have the legal memo on cross-examining him about the disbarment. You prep for him. I'll help, but you should do it."

"What else do we have?" Harry asked. Now my colleagues were wondering if I had any more surprises planned.

"We have Ciafardini lying to his fellow police buddies, including Quitter and White, about his whereabouts on May 8. And calling Moose, his colleague, a stool pigeon when he eventually told the truth. Remember him saying he would get even with Moose? Well, the powers in Newport did get even. Moose was fired from the police department and had to leave town to look for work. He's working in Omaha now, at a motel." I had tried to indict Ciafardini for obstruction of justice early in our investigation, but Silberling thought the evidence wasn't strong enough and we couldn't afford an acquittal.

"I also want to stress Ciafardini's incredible tale about hearing, while in the mens' room, that Ratterman was in the Glenn, overhearing this from an unknown person, and then getting a call for *him* at the police station even though he was off-duty, plus all the questionable facts surrounding the whole arrest: Altogether his story sounds phony."

"One thing, though," Subin reminded us, "he and his buddies almost never came to Newport on May 8. The three of them all agree they almost stayed in Louisville. How would that be so if a staged arrest was planned?"

I was ready with the answer to that question. "Right, but that fact only suggests Ciafardini wasn't in on a plan hatched before May 8. My best guess is that the general idea was to embarrass Ratterman with a picture whenever Tito got him compromised. The plan fell apart late that night, after Ciafardini was in Newport, at the Glenn, when Marty couldn't get the photographer. Then, they send good old Pat to the police station—after the Withrow plan aborts—to get the call. The tactic shifted on the spur of the moment, from private blackmail to public disgrace."

"Sounds good. What else have we got?" Subin asked. My team was involved but getting restless. Despite the hour, I was wide awake, my mind rushing through the key points.

"Well, there's the Ratterman pen with the obsolete address and phone number. These guys were so sloppy they never even noticed their incriminating evidence couldn't incriminate.

"There's other good circumstantial evidence implicating these characters," I added.

"What are the best shots?" Joe asked.

"Ciafardini winking at April when she asked him what was going on during the arrest. Lester's bondsman refusing to bail out Ratterman, a perfect bail risk, but bailing out April who arguably at the time was a bad risk. The whole arrest process was a bad joke: no warrant, no basis for the charges, no investigation, breaking into a private apartment when the door is not locked, charges made with no foundation, no usual health report on the prostitution charge. These cops were beauts."

It was getting very late. My wife had gone to sleep. My partners were looking weary, but were unwilling to complain. I finally began to wind down. "One more point," I added. "On the importance of time, again: Staab's guys pulled some plane tickets and interviewed Tito's friends—the Beckleys—who he met at the Gourmet Room in Cincinnati and later at the Glenn. Something interesting turned up that we didn't have last time. I want to use it this time and we've subpoenaed some new folks so we can. One of you guys can handle these witnesses."

Now they were awake. "When you put together certain times,

Carinci's story has a huge hole in it. He says they left the Gourmet Room around twelve, were at the Caucus Club from twelve to one, and back at the Glenn at one-thirty where he saw the Beckleys and their party. But the Beckleys say they left Cincinnati for Florida on a one-thirty plane, making it impossible for all those three meetings to have taken place. One of them must not have happened, and I'd bet it was the Caucus Club."

"Spell it out; I'm not sure I'm following," Corey asked.

"Well, if they were at the Gourmet Room until around midnight, as many people agree was so, and at the Glenn before one A.M. as must have been the case since Beckley must have left the Glenn around one A.M. to go to the airport to catch a one-thirty plane, which is not in question, how could our three party boys have also spent the hour from twelve to one at the Caucus Club? Maybe they didn't go there, but cooked up the Caucus Club story to prove Ratterman and Paisley were OK and wanted to go over the river—interstate remember, so it could have been a kidnapping—thus giving credence to Tito's version of things."

"That's good," Subin said, "but how do we get around the witnesses at the Caucus Club who remember seeing them there?"

"I can't answer that," I admitted. "If Tito knew these folks and asked them to corroborate his story at the local trial, they might have agreed at first, not realizing this would turn into a 'federal case.' Once committed to the bullshit story, they couldn't get out. Remember, lying to the FBI is a crime. The Beckley party all said, and still say, they saw Tito earlier in Cincinnati and later at the Glenn; Tito agrees to that; but the airline records show a Beckley leaving the Cincinnati Airport at one-thirty. It's not one hundred percent solid, but it's more use of our time chart that can hurt them."

We were getting into early morning, and tomorrow was a work day.

"Do we have time to go over the evidence that cuts against us?" Harry asked.

"I wish Ratterman and Paisley hadn't been out boozing all night. I wish Paisley hadn't been running around with a showgirl. I wonder why Ratterman was willing to meet with Tito *anyplace*, or go to the Glenn at all. That's why I have to put Paisley on the stand. The only way to deal with all that bad evidence is to put it on ourselves, so it doesn't appear to be pulled out of us. Then we do as much damage control as possible, do it early enough in the trial so we can shore it up with stronger evidence that cuts our way, and hope for the best. Putting on Paisley as our witness is going to be as much fun as having root canal work. But there's no alternative."

My colleagues clearly were concerned about the holes in our case— even Ratterman could not provide helpful accounts about questions that needed answering. Yet, I reminded them, hoping to persuade myself, if Ratterman truly was a victim of a drugging, the frame-up story will have worked. His adversaries will have accomplished exactly what they intended, discrediting Ratterman, by putting him in the very situation that raises the questions we ourselves were asking about him.

Silence. Did my partners buy this explanation? Was I truly convinced?

———

We had several months to prepare our case in detail. This was the distinct advantage government lawyers had. In private practice, I'd never have had this kind of indulgence; even other prosecutors, with their huge caseloads, could not put as much preparation into their cases. We had a major advantage: No resource had to be spared to develop and perfect our organized crime cases. But our concomitant responsibility weighed heavily. With all the effort, we'd better win. No one ever said that to me; no one had to.

We worked away in the relative anonymity of Washington, D.C., living the other half of our divided lives. In Washington, we were worker bees, small fish in the big pond of the New Frontier, bureaucrats in the halls of a giant federal department, in an exciting place at an exciting time, living nonetheless relatively quiet, private lives. When we returned to Newport and our trial, we would be celebrities once more, stars in a dubious firmament, characters in an unfolding drama in a strange place that was distant from us in every way.

———

After all the time, and all the preparation, all the anxieties and theorizing, at 10 A.M. on July 15, 1963, the second trial began. Its beginning was more whimper than big bang. As is often the case with celebrated trials, opening day involves little high drama and much low-luster shuffling of people and papers, boring procedures and inane ceremonies.

The courtroom was packed. Judge Swinford and his entourage were in their places. The defense table personnel were the same, with one exception: A new lawyer, Howell Vincent, was to represent Buccieri this time. Subin and Corey were with me at the government's table, along with Frank Staab, who had retired from the FBI but who we'd hired as a consultant for this trial. In addition to his mastery of all the details of the investigation, he was my security blanket.

Judge Swinford had summoned a panel of prospective jurors from the Eastern District of Kentucky in order to assure our choosing a jury that did not know all about this notorious case. Swinford gave the jurors his "call to duty" pep talk about their citizens' sacrifices to assist their government, a speech we'd heard before and admired for its high-minded allegiance to principles of fairness, integrity, and civic responsibility. The judge introduced the players—the government and the defense—and asked initial qualifying questions of the panel, questions about their health, their comprehension of the proceedings, their familiarity with the widely publicized facts in our case. He would not sequester them, he said, but he would rely on their rigorous adherence to his rules of propriety during all recesses. Then he allowed the lawyers to question individual jurors.

My voir dire questions were brief, limited to their personal connections to the government and experience with the Newport scene. I was inclined to quickly state, "The United States is satisfied with the jury," and hope for the best. Really biased jurors are not likely to expose their prejudices, even to facile questioners. By their questioning, the defense lawyers attempted to indoctrinate jurors to the legal principles their clients would rely on. Some jurors were excused for medical reasons, some given with startling candor ("I have hemorrhoids that bother me pretty bad"). Most stated, one way or another, that they'd "heard about the case but were not familiar with the actual facts."

Judge Swinford was liberal about having jurors "stand aside" if they displayed any inkling of being questionable candidates, and in permitting the defense lawyers to editorialize: "Gambling and vice existed in Campbell County for more than a hundred years," Walker reminded them. "You won't be influenced by the fact that the attorney general has sent these three lawyers here from Washington to handle this case for the government, will you?" Steuve inquired. "You won't give any greater weight to the testimony of these reformers than that of the defendants, will you?" Davies wanted to know. Would they "stick to their convictions" even if they were in a minority? Weintraub asked.

As the defense lawyers continued to challenge, I kept saying, "The United States is quite satisfied with the jury," hoping to get the message to them that we were confident, believed in them, and weren't playing any tactical games. We worked at jury selection, pushing and shoving, into the early evening and the next day before settling on our panel and several alternates, who would stand by and sit quietly during the trial, ready to replace any juror who had a sudden attack of, say, bad hemorrhoids.

Joe Corey gave the government's opening statement. It was brief and simple. He read the indictment and explained in plain English what crimes it accused the defendants of committing—a misuse of police power and a common agreement to discredit Ratterman by falsely arresting and charging him. He promised the evidence would fit together "like small pieces of a jigsaw puzzle," no one of which supplies the whole picture. Joe highlighted some of the key pieces of our puzzle, noting why they were important and how they would be seen to fit together. The facts in our case, he promised, were stronger than fiction and would seem like a TV show "composed of politics, intrigue, mystery, false alibi, and sex."

The defense opening statements joined the issue, presenting the other view of the case about to be tried: The puzzle Mr. Corey alluded to has missing pieces; the government's pieces don't fit together; the Ratterman episode was a product of the press and public relations efforts of the reformers' committee, which wanted a widely publicized trial in order to elect their moral crusader, Ratterman; this case should have ended "in the Newport, Kentucky, police court."

With the judge's words, "Call your witness," the trial began in earnest. Christian Seifried, chairman of the Social Action Committee of the Newport Ministerial Association, started our chronology, talking of the formation of the Committee of Five Hundred, the drafting of Ratterman as its candidate for sheriff on April 4, 1961, and their goals to provide good government and eliminate gambling, prostitution, and other illegal activities in Newport. Seifried was a clean-cut, all-American good citizen whose demeanor and image set the scene and demonstrated the division we wished to portray to the jury between the good guys and the bad guys.

But life is not so clear-cut, as our next witness would demonstrate. The first legal squabble arose when I advised the court that we intended to call Paisley as a witness. While we were turning over his statements to the defense attorneys as required by law, we wanted the court to excise all references to "extramarital affairs" as irrelevant. Of course, the defense argued they were "very material" because they concerned the character and integrity of the witness. I offered Judge Swinford the first of our legal memoranda, citing legal authorities to bolster our position, and crossed my fingers.

Paisley testified that he was "unable to remember the sequence of events. I remember very little about being in the Tropicana . . . nor do I remember leaving the Tropicana." He remembered entering and drinking in Tito's room with Ratterman, Tito coming in and going out of the room, and going back to his hotel in a taxi. He recalled Ratterman, fully dressed, stretched out on a bed talking to Tito. The next thing he remembered was the phone ringing in his hotel room in Cincinnati and hearing from Ratterman that he'd been arrested and asking him to come to Newport that morning.

There, we got into the tricky question of Paisley's condition: Was he drunk or drugged? We couldn't prove the latter and didn't want to try, for fear of weakening Ratterman's claim, which we believed was true and provable. Paisley testified that he'd "never had this unrealistic feeling before," that "in the course of my business, I drink with clients and socially, and I have never experienced this before or since, where I was unable to recall periods of time or had this feeling, just from the use of alcohol."

We left things there, after noting that when Paisley was tried in Newport for conspiring with Tito, he had been represented by Tom Steuve, and acquitted. We sat back waiting for the expected attack by the defense on cross-examination, and praying Judge Swinford would not allow them to open Paisley's Pandora's box.

"I am not going to go back into his extracurricular activities . . . to sit here and let this jury hear a sordid story of the infidelities of this witness," Swinford decided. At a bench conference, despite the wrangling of the defense lawyers, Swinford held firm, and I gave our anxious witness a wink of encouragement as I returned to counsel's table. Our first legal brief had paid off.

His was a long, arduous, testy, noisome cross-examination, and while Paisley did not help our case, we came out of his testimony alive, I felt. Lingering questions remained as a result of his testimony: Why had they allowed themselves to get into this mess? Why wasn't Paisley tested to determine if he was drugged? How naive or culpable had they really been? But the worst of our case was over, early, and we could gain momentum by moving directly into our strongest testimony.

My favorite three witnesses—the Withrows and Granny Hay—were as good this time as they had been in the past. I took Tom Withrow through the story of the approach by Lester and his deal with Buccieri to take a picture of a man in a room. Withrow's down-to-earth sense of humor gave credence to his testimony.

Again, our legal research on critical and contested evidence paid off. It was important that Nancybelle Withrow be allowed to testify that it was Marty Buccieri who had called her at 1:30 A.M., saying he needed to have a picture taken right away. Buccieri's identification tied this call to his prior meeting with Tom. At the last trial, Swinford had not allowed her to testify who called because she could not identify the voice. The fact that she'd subsequently heard the voice on television and could then identify it was deemed insufficient. Our legal brief listed cases that had approved the use of circumstantial evidence to identify a voice that only could have belonged to one person. The judge had done his homework this time and ruled in our favor. "I am going to permit her to say what the person said," he ruled. "A person may be identified by voice when the witness hears his voice distinctly over the radio transistor, and is unhesitating in his positive identification."

There was no cross-examination of the Withrows. Granny Hay testified next; she was a dream witness, entirely credible and winningly feisty. With their testimony, we were back on top of our case and, I believed, we had dissipated any of the fallout from Paisley's murky testimony.

The following day, July 18, we continued with three police officers, the two who had traveled back to Newport on May 8 with Cia-fardini—Jones and Bishop—and Sergeant McSorley, whose records showed precisely when he received the anonymous call (at 2:32); sent Ciafardini, Quitter, and White to make the fateful arrest; and every-one involved returned to the police station (at 2:49). The whole thing took seventeen minutes. At 3:15, Lester arrived, bailed out Tito and April, and the three of them left.

Next, we decided to trump some of the cards defendants had played at the first trial. We called a handful of witnesses they had called last time, relatively innocuous witnesses whose testimony could have been avoided; but we didn't want the jury to think they corrob-orated the defense view of the case. So we called them.

We returned to our good-guys-versus-bad-guys lineup with Henry Cook, whose obvious rectitude and courtroom experience permitted us to tie up loose ends and fill in several blanks in our overall testi-monial picture.

Cook explained how Withrow's crucial testimony came to light. A local minister told Mrs. Ratterman that one of his parishioners had come to him in pastoral confidence asking him to let her know that her husband had been framed. The parishioner knew it was a frame-up because he "was supposed to be involved in it." Cook had already heard about it from people at the hospital who'd heard Withrow—there to take photos of newborn babies—say he'd been contacted to take a picture at the Glenn Hotel. Cook had "put the two together," then went to see the Withrow family and persuaded them to testify.

Brock McIntosh testified that on the night of the arrest he was employed by Tito and Marty as a shill at the crap table in the Sapphire Room. Tito announced at 2:30 or 2:45 A.M., an unusually early time to have done so, "That's all for tonight." Usually, they closed an hour later. He figured "there was going to be a raid." He educated the jury about the gambling business, noting that typically there were six shills using house money to keep the game going and only two to four real players in the crap game.

We were building toward the presentation of our central character, keeping up the drama over when he'd be called, and shoring up some of the weaker parts of his prospective testimony. Ann Ratterman testi-fied about the night of May 8 and the morning of May 9 in the Ratterman house.

We moved to higher stakes with Rita Desmond; Bonnie Noe was her new name and housewife was her new avocation. It did not help our case that Rita painted Paisley as a drunken girl-chaser. But she did corroborate April's testimony that Ratterman was clothed and innocent. And she remembered Lester telling April: "This is the pen George Ratterman gave you."

We recessed for the weekend, and returned to trial Monday morning, July 22. Frank Staab described the exhaustive investigation he'd conducted (approximately five hundred interviews throughout the United States), and introduced numerous statements he'd taken from the defendants. Many of them contained remarks by the defendants that independent evidence showed to be lies.

He confirmed, on cross-examination, that there never was a kidnapping investigation, though I wondered why the defendants would want to suggest that such a serious charge was considered.

Clumsy cross-examination permitted Staab to introduce harmful evidence we'd never have gotten in directly: that April had declined to go to the press when she decided to tell the truth, insisting on talking only to the FBI. Staab was better able than April to put her changed testimony into a credible context, even in response to sarcastic questions. Steuve: ". . . [S]he first said under oath that Ratterman was disrobed and the second time she put his clothing on him, is that about right?" Staab: "There was additional investigation made concerning her story, continuously from the time she gave it until the time she came back and said she wanted to change her story and tell the truth."

By our calculations, it was time to call our central witness. Foundations had been laid. Necessary props had been built. There would be time to correct any problems that arose from his testimony. It seemed the right dramatic moment for me to call, "George Ratterman."

A cool, poised witness, George Ratterman strode to the stand, took the oath, and began what would be a long and contentious testimony. To show motive, Ratterman told of the evolution of the local reform group, and how he came to run for sheriff, reluctantly: "You heard this all over the community that the whole movement was useless anyway, because those who controlled our community, the vice and the corruption, had so much money and were so powerful and controlled all of the officials, that nothing could be done, anyway. So I was afraid that if nobody stepped forward to run for this office, the whole movement would die by the wayside, and for that reason when it became obvious that nobody else was going to do it, I offered my services . . . for the post of sheriff of Campbell County." He was "for better government for the community, through honest law enforcement," particularly to fight wide-open illegal gambling and prostitution: "It would be my duty to stop them and I intended to do that." We hoped this introduction to applied civics would impress the jury with the fact that Ratterman was the representative of good in the ensuing battle with evil forces.

Ratterman tried to describe the indescribable: "I can recall various things that happened with no continuity, that is, there are blank spots and then things that I can remember. It is somewhat similar, you might say, to watching a movie and having certain portions blacked out . . ." Then he related his incomplete and hazy recollection of the event that had brought us all to this point. I would provide the missing segments of his story with the strong witnesses who followed. Then I left him to his cross-examiners, hoping he'd be as strong a witness as he had been at the first trial and that they'd be as ineffective.

Questioning continued all day, and went exhaustively into every detail. Ratterman held up. His failures to recollect certain facts could be viewed as evasiveness in an embarrassing situation, or more innocently, that his rendition was not pat and contrived, because he had been drugged. If only we could crawl into the heads of the jurors and know how they were seeing this critical part of our case.

Ratterman was patient and direct with all his answers, though he gave no ground. His quickness and sense of humor were evident. When asked by Davies how he could say there were few reformers in Newport during the past forty years when he wasn't forty years old, Ratterman replied: "I also know Washington was our first president and I wasn't living then either."

On redirect, I concluded by having Ratterman note that though there were five thousand members of the Reform Committee, he received thirteen thousand votes in his winning election, and that "there has been no open gambling in Newport" since he was elected. Finally, we had finished this essential part of our case. It may have been entitled *U.S.* v. *Lester et al.* in the official records, but it was always publicly referred to generically as the Ratterman case. If he was innocent, they were guilty.

It was time for April Flowers. April was poised, pleasantly dressed, tanned; she could have been a Kentucky matron rather than an "exotic dancer," as she described herself. She'd been through this routine once before, had had her dress rehearsal. She'd spent the week awaiting her time to testify relaxing by a local motel pool.

As she told her basic story, the courtroom audience was rapt. I prompted her to tell the jury why she went along with the hoax at the local trial. "I was afraid not to . . . I was to go along with the policeman and this was held in Newport Police Court and they were Newport policemen. They were lying; I couldn't get up and tell the truth then; I was afraid. So I went along with their lies. I said exactly what they said."

She left Newport in June and worked first in Louisville, later in Alabama, and then in Port Huron, Michigan. In September, she decided to call the FBI because "my conscience bothered me very much and I wanted to tell the truth." Steuve interrupted: "Your what?" April bristled: "Conscience, shall I spell it?" On redirect, I asked her to explain her turnaround. "I felt very badly because I had lied and discredited a man that was innocent and in doing so, I discredited myself."

The credibility of April's story was the key to winning this case. If the jury believed her recantation, we'd win, I had felt all along. So she had to be open and believable. After getting her story on the record, I stopped and waited for the inevitable blasts of cross-examination, hoping her basic honesty about this episode would shine through. April had cried the first time she told me the story of her conversion. Her mother was very ill, and she'd done some soul-searching and wanted to clear the record for her own peace of mind. When I saw her real tears, I decided to stop my rehearsal. I hoped, if she didn't go over and over this part of her story and become hardened, she'd cry again on cross-examination, and if she did the jury might react sympathetically, as I did. So, after a light and precise questioning that made the points we had to make, I announced: "You may cross-examine."

Dan Davies jumped in, probed, drew no blood, and stopped. Weintraub picked up the cudgel. More about the arrest, the arrangement of Tito's room, who did what when the police were in the room, Ratterman's condition. He became pedantic. Why did she say Ciafardini gave her "sort of a wink" at the last trial and "a wink" this time? April's simple candor seemed disarming: "A wink's a wink." To my surprise, after only a light and brief cross-examination, Weintraub announced: "That's all." When Steuve asked April where she was currently performing, she replied Houston, "because my mother is dying of cancer and I'm trying to support her," and she began to cry.

April had been tough but sincere in responding to Steuve's questions about her motives and her veracity. Her son had been threatened. She'd received anonymous calls. "I was just tired of lying and being afraid of these people." When her questioner sarcastically referred to her "different story" about what happened, April corrected him: "Not a different story, the truth."

Before Howell Vincent concluded his cross-examination, he'd stepped into the second trap we set. I had carefully prepped April to not say anything on direct examination about passing the FBI's lie detector test; but if the defense opened the door, she should step right in and hammer them with it. I explained how it could and could not be done so there would be no prejudicial mistakes. Sure enough, at the end of his cross-examination, Vincent asked April about her testimony in the Newport Police Court that she knew nothing about Ratterman being framed. To attack her credibility, he asked if she hadn't said then that she would take an oath and would take a lie detector test. "Did you make that answer?" "I did." Then Howell opened the door, and April marched in.

MR. VINCENT: You tell this jury now what you testified to in police court under oath is perjury?

MISS HODGES (FLOWERS): I perjured myself in Newport Police Court and when I came back in September to make a true statement to the FBI, they suggested that I take a lie detector test before talking to the Federal Grand Jury so that there would be no embarrassment. I did take a lie detector test.

MR. VINCENT: If the Court please . . .

MISS HODGES (FLOWERS): And I passed it. Thereafter I talked to the Federal Grand Jury and that's why I am here now telling the truth.

Of course, the defense attorneys hollered as if stuck and the judge cautioned the jury that this testimony about her passing a lie detector test "should carry no implications as to her testimony in this case." I smiled to myself, knowing that an instruction like this was, in Mark Twain's words, like telling a child to stand in the corner and not think about a white elephant.

To my delight, the last words the jury heard from April were about her fears, the threats to her son, comments that "if I knew what was good for me, if I wanted to stay healthy," that "people that don't play along will be thrown in the river . . . in other words, they will be floating." If I could have written the script, I'd have ended it on this note.

When a weary but unwounded April Flowers stepped down from the witness stand at the end of over two grueling days of testimony, I felt strongly that the most important chapter of this trial had been written. There were three key parts to our case, the Ratterman-Paisley-April segment, the Withrows, and the doctors. We would soon get to the third key segment.

I turned next to our medical and expert witnesses. Drs. Anderson and Tanner laid the foundation for Dr. Cleveland's critical testimony. I took Dr. Cleveland, carefully and thoroughly, through his credentials, the toxicological nature and effect of chloral hydrate as a sedative and hypnotic drug, his supervision of the analysis of Ratterman's specimens, his conclusion that Ratterman's blood specimen the morning after contained 8.1 milligrams of chloral hydrate, and how the body absorbs, metabolizes, and eliminates the byproducts of that drug through blood and urine.

Then we got into the controversial subject of when the chloral hydrate was ingested. I posed my carefully prepared, long hypothetical question, based on testimony already in evidence. An expert witness may be asked his opinion if his credentials are appropriate and if the question is based on evidence before the jury. This time the judge let him testify about the timing of the drugging. Dr. Cleveland's response made our case. "It is my opinion that . . . this ingestion would have been in the order of ten to eleven P.M. on May eighth."

Illustrating his points with a chart on a blackboard, he showed why the drug could not have been ingested, as the defense was suggesting, any time between 1 A.M. and 2:45 A.M., because, by then, Ratterman already showed the peak effects of the drug. Since byproducts of the drug were found in Ratterman's blood and urine at 9 A.M. and it all was gone by 3 P.M., the metabolism was complete, and one could rewind to the likely time of ingestion—about 10 P.M. the night before.

I was elated; and the defense lawyers were agitated.

Clumsy cross-examination permitted Dr. Cleveland to add a clincher. Pressed to explain why he didn't fix the time of ingestion at the first trial, Dr. Cleveland responded: "At the previous trial I was not permitted to answer the question."

"Our show played well in Cleveland," I whispered to Subin as our witness stepped down. I was so pleased with the way Dr. Cleveland's testimony had gone that our plans to call other witnesses would have made them seem anticlimactic. I wanted to end on a high note. I leaned over to confer with Corey, Subin, and Staab. "I want to stop now," I whispered. "Have we missed anything important?" When they said no, I rested the government's case. I felt relieved and elated about how the case had gone in. Now, it was our job to screen the defense, sum up, and pray.

Judge Swinford cleared the jury from the courtroom for the predictable defense motions for acquittal, which always came at the close of the government's case. The prosecution was based on "suspicion, surmise, and suggestion," they argued. There was no proof of any agreement between the defendants. Judge Swinford denied the motions and recessed over the weekend. On Monday morning, July 19, we returned to the trial, and the defendants each took the stand to deny the charges and defend themselves. They had no surprises, no new moves.

When it came time for cross-examination, I jumped in aggressively, with a first question that even surprised me. "Mr. Carinci, Dr. Cleveland has testified that chloral hydrate was ingested into George Ratterman between ten and eleven P.M. Can you be more specific and tell us precisely when?"

MR. WALKER: Now, I object to that question, if the court please.

THE COURT: Objection sustained.

MR. GOLDFARB: Yes, sir.

I delved into Tito's so-called Derby friends because they included Gil Beckley, who one of my colleagues had indicted in New Orleans for running a nationwide lay-off betting setup out of the Glenn Hotel. Beckley provided another entry for our time chart. When Tito, Paisley, and Ratterman left the Gourmet Room, Beckley said he'd see Tito later at the Glenn. Since Tito testified that he was certain he saw the Beckley party at the Glenn while Ratterman was in Room 314, how could the three revelers have been at the Caucus Club between 12 and 1? The Beckley party had left the Glenn at 1 A.M. to catch a plane to Florida!

Tito had testified they had gotten to Room 314 around 1:20 A.M. and he'd seen the Beckley party downstairs later when he was running around getting the drinks and girls. What he did not know was that this time we had airline documentation showing the Beckleys must have left for the Cincinnati airport about 1 A.M.; the airport was a half-hour drive from the Glenn.

At a bench conference I persuaded Swinford, with the help of the *Kansas Law Review* article Corey had found, to allow us to bring out Lester's being reprimanded on several charges by the Kentucky Court of Appeals. "He has testified as to his professional erudition and you have a right to attack it if you can," Swinford ruled. "He may offer any explanation that he wants to give." The judge was probably outraged, as we were, by Lester's self-portrayal as a fine and respected lawyer.

Lester admitted that he had indeed been reprimanded "thirty years ago" for what he called "imprudence," which Corey corrected from the record to "non-professional conduct." Lester pontificated that his prosecution was a political reprisal that "tore down the temple of justice."

On rebuttal, we returned to my compulsion about times. Mrs. Ellis Seith, a Miamian, testified that she and her husband and three other couples, including the Gil Beckleys, were at the Tropicana on the night of May 8, having arrived "I would say between eleven-thirty and twelve, twelve-thirty." She remembered seeing Tito there. The Beckleys left "I would say approximately one o'clock . . . to get a plane . . . around one-thirty . . . they talked about the time and as well as I can remember, it was around one-thirty." This fact would eliminate the Caucus Club episode, putting the three cavorters in the Glenn earlier than Tito had reported.

We tightened her testimony with that of John Cook, chief ticket agent and custodian of records at the Cincinnati airport. There was a flight from Cincinnati to Miami that night; it was scheduled to leave at 1:42, the actual departure was 1:51; and his records showed one passenger named Beckley was on that flight.

IRS agent Vincent Brennan repeated his testimony that Charles Lester had gratuitously made disgustingly obscene remarks to him about Ratterman, too disgusting to repeat in court. He'd found these remarks "shocking," "filthy." He also said that Lester told him he'd "been up since two o'clock when this Ratterman deal broke," and that they were going to charge Ratterman with committing unnatural sex acts "if he thinks he's going ahead and run for sheriff."

Mitch Meade, who during the early days of our investigation was an assistant U.S. attorney in Lexington and was now counsel to the Kentucky State Bar Association, delivered the coup de grâce. We called him as a character witness to testify about Lester's general reputation for veracity in the legal community. Walker objected, which in and of itself must have looked terrible to the jury, but Swinford let Meade testify. "Whenever a person takes the witness stand, he puts his truth and veracity in issue. Now, you limit it to that question, not as to his general reputation." That ground rule established, Meade made his deadly declaration.

> MR. GOLDFARB: Do you know his reputation for truth and verac-
> ity in the community in which he lives and among the people
> who know him best?
> MR. STEUVE: Objection. The means of knowing, not whether he
> knows it. Does he have the means.
> THE COURT: No, overrule your objection.
> MR. MEADE: Yes.
> MR. GOLDFARB: And is his reputation for truth and veracity good
> or bad?
> MR. MEADE: Bad.

Meade could only say yes or no on direct, but he could explain his answers if pressed on cross-examination. Walker obliged by questioning Meade and allowing him to add: "My information is based upon . . . my discussions with attorneys in this area." With that bullet to Lester's heart, we ended our case.

I'd be making the summation for the government, after the defense counsel made theirs. We were entitled to open first and close last. I advised Swinford that I intended to use my time chart, "a customary device in making summation." But, to my astonishment, Swinford refused to allow me to use the chart, a ruling out of line with precedent and a disruption to my final fling in this case that had haunted me for three years. I had raised the large, artfully composed chart onto a lectern to show the judge. Swinford, possibly trying to overprotect his record on appeal, ruled that the chart would overemphasize the items of evidence it referred to and give the jury a wrong impression that it was an exhibit of evidence. I was crushed.

We adjourned over the weekend, to fret and prepare to wrap up the case the following Monday. Judge Swinford allowed the jurors to go home over the weekend but told them to come back with their overnight bags because he would sequester them once they went into deliberations, where they would remain until the case was concluded. They were to scrupulously avoid any outside communications or media coverage of the case while on their own.

After summations, the court would give its instructions and the jury's deliberations would begin immediately. If the jury did not reach a verdict that day, they'd be sequestered at a local hotel, guarded by three marshals and allowed to see no one else. The alternate jurors would be excused once the case was submitted to the jury, so if anything happened to any of the final twelve there would be a mistrial. At this stage, the court wanted that about as much as we on the government side did, so he was being extra careful. In view of the experiences of my colleagues in the Marcello and Hoffa cases, we were worried someone would contact one of our jurors, if only to cause a mistrial. Subin, Corey, and I knew how easy this would be in view of Swinford's easy-to-circumvent honor system for jurors.

Dan Davies's summation was in keeping with his style throughout the trial: kindly, low-key, unpretentious. His clients were innocent, veteran policemen, sent out on an assignment in the middle of the night and now entwined in a parochial political battle they had nothing to do with. They were cops who made a mistake; that happens, but you don't go to prison for it. How could anyone say Ratterman was deprived of his rights when he was tried and acquitted? Now all the king's horses and men—another reference to the Kennedy intrusion—are joined against them. Release them! They are innocent!

Weintraub, too, was characteristic in his summation: excessively florid in a malapropistic, long-winded flyover of the evidence. He held on to the shirttails of the less implicated Quitter and White, and made Ciafardini's escapades on May 8 sound like nothing more than a soap opera of infidelity and a travesty of Keystone Kops. He berated the carpetbaggers who were in Kentucky on a misguided crusade; the jury should send us home empty-handed.

Vincent and Steuve spoke relatively briefly, spewing various theories of Ratterman-invented conspiracies to entrap Tito for political reasons. They reminded the jury, to my embarrassment, of Paisley's peccadillos and Ratterman's nights on the town.

Walker told them he had "a dual obligation," because he was representing a lawyer, not just any defendant. He told them—improperly—that he knew Lester and could attest to his honesty as well as to his legal skills. Most of the witnesses they'd heard had said nothing about his client, Walker recalled, suggesting that the jury should apply some quantitative test of the evidence. Lester's meetings with the other defendants that night were all circumstantial, "just one of those things that happened." His actions were those of a lawyer working on a case. April "is a perjurer and a liar and unworthy of belief." Agent Brennan was part of the political war and entrapped Lester. Ratterman was an "egocentric or an egotistical absurdity," a villain and an evil mastermind who cooked up his story to explain his night out to his wife and public.

Walker's final crescendo about Lester sent my temperature rising: "Everything that Mr. Lester did, he did as a lawyer . . . And we're from Kentucky, you're from Kentucky and I'm from Kentucky, and we may be ignorant, but we know that zero plus zero equals zero . . ." He was sure this good Kentucky jury of twelve Christian men and women "would not destroy and disgrace this fine lawyer in his twilight hours."

We asked for a bench conference first and pointed out to Judge Swinford that Charles Lester had been indicted for attempted rape and pleaded guilty to assault and battery. Since that was a misdemeanor, the law forbade our bringing out that fact. But, Corey argued, Walker had misled the jury about his client's record and we ought to be able to correct that misstatement because it would leave "a totally unfair impression with the jury about this man." Judge Swinford's face was white, but he ruled in tightly controlled words:

"Mr. Walker made an improper statement. That addresses itself to his sense of ethics . . . but I can't permit counsel to comment on something that is not a part of the record . . . There is nothing the Court can do about it as far as the jury is concerned . . . This is just one of the things that happens in a lawsuit." He was right; Walker had been a sleaze, though he stated, "I hope to die this moment if I knew anything about it . . ."

When I stood to sum up our case, I was livid about this last stunt. Let us leave these "five blasts of smoke and dust," I began, this crazy fog of slurs, and talk about time. If who was telling the truth was the question the jury faced, "nobody can lie about time." Whether you are a Kentuckian or not, I commented in wry response to Walker's chauvinistic pitch, if somebody is known to be someplace at a certain time, they can't be someplace else at that same time. One can adjust the facts but no one can jiggle times. Tito could not have been at the Caucus Club and at the Glenn. Either the Caucus Club witness lied about seeing them there or Beckley wasn't on the 1:42 plane, and how could the plane records lie? I was going to push my thesis: You can't argue against *time*.

Time also implicated Lester. How could he have gotten from his warm bed in the next town to the Newport police station in the few minutes that elapsed between the uncontroverted times in evidence: The defendants arrived there at 2:49, and left at 3:25. Given all that had to have been done during a very few minutes, I hammered and repeated, Lester could not have been called at 3 A.M. and done what he said he did.

If time undid the bail story, time made the arrest story preposterous. The tip came over the phone, records showed, at 2:32 and the parties were back at the station at 2:49—seventeen minutes to recruit the investigating team, get to and from the Glenn, and make three burlesque arrests! To underscore the time element, I advised the jury that I'd been talking to them for seventeen minutes already at that point, and all that happened during the entire event in this trial was alleged to have taken place in the same brief time period.

Ratterman was not found guilty in that case, I admitted, "but it wasn't because they didn't try." He was found not guilty "despite these defendants, not because of them." It was Judge Rolf who changed the bail and ordered a local investigation and prosecutor

Hirschfeld who threw out the case against Ratterman when the smell got too strong—"It stank to high heaven and he didn't want to contaminate himself."

I walked over to where Lester was sitting, stood right in front of him, and glowered at him. "This 'paragon of the bar,' " I said, my voice dripping with sarcasm, conjured up a cockeyed story to drag Ratterman in the muck and discredit him. Instead, he discredited himself. He told Hirschfeld not to throw out the case, "he'd think of something." What he thought up was the story of the circus we've heard at this trial. Believe him, or believe Granny Hay and her family. You cannot believe them both. Believe Tito, or the doctors we relied on, I implored.

Next, I tried to deal with the defense lawyers' blatant chauvinism. Whether it is a Tennessee or a Texas jury, or any normal twelve people in their right minds, I argued, the preposterous defense story is not believable. Only twisted minds would believe Ratterman concocted this event for the publicity. What kind of good publicity was his arrest and all the snide shots he had to take as a result of it? Their summation, I pleaded, should have started, "Once upon a time," it was so much a fiction.

Each of the five defense lawyers had bombarded the jury with anti-Washington, anti-Kennedy, and anti-Goldfarb pitches: "You all remember when you get into that jury room," one lawyer railed, "that you are good Christians and we don't need Bobby Kennedy to send Mr. Goldfarb here to come down here from 'Worshington' to tell us how to do things." For my summation, I wanted a good story that members of the jury could relate to and that would dispel the undercurrent of xenophobia the defense lawyers had tried to create. On one of my trips back to Washington, I had asked Paul Porter, a native Kentuckian, celebrated lawyer, and renowned storyteller, for a yarn that would work. "Ronald," he said, "I have the perfect story for you."

The defendants have three problems with our case, I told the jury, setting the stage for Porter's fable. They say that April is not believable, that Paisley was the bait that trapped Ratterman, and that Ratterman was staging a publicity stunt. Well, recall the story of the sparrow and the fox (I think I said "sparra bird," sliding into a bad Kentucky accent): "A farmer walking across a field saw what looked like a dead bird lying on the ground. He noticed the bird stir, showing a sign of life. Wishing to be helpful, he placed the bird in a pile of manure, packing it around the bird, leaving its head free, hoping the heat and chemicals would be resuscitative. It worked; and in a little while, the bird moved its head and began to sing. Across the field, a fox—who would never have seen the bird but who heard the singing—followed the sounds, found the helpless bird, and gobbled it up."

I told the story with as much of a local twang as I could master. The jury seemed intent. Then I used my—Porter's—punch line. "There are three morals to the story. The first moral is, *it's not always your enemies who get you into it* [Yes, Ratterman's friend had gotten him into trouble]; the second is, *it's not always your friends who get you out of it* [April Flowers had saved him]; and the third is, *when you're up to your neck in manure, you ought to keep your mouth shut* (being busted with a stripper in a gambling joint was not the best material for a reformer's publicity campaign]."

The jury had a good laugh; two jurors actually slapped their legs; and the courtroom rippled with laughter.

I thought I had them so I kept hammering back at the defense lawyers' arguments. "These fellows say Bob Kennedy has made a big deal out of this case. If he had, would he have sent a young fellow like me—not yet thirty years old—to go up against these famous veteran trial lawyers?" I inquired self-deprecatingly.

I dwelled on the veracity of April. If she perjured herself at the local trial (the defense lawyers all had labeled her a perjurer), she *must* be telling the truth now. And the defendants must have perjured themselves, then as now, because they told the same perjurious story. As Paisley had been the friend who got Ratterman into trouble, it was this unlikely former enemy who was now getting him out of it—like the fox and the sparrow, I smiled. I wish I could bring in Eleanor Roosevelt to testify in this case, I told the jury, but it is not likely in criminal cases that we get virtuous people to testify. But all the believable evidence in this case combined to give credence to April's testimony, and she should be believed. Ratterman must be believed, too, or these conspirators will have accomplished just what they set out to do—discredit a good man. "Somebody hits you in the arm, you can come in and show the bruise. Somebody tears your clothes, you can show the rip. But if somebody destroys your reputation, what do you do about it? It follows you for years, just like this has followed Mr. Ratterman for years."

I went back to Granny Hay one last time and read the jury something she had sent me in a letter: "I shall pass this way but once. Any good thing, therefore, that I can do or any kindness that I can show, let me do it now. Let me not defer it or neglect it for I shall not pass this way again." I asked them to line up with her and Henry Cook, and the decent doctors who testified, along with April and Ratterman.

Then, with a rhetorical rush of purple prose, I concluded: "From the time this arrest of Ratterman took place, a Pandora's box of slimy insinuations, accusations, lies, nastiness, attacks at good people's reputations, have been dragged in front of the public. That includes Chris Seifried, Granny Hay, George Ratterman, and it includes all these people who you heard attacked in the course of this trial. All I want you to do in this case is, for the first time in two years, will you shut this Pandora's box of slime once and for all and judge these six defendants—because it has been open for two years and it is contaminating and you can shut that box like no one else could in the world—with one word, guilty."

I sat down, totally spent, empty, finally done with this case. It had preoccupied three years of my life. I'd done what I could do. The final words and acts would not be mine.

I listened in admiration to Swinford's instructions to the jurors. This was "the most important part of this case . . . your decision." Remembering the frustration of our last trial, he lectured them that it was no compliment to juries that "hang," that it was their duty as good citizens not to be stubborn, that all comes to "nothing if the case cannot be concluded." He could only urge them to do so, he could not require it. "I couldn't if I would and I wouldn't if I could," he stated. But "some jury some day is going to have to decide it," and the buck must stop here.

Swinford was a wonderful storyteller. He told them about the instruction Andrew Jackson gave juries when he was a district court judge in Tennessee: "Go out and do right between these people." Then he eased into his own—more detailed—instructions, based on established law but presented in a commonsensical style he had honed through the years. "I don't care the snap of my finger," he told them, "who wins this case," recording his impartiality a bit more than I'd have wished. They would have nothing to do with the sentencing, he explained; they only had to decide the facts. They should do that by thinking as they do in determining the ordinary affairs of their lives.

On proving a conspiracy: "Science has not reached the place where you can open a man's head and look into it" to see his intentions. He told them conspiracies need not be proved by showing the parties sitting around a table drawing up an agreement. Things in real life do not work that way. They should presume that people intend the natural consequences of their deliberate acts.

Don't get hung up in the jury room on inconsequential questions, he told them, and he made his point with another story. He recalled a slander case he'd tried in Kentucky years ago. One of the lawyers told the jury that in Shakespeare's words, "Who steals my purse steals trash . . . but he who filches from me my good name robs me of that which not enriches him and makes me poor, indeed." His opponent argued that he knew as little about Shakespeare as he did about his case—it was really Jesus Christ who said that. Later, when the jury seemed endlessly hung, the judge called them back and asked if they needed help. "We're hopelessly hung," the foreman reported, "half say Shakespeare and half of them say Christ." Everyone in the courtroom laughed, and I hoped our jury got his point.

He summarized our theory of the case, a plan to discredit the reformers by people with a stake in local vice and crime. "This plan was conceived primarily in the mind of the defendant, a shrewd and capable and experienced lawyer, who was the friend and counselor of the night life," he told them, and thus Lester "was the force behind the planning of the execution of this crime." Subin kicked me under the table when Swinford told the jurors that if a defendant joined the conspiracy after it was formed, knowing its existence and purpose, he was just as guilty as the one who originated it: That would surely cover Quitter and White, we both thought.

Ciafardini, a policeman who hung around at the Glenn and did nothing to enforce the laws there, "was at the right place at the right time" when the picture-taking scheme fell through. The three police officers falsely arrested a comatose Ratterman, then perjured themselves at the local trial. Swinford obviously understood our case; if only the jury would.

When he was done, Swinford released the two alternate jurors. "You have had all the fun of trying the case without the responsibility of deciding it," he told them, thanking both for their service. He told the remaining twelve jurors how to write their verdict, and ended with one final instruction: "Stay in good humor." Then we recessed for the night and three U.S. marshals took the jurors to the hotel.

That night, we weary prosecutors treated ourselves to a good dinner in Cincinnati and took our first night off in over a month. We went to a movie after dinner to try to divert our minds from our concerns about the verdict. No sooner did we sit down in the dark theater than Subin grabbed my arm and in a hushed but alarmed voice said: "Let's get out of here!" I didn't know what was happening, but instantly he and Joe Corey each lifted me by an arm and guided me down the aisle into the lobby.

"What the hell is going on?"

"Three jurors just came in and sat down beside us; that's all," Subin reported. We had a panicky laugh, and moved to another part of the theater. It was going to be a long weekend.

Monday was an endless day as we sat, paced, drank coffee, closed files, called Washington to keep our bosses advised. By Tuesday, we were starting to worry. To deflect our growing depression, we waited at the motel, where we could pack and be comfortable. We ordered pizzas and we set them on top of the lampshades to keep them warm. Someone brought beer that we kept cool in the cold water in the tank behind the toilet. Someone had cards and we started a nickel-dime poker game. The room filled up with smoke from the agents' cheap cigars. As I looked around the room at this sordid scene—FBI and IRS agents with their weapons strapped on, sitting around gambling with prosecutors who had tried the biggest excise tax evasion trial in history—I had to laugh. "Could you imagine the Newport police barging in on us now," I asked, "What would we say?" One agent had the answer. "I'd tell them we are having a training session!"

After a while, I couldn't stand the suspense one minute more. "Let's go see Judge Swinford and ask him to give the Allen charge," I said, and we all filed out of the motel and drove to the federal courthouse in Covington. We had prepared the standard instruction a judge may give to a jury that is showing signs of being hung. It pushes them gingerly, without infringing on their independence, to make a decision.

Judges do not have to give the Allen charge, though its wording has been approved by appellate courts and many judges use it in situations like this. Judge Swinford would not. He knew his jurors, he told us in his chambers where we met with him and the defense lawyers, who predictably opposed pushing the jury. If they didn't get an acquittal, they hoped it would be deadlocked.

"Have patience, Ronald," Swinford admonished in his typical kindly fashion. "I know these folks and they won't be pushed, but they'll make their decision in their own fashion and in their own good time," he predicted. Then he told a country story I've often repeated about the wisdom of the average citizen sitting as a juror. Seems a traveling judge in a rural area of Kentucky had finished all the work he had to complete before moving on, except one small civil case for breach of contract. There were no more jurors around to hear the case, however. So the judge asked the parties if they'd agree to let him round up some lawyers from around the courthouse to sit on this one jury. They agreed. The clerk gathered some local lawyers who were working in the building. The case was tried quickly, the judge instructed the jury, and they retired to decide the case. After five hours of deliberations, it was getting late and everyone else had gone home; the judge summoned the jurors.

They filed into the courtroom in a semicircle in front of the bench. The judge asked: "Are you getting close to a verdict? We've been waiting five hours. The whole case took only one hour to try. All that's involved is a few-hundred-dollars claim. Without pushing you, I just want to know if you are almost ready to report." Whereupon one of the jurors stepped forward and said, "Your Honor, we're not done with the nominating speeches for foreman yet."

We all had a good laugh and retired to the hallways for more pacing and praying. Swinford had been around a long time and had faith in the jury system. Most of the time it worked well.

Eventually, three days after they first retired, the jury sent word they were ready to report. Notice was sent to all the defendants and lawyers. The courtroom was abuzz. Reporters rushed to their tables, looking at their watches to calculate the time they had before their deadlines. The jurors filed in, eyes straight ahead, sober countenances telling nothing about their decision that I could divine.

When everyone was seated, the courtroom was eerily quiet. As

Judge Swinford asked if they'd reached their verdict, he admonished, "I want no demonstrations," and warned that any disruption would be treated as a contempt subject to disciplinary action. The tension was palpable. "Read the verdict," Swinford ordered the marshal.

"We, the jury, hereby find Charles E. Lester and Edward Anthony Buccieri guilty under Count One of the indictment and innocent under Count Two," she reported. "We find Tito Carinci, Patrick Ciafardini, Joseph Quitter, and Upshire White not guilty on all counts." The jurors were polled; the verdict was indeed unanimous. My face was flushed, my heart was pounding, my mind was racing with conflicting emotional charges: relief and a sense of accomplishment for the guilty verdicts and disappointment and bemusement about the incomprehensible acquittals.

Swinford immediately released the four defendants who had been acquitted and called Lester and Buccieri to the bench. Walker moved that the two should be acquitted "on the grounds that no police officer has been found guilty, and therefore there could be no acting under color of law, and therefore could be no violation by private citizens."

Judge Swinford ruled immediately that "these two defendants can be found guilty under this conspiracy charge, even though they may not have been officers and may not have actually made the arrest. The charge here is a conspiracy and therefore each conspirator to the offense may be found guilty, irrespective of a finding as to the other alleged conspirators . . . it is possible for a person to conspire to have someone arrested under color of law and yet the actual officers making the arrest may not even know of the conspiracy. So I think there is no question but what the verdict is correct and it is sustained by the evidence." The two convicted defendants were ordered into the custody of the marshals until bail was made, and everyone else was dismissed.

Swinford had presentence reports and was ready to pronounce his sentence. The government made no recommendation about what it should be; that was the department's practice, though Swinford must have known we wanted the maximum. Buccieri had nothing to say. Walker spoke on Lester's behalf, asking the court to "deal mercifully with him."

Swinford: "I believe the verdict is supported by the evidence . . . I feel it is a very serious offense. Of course, we do have a situation of an attorney-at-law, which in my judgment makes it even more significant, with knowledge of the full import of these acts. It's a serious thing to cause a person to be arrested, an offense against him, against his family, and against society . . . It will be the judgment of the Court that each of them be sentenced to twelve months in prison."

The judge had given them the maximum sentence. I felt relief. I would not go home empty-handed. My pushing to prosecute a second time could not be viewed as youthful overzealousness or egotistical indulgence. The government's money had not been wasted. We did get our kingpin; everyone had viewed Charlie Lester to be the biggest catch in our case.

But I was shocked at the acquittals, especially of Carinci and Ciafardini. How could the jury have let those people off? How could I have batted .333 when I expected to go at least 2 for 3? I was outraged that people I viewed as scoundrels, whose defenses had been feeble, could have gotten off!

With some distance and detachment from the trial, it became clear the government had won the case, however many defendants escaped conviction. If we could have gotten one defendant of them all, no doubt we would have chosen Lester. More important, Newport was now a different place. That was the real goal, and it was clear we had achieved it.

Hundley and my colleagues at home were delighted. Kennedy called me at the courthouse immediately to say congratulations and to invite me to come tell him all about it when I returned to Washington. The press coverage was prominent and positive.

Not everyone applauded our success. The weekly booster magazine left free at every hotel bedstand, *This Week in Cincinnati*, had an editorial urging my swift return to Washington so the area could recover its reputation as the Queen City of the Midwest and lose its image as the outskirts of Gomorrah.

But one touching encounter left me with a sweet recollection of the good people of Newport. As I walked down the street one day after the trial, an elderly lady stopped me. "I know who you are," she said. "You're that prosecutor of the Ratterman case, Mr. Goldfarb, aren't you? I read about you every day in the papers and see you on the nightly news." "Yes, I am, ma'am," I replied, wondering what was coming next. "Well, I want you to know, Mr. Goldfarb, that I've lived in Campbell County for seventy-five years and we good people here go to bed each night thanking God for sending us a good Christian boy like you to clean things up."

—

Exhausted by an ordeal that had lasted almost three years, disappointed about losing some of the defendants, suffering the inevitable letdown one sustains when any major effort ends and the congratulations are over, dumped from the front pages and TV leads of the local media to the relative quiet and invisibility of the halls of the Justice Department, I returned to Washington. Then I questioned exactly what we had accomplished.

Hundley and Petersen noticed my pensive mood and promised they'd find me an interesting case to arouse my creative juices and engage my professional energies. "You've got no reason to sulk," they told me during one pep talk in Hundley's office. "What you accomplished is the classic example of what we set out to do, and the attorney general will now use the Newport experience in his speeches as proof of the validity of our program."

"Come on, you guys sound like my parents," I sighed. "We spent years and a fortune to move a mountain, and what do I come home with? Two misdemeanor convictions, out of six."

"You're missing the major points," Petersen chimed in. Henry was not in my personal clique, but he was an unromantic professional prosecutor whose views on these matters I respected. "Bob Kennedy told Congress early in '61 that Newport was a prime example of the problem he wanted to deal with. Now, Newport is closed down. We can turn over law enforcement to a local sheriff who's committed to do his job. You've put in prison a bunch of bad boys, crooked lawyers, hustlers, and closed the biggest gambling setup in the area. The citizenry is coming out of the woodwork and taking back their city. The federal law enforcement establishment there is working together for the first time. And you're crying over a spilt defendant? Come on, this is a rare case where we can walk away and feel the job is done."

Hundley showed me a letter Frank Staab had sent to Robert Kennedy, who had sent it to our office to be put in my personnel file.

Coming from one I had so admired, it touched me very personally. Staab had explained to Kennedy the importance of Lester's conviction, describing him as "the nucleus of the cancer which has existed in northern Kentucky for many years." He had ruthlessly used his skills to protect the criminal element and to destroy those who dared to take a stand against vice and corruption, Staab reported. He was feared by other lawyers, by public officials, and by the police, Staab added. In thanking the attorney general for the privilege of being part of the team that broke "the stranglehold of the forces of corruption in Newport," Staab had very kind and touching words about me.

"Stop feeling sorry for yourself and give the appeals group some help. And take a look at this case." Petersen handed me a huge file and asked for my opinion whether we had any case to bring. It was potentially a big case involving a major Mafia figure in Philadelphia. I left his office placated.

———

Certainly, I did not want the two fish we did catch in this case to slip away. From the moment we heard the jury's odd decision, we realized the potential reversible error we had taken such pains to avoid in preparing for the trial had been provided inadvertently by the jury. There could be little doubt the convicted defendants would appeal, claiming inconsistent verdicts. Since the jury had not convicted the three police officers, how could there be a conviction under the Civil Rights Act against the two it did convict? Lester and Buccieri could not act "under color of law"; only the policemen could, and the jury unaccountably acquitted them! There would be another chapter to our long saga, and the conclusion was not clear.

Not only did the attorneys in the Organized Crime and Racketeering Section usurp the investigations and trial work of the U.S. attorneys around the country; we also handled our appeals. Traditionally, lawyers in the appellate section of the Department of Justice and in the U.S. attorney's offices around the country wrote briefs and argued appeals in the Courts of Appeals. We held on to our cases, including their appeals. So, on returning to Washington, after all the congratulations, we turned our attention to the imminent appeal.

The key issue at all criminal trials is one of fact: Did the defendant do the act charged? On appeal, the facts are presumed from the trial record and can no longer be questioned, and the only issue before the appellate court is one of law; and that legal question may never have arisen at the trial. While sometimes the issue on appeal is whether the trial judge erred in deciding a particular question at the trial, and thus is a replay of the same legal question that was raised at the trial, this was not the case in our appeal. Often, as here, a legal question is raised in an appeal that was not—could not have been—raised at the trial.

For someone who is not trained in the theories and rationales of the law, some of its postures and procedures must seem strange, even illogical. Even for someone who is trained in the law—by this time I had three law degrees—the workings of jurisprudence can be baffling. It seems perverse to switch gears after a trial and adopt a different view of one's case in order to adapt to the exigencies on appeal, especially when that view differs from the government's view at the trial. But we had to proceed on appeal as if Carinci, Quitter, White, and Ciafardini were innocent. Unless we did, however at war this was with our view of the case, we faced the bootstrapping argument that the two convicted defendants couldn't have committed the crime without the acquitted three policemen, and thus should be released.

The government had to come up with a theory on appeal that was consistent with the jury's verdict, even if it was inconsistent with our view at the trial, or lose the two defendants we did convict. As a result, our theory on appeal shifted: Now the government must urge that Lester and Buccieri deprived Ratterman of his civil rights "by causing the police, as their innocent dupes, to make an unwarranted arrest" knowing that it would "lead in turn to a sham prosecution."

Left with the jury's weird verdict, we carved out an ingenious conspiracy: "Lester and Buccieri conspired to cause the police to arrest Ratterman on false information, and to cause his false prosecution." We listed every act by Lester and Buccieri to demonstrate the strained conclusion "that the two convicted defendants conspired to use state power, from the arrest through the trial, with the basest of motives and with the intent to deprive George Ratterman of his basic constitutional right." The two convicted civilians—Lester and Buccieri—acted willfully in causing harmful acts, and the three acquitted policeman had the legal capacity to act under color of law.

Combine the willfulness of one group with the capacity of the other, and together the statutory requirements are met.

We argued that one can aid and abet in the commission of an offense one is incapable of committing oneself by causing another person capable of committing the offense to do so. Thus, by the magic of the appeals process, our three once-crooked cops became innocent conduits, deceived by Lester and Buccieri's scheme into misusing their police powers.

A not-guilty verdict does not mean a defendant was deemed to be innocent, only that the jury decided there was inadequate proof of his guilt. It was in this never-never land that the government pursued developing its after-the-trial theory.

We hoped that the Sixth Court of Appeals might be swayed because the facts of the conspiracy were so strong that there might be a subconscious undertow toward upholding the convictions to assure that everyone involved in this crime would not go free. It would take psychiatrists, more so than lawyers, to ever prove that judges, like juries, may wittingly or unwittingly nullify the pure law in a case to arrive at a "just" decision. The department's brief would play that card emphatically.

The defendants' briefs were long-winded, but their point was impressively argued: We had revamped the theory of our prosecution. It is legally impossible to conspire to violate this section of the Civil Rights Law without a co-conspirator actually violating it. An accessory can only be found guilty if the principal is guilty. Since the three policemen were acquitted, an S.242 violation could not be committed because there was no "state" action; and that being so, the crime couldn't be conspired about or abetted, either.

"Upon this record, whom did appellants aid or abet or counsel or procure or cause to commit an offense against the United States? The jury said: 'No one.' Put another way: If the police officers did not conspire with petitioners, how could petitioners conspire with the police officers?"

By the time the briefs were filed and the case was ready to be argued, I had left the Department of Justice and was in private practice. Subin argued the case before the Court of Appeals in Cincinnati with a tremulous feeling in the pit of his stomach. One of the judges had asked Subin during his argument, "That wasn't your theory at trial, counselor, was it?"

The court issued its decision on July 8, 1966, almost two years after I'd left the Department of Justice. A majority of the three-man panel upheld the convictions of Lester and Buccieri. "Appellants were fairly tried and fairly convicted," they concluded, adding that "one reading the record before us might find it difficult, perhaps even impossible, to comprehend how the jury could have acquitted all the police officers of the conspiracy offense." They agreed with the government that "the evidence was ample to sustain a conviction of all defendants on both counts."

The court followed a venerable rule that even though "a defendant may be incompetent to commit an offense as principal by reason of not being of a particular age, sex, condition, or class, he may be punished as procurer or abettor." A conspiracy is merely an agreement to commit an illegal act; the agreement itself is the crime. Thus, one can be guilty of conspiring regardless of the unsuccessful completion of the crime planned.

One judge (a senior trial judge, not a regular member of the Court of Appeals) dissented. To convict only one conspirator while exonerating all the others allegedly conspired with is improper, he argued; "essential facts" would be missing in that situation. Even the lone dissenter stated "there was abundant evidence from which the jury could find that they wickedly conspired to disgrace Ratterman; that Lester, as a lawyer, suborned perjury; and that both, by malicious artifice, led the officers to arrest the innocent Ratterman." But this would amount to violations of state laws, he concluded, not the federal Civil Rights Act. He concluded that "our vaunted legal system" demanded that the convicted twosome should be acquitted and discharged.

However strained our appellate view of the case, I was satisfied we did the right thing by preserving this conviction and preventing the compounding of the jury's mistaken verdict. In fact, this case has been cited for decades as the legal authority for the crime of "causing an innocent agent" to violate the law. Pragmatics had been the parents of creative jurisprudence, although such a result was never our intent.

Buccieri decided to forgo the costs of further appeals and went off to serve his sentence. Lester had more at stake, including disbarment and public disgrace, so he appealed further: first, to the Court of

Appeals for a rehearing before the full nine-member court, a procedure reserved for unusual cases (it was denied immediately), and then to the United States Supreme Court.

Buccieri probably felt that serving a year (less with the reduction for good time) for a misdemeanor was part of the risk of his work. He'd "do the time" as a badge of honor and presumably be rewarded by those he represented when he was released. For some people, serving a prison sentence under certain circumstances is not as horribly unthinkable as it would be for others. But that was not the situation with Lester.

Most cases appealed to the Supreme Court never get there. At that time, about one in twenty petitions to the Supreme Court were granted. To winnow its caseload to a manageable number, the Supreme Court takes only those cases raising issues of national import, those making important precedents, and those where lower appellate courts are divided in treating a recurring question and uniformity is needed.

It takes four votes of the nine justices for the Supreme Court to take a case (or, as they say, to grant *certiorari*). That does not mean that the four voting to hear and decide the case have indicated which way they will rule. It only means that four members want the Court to decide that case.

Lester did not find four justices interested in hearing his appeal. On June 9, 1967, his petition to the Supreme Court was denied. A later Petition for Rehearing was also denied. Lester told the press at the time that "If I were someone else . . . they would have granted our writ . . . We were tried in the newspapers."

———

At last, the case was over. Bill Lynch, by then a senior attorney in the Criminal Division, called me in my office in Washington to let me know.

Buccieri served his sentence and was released on parole before the Supreme Court delivered its opinion. Charles Lester served his sentence and was later disbarred.

In 1965, Tito Carinci was convicted of income tax evasion and sentenced to a term in prison. The three policemen finished their careers on the Newport police department during Ratterman's tenure as sheriff. After completing his term as sheriff, Ratterman and his family moved to Colorado, where he became an investment counselor. Bill Lynch spent his career in the Justice Department, becoming chief of the organized crime section. Harry Subin left the department and teaches criminal law at New York University Law School. Joe Corey died several years later.

In many ways the Ratterman case was over long before 1966. As I had come to realize, Newport had changed in ways we, and the good citizens of Newport, Kentucky, wanted.

Chapter 10

A Meeting in Kennedy's Office

The organized crime section met on the morning of November 22, 1963, in the attorney general's office. It was a bigger group than usual and included some guests. For several hours, we reported the status of investigations, described new indictments and recent convictions, and responded to Kennedy's occasional inquiries.

Most of these battles were never won finally or permanently, of course. But, state by state, Robert Kennedy's goal was being approached. Federal law enforcement agencies were coordinating their efforts to deal effectively with organized crime cases. Our (Wyn's) intelligence unit was growing more sophisticated. Our group of special prosecutors occupied a prominent place in the national law enforcement world. We were all very busy investigating, preparing, and trying cases. Helpful laws had been passed. More funds were being allocated to our work. Valachi's testimony on national television had given wide exposure to the systematic and dangerous workings of the Mafia. A cycle was being played out. We were raising hell with the forces of evil from the hellish subculture of crime.

As we listened or reported, and I sipped my coffee, the roomful of lawyers exuded confidence and excitement. We had a wonderful sense, quite wrong of course, that we were part of an invincible force. It was heady.

But we were wreaking havoc, more than we could possibly have realized at the time. Our leader at Justice, Robert Kennedy, was emerging as a national figure himself, no longer merely the brother-of. Every reasonable presumption was that we would continue our work indefinitely, certainly into President Kennedy's next term. The future was unlimited.

Any questions of personal risk were uniformly discounted. Our villains killed each other and would do anything to beat their prosecution, but they would not dare harm a federal prosecutor, especially a special assistant to Robert Kennedy, the myth promised. The bigshot criminals we were pursuing would be afraid of incurring the awful wrath of the federal government if that happened.

Henry Petersen opened this meeting with an impressive statistical summary of our group's activities since we began. Raw data lacks feel and flavor, but it shows direction and defines activity.

"Bob, I hope you'll be impressed with some of the facts I've pulled together. Our special intelligence unit—Wyn Hayes's baby"—Henry smiled in the direction of Wyn—"has coordinated data from twenty-six intelligence agencies bearing on over three thousand major rackets figures. The number of lawyers in our section has tripled since you arrived—we're over fifty now, we should be around sixty next year. And they're not shuffling papers in Washington; the increases in the days our lawyers have spent in the field, in grand juries, and in court on our cases have risen dramatically. So have organized crime indictments and convictions. We've got permanent field units in four cities: New York, Chicago, Miami, and Los Angeles. You've visited a few of them. And we've set up temporary special units in a number of other cities, Las Vegas for one. After eighteen months of overseeing them, we're authorizing the U.S. attorneys to file cases under the new statutes. They're required to get our approval only in exceptional cases or where official corruption is involved.

"Speaking of that, recent official corruption cases have snagged three state supreme court judges, five mayors, two police chiefs, three sheriffs, and a ream of state legislators, district attorneys, vice squad officials, and others."

Henry went on with his survey. "The IRS Intelligence Division pulled together information about wagering tax investigations it has conducted since you took over, and the numbers are impressive. The action is up. The number of investigations rose from 580 in 1960, to

890 in '61, to 1,133 last year, to 1,245 this year. Convictions jumped from 385 in '60 to 503 to 568 to 645. And the value of property seized in these gambling raids went from about a quarter of a million dollars in 1960 to two-thirds of a million this year."

Petersen continued, "Our program is more than paying its own way, across the board, Bob."

"What do you mean?"

"Well, Mortimer Caplin prepared some IRS economic studies for us, and his findings are very interesting. His figures show our program more than pays its costs through its revenue-producing features—fines, penalties, and confiscations of property. That's not the reason for doing all this, of course, but it's interesting that our work is not costing the taxpayers anything."

Grinning, Kennedy mused: "Mort once told me that virtue is its own reward . . ."

Walter Sheridan's staff had come to the meeting with a large chart and larger smiles. We learned why. Sensitive to claims that we had spent an inordinate amount of resources "getting Hoffa," our colleagues had prepared for the attorney general a list of prosecutions of Teamsters officials and associates since we started our efforts in 1961. The list they unfurled was imposing.

Since early 1961, in addition to other major convictions of crooked national labor leaders such as bakers' union chief Cross in Washington, D.C., and UAW union boss Gosser in Toledo, which other lawyers had reported, the Teamsters convictions racked up as a result of our group's efforts made a list that ran on for pages. Interstate theft by Felix "Milwaukee Phil" Alderisio; labor management conspiracy in Philadelphia by Morris Abrams; embezzlement by a business agent in Charlotte, North Carolina; Taft-Hartley violations by another agent in Los Angeles; obstruction of justice by a local president in New York City; probation violation of a Hoffa associate; embezzlement by a local union official in Kansas City; perjury and grand larceny in Hoboken, New Jersey; tax law violations by a Teamsters attorney in Detroit; mail and wire fraud by a New York City Teamsters accountant; their list went on and on. In Puerto Rico; Miami; Louisville, Kentucky; Chicago; Pontiac, Michigan; San Francisco; Nashville; Newark; Detroit; and Syracuse, Teamsters officials, lawyers, and business agents had been caught, tried, and convicted for violations of the Taft-Hartley Act and labor management laws, for obstructions of justice, conspiracies, perjuries, frauds. Sheridan's team's list was a rogues' gallery of Teamster misdeeds.

All over the country and all the way up the union leadership ladder to Hoffa himself, our people had exposed the extensive illegality and corruption of the top echelons of the union. After three years of defending ourselves from claims of carrying on a brutal and unfair vendetta, the facts made it clear that Kennedy's claims about the union's vulnerability to honest investigation were sound. Our demonstration of Hoffa's consistent and cavalier meddling with juries and the trial system explained his earlier ability to avoid convictions. His onslaught of political and media pressures showed that only an equal effort could have disclosed and ended his broadscale criminality. Two trials of Hoffa himself were scheduled for next year: the first in January 1964 in Chattanooga, Tennessee, and the second the following April in Chicago, Illinois. We were ready for our face-off with Hoffa himself.

Wyn Hayes went next: She had compiled interesting data on our gambling cases. A combination of exciting IRS raids and increasing use of our new interstate gambling and travel laws had led to a veritable revolution around the country. And since gambling profits were a large part of organized crime's bankroll, our efforts had to be making an impact.

"General," Wyn reported, "arrests, trials, and convictions for failing to register and tax evasion are happening all over the country. We're hitting operations in hotels, bars, casinos, social clubs, barber shops, fashionable apartments, even a Democratic Club." Titters around the room at that last. "One day alone, March 7 this year, General, the IRS ran raids in 158 locations in 59 cities in 20 states. They rounded up and arrested 127 people, seized $43,867, 44 machines and 12 automobiles.

"And big money is involved—millions, wherever we've gone. A $100,000-a-day gambling operation in one Seventh Avenue hotel in New York City, a $250,000-a-day operation in Miami, a $2-million-a-year setup in Lansing, a $2-and-a-half-million-a-year horse-book operation in Atlantic City, a $3-million-a-year operation in Chicago; in numbers alone, $4.5 million a year in Detroit and $2 million a year in Indianapolis. In the Catskills, a $13.5-million-a-year bookmaking operation. It's big money wherever we've gone: Terre Haute, Indiana; Reading and Pittsburgh, Pennsylvania; Wheeling, West Virginia; Miami, Florida; Louisville, Kentucky; New York City; Providence, Rhode Island; Detroit; Indianapolis; Los Angeles; Las Vegas—"

A kibitzing voice interrupted. "You sound like a railroad conductor, Wyn." We all laughed; Wyn talked fast, was excited by her report, and did sound like she was about to call out, "All aboard!"

"We're catching citywide and regional interstate numbers operations, dice games, *bolita,* horse races, casinos, lotteries, bookmaking, slot and pinball machines, monte. They're usually traveling interstate, from Illinois to Tennessee and from Tennessee to Arkansas, from Connecticut to Richmond, Virginia; Portland, Maine, to Boston; from Tuxedo, Maryland, to McLean, Virginia [laughs around the room, as this is Kennedy's home]; West Virginia to Pennsylvania and Ohio; even from Harrisburg, Pennsylvania, to New York City to Haiti."

"We're getting convictions in most of these cases, Bob," Henry added to Wyn's comments. "And the locals in some places are wanting to join us. In Washington, eighty-two thousand signatures petitioning against a legalizing gambling law were stolen from a safe *in the state house.* We're letting the state handle it, but the FBI and U.S. attorney are staying in touch."

"We're picking up rumors that one gambling operation is moving to Europe; another group is planning to build a plush casino in Elliot Key, Florida, on a man-made reef four miles out. Jimmy 'the Greek' Snyder closed down his Las Vegas operation altogether," Wyn added.

Kennedy smiled, peering over hands clasped cathedral-like before his face, his feet up, shirt sleeves rolled high; he was clearly pleased with the results he was hearing about.

"How about payoffs?" Kennedy asked.

"Most cases, there are kickbacks," Henry answered. "We're arresting cops on the scene at some of the raids. Where we can, we're including conspiracy, bribery, and tax evasion counts to bring in police, district attorneys, city officials, legislators on the take."

"Another thing," Wyn added. "We're also showing that not only are these operations illegal, as we knew, but sometimes they're crooked, as well. We've raided and arrested the nation's leading peddler of crooked gambling devices in Chicago. Four women on his premises were marking the backs of playing cards with a chemical only visible through special glasses. In White Sulphur Springs, our agents discovered that the dice table confiscated at a raid was rigged. Lynch and Goldfarb discovered the Cincinnati numbers operation run by Screw Andrews was fixed. With past-posting, racing results are rigged. You can't trust anybody!"

Smiles around the room. Henry Petersen reported that John Diuguid was in New Orleans awaiting the jury's verdict in the latest Marcello case. John thought the evidence had gone in strong; our lawyers there were anxious but optimistic. John was going to call and report as soon as he knew the verdict—perhaps while we were meeting this morning. Angie Novello—Kennedy's secretary—would interrupt if John's call came during our meeting. Marcello would be another big timber to fall as a result of our program, and there was special departmental interest in this very legitimate case, even if it was the result of our earlier gross procedures in deporting Marcello. (The call came later; Marcello was acquitted. Another jury-fixing case soon followed.)

We were even getting into international diplomacy in the course of several investigations, and here Kennedy would be sensitive to non–Justice Department considerations, as occasionally he was called upon to intervene with appropriate officials elsewhere in the government. We'd contacted the Department of the Army and all military commands in Europe and the Far East to bar a company from placing its gaming devices in service club installations, and to assist in our investigations of bribes to military club managers.

Our ambassador to Panama was working with us to snag a Panamanian United Nations official who was acting as a courier and transferring New York and Las Vegas gambling funds to secret, numbered foreign bank accounts, while maintaining cordial relations with the Panamanian government. At the same time that two of our lawyers were meeting in Monaco to negotiate a deal with the Panamanian to testify about one major transaction involving New Yorkers we were investigating, others were attempting to persuade the Swiss banker who had a controlling interest in the Panamanian bank to permit an exception to the banking secrecy laws and allow disclosure of the real parties in interest in the accounts in question.

Our ambassador to Rome was working with the Italian government to allow us to quietly deport Paul "the Waiter" Ricca (alias Felice de Lucia) to Italy, whose government finally agreed to accept him if ours would do it quietly (no press announcements) when the Italian parliament had adjourned. We'd worked with the INS on this case. Kennedy told us that eventually he had to write the Secretary of State to emphasize our "special interest." Our big narcotics case that started in Laredo, Texas, already had involved us in complicated fugitive and bail negotiations with the Royal Canadian Mounted Police, crown prosecutor, and minister of justice. These cases posed tricky problems of diplomacy, immunity, and international political trade-offs, which were over our heads, but not Robert Kennedy's. He was invariably helpful to us, and effective in making the necessary entreaties to enable our work to not be compromised.

Between the FBI's extensive electronic surveillance of major racket figures and Joe Valachi's disclosures about the inner workings of the mob, the Mafia was besieged like Dracula dragged suddenly into the light of day. The federal government was building a massive skimming case in Las Vegas. The big bankruptcy fraud case in Detroit was set for trial. (There would be convictions the next year in that case and in the New York bankruptcy fraud case we brought.) An IRS report disclosed ninety-three tax convictions. An interstate prostitution ring in Georgia had been busted and the proprietors sentenced to prison terms, another big one in the Pittsburgh area had been closed, and charges were pending involving the biggest prostitution ring in Reno. We'd indicted major East Coast loan sharks, West Coast counterfeiters, extortion artists, and Las Vegas money launderers. Everyone everywhere knew the pressure was on.

Syndicate bigwigs were fighting among themselves, when they were not fighting our inquiries and trials; their political connections were becoming shy. An FBI tape in May 1962 had turned up a remark to New York syndicate member Sal Profaci from his cohort Michelino Clemente: "Bob Kennedy won't stop today until he puts us all in jail all over the country. Until the commission meets and puts its foot down, things will be at a standstill." We never dreamed what awesome acts that remark would foreshadow.

Herb Bates reported next. Bates, sitting in front of the group close to Kennedy's desk, presented a long report—complete with a large chart listing his local scorecard—on his continuing investigations in

Detroit. The biggest numbers operation had been closed down, the investigating agencies, originally competitive with each other and combative toward us, were cooperating, and the heat was being felt. Herb told of one gambler who asked him how long our efforts would continue; he was planning to get out of the rackets and even out of town.

"It's the constant pressure that's making the difference, General," Herb concluded. "They've never seen anything like it." Herb told Kennedy of a recent comment by the chairman of the Mafia board in Detroit, Joe Zerilli, that "the mob should play things legitimately until the heat is off, then we'll get back in."

"When is that going to be?" Kennedy asked.

"I guess when you and the president are out of office," Bates speculated, unaware then of the eerily prophetic nature of his intended light remark.

The conversation moved from Detroit to Las Vegas. One of our investigations had unearthed an interesting discovery. A big-time New York gambler had explained to one of our colleagues working in New York, how the gambling casinos avoided records of their winnings. Gamblers travel to Las Vegas and gamble on credit. When they lose, they return home, cash a check and give the money to a designated casino representative whose identity is not disclosed, and the casino cancels the debt. But there is no record of the money lost by the gambler to the casino. That information was given to our Las Vegas investigators, who would pursue this new trail. Coordination by our lawyers was producing results.

Henry Petersen gave an update on the intensified Giancana investigation. The report was a mixed bag—it was all-out warfare between the pursuers and the pursued. Sam Giancana must have been bemused by our constant investigations and harassments, particularly in view of what he—not we in the organized crime section—knew about his secret recruitment by the federal government in a confounding anti-Castro caper. We know he was outraged by the pressures placed on him by us and the Chicago FBI. "This is like Nazi Germany and I'm the biggest Jew in the country," he was overheard complaining.

Bob Blakey made an interesting proposal. He'd finished his cases in Pennsylvania with Hank Ruth and Tom McBride and was hankering for some new action. He proposed going to Chicago to work on the elusive Sam Giancana, and he suggested a gimmick. If he could be assigned as a Social Security Administration hearing officer, to conduct an investigation of bars and bar girls, he would use the Social Security law immunity statute to try to get to the top of the Chicago mob and their public payees in the police by immunizing all the prostitutes and lower level rackets figures who probably had never paid Social Security taxes on the prostitutes' wages.

Kennedy liked Blakey's proposal, and said, "I'll take care of it." There were smiles around the room as we pictured another of our colleagues moving his life to Chicago after Kennedy made a tactical phone call to the head of Social Security.

Like a summer storm, there was electricity in the atmosphere. We were hot. Two months before, the televised Valachi hearings put the organized crime section on the map. In his own testimony on September 25, 1963, introducing those hearings, Kennedy had described our work and asked for new weapons to enable us to expand our efforts—wiretap and immunity laws in particular—to follow up on the interstate travel, shipment, and communications laws he'd gotten from the Congress earlier. I felt a special touch of pride when Kennedy had cited the work in Newport to the committee as a notable example of our program's success.

For a time, I had been looking into a potential case in Tampa, Florida, involving a local underworld character named "Big Joe" Sanfratello. It produced the only moment when I experienced a personal threat. In the middle of the night, upon returning from an investigation in Tampa, I was awakened by a caller, purporting to be from Tampa. He said, gruffly: "Tell your wife to come outside, Mr. Goldfarb."

I reported the call to Hundley, who contacted the FBI; fortunately, nothing more happened and we put the incident behind us.

It was a different case, however, that brought me face to face with RFK at our meeting that morning. A few months before, knowing I was bored and looking for something to get my teeth into, Bill Hundley had given me a cold file and suggested I review it to confirm an earlier recommendation that it be closed, or else come up with a second opinion. After reading, I detected one chance to turn the inves-

tigation into a prosecution, but it required the unlikely possibility of
getting an attorney to admit he was part of a criminal conspiracy that
implicated a big-shot East Coast Mafia boss. That possibility, along
with my intense dislike of crooked lawyers, prompted me to ask
Hundley for authorization to convene a grand jury in Miami. He
agreed. Harry Subin and I were off again, this time headed south to
catch a big-time crook who lived in the North.

There was one dishonest lawyer in this case, not a Svengali-like,
behind-the-scenes power like Charlie Lester, just a guy who was ready
to cheat if the price was right. I had the feeling he might talk if
squeezed hard enough. Armed with a departmental memorandum
describing our policy of alerting state bar associations about misconduct by lawyers, and the authority to offer this fellow immunity if he
told the truth in the grand jury and the trial, we subpoenaed him.

Early the first evening after we arrived, we had a preliminary interview with the lawyer in the U.S. attorney's office in downtown
Miami. I told him that we knew what he had done, deplored it, and
were ready to advise the Florida Bar Association; but that he had one
chance to come clean. If he did, we would give him immunity. If he
did not, I would recommend that he be prosecuted with others on
multiple felony counts. Immediately, he started to provide all the
missing links we needed to make our case. Subin sat transfixed as his
story unfolded. I leaned over and whispered: "Harry, get this down.
It's called a confession!"

With this new testimony, we continued our investigation in grand
juries in Miami and New York City. We were able to prove that a
purported sale of a vending machine business by a Floridian to an
East Coast mobster had been backdated to appear to precede the
vendor's death. The vendor was a front for the mobster who didn't
want to lose control of the business when his front suddenly died.
Subin and I returned to Washington and prepared an indictment. It
could be a big catch, and there was excitement about the case in the
organized crime section.

Our proposal was approved by Bill Hundley and his boss, Jack
Miller, the head of the Criminal Division. But there was a problem.
Because we meant to indict under the estate tax laws, a copy of my
proposed case went to Louis Oberdorfer, head of the Tax Division.

And Oberdorfer had a problem with it. He thought my use of the criminal provisions of the estate tax laws under these circumstances was a misuse of the revenue laws and thus bad policy, even if technically we could prove there had been a legal violation. With two department division heads disagreeing, the call was for Bob Kennedy to make. Oberdorfer had been invited to attend this next group meeting with Kennedy.

I was exhilarated, waiting my turn to push for indicting one of the biggest names in the Mafia. This could be a coup; I had been treading water, looking for a new case, even considering leaving the department unless something big came along to induce me to stay. But I might have struck gold in a case others had given up on.

Interesting as our meeting was, I was impatient to make my pitch. After several hours of listening to others, Hundley invited me to describe my proposed case to the attorney general. After hearing me out, Kennedy asked Miller, "What do you think, Jack?" Miller said he had approved the prospective indictment. Hundley reported that Oberdorfer had a problem with my proposal. "What is it, Lou?" Kennedy asked Oberdorfer. He made his case. Technically, what I proposed was legal; but policywise it strained the symmetry of the revenue laws. "This wasn't what this law was designed to accomplish."

"Ron, what do you say to this?" Kennedy turned to me.

"Let me ask Mr. Oberdorfer one question," I replied. "If you were the trial judge in this case, and I presented my evidence, and the defense counsel moved for a directed verdict because there was no legal case to go to a jury, would you grant that motion?"

Oberdorfer thought, then replied: "No, I would not."

"Well, General, I rest my case. I can present a case that the best minds in this room agree is enough to go to the jury, against a big-time mobster we've been after for years. We *have* to go with it. This guy isn't going to murder someone in broad daylight and in public. This is the best prosecution of him we're going to get. Let me put it to a jury."

It was getting close to lunchtime. The attorney general had guests for the day, Robert Morgenthau, the U.S. attorney in New York City, and his assistant on criminal cases, Silvio Mollo. There was a rumor that Kennedy would resign soon to run his brother's reelection campaign, and Morgenthau might replace him as attorney general. They were going to Hickory Hill, Kennedy's McLean home, for lunch. "Let's break early," he said. "I'll think about it. We'll decide this afternoon."

We straggled out of Kennedy's office and returned to our offices on the second floor. My mind was on my case: Would he go along with my proposed prosecution? Though I knew Kennedy had a high regard for Oberdorfer, I was sure he would authorize my case going forward. Oberdorfer might have been right in a pure policy sense; but so was I on a pragmatic level. Considering the defendant in this case, I knew where Kennedy would come out.

As I stood at the desk in my second-floor office looking over phone messages and reviewing my notes, someone opened the door and shouted: "Have you heard? The president was shot!" My first impression was that this must be a sick joke, and not funny.

We all ran to a nearby office that had a radio and huddled around it listening . . . to what turned out to be a horrible report from Dallas. Gerry Shur, Bill Fowler, and Herb Bates were huddled together having a hushed conversation. Henry Petersen walked by, cursed, and smashed his fist against the wall. Slowly, quietly, the building emptied. Eventually, I left for home, confused, frozen in the uncomprehending paralysis of what it all meant, unsure what to do. While I had no contacts with JFK professionally, my vicarious tie through RFK made the incident seem somehow more personal to me than what every American must have felt upon witnessing the murder of their young president. I didn't return to the department for days, until after the funeral. Washington was a citywide wake.

When Bob Blakey heard the news of the assassination, he'd walked into Henry Petersen's office. Henry, an ex-Marine, was looking out his window, weeping. Crying was very out of character for him, but Henry sensed that with JFK gone, Lyndon Johnson as president, it would never be the same. Once, not long before and while our work was picking up speed, Henry Petersen had talked to Robert Kennedy about how tenuous our whole operation was and how important he thought Kennedy's work with our section was. Kennedy had promised: "Don't worry: We're going to win the next election. We're not going anywhere. We're going to finish this."

Now Kennedy's promise to Henry that he'd see this fight to the end was never to be fulfilled.

It struck Blakey then that he would not go to Chicago—and he didn't. "Suddenly, it occurred to me," he reminisced years later, "it all depended on Robert Kennedy. And Robert Kennedy depended on John Kennedy. And the day the assassination went down, all that was over."

"That was it," Herb Bates remembers thinking. "The bubble has burst."

Robert Kennedy heard the news when he reached home to have lunch with his wife, Morgenthau, and Mollo. Painters at work on the house first heard something on a portable radio. Tentatively, they approached the group eating soup and sandwiches near the pool at Hickory Hill, while the attorney general was taking a quick swim. Just then, a phone call came from J. Edgar Hoover on the White House phone, at around 1:45. "I have news for you," Hoover reported coolly to the attorney general. "The president's been shot. I think it's serious." Bob Kennedy clapped his hand to his mouth. They all ran to the house. About a half hour later, Hoover called again to tell a dazed and horror-struck Robert Kennedy: "The president's dead."

Jack Anderson reported that the family priest came to Hickory Hill to console Robert Kennedy as soon as he heard the tragic news, but waited for three hours while Kennedy talked privately to John McCone, a top CIA official whom he trusted.

Just hours after the assassination, about 3:30 or 4:00 P.M., Robert Kennedy called Harry Williams, his closest contact with the anti-Castro Cuban contingent, at his room in the Ebbitt Hotel in Washington, D.C. Williams was meeting with Washington author Haynes Johnson, who was writing a book about the aborted Cuban invasion. When Williams hung up, he told Johnson that Kennedy had said: "One of your guys did it." Kennedy's first presumption was that Oswald was an anti-Castro activist who was angry at the weakness of the administration's Cuba policy.

Later that afternoon, as he walked with his friend and aide Ed Guthman on the lawn behind his house, Kennedy said: "I thought they would get one of us. But Jack, after all he'd been through, never worried about it." Kennedy told Guthman he'd received a letter from someone in Texas the week before warning the president would be killed if he came to Dallas. Kennedy sent it to Ken O'Donnell, "but I never thought it would happen."

Stunned, speaking softly to his confidant, he said, "I thought it would be me."

Chapter 11

HIDDEN VILLAINS,

TRAGIC HEROES

This did not set out to be an assassination theory book; but it would be naive to ignore any link between that event and what we had been doing in the organized crime section of the Justice Department for almost four years. Events and disclosures since November 1963 and continuing to this date raise the speculation that there was such a connection, although the available evidence does not yet and may never support that thesis with dispositive proof. The facts we do have, however, are disquieting. And, as the Greeks said and Robert Kennedy himself privately noted, "All things are to be examined and called into question. There are no limits set to thought."

The vast and intriguing postassassination literature quite simply contains shocking and controversial disclosures bearing on the relationship between the work of the organized crime section and the JFK assassination. None of this information was known publicly while I worked at Justice, nor when I first considered writing this book. While some of these disclosures are embarrassing and many are questionable, not all can be ignored or automatically discredited as scurrilous examples of exploitative commercialization or mere celebrity voyeurism. Taken together they form a thesis that has to be pondered.

THE THESIS

The thesis is that top mob members wanted Robert Kennedy and later John Kennedy murdered. First, they were outraged by the brothers' hypocrisy, and second, they were alarmed at the increasing danger of being further investigated and prosecuted. The hypocrisy they saw derived from their notion that Joseph Kennedy's history with organized crime figures plus some racketeers' support of JFK's election warranted protection from, not their selection for, aggressive prosecution. This compromising history was compounded by the administration's later use of mob members in its attempts to deal with Castro. They delivered, and they expected appropriate acknowledgment of their cooperation. That's how it was supposed to work. The confounding thing was that rather than laying off, the Justice Department was piling on. Major mob leaders were outraged and planned revenge.

What is the factual basis for this thesis? Can this case be made as a matter of credible history, or confirmed by rigorous prosecutorial standards?

Start with the father. Under this theory, Joseph Kennedy had unleashed a tragedy of horrible proportions in his uncontrolled quest for one of his children to become president. As Joseph Kennedy biographer Richard Whalen has written, the hungers of the "founding father" fueled the rise of his sons as his "flaws perhaps caused their fall."

The elder Kennedy's mob connections reportedly began during the Prohibition era, when—like the mobsters themselves—Joseph Kennedy made a fortune in the whisky business. He reportedly maintained some of those contacts with underworld figures.

In the episode of the PBS series *The American Experience* about "The Kennedys," which provided an overall sympathetic treatment of the Kennedy family and a fascinating history of Joseph Patrick Kennedy, the elder Kennedy was described as a ceaseless philanderer and a consort of bootleggers. The Kennedys were "a tribe that lived by its own rules," the report noted, and Joseph Kennedy used his extraordinarily vast fortune "to reach anybody," "do anything," in the words of host David McCullough. When Joseph Kennedy imported illegal liquor during the Prohibition years, he "forged alliances with the underworld that would endure all his life." His life-long pattern of risky behavior, and his credo that money does miracles and he could reach anyone with it, led him to go to the mob in his quest to win the critical West Virginia presidential primary for his son.

A respected J. Edgar Hoover biography revealed that FBI bugs uncovered the fact that Frank Sinatra had asked Giancana for help with the Kennedy campaign in Illinois in the 1960 election, and the organized crime figure had provided it. Giancana had also raised money for JFK's crucial West Virginia primary campaign at the request of Joseph Kennedy, Hoover told Robert Kennedy in December 1961, and later felt he was "not getting his money's worth." Giancana later cursed John Kennedy to Santos Trafficante, Jr., according to his lawyer, Frank Ragano, complaining, "We broke our balls for him and gave him the election and he gets his brother to hound us to death." In the close presidential election, which Kennedy won by one-tenth of 1 percent, crime boss Sam Giancana's control over key wards in Chicago was credited by some as critical in tilting the balance. The Kennedys had erred by taking money and assistance in their political campaigns from what turned out to be a deadly PAC.

Judith Exner told Larry King and his television audience in 1992 that she repeatedly carried satchels of money from JFK to Sam Giancana for his use in Kennedy's West Virginia primary. She was not to ask questions, but she'd be looked after. She'd not said this earlier, she explained to cynical questioners, because she was afraid to talk about it. She said that Sam Giancana bragged to her, "Your boyfriend wouldn't be in the White House if it wasn't for me." Exner added, "They hated Bobby." What an irony of history it would have been if organized crime was a factor in the close 1960 election, Harris Wofford pointed out; it would not be an irony "Robert Kennedy would have enjoyed."

The president recklessly gave their arrangement his implied acceptance by presuming he could continue to flirt with and use the mob as if it were just another controllable liaison. "The Kennedy children were an extension of their father's incredible ego and lust for power," Richard Whalen wrote. "Jack, like Joe . . . believed in essentially nothing beyond himself and his family. Father and son were solitary adventurers." Hoover biographer Anthony Summers adds the melodramatic speculation: "Kennedy may have paid the ultimate price for his dalliance with Giancana," adding, not so speculatively, "The Mafia, which does nothing for nothing, takes vicious revenge when it considers a pact has been broken."

According to Giancana's brother Chuck and to his godson, Sam Giancana, in their 1992 book, *Double Cross*, "Mooney," as they referred to their mobster kin, had markers from Joseph and Jack Kennedy, and anyone who owed him "was more involved than he imagined." The father had "danced with the devil" for many years and made a direct deal with Giancana, and Jack knew of it, according to their account. Giancana railed to his brother while the McClellan Committee hearings were going on, "Bobby is gonna go for the throat," and his appointment as attorney general came "like a rabbit punch in the dark." The deal—protection and access—made by the father was guaranteed when some of JFK's dalliances were arranged by the mob, whose discretion could be assured by cooperation.

Sam Giancana theorized, his family historians reported, that Joseph Kennedy had conceived a diabolical scheme, positioning his vehement son as attorney general "to systematically erase all markers"; and if there was to be a mobster list for prosecutors to pursue, Mooney knew "he'd be on top of the list." "It's a brilliant move on Joe's part," said Giancana ruefully. "He'll have Bobby wipe us out to cover their own dirty tracks and it'll all be done in the name of the Kennedy 'war on organized crime.' Brilliant. Just fuckin' brilliant."

What markers? Their book states that Joseph Kennedy was saved twice from mob wrath—once in a scrape with the Purple Gang in Detroit, and again in 1956 from a vendetta by Frank Costello in New York. Kennedy came to Giancana in the second instance, pleading for his intervention to cancel the contract Costello had put out on Kennedy, according to Giancana's literary heirs, and promising, "He'll be your man . . . my son . . . will owe you . . . he won't refuse you, ever." Giancana thought he had a very valuable deal, and told his brother that he and the Kennedys had a lot in common: "The good thing is, nobody knows it."

After helping the JFK presidential campaign, and the CIA in its Castro capers, Giancana drew the conclusion that they were top-level partners and he'd be immune from prosecution. "Bobby Kennedy is just too far down the ladder to know about it."

The Giancana-to-Giancana conversations, allegedly held over a lifetime, are impossible to confirm.

From the father, the circumstantial evidence under this theory moves to the sons. Why did the brothers choose labor racketeering as the public issue that would showcase JFK's presidential candidacy; and why, once succeeding, did RFK pursue it above all other subjects when both brothers were in office? Could they not have known about their father's past? There were hints of Teamsters support of John Kennedy's candidacy if Robert Kennedy would "play smart," Theodore C. Sorensen has reported. Yet, in their legislative partnership and in their executive lives, JFK and RFK pursued the rackets aggressively.

The thesis continues—that Robert Kennedy as attorney general burned his candle at both ends, pursuing and exploiting the mob at the same time. In 1974, a senate investigation disclosed outrageous Cold War abuses by the CIA that seemed to compromise both brothers, particularly Robert Kennedy. Referred to as the Church Committee after its chairman, Idaho Senator Frank Church, the Senate Select Committee to Study Governmental Operations with Respect to Intelligence Activities issued a report in 1975 describing a program of governmental malfeasance. The Church Committee called it "an aberration" that could be explained only as a result of "the pressures of the time." One of its carefully documented and confounding exposés was that "U.S. Government personnel plotted to kill Castro from 1960 to 1965. American underworld figures and Cubans hostile to Castro were used in these plots and were provided encouragement and material support by the U.S." Recently declassified FBI and CIA documents provide further illumination of this sordid revelation.

The CIA's "hairbrained schemes, including using the Mafia to gun Castro down," began under Eisenhower, according to his biographer Stephen E. Ambrose, though he could not say whether Eisenhower actually ordered it or even knew about this particular scheme. All Kennedy White House officials questioned by the Church Committee denied knowing of plans to use underworld figures to eliminate Castro, and testified that the president was unaware of it. CIA records describe two meetings with Kennedy administration officials: one in August 1962, another (after JFK's death) in July 1964; and they note a White House environment that pressed for decisive action against Castro. Might the president's aides have provided their mentor with a winking, technically accurate, "deniable" knowledge of activities? Would presidential subordinates condone such extraordinary action without permission? Whatever JFK knew, the Church Committee reported years later that the caper continued during his watch.

After initiating other attempts to sabotage the Castro regime in early 1960, in August of that year the idea was hatched that the underworld be recruited to assassinate the exasperating Cuban leader. An ex-FBI agent then in the private investigation business was approached by the CIA as "a cutout," one having access to the underworld. He in turn recruited Johnny Rosselli, a California rackets figure with Las Vegas ties and a criminal record for labor shakedowns of the movie studios. Rosselli felt it was his patriotic duty to help. Though the CIA had budgeted $150,000 for this assignment, the mob "never took a nickel," the CIA reported; Rosselli said it was the least he could do for his country.

Along with Cubans who were hostile to Castro, Rosselli recruited two friends, "Sam Gold," who turned out to be Giancana, and "Joe," a.k.a. Santos Trafficante, Jr., the Mafia's man in Cuba before Castro jailed and then deported him. Rosselli's two rackets friends had the needed contacts in Cuba. Trafficante was less a patriot; though he later claimed to have acted in his country's interest, he was also personally interested in reestablishing his gambling, prostitution, and narcotics monopolies in Cuba if Castro could be eliminated.

The Church Committee discovered evidence "of at least eight plots" involving the CIA from 1960 to 1965 to assassinate Fidel Castro. "One plot," it reported, "involving the use of underworld figures, reportedly twice progressed to the point of sending poison pills to Cuba and dispatching teams to commit the deed."

FBI documents indicate it had information as early as October 1960 that Giancana had told friends that Castro was "to be done away with very shortly," probably around November 1960, and that the Chicago rackets figure "had already met with the assassin-to-be on three occasions."

The CIA-mob liaison came unraveled, however, under the bizarre circumstances of a bungled Giancana tap. According to the Church Committee, in October 1960 Sam Giancana had privately arranged the monitoring of a Las Vegas hotel room. Its fortuitous discovery led to a possible prosecution that could have made public an embarrassing story. That bugging was described later by one CIA official as a Keystone Kops comedy.

The apartment in the Riviera Hotel was supposed to be bugged to discover if Giancana's girlfriend was carrying on an affair there with comedian Dan Rowan. A maid discovered the electronic tap of Rowan's phone and reported it to the local sheriff. The sheriff found a bug behind the bed, along with seventeen lock picks, two telephone-bugging devices, one earphone, one miniature transmitter in a cigarette case, a Minox camera, and other monitoring devices and tools of the trade. Unfortunately, the phone taps included conversations of Giancana himself discussing his efforts to assassinate Castro by poisoning him. Indeed, Giancana had gotten the tap placed by telling his contact with the CIA that the CIA owed him a favor as a result of Giancana's assistance on the Castro assassination operation.

On October 18, 1960, Hoover advised his CIA counterparts that the FBI had received this information from the local law enforcement officials working on the case. In December the Criminal Division requested a full FBI investigation into that illegal wiretapping, according to top secret bureau records. In January 1961, the local U.S. attorney, who would be prosecuting any case that might be authorized, sought a prosecutive opinion from the Justice Department. This unwelcome political hot potato was dropped in the lap of the Kennedy administration as it came into office.

Local charges were dropped on April 24, 1961, because the complaining witness (Rowan) did not desire to prosecute. In April 1961, the CIA sought help from the FBI to persuade the Justice Department not to prosecute the wiretapper for fear that its "dirty business" would be disclosed during any criminal trial. An FBI memorandum dated April 25, 1961, stated that it was conducting an investigation into the wiretapping, "at the [Justice] Department's request," and indicating that the Criminal Division was being supplied with information about the investigation. A later FBI memo noted that information about Giancana should be limited within the department to those with "a need-to-know."

The department officially declined to prosecute the wiretap case on April 24, 1962, a year later. The statute on which any indictment might be based required not only *interception* of a phone message (which had occurred) but also *publication* (which had not occurred). There was a straightforward basis to deny prosecution. Criminal Division chief Jack Miller noted to Kennedy that "it is clear that the national interest will preclude any prosecution," alluding to the CIA's request for forbearance.

What did Robert Kennedy know and when did he know it? as the probing, classic question has come to be put, repeatedly. On May 22, 1961, not half a year after RFK had become attorney general, Hoover had sent him a memorandum advising him of the CIA's admission of the Las Vegas wiretap and the use of the underworld in clandestine Castro plots. Courtney Evans, the liaison between Kennedy and Hoover, recalled to me: "I hand-carried all memos over [Hoover to Robert Kennedy], and I'll tell you, I read 'em even if I didn't write 'em." Yet a later CIA internal investigation into the episode concluded that Robert Kennedy did not know about the Castro assassination plan using organized crime figures until he was informed about it by the CIA in May 1962. This, despite an FBI document dated May 21, 1961, stating that a CIA official told Attorney General Kennedy about "the use of Giancana and the underworld against Castro" during a "recent" briefing.

Thus, while our extraordinary efforts against organized crime were only beginning, a few department officials were discreetly looking into these compromising events and the Criminal Division was being implored by the CIA not to prosecute the wiretapper for fear that a trial would expose the whole story and "embarrass" the U.S. government. On June 3, 1961, on one of the memos between the Justice Department and the FBI, Kennedy scribbled a note to FBI liaison Courtney Evans, "I hope this will be followed up vigorously." It was, but it remains unclear precisely who at Justice—beyond Hoover and his closest aides—knew what information, and at what time.

News of this potential high-level fiasco was emerging from other sources, as well. A February 27, 1962, FBI memo to Robert Kennedy and White House aide Kenneth O'Donnell disclosed the dangerous liaison between the president and Judith Exner, a friend of John Rosselli and Sam Giancana. One of our colleagues had discovered the records of their phone calls while following a paper trail of racketeers' phone records; he reported that fact to Robert Kennedy at one of our meetings with him, and the attorney general advised the president. Then, on March 22, 1962, Hoover lunched privately with President Kennedy at the White House, and hours later the long history of White House phone calls between the president and Exner (seventy since the inauguration) ended.

In the interview with talk show host Larry King on February 4, 1992, Judith Exner said that she was a longtime lover of Kennedy before and while he was president and had a brief affair with Giancana after Kennedy was killed. She also said that the attorney general knew about the president's reckless relationship with her.

Exner also told King that President Kennedy knew about the CIA's use of Giancana in the Castro assassination plot. "I carried the intelligence material between Jack and Sam . . . at Jack's request." Her cloak-and-dagger description of those alleged events was never reported in her earlier book nor in her sworn testimony to the Church Committee. Her story on the King show in 1992 was told then, she stated, and not earlier to the Church Committee, because Rosselli was killed after he testified, Giancana had been killed a few weeks before he was to testify, "and I was afraid . . . terribly afraid."

Eventually, on May 7, 1962, the attorney general met with CIA officials and was briefed about the CIA's use of John Rosselli and Sam Giancana to assassinate Castro. The Department of Justice had not been informed of this plot, Kennedy was told. Robert Kennedy was "disturbed," according to CIA counsel Lawrence Houston: "If you have seen Mr. Kennedy's eyes get steely and his jaw set and his voice get low and precise, you get a definite feeling of unhappiness." The CIA had never cleared its program with the Department of Justice or the FBI. Kennedy told Houston, later, that there was not to be any further contact with the Mafia without prior consultation with him: "If you even try to do business with organized crime again—with gangsters—you will let the attorney general know." Kennedy told Hoover, "It would be difficult to prosecute Giancana or [Robert] Maheu then or in the future."

Jack Miller, who ran the Criminal Division, and Courtney Evans have no recollection of Kennedy having any information about or conversations concerning the use of the mob in a Castro assassination plot. They both say now that Kennedy may have known in early 1961 that the CIA had an alliance with rackets figures to help political destabilization efforts in Cuba. Why wouldn't we do everything possible, unashamedly, if our national security was endangered, they ask? But there is no proof Kennedy knew the assassination of a national leader was part of those plans, they argue, until he was told so in May 1962 by the CIA's Houston and Sheffield Edwards.

For this hear-see-and-speak-no-evil position to be so, one would have to believe that the FBI and CIA never told Robert Kennedy—to whom both agencies reported—about this one extraordinary feature, despite documents contemporaneously prepared that demonstrate that some top officials at both agencies knew about this fact. Miller and Evans urge that this is exactly what happened. Refreshing his present recollections with extensive FBI and CIA internal reports of these events, Miller wrote to me:

> Assuming this report is true, and it was an exhaustively researched report, I gather, (1) Kennedy was not informed of the assassination plot until May of 1962; (2) I was not informed of the assassination plot; and (3) whatever the situation was there were no reservations imposed or attempted to be imposed by the CIA on any prosecution of Giancana or anybody else.

The Church Committee reported that in April 1962, while this anguish continued, a CIA official—William Harvey—continued to actively work with Rosselli to arrange the assassination of Castro. The CIA has concluded that this second phase of the Castro caper was unknown to Robert Kennedy and to most others in the Kennedy administration, and indeed to the CIA itself. It also concluded that while Rosselli was used in phase two, Giancana and Trafficante were not. Phase one was carried out from August 1960 until May 1961; phase two from April 1962 until February 1963. Phase one involved the use of organized crime figures, and phase two used Cubans, but Rosselli was involved in both phases. The plan was on hold for a while during the interim between phase one and phase two due to the Bay of Pigs fiasco.

CIA officials who testified years later before the Church Committee admitted their "unsavory" contacts with the syndicate were likely to be manipulated in turn by organized crime figures "for their own self-protection or aggrandizement."

When Rosselli later faced deportation and indictment for fraudulent gambling activities, he called in his chips, and sought help from his former government "associates." Sheffield Edwards, the CIA official who had opened the contacts with organized crime, later told Rosselli that he'd mentioned to Attorney General Kennedy how Rosselli had acted in the national interest. If Edwards did so, it did Rosselli no good. He incurred the wrath of the mob in addition to his problems with the government, and survived neither. Rosselli did time in prison, testified before the Church Committee, and was killed gangland-style in 1976.

Giancana certainly was cocky about his secret chip. When FBI agents stalked him at O'Hare Airport on July 12, 1961, an irked Giancana railed at them that he knew about the Kennedys "and one of these days we are going to tell all" about your "boss" and your "superboss." In August 1963, a Chicago newspaper reporting on the FBI's surveillance of Giancana quoted the gangster as saying: "Why don't you fellows leave me alone? I'm one of you!"

Columnist Jack Anderson takes the basic thesis to an extreme conclusion in his theory about the assassination of JFK. Anderson says that John Kennedy acknowledged to him that the mob stole the 1960 election for him and that Nixon was magnanimous in their postelection conversation. Thereafter, the young president, wanting to dramatize that he was not beholden to the mob, authorized Robert Kennedy to aggressively pursue his war against organized crime. The mob became disenchanted with Kennedy and eventually grew to hate him.

President-elect John Kennedy was briefed verbally "in oblique terms" by the CIA's deputy director, Richard Bissell, about the plot to kill Castro, according to a document recounting this briefing, which Anderson says he has seen. A responsible British historian and expert on international spying, Christopher Andrew, recently reported that Ike himself, along with Bissell, briefed JFK early in his presidency about the Cuba strategy, and that CIA director Allen Dulles did so in November 1960, before the inauguration. The new president went along with the CIA until the Bay of Pigs fiasco, after which he asked Robert Kennedy to find out everything that was going on at the agency concerning Cuba and to take charge.

Johnny Rosselli, who brought Giancana and Trafficante into the "program," told Anderson that the racketeers' role was a charade. According to Rosselli, Trafficante went to Castro and offered to save his life by tipping him off about assassination attempts; in return, he was paid off for the confiscation of his casinos. In effect, Trafficante was a double agent. Castro recruited Trafficante "to turn the Mafia's guns against President Kennedy," according to Anderson, a scheme that appealed to "Castro's Latin sense of irony." When the CIA found this out, they stopped dealing with him and Giancana. Trafficante hated John Kennedy, and was a violent man who, Giancana said, thought the solution to every problem was "kill, kill, kill." Trafficante recruited Marcello to assist in arranging the assassination of John Kennedy, Anderson says.

On September 7, 1963, Fidel Castro told Associated Press reporter Daniel Harker at an impromptu interview at the Brazilian Embassy in Havana that he knew the CIA was attempting to use terrorists to assassinate "Cuban leaders," and he warned JFK and RFK, "We are prepared to . . . answer in kind"; if American plots continued, he added, "United States leaders would be in danger . . . they themselves will not be safe." Recently released CIA reports disclose that on the very day of JFK's assassination its agents were meeting in Paris with a Cuban agent they were paying to kill Castro.

In a Latin American tour in 1965, then senator Robert Kennedy told an audience of students who were complaining about American treatment of Castro, "I saved his life." Kennedy was referring to his orders to the CIA to stop their use of the mob to assassinate the Cuban leader, according to his then press secretary, Frank Mankiewicz. Castro told Mankiewicz in 1974 that he had no animosity toward Robert Kennedy; indeed, he respected him and his brother. Castro said he believed John F. Kennedy was making exploratory gestures toward possible reconciliation at the time of his assassination. Self-servingly, Castro told Mankiewicz that he was saddened by his adversary's "tragic ending"; that he thought the deceased ex-president was reconsidering his Cuba policy, one he had inherited and came to regret. Castro wished all records were made public so it would be quite clear that Oswald's act was not a counterrevolutionary act of the Cuban government, and called Jack Ruby's murder of Oswald "incredible, inconceivable. That does not happen even in the most mediocre of movies."

Anderson's sources told him that Jack Ruby was told to kill Oswald, an instruction he was not in a position to ignore. Ruby had access to the police station; Oswald was not protected; Ruby couldn't miss. Anderson agrees with Oswald's remark, "I'm a patsy," citing Nicholas Katzenbach's assessment to Bill Moyers at the time of Oswald's arrest, "It's too pat . . . too obvious . . . too good to be true." But Anderson concludes, with Hoover running a one-man investigation of the assassination that skirted all these known complications, and Dulles on the Warren Commission to be sure no conspiracy theories were taken seriously by his colleagues, LBJ avoided a potentially cataclysmic confrontation with Khrushchev over Cuba.

Could Robert Kennedy not have known of the CIA's use of Mafia figures in the assassination efforts, given his micromanagement of Mongoose, a covert anti-Castro plan that included assassination, and the FBI's reports to him in 1961 and 1962? Arthur Schlesinger, Jr., who knew both men well and who wrote biographies of JFK and RFK, has noted that "the President trusted him [RFK] more than anyone else to get to the bottom of an idea or a project, to distinguish what was operational and what was literary, to anticipate consequences, to ride herd on execution, to protect the presidential interest . . ."

Richard Reeves, the author of *Kennedy*, concluded to me: "There's no doubt in my mind that Bobby was the director and manager of Mongoose and the attempts to assassinate Castro. And the driving force behind him was his brother." Reeves's book reported a Robert McNamara remark to Richard Goodwin shortly after the Bay of Pigs invasion in April 1961, about eliminating Castro. Goodwin described that conversation as "the first and only time that I heard a serious suggestion of assassination"; though the terminology used was "Executive Action," "its meaning was instantly apparent. Assassination." Goodwin sets the time as "around the middle of May."

In McNamara's memoir, *In Retrospect*, he reports, "During my seven years in the Defense Department . . . all CIA 'covert operations' (excluding spying operations) were subject to approval by the president and the secretaries of state and defense, or their representatives. The CIA had no authority to act without that approval. So far as I know, it never did." Thus, Reeves concluded, "liquidation was off the record. But it was never off the table." Reeves's review of CIA records of its own involvements at the time includes Richard Bissell's statement that he had "no doubt that it was fully known to the Attorney General."

Cambridge University professor Christopher Andrew concluded in a recent book:

> In keeping with the doctrine of plausible deniability, the agency left no smoking gun to link the assassination plot with the White House. But it is difficult to believe that the president was not informed the plot was under way, even if he was not told (and probably did not wish to know) all the details. Kennedy inherited from Eisenhower a system designed to ensure that major covert operations did not proceed without presidential approval. The plot to kill Castro was not a momentary aberration by a handful of agency deviants.

Professor Andrew described Robert Kennedy's active assumption of control over the administration's covert Cuban machinations as "a dark side to Camelot."

These cowboy CIA operations not only violated the most minimal notions of morality in foreign policy but also appear to have clashed with the heart of our ongoing organized crime program. And, if those events weren't perplexing enough, a recent disclosure suggests that Robert Kennedy's involvement with the CIA and the mob didn't stop with this inherited mess.

Two articles in 1994 by Max Holland, a reputable Warren Commission historian, state that in November 1961, after the embarrassing Bay of Pigs disaster, JFK put his trusted brother RFK in charge of Mongoose, which had high Kennedy administration priority; it was a no-holds-barred operation; and Robert Kennedy was applying intense pressures. According to Holland, Robert Kennedy's intimate involvement with the CIA's Cuba plans began "two days after the inauguration." And after the aborted invasion in April 1961, he "immersed himself in Agency affairs."

While leading our organized crime efforts, Robert Kennedy was managing another CIA caper with Mafia members, according to former CIA staff member Samuel Halpern. The creator of the cryptonym Mongoose, Halpern was William K. Harvey's executive assistant at Task Force W., created in November 1961 to respond to the Kennedy administration's strong concerns over Cuba.

Halpern told me that Robert Kennedy had asked the agency to assign a full-time staff officer to meet with rackets figures he identified at times and places designated by him. Halpern remembers not liking the idea because it ran counter to CIA procedures: The agency preferred to choose the time and place of all its agents' meetings. But Halpern had no choice. So early in 1962, he selected a big, husky, savvy guy (now deceased) "who knew how to take care of himself" to work as the case officer with Kennedy. Several times each month, when Robert Kennedy or his secretary, Angie Novello, called on a special secured phone, he would leave, stopping by Halpern's office to say: "I'm off again, Sam." He'd see or talk to Robert Kennedy and be gone for several days, sometimes a week or more, to cities all over the United States and Canada.

This private project was not part of the earlier and continuing program to use the mob to assassinate Castro. It was done to locate Mafia networks left in Cuba from earlier days, "stay behinds," "rat lines," to help the general destabilization of Cuba.

This private program ended in October 1962, after the missile crisis. CIA funds paid for this project, though Halpern remembers it netted nothing: "We never put out a single, solitary piece of paper on it; we had no intelligence for our community. It was the craziest part of Mongoose. But the attorney general wanted it and we all knew he spoke for Jack. In my business, you don't ask questions."

Halpern wondered with colleagues at the time how this odd and useless adventure lined up with RFK's organized crime drive. "We were working with him and reading headlines all the time about what Kennedy was doing against organized crime, and we couldn't figure it out. I'm no lawyer, but if the Justice Department developed any cases against these guys, they could have brought all this out in court. But, we were under orders."

A retired CIA officer, Scott D. Breckenridge, described these events in his 1993 memoir, *CIA and the Cold War:*

> Among the initiatives emanating from MONGOOSE was one arising from a theory entertained by the Attorney General that the criminal syndicate, the Mafia, must have channels into Cuba

to protect such remaining assets as they might have there. CIA was directed to provide an operations officer to meet with Mafia figures identified by Kennedy under circumstances over which CIA had no control. It was not all that easy or comfortable for CIA operations officers to carry out unprofessionally conceived clandestine activities run by a young man who spoke for the president as few, if any, could. The Attorney General's initiative in involving the syndicate is interesting, given his apparent disapproval of such connections when members of the syndicate were involved in planning to eliminate Castro . . . for some it will suggest the genesis of CIA's decision to approach the syndicate again in its plan against Castro during the Kennedy administration."

There are no CIA records to confirm Halpern's story, nor Justice Department records to dispute it: Those kind of records generally aren't kept.

In October 1994, I asked Angie Novello about this charge, and she stated she knew absolutely nothing about the arrangement described by Halpern and Breckenridge. If she placed such calls for Kennedy (she placed thousands as his aide at Justice for four years), she would have placed them without any knowledge of who she was calling and why, she told me. Arguably, Novello would be presumed to be protective of her former employer—a man whose memory she holds in the highest regard—but she spoke to me in circumstances from which I presumed she was telling me the truth as she knew it.

Kennedy's close aide and friend John Seigenthaler—one of those he was most likely to confide in—knew nothing of the allegations that Kennedy used rackets figures to pursue cold warrior gambits, and surely not to assassinate another country's leader. Seigenthaler recalls Kennedy expressing disgust with the CIA when he heard of their use of assassins, and telling John McCone and Richard Helms he thought it was disgraceful and that it should be stopped. Seigenthaler also presumed the heavy pressures the department placed on Giancana were Kennedy's way of sending a message that there would be no compromises.

James Symington followed Seigenthaler as Kennedy's administrative assistant from May 1962 until June 1963. He knew nothing about the Mongoose caper or the Halpern story. If it happened, Symington told me, it was "over my head and outside my door." But the notion that Bob Kennedy might have compromised organized crime cases is impossible for Symington to believe. "Compromise wasn't a word Bob would use, it wasn't in his vocabulary, especially in organized crime cases." Kennedy was a meddler, Jim remembers, and he dabbled in areas outside his Justice Department bailiwick at his brother's request. But, Symington is sure, "I know how Bob was with causes; he had a razorlike commitment to organized crime and civil rights cases that he'd *never* have compromised."

Furthermore, Symington mused, if Kennedy *had* suggested that any case be compromised, Jack Miller would have resigned, and so would Bill Hundley. So would we all.

John Nolan was Robert Kennedy's next administrative assistant and remained so until July 1964; he traveled with him often and worked very closely with him regularly. Nolan says that he knew nothing about any of these events, but he has speculations about them based on his close contacts with RFK.

Nolan recalls Kennedy's predilection to use "meta diplomats," trusted private minions, to get things done outside existing institutions. But he also remembers the loathsome light in which Kennedy viewed Giancana, so much so that Nolan believes Kennedy could not have dissembled about any contacts with him. He sat in on countless private, insider meetings that dealt with Giancana and remembers that Kennedy regarded him as "beneath his consideration." For Robert Kennedy to have worked with Giancana, Nolan says, "is inherently implausible; it just doesn't ring true."

Nolan's construct of what may have happened is that any specific knowledge in the department of collaboration with Giancana would have stopped before it got to Kennedy.

Anyone who knows Bob Kennedy's history and practices knows that if he had conducted *any* investigative work such as this—and anyone else was involved—he would have worked on it with Walter Sheridan. Walter was his key investigator for about ten years, on the McClellan Committee and at Justice; he called on him invariably in key situations and trusted him completely. I asked Walter about these accusations in December 1994, just weeks before he died. I discussed with him all the available FBI and CIA reports about the use of the mob in the plans to assassinate Castro, and read him (he was losing his sight) what Halpern told me and what Breckenridge and Holland had written. Sheridan said he knew nothing about any of it and unequivocally doubted the existence of the latter scheme.

Of course, Sheridan might have been kept in the dark by Kennedy, or he may have withheld from me what he knew; he was renowned for his "discretion." Devoted friends have reflected that he probably took secrets to his grave. But the circumstances of our conversations, and my instinctive reading of my former colleague's remarks and reactions, lead me to believe he was not dissembling to me. None of this resolves the question, I understand, but it undermines the credibility of Halpern's story. Much of his tale is hearsay, but I know of no reason Halpern would have to lie. Halpern's story, if true, would have to be one Bob Kennedy kept totally to himself at the Department of Justice.

Whatever else he did, RFK kept the prosecutorial pressures on all these conspirators-in-hindsight as if he knew nothing of any of these recently revealed facts. If the evidence shows that Robert Kennedy participated in secret capers with mobsters, then he can be accused of cold warrior recklessness. But I know from personal experiences that he cannot be charged with compromising our mission to prosecute all members of the Mafia. He never let up on that mission, nor suggested that any of our lawyers pull their punches.

I recall a revealing moment of truth when Henry Petersen called me to his office one day (before I left) to ask my opinion about a strategic question concerning our pursuit of Giancana. What if we were to question him before a grand jury, knowing he was unlikely to answer our questions? We'd give him immunity; he'd refuse to answer, and we'd jail him for contempt. As an expert on contempt, what did I think of the legality of recalling him as a witness after the first grand jury ended its eighteen-month life and a second grand jury was impaneled? Could we ask the same witness the same question, with the same likely result? Theoretically, in such a scenario the witness could be jailed forever—for consecutive eighteen-month periods.

I knew what Henry had in mind. While I shared his goal of disempowering mob leaders, my conscience recoiled at the idea. "Legally, you could do it," I told Petersen. Courts had held that there is no double jeopardy if the offense, while similar, is not the same. And, in the most technical sense, each contempt is a separate offense to a different grand jury, a separate affront to the sovereign government, I had to admit. "But I advise against it. It's ingenious, but it's going too far. It's overreaching," I advised, hoping I wasn't alienating my tougher boss. To my relief, Petersen agreed.

That experience confirms to me that whatever private arrangements Kennedy had with mobsters such as Giancana did not, miraculously, get in the way of our section's aggressive pursuit of these less than subtle men who were not likely to have held back compromising information that would keep them out of trouble.

Bill Hundley remembers a similar situation. Hundley recalled to me the time he met with Edward Bennett Williams, who was representing Giancana vigorously, as Williams always did. "Williams was arguing and screaming, but never once said anything about Giancana having cooperated with the government. He never played that card. The subject never, never, never came up," Hundley remembers. Surely, if any case could have been made to save Giancana from prison, it would have been made. Bill Hundley recalled, as I've observed, "Bobby pushed to get Giancana at any cost."

In retrospect, despite these insiders' insights, it is hard to fathom how the attorney general could have been prodding our group of prosecutors to pressure and prosecute some of the very gangsters the government was in cahoots with, while these foreign intrigues were going on, some or all of which he had to have known about. He was not forthcoming to the Warren Commission or the Church Committee (nor to anyone else on the record) about these CIA capers. Thus the haunting speculation that while acting publicly as a vigorous prosecutor, Robert Kennedy had privately been a player. If so, Robert Kennedy's brooding agony over the assassination is understandable on another level than his obvious personal grief; the government's secret dealings with the mob might have led to his brother's murder.

There is more.

EXTENDING THE THESIS

The undercover use of the mob in Kennedy politics and by our government in deadly clandestine shenanigans was not the only perilous undercurrent of which we were unaware. If the sins of the father and the brothers gave rise to the mob's fury, so too did the virtuous work of the attorney general.

Our pursuit of Jimmy Hoffa had driven him to think of murder. Ed Partin, our key witness in the Hoffa trial, one for whose veracity and credibility we had vouched, told a Louisiana police official and department investigators of a chilling conversation he'd had with Hoffa in Hoffa's office in Washington in August 1962. This incident was reported by Teamsters biographer Dan Moldea, in *The Hoffa Wars*.

Hoffa had been thinking out loud, weighing the merits of two separate murder plans aimed at Robert Kennedy.

The first plan, the one Hoffa was then leaning toward, involved firebombing Hickory Hill, Robert Kennedy's Virginia estate, with extraordinarily lethal plastic explosives. Hoffa was careful to note that even if Kennedy somehow survived the explosion, he "and all his damn kids" would be incinerated, since "the place will burn after it blows up."

The second plan was apparently a backup scheme, and in retrospect it is "the kind of thing that makes you wonder just a little bit," . . . Kennedy would be shot to death from a distance away; a single gunman would be enlisted to carry it out—someone without any traceable connection to Hoffa and the Teamsters; a high-powered rifle with a telescopic sight would be the assassination weapon.

Hoffa told Partin that he had a .270 rifle "which will shoot flat and long." He thought, Partin reported, that "the 'ideal setup' would be 'to catch [Robert] Kennedy somewhere in the South,' where extremist 'segregation people' might throw investigators off the track by being blamed for the crime. The 'ideal time' to hit Kennedy would be while he was driving his convertible . . . Somebody needs to bump that son of a bitch off," Hoffa told Partin.

The plot went beyond mere talk, according to this account. "While Partin was at a Holiday Inn in Baton Rouge, federal officials taped a telephone call between him and Hoffa, who was in Pittsburgh, in which Partin told Hoffa he had gotten the plastic explosives and Hoffa asked him to bring them to Nashville."

News of this threat was known to close Kennedy aides at Justice.

Partin had called Charles Smith, who passed on the witness to his superiors in Sheridan's group. Criminal Division chief Jack Miller remembers the threat and viewed it as "damned important; we took it seriously." President Kennedy confided to his friend Ben Bradlee, then with *Newsweek* magazine, at a party in February 1963 that Hoffa planned to have a trusted assassin shoot and kill Robert Kennedy. Bradlee noted at the time in his diary, "The president was obviously serious."

The Hoffa Wars recounts how the plot to kill the attorney general escalated to one aimed at the president. In 1979, the House Assassination Committee picked up and expanded on this disclosure. "There is solid evidence . . . that Hoffa, Marcello, and Trafficante— three of the most important targets for criminal prosecution by the Kennedy Administration—had discussions with their subordinates about murdering President Kennedy. Associates of Hoffa, Trafficante, and Marcello were in direct contact with Jack Ruby, the Dallas night-club owner who killed the 'lone assassin' of the President. Although members of the Warren Commission, which investigated President Kennedy's assassination, had knowledge of much of this information at the time of their inquiry, they chose not to follow it up. Marcello and Trafficante continued to support Hoffa after his convictions, offering bribes to a key witness to recant his testimony against Hoffa."

Enough clouds had cast shadows over the Warren Commission's key conclusion for a new official inquiry to be begun. A special committee of the House of Representatives was created to investigate the assassinations of John F. Kennedy and Martin Luther King. After an intensive and thorough investigation (its counsel, Bob Blakey, was a graduate of our organized crime section), the House Select Committee on Assassinations questioned some of the Warren Commission's conclusions and suggested one that supported the thesis that the mob was in on the assassination.

Among its important findings, the committee reported that "scientific acoustical evidence establishes a high probability that two gunmen fired at President John F. Kennedy," that there was "seemingly irrefutable scientific evidence of two shooters in Dealey Plaza," and that Kennedy "was probably assassinated as a result of a conspiracy." While the congressional committee was not able to name the other gunmen or conspirators, it did rule out the key theories suggested elsewhere blaming the Soviet government, the Cuban government, or anti-Castro groups. The committee concluded that the Warren Commission investigation failed "to explore adequately possible conspiratorial activity in the assassination."

The committee believed that individual members of the national organized crime syndicate may have been involved. The committee speculated that New Orleans Mafia leader Carlos Marcello, Tampa Mafia chief Santos Trafficante, Jr., and the notorious Teamsters chief Jimmy Hoffa had "the motive, means, and opportunity to assassinate President Kennedy."

The House committee examined FBI electronic surveillance of the mob in 1963–64, for the period eight months before and six months after the assassination, to ascertain whether there was any evidence of its involvement in the assassination. They found extensive references to our program, expressions of outrage and betrayal, even comments about "wacking out" Kennedy. In May 22, 1963, one Mafia figure from Buffalo, New York, Stefano Magaddino, complained of the pressures on the mob, and hysterically warned in a telephone conversation that was tapped: "They should kill the whole Kennedy family." New York mobsters fretted that same month that RFK was out to jail the Mafia, which better take action. Philadelphia crime boss Angelo Bruno was told by an associate around that same time, shortly before the assassination, "With Kennedy, a guy should take a knife. Somebody should kill the [expletive]. I mean it. Honest to God. Right in the White House. Somebody's got to get rid of this [expletive]."

"There's just this unremitting and unmitigating hatred being expressed for President Kennedy, Robert Kennedy, and J. Edgar Hoover," Blakely recalled to me. Because the committee's review of the FBI surveillance of the mob around the time of the assassination was both extensive and exculpatory in the North and East, Blakey excludes from the possible conspiracy such Mafia chiefs as Giancana, Bruno, Magaddino, and others. However, because there was inadequate coverage of Trafficante, and none of Marcello and Hoffa, he draws no conclusion—inculpatory or exculpatory—regarding them from the bugs.

While the House Assassinations Committee speculated that Marcello, Trafficante, and Hoffa were behind the assassination, its expert on organized crime, Ralph Salerno, concluded his consultant's report with this qualification: Though he could not preclude the possibility from the facts known, and despite clear and unique provocations by our organized crime section, "it is extremely unlikely that the national commission of La Cosa Nostra was involved in any plan to kill the President." Salerno concluded that the methods used were unusual, there was no precedent for assassination, and they were besieged by inner turmoil as well as our own provocations. But, the experienced Salerno agreed, the possibility that Marcello and Trafficante acted on their own, perhaps at the instigation of Hoffa, could not be ruled out.

A key House Assassinations Committee finding, based on acoustical evidence, indicated Oswald had not acted alone. The committee's acoustical experts concluded that in addition to Oswald's fatal shots, there were gunshot sounds coming from the notorious grassy knoll, and thus two gunmen fired at President Kennedy. Blakey's guess is that that person was a mob representative.

The Committee on Ballistic Acoustics was established to look into the House's acoustical finding. Composed of prestigious scientists chosen by the National Academy of Sciences, the Ramsey Committee (named for its chairman, Norman Ramsey) reported in November 1982 that its analysis of the House committee's experts' report and the acoustical evidence it relied on did not persuade them that there was adequate evidence of a second shot coming from the grassy knoll.

House committee counsel Blakey questions the Ramsey Committee conclusion. It does not contradict the House's acoustical experts' technical analysis of recorded echo sounds, he argues; rather, it sidesteps their technical conclusions by accepting a fallacious threshold premise. The Ramsey Committee's conclusion presumed that the sounds analyzed by the House committee experts occurred at a point in time when they could not have been gunshots at the president. Therefore, they did not do the kind of analysis the House committee experts performed that led them to conclude that the recorded sounds and echoes were gunshots, and that the direction of one of the four shots came from the knoll. The Ramsey Committee concluded that the sounds analyzed by the House experts came *after* Kennedy was shot and therefore there was no need for it to analyze the sounds in issue to ascertain their direction.

The Ramsey Committee never undertook to consider corroborating eyewitness or earwitness testimony independently, nor to tie that direct evidence to the acoustical evidence analyzed by the House committee experts. Blakey argues—and others agree—that the Ramsey findings, like those of the Warren Commission, ignore eyewitness and earwitness testimony of five credible witnesses who heard and saw gunshots coming from the grassy knoll in addition to those coming from the book depository.

Combining the committee's acoustical evidence with the other circumstantial evidence, including testimony of credible people who heard and saw evidence of shots from the knoll, Blakey remains convinced that Oswald was not acting alone. If the film, the autopsy, the ballistics, and the witnesses confirm Oswald's three shots from the depository, Blakey asks, why not accept the same kind of evidence about the fourth shot? That final acceptance would demonstrate that Oswald was not the only shooter.

Blakey's rationale to me is that principled analysis should be made of *all* existing evidence. As there are conspiracy nuts who see a conspiracy where supporting evidence is insufficient, there also are what he calls coincidence nuts, those who explain away as mere coincidence what rational evidence suggests might be a conspiracy. Applying similar, appropriate standards to all the evidence, Blakey concludes there is evidence beyond a reasonable doubt that Oswald was the shooter and killer, along with evidence of the probability that there was another shot by someone else, and thus it was to be a joint murder or was a conspiracy.

The assassination, however, "is cursed with too many theories," Blakey admits. The best overall paradigm, based on observation and verification, Blakey and the House Assassinations Committee concluded, is that the conspirators were the mob in New Orleans and Tampa. Here, though, their theory becomes speculative, however logical. The mob was a certain beneficiary of the assassination. Blakey speculates that "the most plausible explanation for the murder of Oswald by Jack Ruby was that Ruby had stalked him on behalf of organized crime, trying to reach him on at least three occasions in the forty-eight hours before he silenced him forever." Oswald and Ruby both had ties to the organized crime world in New Orleans and Dallas. "The fingerprints of organized crime are all over Jack Ruby."

Bob Blakey concluded at the time of the House Assassinations Committee's report: "The mob did it. It's a historical fact." In 1992, with co-author Richard Billings, he repeated and expanded on that conclusion. "Oswald was acting in behalf of members of the mob, who wanted relief from the pressure of the Kennedy Administration's war on organized crime led by Attorney General Robert F. Kennedy; Ruby killed Oswald on mob orders—he stalked his prey for forty-eight hours—to silence him."

Whatever one concludes about the single assassin debate, the question remains whether Oswald had collaborators, even if it was Oswald alone who shot the president. Those who would close the case and accept the Warren Commission's conclusions argue that the best evidence indicates that Oswald acted alone. But even if that is so, two perplexing possibilities remain: Oswald could have been part of a conspiracy without there having been two shooters in the Plaza; and, he might not have known about any conspiracy, even if there was another shooter. Mafia members and Hoffa could have conspired to kill Kennedy, whether or not they were the instigators of or collaborators with Oswald.

———

Startling disclosures supporting the theory that there was a conspiracy to kill President Kennedy were suggested by a former mobster lawyer in 1992. *New York Post* columnist and Robert Kennedy biographer Jack Newfield first disclosed the story in the *Post* and on public television. Newfield interviewed a longtime Tampa-based lawyer for Trafficante and Hoffa, Frank Ragano, who told of chilling conversations with his two clients and with Carlos Marcello. Ragano published a book in 1994 expanding this story of Mafia-Hoffa intrigue and adding credence to earlier speculations.

According to the aging lawyer, who purportedly wished to atone for his life with the mob and to set the historical record straight, Hoffa and Trafficante (Ragano had served them both as counsel for many years and became their social friend) conspired with Marcello to kill the president. Each of the three had strong motives for revenge and survival; each of them had been harassed and endangered by Robert Kennedy's organized crime drive; each was fighting for his life and fortune.

Ragano reports discussions with Hoffa in 1963 before the assassination in which an enraged Hoffa railed that he'd like to have Robert Kennedy killed. "This has to be done," Hoffa told Ragano.

In March 1963, during a long dinner meeting in New Orleans that Ragano attended with Trafficante and Marcello, after discussing Hoffa's troubles with Robert Kennedy, Marcello said it was a shame what the Kennedys were doing to Hoffa. "You, Jimmy, and me are in for hard times as long as Bobby Kennedy is in office. Someone ought to kill that son-of-a-bitch. That fucking Bobby Kennedy is making life miserable for me and my friends. Someone ought to kill *all* those goddamn Kennedys," Marcello told Trafficante. Threat, or racketeer rhetoric? Later that evening over a brandy nightcap, Trafficante complained to Ragano about the hypocrisy of the Kennedy family: "Here's this guy, Bobby Kennedy, talking about law and order, and these guys made their goddamn fortune through bootlegging. Bobby Kennedy is stepping on too many toes. Che, you wait and see, somebody is going to kill those sons-of-bitches. It's just a matter of time."

One evening early in 1963 when Ragano was with Hoffa and other Teamsters officials and lawyers playing cards in his suite at the Edgewater Hotel in Florida, Hoffa asked his cohorts what they thought might develop if something should happen to Bobby, Ragano reports. They agreed the president would go after his enemies with added determination. What if something happened to the president, Hoffa asked? LBJ would get rid of Bobby, one of Hoffa's lawyers speculated. "Damn right he would," Hoffa replied, according to Ragano. "He hates him as much as I do."

Ragano also described a bizarre meeting with Robert Kennedy in Washington in July 1963. Teamsters lawyers had come to the Justice Department to inspect government records in the pending Sun Valley case and were told they had to talk to Kennedy first. Hoffa was enraged when he was kept waiting for forty-five minutes by his nemesis. When Kennedy arrived with his dog on a leash, Hoffa cursed at Kennedy. Suddenly he lunged at Kennedy, according to Ragano, knocked him against the wall and choked him, screaming, "I'll break your fucking neck! I'll kill you!" Three of Hoffa's lawyers had to pull him off Kennedy.

It is hard to imagine Jimmy Hoffa arriving unnoticed at the Department of Justice in those days. It is harder still to visualize the attorney general—especially this feisty one—simply walking away from such an incident and doing nothing. And it is impossible to conceive of his attending a meeting with Hoffa and his lawyers without some—probably-high level—Justice Department lawyers in attendance. That was not how things ever were done, and for very good reasons. If this dramatic part of Ragano's story is phony, can we believe the rest?

The rest is still more sinister. On July 23, 1963, Ragano reports, he was in Washington with Hoffa working on his cases when Hoffa asked him to tell Trafficante and Marcello when he saw them next, "Something has to be done. The time has come for your friend and Carlos to get rid of him, kill that son-of-a-bitch John Kennedy. This has got to be done. Be sure to tell them what I said. No more fucking around. We're running out of time—something has to be done." Ragano passed on Hoffa's message (to Santos and Carlos), and told Hoffa he had done so when in August he saw him again in Washington.

Ragano states that when he told Trafficante and Marcello that Hoffa wanted Kennedy killed ("I want him dead"), they indicated to him that they thought it was an acceptable idea. "They looked at each other in a way that scared me," Ragano told House Assassinations Committee counsel Bob Blakey. "They took it seriously."

After the assassination, Hoffa told Ragano that he was delighted. "Did you hear the good news? They killed the son-of-a-bitch bastard." This meant that LBJ would get rid of Bobby, Hoffa rejoiced. Hoffa pulled down the flag hung at half mast at Teamsters headquarters; he'd not display even a token formal honor of the dead. Hoffa told one reporter, on the day Ruby killed Oswald, "Bobby Kennedy's just another lawyer now."

Ragano told Dan Moldea that he had talked to Marcello and New Orleans district attorney Jim Garrison and "got the distinct impression they were friends" and that Garrison's 1967 probe was "a deflection to shield Marcello and divert suspicion from him." Others have criticized the Garrison investigation and noted his connections with Marcello.

The night after the assassination, Ragano said, he celebrated with Trafficante, who toasted the news: "Our problems are over. I hope Jimmy is happy now," he quotes his client as saying. "This is like lifting a load of stones off my shoulders," he said. "Now they'll get off my back, off Carlos's back, and off Marteduzzo's back [Trafficante's nickname for Hoffa]. We'll make big money out of this and maybe go back to Cuba. I'm glad for Marteduzzo's sake because Johnson is sure as hell going to remove Bobby. I don't see how he'll keep him in office."

Several days after the assassination, while the country mourned and Hoffa worked with his lawyers on his trial defenses, he took Ragano aside, saying: "I told you they could do it. I'll never forget what Carlos and Santos did for me." A few weeks later, in New Orleans, Marcello, who was waiting for approval of a huge Teamsters pension fund loan, told Ragano, "When you see Jimmy, you tell him he owes me, and he owes me big." Ragano's conclusion: "They had actually acted on the message I had delivered to them from Jimmy and now they wanted payoffs from him."

Years later, when Ragano was using Melvin Belli as his lawyer in a case, Trafficante said to Ragano: "Che, whatever you do, don't ask him about Jack Ruby. Don't get involved."

Ragano says Trafficante told him, in a conversation shortly before he died in 1987, who in the mob had gotten rid of Hoffa, and confirmed that his assassination fears were correct. This last, incriminating revelation has been challenged by Trafficante's family as impossible because they say Trafficante was someplace else when Ragano reports they talked; Ragano says he has witnesses to support his dramatic story. According to Ragano, on March 13, 1987, knowing he was going to die soon, Trafficante confessed to his longtime counsel that he had escaped government retribution for his part in killing the president, and speculated in his native Sicilian: "*Carlos e'futtuti. Non duvevamu ammazzari a Giaovanni. Duvevamu Ammazzari a Bobby.*" Translation: "We shouldn't have killed John. We should've killed Bobby." Trafficante had said this to Hoffa, too, consoling him on the eve of his imprisonment: "Maybe he [Robert Kennedy] should have been the one to go instead of his brother."

Three witnesses support Ragano's extraordinary version. An FBI informant, Jose Aleman, Jr., told House Assassinations Committee investigators that he talked several times with Trafficante in 1962, seeking help in obtaining Teamsters loans. During one of those talks, the mobster told him that Kennedy was "not going to make it to the election. He's going to be hit. Mark my words, this man Kennedy is in trouble, and he will get what is coming to him." Trafficante exclaimed that John Kennedy was a dishonest politician who took graft and did not keep a bargain. Then, according to two biographers, Trafficante said to Aleman: "Have you seen how his brother is hitting on Hoffa, a man who is a worker, who is not a millionaire, a friend of the blue collars? He doesn't know that this kind of encounter is very delicate."

Aleman later recanted, refused to tell the same story to the committee under oath, changing this story in a most suspicious way. Aleman had confirmed the story of Trafficante's remarks to the FBI and to committee investigators. But when he was interviewed prior to testifying in public, he became very agitated, fearful that testifying would result in his being killed. When he was called as a witness, he twisted his earlier words, "Trafficante said Kennedy would be hit by votes in the next election" was all he'd meant to suggest. Blakey leaned over to Congressman Stokes and remarked, "You've just gotten a demonstration of the power of organized crime in this case."

Sam Giancana's brother said he boasted, "We took care of Kennedy . . . the hit in Dallas was just like any other operation we'd worked on in the past," though the grandiosity of his explanation included features that were credible along with others that were not. On the eve of his interview with Senate committee staff investigators, Giancana was shot six times in the neck and mouth, symbolic mob talismans for victims who are talking to the government.

A Las Vegas– and Los Angeles–based "entrepreneur," Ed Becker, reported a conversation he overheard in 1962 at Marcello's farmhouse. In front of two other Marcello associates, Marcello blurted out a Sicilian curse: *"Livarsi na pietra de la scarpa!"* ("Take that stone out of my shoe!"). Then he exclaimed: "Don't worry about that Bobby son-of-a-bitch. He's going to be taken care of." Marcello told his listeners that he would recruit some "nut" to kill President Kennedy so it couldn't be traced to him, "like they do in Sicily." Marcello told Becker that "the dog [President Kennedy] will keep biting you if you only cut off its tail [the attorney general]," but the biting would end if the dog's head was cut off. Marcello reportedly told Becker and the others at that farmhouse meeting that if they got Bobby, the president would use the Army and Marines to get them, but if they got the president, Bobby would lose his power. Marcello denied Becker's story when he appeared before the House Assassinations Committee.

This circumstantial evidence suggests that there was a switch in targets, from the troublemaking attorney general to his source of power, the president. Becker claims he reported to the FBI the information that Marcello was going to arrange the murder of President Kennedy; but the FBI has stated that it has no records of either the Marcello or the Trafficante threats. Nor does it have records of reported wiretapped remarks of Trafficante and Marcello in 1975 saying, "Now only two people are alive who know who killed Kennedy." That remark is intriguing. Marcello had a sign in his office that said, "Three people can keep a secret, if two are dead." Who might have been the third person? A Hoffa confederate? An accomplice of Oswald? Giancana?

Ragano told John H. Davis, a Marcello biographer, that Marcello was "the central planner" of the assassination, and that Trafficante and Hoffa supplied "the shooters." Ragano told Dan Moldea's attorney (in 1978) that Hoffa, Trafficante, and Marcello plotted the JFK assassination.

While the House Assassinations Committee was operating, an assistant director of the FBI told Blakey that it had 1,350 reels of tapes of Marcello, including some of him discussing the assassination. But the FBI would not turn over the tapes to the House committee. Marcello's biographer, John H. Davis, sued the FBI to gain access to 161 excerpts of tapes compiled by prosecutors who used them when they tried Marcello for racketeering in 1981. The federal district court in Washington agreed he should have them, but allowed the FBI to refuse to turn over the half dozen tapes the court had sealed, which allegedly include incriminating remarks by Marcello about the assassination.

Moldea reported in his 1993 postscript to *The Hoffa Wars* that on one of these tapes, Marcello boasted, "We own the Teamsters," a proprietary claim consistent with Ragano's report that Hoffa used the mob and paid them off, to rid himself of Robert Kennedy's crusade.

THE CONCLUSION OF THE THESIS

House Assassinations Committee counsel Blakey speculates that President Kennedy's fatal flaw, his affair with Exner, "left him vulnerable to assassination by organized crime." Harris Wofford also has commented on the dilemma caused by JFK's private life and RFK's public work:

> What surely shocked the Attorney General was the recognition, as he put the facts together, that his brother and the government of the United States were entangled with the most evil forces he could imagine, and that Sam Giancana, John Rosselli, and their like held an enormous power to blackmail not only John Kennedy and his family but any government of the United States. The Mafia leaders were privy to what may have been the worst national secret in the history of the United States, and the most embarrassing personal secret about John Kennedy. Nothing could damage the reputation of the United States government and of the Kennedy administration more than disclosure that it had conspired with organized crime to murder the head of a foreign government. Nothing could damage the personal reputation of John Kennedy more than detailed and public allegations of a sexual liaison, while in the White House, with a woman who at the same time was having an affair with a notorious Mafia chieftain.

A recent book expanded on this intriguing thesis. In their biography of Johnny Rosselli, *All American Mafioso,* the authors note that the mob traditionally lived in an implicit peace with gangbusters; they "took the heat" as part of the price of operating. But this scenario was different with the Kennedys. Joseph Kennedy and John Kennedy had made a pact, they speculate, and Robert Kennedy had violated it: ". . . the Kennedys . . . had crossed the line dividing the underworld and legitimate society. They had accepted favors from the mob, had cavorted with their women, had employed their services in intrigues at the highest level of government. Bobby Kennedy's war on crime was more than an assault, it was a betrayal, a double-cross that violated the core of the Mafia ethic. *Onore* required vengeance. Having enjoyed the beneficence of the mob, the Kennedys then spurned them. The mob's reaction was inevitable. As Roselli exhorted Sam Giancana, 'Now let them see the other side of you.' "

No doubt, Robert Kennedy unleashed the mob's fury by attacking it and its leaders as they had never been attacked before, and under the most provocative circumstances. They thought they had a deal with the family, and were infuriated when Robert Kennedy became their nemesis. In hindsight, the events that transpired do not seem so surprising. In the philosophical words of the existential "social historian" Judith Exner, musing in her own memoir, "Some people are deadly serious about the games they play . . . Life in the underworld of crime and the netherworld of politics is cheap . . . it is impossible to tell the good men from the bad."

Mob lawyer Ragano also believes that "the double-cross factor" was what provoked the drastic action against the president.

> The new administration, instead of continuing the status quo and allowing the rackets to flourish, dared to undertake an unprecedented crackdown against the Mafia's hierarchy. Nearly all the godfathers felt betrayed and blamed the Kennedy sons, not the father, for their predicament . . . By reneging on a bargain, the Kennedys became fair game for the savage vindictiveness of the Mafia rulers, despots who survived through a polluted code that obligates them to avenge the merest slight. Had no bargain been struck, it is quite possible that John F. Kennedy would be alive today. The mob would have regarded him as an adversary, but they would not have felt the compulsion to eliminate him as a double-crosser.

This earthy theme was also developed in more elevated language by Kennedy family biographers Peter Collier and David Horowitz. "In the service of his brother's presidency," RFK "had led the administration into dangerous places," they noted in *The Kennedys: An American Dream*, "daring the gods of the underworld and seizing the fire that finally erupted into anti-Kennedy hatred."

A family friend, Mary Bailey Gimbel, described Robert Kennedy's fascination during those obsessed days after the assassination with the story about the poet Gerard de Nerval who walked with a lobster on a leash because "he knows the secrets of the deep." Collier and Horowitz wondered whether "Bobby, like Nerval's lobster, knew the secrets of the deep. He knew what had happened beneath the surfaces of the administration; he knew the role he himself had played . . . and the nightmare marriage between the intelligence services and the mob." Columnist Jack Anderson also speculated whether Robert Kennedy was "tormented by more than natural grief," wondering if acts he condoned "put into motion forces that may have brought about his brother's martyrdom."

Jacqueline Kennedy gave Robert Kennedy one book other than the volume that opened this story. When he was grieving the murder of his brother, she suggested he read Edith Hamilton's *The Greek Way*. People close to him reported he read it and reread it, and often carried a worn copy with him. Lines from that book appeared regularly in his speeches; it obviously was enlightening to him. How raw his reaction must have been to read there the words of Euripides' Electra: "Brother, mine is the blame . . ."

THE CREDIBILITY OF THE THESIS

How credible is this theory that the assassination was planned, if not executed, by key organized crime figures? Some of the sources are, as they usually are in criminal cases, questionable characters with motives to lie. Much of the evidence is circumstantial and arose long after the events it describes. However, prosecutors often prove their cases with circumstantial evidence and witnesses who have questionable pasts and compromising involvements.

Serious questions can be asked about Frank Ragano's recent disclosures. But admissions by clients to their attorney in a confidential setting, however ethically questionable their disclosure may be, usually are deemed to be made in circumstances suggestive of candor and accuracy. Though the attorney-client privilege ordinarily precludes a lawyer disclosing incriminating comments by his client, the rule does not apply in situations where the lawyer is assisting the client in criminal conduct. Though he sometimes represented them, Ragano was not counseling Trafficante or Hoffa regarding their plans to kill either John or Robert Kennedy; indeed, he was a message carrier between them and Marcello in their conspiracy, and thus arguably a participant in their crime. For these reasons, his testimony about these conversations would probably be allowed.

It can be argued that Ragano's late-life conversion to candor may be an attempt to cash in on the public's insatiable interest in the

Kennedy assassination, or that it's the latest example of the emerging literary genre, books by crooks. But his co-author is a reputable *New York Times* crime reporter, Selwyn Raab, who checked all Ragano's stories and lent his name and reputation to them.

While the witnesses who reported the threats by Marcello and Trafficante and Hoffa might have made their reports to gain advantages or to sell books, admissions by defendants are classic exceptions to the hearsay rule. Generally, they are admissible in court, though they are subject to cross-examination and their value may be questioned.

The mobsters who bragged that they had killed the president may well have been claiming false credit for Oswald's act. In their underworld such a claim would have its weight. But were they alive and defending themselves in a criminal case, there is little question that, however questionable, their admissions would be admissible evidence, and damning.

In his recent book *Oswald's Tale,* Norman Mailer attempts to interpret the assassination so that it can be viewed as "tragic rather than absurd." He posits two theories about Jack Ruby's murder of Oswald, a crime, he concludes, that on its face belongs to the Mafia. Because they had the motive, had at least spoken about killing the president, and could be tied to Oswald through his connections to Marcello, and because they stood to gain from Hoffa if he believed they were behind the assassination even if they were not, Mailer theorizes: "If Oswald had been the hit man, he could not be relied upon. And if he were innocent, that might be worse . . . Hypothesis One and Hypothesis Two may be at great variance, but they come to the same conclusion."

If all the parties were alive today—Hoffa, Giancana, Marcello, Trafficante—would there be enough circumstantial evidence to bring a criminal case against them for conspiracy to kill the president? As could be said of many others, all had the motive and means to commit the crime. Could one conclude from the existing credible evidence that there was a criminal conspiracy to kill the president, even if the best evidence to date indicates Oswald acted as a lone assassin, and there is inadequate evidence of a link between Oswald's act and such a conspiracy? To consider this question, one must understand that a conspiracy is simply an agreement; the goal need not be reached for the crime to be proven. Along with the agreement, one overt act—possibly innocent in itself—in furtherance of the object of that conspiracy is all that needs to be proved to make the case.

I can imagine a hypothetical scenario where the organized crime section meets in Robert Kennedy's office to consider a prospective prosecution of major rackets figures for plotting to kill government officials—not for actually doing it, but for planning it. Suppose, for example, top Mafia chiefs had planned to kill a governor or his state rackets prosecutor to stall the latter's campaign to rid the state of organized crime. Suppose further that the governor was later killed under circumstances where the connection between the killer who was caught and the plotters was unclear.

Arguing against such an indictment for conspiracy at our imagined meeting, skeptical lawyers would point out that someone else actually committed the murder and only tenuous connections, probably inadmissible as evidence, tied that person to the alleged conspirators. They'd also argue that if any conspiring occurred, at first the agreement pertained to one proposed victim (the governor) and later it pertained to another (the rackets buster). What kind of agreement was there, skeptics would ask, and what exactly was its purpose? One of my former colleagues at Justice, now a law professor, remarked about such a proposed case: "Conspiracy may be the darling of prosecutors, but as the Apalachin case demonstrates, prosecutors can not push the conspiracy theory too far. Far worse than bringing a case like this is losing it, and it surely would be lost."

More aggressive prosecutors would argue that for such a serious crime by notorious crime figures, the evidence of a plot was strong enough to persuade any jury that wasn't fixed. The motive was clear. The admissions between the conspirators were repeated and unambiguous: Witnesses would swear there had been several conversations between the conspirators whether to kill the chief prosecutor who was causing their immediate problems or the chief executive who owed them and did not rein in the chief prosecutor. We would be reminded of the embracing nature of conspiracy law. Steps were taken—not so innocent—to advance the conspiracy.

Ragano's reports about Trafficante's and Marcello's and Hoffa's incriminating remarks, along with Partin's testimony about Hoffa's threats, and Becker's report of Marcello's warning, and Giancana's brother's reports of their conversations and his boasts, combined with the fact of the killing and the clear motive, arguably constitute a case of conspiracy that a jury might believe. I think if we had discussed a comparable case in one of our meetings in Kennedy's office, we would have presented a special grand jury with a proposed indictment of these conspirators for conspiracy, though not, with the evidence to date, for the assassination. Of course, that can never happen.

Certainly, a case can be made to consider all the available evidence in a court of public opinion, in a congressional hearing, for example. Such an inquiry would add an important postscript to the official history of the assassination. A congressional investigation of the surviving witnesses under grants of immunity would preserve this record under oath and subject their story to rigorous cross-examination. A private inquiry by a prestigious body might serve this purpose, but it would not have the power to subpoena documents or order witnesses to appear.

Though the likelihood of some further decisive revelation fades with time, it is still conceivable that, even at this late date, missing pieces to the "thirty-year jigsaw puzzle" about the assassination, will be found. Few known sources of corroboration remain to be plumbed, however.

The President John F. Kennedy Assassination Records Collection Act of 1992 established a five-member review board to be appointed by the president to ensure the preservation and to facilitate the public disclosure of all government records relating to the Kennedy assassination. That board is slowly but surely opening up remaining sources of information. It could hold hearings on this subject to complete the public record, and it should do so soon.

The fundamental fact remains that for over three decades, no one has satisfactorily answered the key question: If not Oswald alone, who else? Some appropriate responsible inquiry should place on the record all the evidence that has emerged since the House Assassinations Committee bearing on these haunting and persistent questions: Was there really a criminal conspiracy by Hoffa and top mob leaders? Was it related to Oswald's acts? If nothing more, the cynical atmosphere surrounding the Warren Commission Report would be cleared in a decisive, public forum, for the future generations that will have no personal memory of these historic events and for those of us who have wondered about it for decades. Without it, the case will never be closed!

Why shouldn't the case be closed? What motive would the prestigious Warren Commission have had, supporters of its conclusions ask, to assemble the facts and then dissemble about the truth of the matter? If mobsters had the president killed, why wouldn't the national law enforcement agencies investigating the murder want to bring them to justice? Why would the powerful and profoundly interested attorney general, known as a persistent, some said ruthless, investigator, permit an inadequate investigation and an erroneous conclusion about a subject of such painful personal interest to him?

While he remained attorney general and putative chief of the federal government's law enforcement world during the period of the Warren Commission's work, and though he continued to be influential and informed, Robert Kennedy was far less powerful after the assassination than appearances suggested. He was in deep shock and preoccupied with his personal grief and family obligations during the important days in the immediate aftermath of the assassination. For a month, he didn't appear at the department.

Kennedy delegated to his deputy, Nicholas Katzenbach, the job of coordinating the department's work with the Warren Commission. He had friends on the commission whom he could trust. The Criminal Division provided lawyers to the Warren Commission, and one of them, Howard Willens, told me "unless there was a clear and important reason to talk to the attorney general, this was not a subject to raise with him. As a messenger between the department and the commission, I would bring anything special to his attention, so he had the assurance that everything was being done."

The new president and the director of the FBI were personally hostile to Robert Kennedy, and were keenly interested in their own agendas and in public perceptions about the transition of power following the assassination. Finally, we now know that Robert Kennedy knew things that must have haunted him, things he would not wish to become public.

For Lyndon Johnson, it was important to have a credible and distinguished investigating body and as quick and as innocent an explanation as possible in order for the governmental transition to take place smoothly. It was in the national interest for the case to be closed and for this superpower world leader to appear in control of its affairs and the country invulnerable to further disruption. A long congressional investigation or a fractious Texas board of inquiry could highlight dangerous rumors of foreign intrigue that might lead to a war, many feared.

J. Edgar Hoover, whose investigators the Warren Commission relied on, had his own self-interest. It was in his institutional interest to attribute the assassination to an isolated, flaky crackpot, and a national security risk at that, rather than to an organized criminal plot his agency arguably should have known about. In the cases of Carlos Marcello and Santos Trafficante, Jr., and Joseph Francis Civello (a Dallas rackets figure) there had been inadequate surveillance, experts advised the House Assassinations Committee. Indeed, Hoover took disciplinary action against seventeen FBI agents for derelictions in the assassination investigation; five of the actions were severe, including the one against Dallas agent James Hosty for his handling of Oswald himself. The CIA, which assisted the FBI in the Warren Commission investigation, also had compromising misconduct to hide. The agency did not want its collaborations with organized crime characters in clandestine operations in Cuba to come out.

The Warren Commission members only knew the facts its investigators provided. Through the intervening years, increasing information has cast doubt about the adequacy of the FBI and CIA investigations upon which the commission relied. One recent memoir by a high-ranking FBI official candidly concluded that "each agency circled the wagons to defend its own personnel and reputation."

After the trauma of the assassination, and after ceremonial events were completed, the attorney general left office on September 3, 1964. Hoover's hold over the FBI became absolute again, supported by President Johnson, whom Hoover could more readily control. Furthermore, the Warren Commission was unlikely to welcome suggestions years later that its findings were based on flawed investigations.

With time, critics—some responsible, some reckless—would question the Warren Commission's fundamental finding that Oswald acted alone. In 1966, for example, Edward Jay Epstein's *Inquest* puzzled the public with its challenging analysis of the ballistics evidence surrounding the assassination and made a convincing case that the single-bullet, single-assassin theory of the Warren Commission was flawed. That thesis fueled a generation of books (hundreds, perhaps thousands according to one count).

Eventually, knowledgeable observers including credible insiders began to question some of the conclusions of the Warren Commission. Recent reports quote Warren Commission members Senator Richard Russell and John McCloy as questioning the single-assassin conclusion, and involved law enforcement figures from the Secret Service, FBI, and the Dallas police also questioning the commission's conclusions.

LBJ publicly endorsed the Warren Commission findings but told several people that Castro was responsible. LBJ told his aide, Joseph Califano, that he thought Robert Kennedy spearheaded the Kennedy administration's policy to assassinate Castro and that as a result JFK was murdered. "President Kennedy tried to get Castro, but Castro got Kennedy first." LBJ didn't believe that only one person assassinated Kennedy, he told Califano. In the course of a private interview, he blurted out to ABC-TV commentator Howard K. Smith, "Kennedy was trying to get Castro, but Castro got to him first." Smith told me he almost fell off his chair when the former president said this, but despite Smith's prompting, LBJ would not return to the subject. "It was amazing," Smith recalls.

A recent book about the hostile competitiveness that has characterized the history of intelligence gathering by the CIA and FBI describes how that feud led to a "failure to prevent or properly investigate the death of a young president." A combination of what the author, Mark Riebling, called "Hoover's duplicity" in dealing with the Warren Commission, and the CIA's machinations in dealing with the FBI, prevented the facts we knew at the time about the assassination from coming out and possibly the whole truth from ever emerging. A later FBI director, Clarence Kelley, concluded the CIA's failure to cooperate with the FBI "cost JFK his life."

Robert Kennedy himself confided to close aides that he doubted the single assassin thesis of the Warren Commission. "There's been so much bitterness and hatred, and so many people who might have said something have remained silent." Kennedy's press aide in the Senate, Frank Mankiewicz, wrote to me: "It seemed clear to me that he did not believe the Warren Commission's conclusions—a lone gunman, etc.—," though Kennedy never revealed to him "any indication of where he thought the responsibility lay." Kennedy told Ed Guthman that he doubted Cubans did it, and guessed it might have been the mob. In 1966, he told Arthur Schlesinger, Jr., his biographer, that he thought the Warren Commission report was "a poor job" but while he would not endorse it, he didn't want to criticize it and "reopen the whole tragic business." In 1967, he said to former White House aide Richard Goodwin that he thought "the mob guy in New Orleans" was behind the assassination, according to one of his biographers, Jack Newfield. Biographer Anthony Summers quotes Kennedy telling Goodwin in 1966, "If anyone was involved, it was organized crime."

There have been rumors that Robert Kennedy conducted his own private assassination investigation. A campaign aide was quoted as saying Kennedy told him, days before he was killed, "I would like to reopen the Warren Commission" if elected president. I questioned every one of his closest aides, people he most trusted and undoubtedly would have used for such an investigation, and they all deny knowledge or the likelihood of it.

MY CONCLUSIONS ABOUT THE THESIS

I realize now, from the vantage point of a quarter-century's hindsight, how innocent we were of hidden forces swirling around us that unwittingly could have conspired toward a tragic end. Nonetheless, there is a haunting credibility to the theory that our organized crime drive prompted a plan to strike back at the Kennedy brothers, and that Robert Kennedy went to his grave at least wondering whether— and perhaps believing—there was a real connection between that plan and his brother's assassination.

How, one wonders, could this sophisticated man not have realized that what he was doing as attorney general and what his brother was doing as president were on a collision course? RFK knew of Hoffa's death threats toward him and he knew of Giancana's and Trafficante's roles with the CIA. Because he alone was aware of these furtive undercurrents, might Robert Kennedy, wittingly or unwittingly, have preferred to accept the simple conclusion of the Warren Commission so as not to open up compromising family and government secrets? As critic Max Holland has stated: "Full disclosure undoubtedly threatened the emerging Camelot view of the Kennedy Presidency, and, it must be said, RFK's political future as well."

How could Robert Kennedy not have surmised after the assassination that his and our intensive crusade had something to do with that event? How could he have compartmentalized his knowledge of our work prosecuting the rackets and his work as a cold warrior? What a profoundly agonizing weight he must have borne knowing the secrets he knew and, anguishing, as he must have, over their possible consequences. Not one of his closest aides knew of these secrets Kennedy carried with him, or if they did, would admit it. Walter Sheridan, who was as close as anyone, told me: "Bob and his brother confided with each other on some things, and no one else." John Seigenthaler agrees: "Whatever Jack knew, he told Bob."

We in the law enforcement world were ignorant of these undercurrents and of the risks they created. We believed that the battle lines between the "good guys" and the "bad guys" were clear-cut, along with the well-advertised dictum that no one would dare hurt us, that the Mafia was too smart to try such a thing. Might it be, as one of Kennedy's aides speculated, that he thought he had no choice except to remain detached from the Warren Commission investigation. If killers could strike his brother while he was president, what could stop them from killing an emasculated attorney general? Wouldn't it be wiser and safer if he waited until he regained power as president before seeking the real killers?

When the president of the United States was shot and killed, we knew we had lived an illusion, that the world, even for a popular and powerful president, was not a safe place, that anything was possible. Given what followed for the next three decades—murder and mayhem in the United States on an unprecedented scale—it seems a reasonable speculation that when we opened Pandora's box, the settled forces we had attacked would strike back violently and decisively.

———

On the basis of the credible postassassination literature, my interviews with knowledgeable insiders, and my personal experiences at Justice, I draw the following conclusions about this strange chapter of Robert Kennedy's attorney generalship:

1. Robert Kennedy participated in, and at times managed, clandestine cold warrior escapades in foreign affairs that were unwise and outside his jurisdiction as attorney general. These acts created an appearance of conflict with his authority over the department's organized crime program. He was not candid with his colleagues or any public inquiries when candor could have been relevant.

2. From personal experience, I *know* that our organized crime program was not compromised by these unwise actions, hard as that conclusion may be to accept.

3. Based on circumstantial evidence, the likelihood is that our organized crime program prompted Hoffa, Marcello, and Trafficante to plot an audacious assassination: First it was to be of Robert Kennedy, and later the plan shifted to JFK. To date, conclusive proof is missing, although some circumstances suggest that their plot could have been connected to the deadly acts of Lee Harvey Oswald.

Chapter 12

JUSTICE AND PASSION:

A PORTRAIT OF

ROBERT KENNEDY AS

ATTORNEY GENERAL

The organized crime section never got back to what was to be our last meeting with Robert Kennedy, to the decision about my proposed case, or any other. By the end of 1964, our group of lawyers was there in body, but not in spirit.

Our work was at an impasse, and the world had changed. At that brief stop-frame of time during the first half of the 1960s, John and Robert Kennedy had demonstrated the vigor of youth, the vision and value and the attraction of government service, and a sense of mission that young people setting out in the world found striking and energizing. My contemporaries and I were children of the 1950s, raised in a time of what now seemed innocence, relatively; most were subscribers to our parents' vision of the American dream, prepared to work hard and be rewarded, to serve for high purposes, exploited—in the best sense of that word—by John F. Kennedy's exhortations about doing what we could for our country.

The period from 1961 to 1964 was longer ago for those of us old enough to remember it (and longer still for those younger, who have read about it as history) than the passing of only three decades suggests. The United States was another place then—before the profound social changes wrought by the civil rights and women's revolutions, before the divisive disaster of the Vietnam War, before scandal epitomized by Watergate became the common currency of government and the obsession of the media. We who were entering adulthood and beginning families and careers—after school and military service for most of us—are ending our middle age now in a time of public cynicism and drift and endless analysis. The traumatic killing of JFK ended an era. The brilliantly perceptive Daniel Patrick Moynihan said at the time, "We'll just never be young again," and he was profoundly correct.

In his death, as in his life, President Kennedy was the epitome of the multimedia president. Handsome, smooth, elegant, comfortable before questioners and cameras, he used media to win his critical election debate, and to charm reporters once elected. His assassination, the first time a national calamity was exhaustively covered by television, brought every American into that event in a uniquely personal and intense way. We also saw his killer killed before our eyes, right in the police station, by a second-rate hoodlum. These events traumatized the nation's psyche. Having seen a vital, attractive president slain, over and over again and from every angle, we then watched his widow and young children grieve, and his young brother and alter ego transformed before our eyes, it seemed instantaneously, from the tough, political kid his detractors feared into the soulful, reflective statesman he became.

When all that occurred, every American not only felt they were an integral part of the event, they realized that every person—even the most powerful—is vulnerable to mysterious forces of evil, and for a time felt that life is a conspiracy, power is illusory, and anything can happen. Thus, for millions of us, it is not melodramatic hyperbole to say the world had changed.

———

Robert Kennedy plunged into despair and introspection after the assassination. Walter Sheridan was in Nashville when the assassination occurred. He came home the following day and went straight to the White House. On Thanksgiving, he went to Kennedy's home. "We need you. When are you coming back?" he asked his friend. "I know," Kennedy replied, "but I don't have the heart for it now." He didn't seem to care about the Warren Commission investigation. Since nothing would bring back his brother, the fatalistic Kennedy didn't really want an endless investigation, Nicholas Katzenbach mused later; it would be too painful.

Robert Kennedy was gone from Justice often, and when present he was tentative, not his former vibrant self. "He was a walking zombie in the Department of Justice from the day of the assassination to the day he left," Bob Blakey recalls. "I remember vividly the day I went up to say good-bye to him. Looking at him was like looking right through him to the wall. When we shook hands, his hand was limp."

After the assassination, biographers Peter Collier and David Horowitz wrote, Robert Kennedy was "incapacitated within a suffering that surpassed anything."

The FBI dealt directly with the White House now, bypassing the attorney general and his aides. When the Criminal Division head, Jack Miller, flew to Dallas, the FBI would not discuss with him what was happening.

The department's work moved forward glacially. Organized crime cases progressed, but those being planned, such as my proposed case in Florida, stalled, at least for a while. Like many of the younger lawyers in our group, I found that I'd lost interest in much of what we were doing. Had I gotten Kennedy's approval to proceed with the next big trial, perhaps I could have thrown myself into action again and regained the drive of the past three years. But that never happened. Some of our lawyers started looking for other challenges. One by one, those lawyers (those who were not planning a career at the department) left the section, to private practice in Washington or in other cities, to other government agencies, to teach, to work on other good causes such as the Peace Corps or the Civil Rights Division at Justice, where things were hot. Walter Sheridan, Jake Tanzer, and Henry Ruth started to work for Burke Marshall on civil rights cases.

The loss of Kennedy's leadership subtly seeped into the department's morale. Attention was being paid to the Warren Commission investigation, to our leader's personal loss and his hoped-for recovery. During the next few years, the lawyers in the organized crime section would spend half as much time in the field, 72 percent less time in grand juries, 56 percent less time in court. For those of us working on cases this energy shift was perceptible; it seemed to be the result of an organizational malaise that followed the depression of the assassination. The impact of Robert Kennedy's presence and command was gone.

As a practical matter, the organized crime section would never be quite the same. The undisguised antipathy between Robert Kennedy and J. Edgar Hoover had existed throughout the almost four years of the Kennedy administration. The instant the president was killed, the power centers of government shifted and Robert Kennedy was no longer more powerful than Hoover, no longer able to demand his allegiance, to call the shots on any issue they might disagree about. Kennedy was distracted, and Hoover was quite ready to seize the moment—and did. The wrestling for supremacy between these two men was over. Hoover was back in charge, and the Federal Bureau of Investigation again became his private fief.

As Bill Hundley recalled, "The minute that bullet hit Jack Kennedy's head, it was all over. Right then. The organized crime program just stopped, and Hoover took control back." Kennedy himself said, "Those people [the FBI] don't work for us anymore." One FBI agent admitted to biographer Anthony Summers, "The whole Mafia effort slacked off again."

Less than two weeks after the assassination, on December 3, 1963, an FBI bug revealed a cynical remark by one Chicago hood to Sam Giancana: "In another two months from now, the FBI will be like it was five years ago. They won't be around no more. They say the FBI will get it [the assignment to be the investigators for the Warren Commission]. They're gonna start running down Fair Play for Cuba, Fair Play for Matsu." Whether in pique over the perceived insult or in cynicism over the major miscalculation, the speaker added: "They call that more detrimental to the country than us guys."

Hoover's obsession with the power politics of the organized crime section is illustrated by one anecdote that came to my attention years later through a Freedom of Information Act request by a client. An FBI memorandum to Hoover by his longtime confidant and chief aide, Clyde Tolson, concerned an article in *The New York Times* of July 18, 1965, that outraged the FBI chief. Three full single-spaced typed pages ranted on about the harmless *Times* article being "a knife in the back" of the FBI. The article quoted me (then gone from Justice) as making the blasphemous—I thought obvious—charge that the department's organized crime program could never be the same after Kennedy left. Much as I respected the intelligence of the new attorney general, Nick Katzenbach, whom I knew personally and admired, it was inevitably different when the attorney general was the president's brother. Kennedy had been a special attorney general.

The FBI's vain and self-indulgent memo discussed me and my remark. Hoover made a melodramatic marginal note at that point in the memorandum: "Another stiletto from Bobby K."

The fact is, Robert Kennedy permanently affected all of us in the Department of Justice. Not only had the world changed, we had. The hot dogs who joined his crusade after law school educations and some early professional careers found a time and place to focus and energize their talents. Even the few drones, whose careers in the department took them in disparate directions—an assignment to the internal security division would be as good as one to the lands division—had come to share the prevailing sense of mission. No doubt, for them, too, these years in the department were their most exciting ones. Many members of our team who left Justice continued their careers in law schools, on the bench, in public affairs, at the top of their profession. But in retrospect, as exciting as it was, we never realized until time and experience had put this episode in perspective just how special, like RFK himself, our work had been.

I began to look around for a new job somewhere else, uncertain what I really wanted to do. I wanted change. But now, having caught Potomac fever, I wanted to stay in Washington, where it seemed my career might be and the life was good. Kennedy had planned a national symposium on reforming the bail system. I worked on it, and wrote about it and other legal issues for *The New Republic*.

When President Johnson decided to lay plans for a national poverty program, he named Sargent Shriver to direct a task force to design that program. Each government agency donated one or two of its members to work on that task force. I let it be known I'd like to make that move, and was assigned by the Justice Department to work on that new project, one that could not have been more different from chasing hoodlums. So, I no longer worked at the Justice Department, even though I remained on its payroll.

I didn't see Kennedy again at the department, but I did fortuitously find myself with him on a shuttle flight from Washington to New York

City one day in the summer of 1964. We sat together but spoke little. He read the sports pages while I reviewed some papers I had been working on. He was met at the airport by a car and driver and offered me a lift into Manhattan. On the drive, he and his aides and I discussed his running for a Senate seat from New York against the Republican incumbent. We all encouraged him to run, sensing his need to get involved again in politics and government despite his concerns about the risks of public life. He gave no sign then that his mind was made up, but soon thereafter he did announce his candidacy.

My life centered on private events. My wife gave birth to our first baby. I began a second book, about the bail system. Kennedy never completely focused again on his job as attorney general. One evening late that summer in 1964, while I was eating dinner at home with my wife, the phone rang. It was Kennedy. Would I be interested in coming to New York City? He needed another speech writer.

"When do you want me to come?" I asked.

"Tonight." Typical.

"Could I come in the morning?"

"Great, we'll see you then. Thanks, Ron."

Until our election-night celebration at Delmonico's in November 1964, I never left the Chatham Hotel in New York City after I got there the next morning.

That was the quiet end of my Justice Department career. I resigned from the department over the phone the day I arrived in New York and talked to Kennedy and his staff. My work at Justice ended as unpredictably as it had begun, both times unexpectedly, both times to work for the same man, both times to enter a new world. This time, however, I had no moral uncertainty about the man for whom I was working.

———

Perhaps it is possible now, near a century's end and a quarter century after Robert Kennedy's untimely death, to assess his place in history. Certainly, the success of his dynamic, dramatic drive against organized crime can be measured, and I hope this book will help others make that judgment.

Our chapter in the annals of national law enforcement is written. The statistics are impressive. In 1960, there were seventeen lawyers in the organized crime section; Silberling's charter was to get us to fifty quickly. And he did. The days our lawyers spent in the field jumped tenfold; the days we spent before grand juries and in court rose even more dramatically; the number of indictments secured and the number of defendants convicted climbed by almost 70 percent. The trend continued throughout Kennedy's tenure at Justice.

During my years at Justice, I answered the nagging questions about the conflict between civil liberties and prosecution, and about Kennedy himself, that had troubled me when I first contemplated joining the department. I became comfortable with our work and proud of what we accomplished. Prosecutorial discretion and tough law enforcement, I discovered, did not need to be dirty words. Excesses that I learned about later, about which all or most of us knew nothing at the time, qualify the completeness of my judgment; but they do not change my overall conclusions.

Today, as the world has changed, the world of organized crime within it has changed as well. Most, if not all, of the Mafia dons of the 1960s are dead, or close to it. With a few exceptions, the grip of the Mafia has been weakened dramatically. "It's twilight, not sunset" for the Mafia, Bob Blakey suggests. Today's law enforcement agencies must focus on Central and Latin American drug organizations such as the Colombian cocaine cartel and Jamaican posses, on Asian gangs, such as the Chinese Triads, Japanese Yakuza, and Vietnamese gangs, even Russian gangs.

Much of what Robert Kennedy wanted to accomplish, he did. Today, the organized crime section remains a large, active part of the department's Criminal Division. The department's intelligence in this field is extensive. Law enforcement agencies regularly cooperate with each other toward common goals. Some big-city federal prosecutors' offices have permanent staffs devoted to investigating and prosecuting organized crime and racketeering. Kennedy's crusade had ample immediate successes, and it changed the law enforcement landscape permanently. As *New York Times* crime reporter Selwyn Raab concluded, "Except for the convictions of Luciano and Genovese and the brief campaign by Robert Kennedy in the early sixties, the Mafia remained unscathed for fifty years. It had enjoyed a singularly untroubled reign of prosperity."

All of our efforts were not successful, and a few of them were not completed. The Chicago FBI, along with members of the U.S. attorney's office in Chicago, working in tandem with our attorneys, had relentlessly kept the pressure on Giancana. The strategy that was discussed earlier eventually was carried out after Kennedy left Justice in 1964. Knowing Giancana would never testify about any subject because it would destroy his reputation among his "peers," the Chicago prosecutors subpoenaed Giancana in May 1965 before a federal grand jury and questioned him extensively. The theory was that he would be forced to either lie and be convicted of perjury or to refuse the immunity he'd be offered and be imprisoned for contempt. There was no way he could tell the truth in public proceedings on the highly sensational series of questions he would be asked. But it was risky because the judge told Giancana that with immunity, he had "a free pass at anything and everything he had ever done during his life."

Predictably, Giancana invoked the Fifth Amendment in response to all the carefully crafted questions that were prepared for this event by our lawyers. The prosecutors took Giancana before the federal judge, who offered him immunity from prosecution (under the Federal Communications Act), which precluded his invoking the Fifth Amendment.

Giancana would not testify; he could not, as everyone knew.

The trial judge ordered Giancana incarcerated at the Cook County jail until he obeyed the court's order to testify, in effect for the remaining life of the grand jury (at that point about a year). "You have the key to your own cell," the judge advised Giancana before he was hauled off to jail; he would be kept there until he agreed to appear and testify before the grand jury. Since federal grand juries were active for eighteen-month periods, Giancana was jailed for a serious period of time, the equivalent of a felony sentence. The court's questionable rationale for sentencing under the summary civil contempt law was that it was coercing the witness's cooperation, not punishing his recalcitrance (which would have been a criminal contempt and handled differently). Giancana reportedly offered a reward of $100,000 for any scheme to spring him from this prosecutorial trap. None was conceived. The appeals court this time upheld the trial judge.

In fact, when Giancana was released a year later, he left the country. Fed up with the government's harassments (though not the gimmick Petersen had sought my advice about), he moved to Mexico to continue his operations internationally, while passing the torch he had received in Chicago from Tony Accardo to Sam "Teets" Battaglia.

Another tactical tragedy, caused by a colossal tripping up of the IRS by the FBI, arose from our long-standing investigation into Las Vegas skimming. Like the inadvertent discovery of the Giancana bug of Dan Rowan's apartment that led to the exposure of the CIA's collusion with the mob to kill Castro, so too did this important investigation become derailed by a fluke discovery.

A lawsuit in the federal court in Las Vegas revealed an astonishing story: While the IRS skimming investigation was going on for years under our section's supervision, unknown to any of us, the FBI had been running an illegal surveillance of its own. Sometime late in 1960 or early 1961 (around the time J. Edgar Hoover decided he had to get into the organized crime business and started his successful hoodlum surveillance operation in Chicago), the FBI office in Las Vegas began a sting of its own. However, this one stung us.

FBI agents had arranged with the local telephone company to lease twenty-five private lines, which were connected to the FBI's Las Vegas office. Bills were to be sent to the Henderson Novelty Company—a fake, nominal entity—at the FBI address and at a designated P.O. box. Bills were paid in cash. The telephone company manager told his employees to provide "whatever service they needed."

One line was connected to a bug placed in the phone in the office of the head of the Fremont Hotel casino. The phone company had induced a problem with the Fremont line; when it received a complaint a "repairman" installed the FBI bug, and the company then "corrected" the problem. But, by chance, the bug was discovered when the phone was moved by an innocent off-duty phone installer during an office remodeling. Research led to the Henderson Novelty Company, and all hell broke loose in Las Vegas. As word spread around town, two more bugs were discovered in the Sands Hotel manager's rooms. Another was found in the Dunes Hotel, then the Stardust Hotel, then the Desert Inn, then the Riviera Hotel. A lawsuit followed, charging the phone company with numerous violations of law, and depositions brought out the compromising role of the FBI.

Senator Robert Kennedy would become embarrassed when in subsequent years it became public knowledge that the FBI had engaged in extensive illegal eavesdropping and wiretapping in Washington, Chicago, Las Vegas, and Kansas City at the same time that Kennedy had been assuring Congress that his department was not doing so. Throughout 1962–1963, while one arm of our investigative team (the IRS) was spending vast resources and manpower assembling our massive skimming case, the FBI was aborting it by wiretapping the offices and homes of some of the very people and places under legal scrutiny. When this information became public, the FBI's specious justification was that the intelligence it gained outweighed the prosecutions we lost, and as long as the information was not communicated outside of law enforcement offices, the law technically was not broken.

Thus, none of our meticulously crafted cases could be brought because the FBI's actions had tainted the evidence (over nine hundred pages of valuable IRS intelligence reports). One estimate put the provable skimmed profits from six casinos at $6 million. Nevada state officials, aware of where their political bread was buttered, exclaimed that Justice Department tactics had violated state laws, and that the FBI's tactics could "destroy almost any economic or social group in this country." The State Gaming Commission issued a report stating that skimming was a media-created phenomenon started by Robert Kennedy, and that it had found no evidence that money was being channeled to syndicate figures. The commission chairman told the press that witnesses from the casinos testified there could be no skimming because there was "tight internal control"; the chairman found any discrepancies "minimal" and probably based on "the limited scope of the sampling coupled with the leeway for human error."

As deals were worked out releasing bugged defendants from criminal charges, their lawsuits against the FBI agents who did the bugging were dropped. Earl Johnson and the IRS agents he'd worked with assiduously and at great expense for years were demoralized about the FBI's rogue operation. Earl Johnson had specifically questioned the FBI about their use of electronic surveillance and was assured it was not being used. Our scorecard had some major losses, and this case was the biggest. What hurt most was that it was unnecessary.

Despite our frustration, Earl thinks there were compensations—or rationalizations—nonetheless. "While there is no doubt the FBI bugging fiasco destroyed our IRS investigation, I often wonder whether it didn't have a lot to do eventually with the mob's willingness to sell a good deal of its Las Vegas interests to legitimate business entities. After all, it was only three or four years later that Howard Hughes bought out the Desert Inn (owned by Moe Dalitz and other "Purple Gang" alumni) and three or four other casinos. Most of the rest of the mob casinos were sold to others during the next decade.

"It may be wishful thinking, based on a desire not to see all that good work down the drain, but I think it is quite possible the intense federal pressure during the 1960s took the profit out of illegal ownership of Las Vegas casinos—or threatened to. That may have played a large role in the mob's decision to sell most of its Las Vegas interests.

"To put it another way," Earl continued, "this time the intensive enforcement effort meant it cost more to operate these casinos as mob-owned enterprises than it did to operate them as legitimate businesses. So these properties were worth more to legitimate operators than they were to the mob. For once, the good guys (comparatively speaking) bought out the bad guys (in both comparative and absolute terms)."

But those frustrations did not typify our experiences. Stopped midstream as we were, the efforts of the Kennedy organized crime program nevertheless did raise the consciousness of the American public and the law enforcement world about organized crime. We had developed and nationalized a model—an intensified, well-coordinated effort. We ad-libbed while we worked, developing laws to fill the gaps we encountered. We stretched the laws we had because we didn't have all the ammunition we needed.

Though our work was stopped short by the assassination, momentum continued to bring about some of the important successes that evolved after our work began. Many of our successes were individual successes; a few were systemic. Hoffa and many of his crooked cronies were convicted, but it took two more decades for the Teamsters union to clear its house. But it finally did, and our earlier work helped create conditions to make it possible. Federal investigative agencies continue to collaborate as they had not before. We started strike forces in some cities, and several years later the strike force concept had become institutionalized and was in practice in most big cities. (Unfortunately, several administrations later, the strike force program was dismantled.) A few of the cases we brought led to widespread political reform—Newport, Kentucky, was one— but there were not many others.

Some of our graduates continued the battle and finished their careers at Justice. Nick Katzenbach tried to keep the organized crime section a special place. And he appointed our colleague Henry Ruth to head the President's Crime Commission study of organized crime. Bob Blakey worked for the McClellan Committee, and it introduced legislation providing many of the statutory weapons we had learned were needed to fight organized crime: a general immunity statute, special longer-standing grand juries, a witness-protection program, a law permitting wiretapping and bugging in organized crime cases, and finally, RICO, the ultimate weapon against patterns of behavior and organizations of criminals, an antitrust-type remedy to deal with institutional crime and systemic corruption. Individual criminals commit crimes, Blakey had convinced the committee, "but organizations make organized crime possible." Another of our colleagues, Brian Gettings, also worked on the drafting of the RICO statute after he left our section and worked for the House Republican Crime Task Force.

In 1994, I asked Bob Blakey—now a Notre Dame law professor— his assessment of our work, of Kennedy's crusade. His career has been devoted for three decades to studying and fighting organized crime.

"What's the story on political corruption, crooked labor unions, and the mob today?" Blakey answered. "I can tell you that in virtually every metropolitan area in this country, in Boston, in Philadelphia, in New York, in Cleveland, in Chicago, in Los Angeles, in New Orleans, the heads of the families, whole families, have been decimated. We may have been prevented from finishing the job personally, but it was Kennedy's program that made all this possible; without it, none of these things would have happened."

As I had learned from my experiences in Newport, life isn't neat and victories are rarely complete. There can be no total victory; there can only be progress, reform, and qualified positive experiences. Our cases were tough to win and tougher to lose, but the effort was made.

We tend to talk about national efforts like this as if they were wars; but they are not won as dramatically as a world war, with surrenders and public ceremonies. As the veteran crime reporter Miriam

Ottenberg concluded after following our program closely for years, our war might be viewed as a war of liberation: rank-and-file union members liberated from crooked leaders who stifled their democratic processes and plundered their hard-earned savings; honest employers and contractors relieved from paying off exploitative union thugs and crooked politicians; American citizens freed from extorting racketeers and venal public officials; communities returned to the likes of Granny Hays and her fellow citizens of Newport who were liberated from the contaminating influences to which organized crime subjected their community.

Did we cross lines in an immoral, ends-justify-the-means rationalization when we targeted individuals for prosecution? Did Tony Provenzano laugh up his prison sleeve when the ACLU filed an amicus brief on his behalf in the labor extortion case in which we convicted him? It said nothing about the government witness who was killed on the first day of his trial. Did we come too close in using Partin the way he was used to finally snare Hoffa? Was the Chicago FBI guilty of outlawry in harassing Giancana? Would I have arrested Marcello and shanghaied him the way he was? Did Kennedy look the other way and burn his investigative candles at both ends when the FBI hit Las Vegas skimmers low while the IRS was hitting it high? Did he object only to the means used in the CIA attempts to kill Castro, and not to the end?

I personally would say yes to some of those questions, no to others. I blanch at the Marcello deportation arrest, but not at our persistent pursuit of him. I think the right thing was done with Hoffa. Juries and appellate courts agreed with every conviction we secured, and spanked us—appropriately—in the few instances when we did exceed fair bounds. All the cases Kennedy brought with him from the McClellan Committee ended in convictions. I believe our record on labor cases vindicates Kennedy from charges that he had a vendetta against Hoffa and the Teamsters.

The geometry of life is not all straight lines; what is critical is that in law enforcement they may not be crooked. But is it crooked to indict someone who shot an informant in a narcotics case for obstruction of justice as we did in Kansas City, or a brutal Mafia kingpin in Chicago for not paying his taxes when we really want to stop his killing and stealing? When we kept discovering bribery of public officials to keep criminal cases from getting to courts, the brutal elimination and threatening of witnesses (and their families), destruction of documents, and tampering with juries once cases did get to court, how could we not take some extra steps if we were to accomplish our legitimate goals? History will judge the correctness of those steps. Juries and appellate courts gave us a 96 percent success rate.

There were also excesses we—or at least I, and I believe all my colleagues in the organized crime section—did not know about, and learned about much later. The use of mobsters to attempt the assassination of Fidel Castro, which Robert Kennedy and the president did not initiate but may have known about and continued, the alleged CIA-rackets connection recently exposed—these troubling actions would have seemed incredible—as would Hoffa's death threat to Robert Kennedy—if we had heard about them. They still do.

Knowing what I now know about Robert Kennedy's private dealings with the CIA, I am confounded as to how he could have so compartmentalized his two lives, as rackets buster and cold warrior. What I *know* from personal experience is that he never compromised any of our cases because of these complications. Quite the contrary, while it would appear that he would have had to account for his dealings with mobsters who were our section's targets, he never did. I cannot imagine how he planned to cope with their inevitable extortions if they were prosecuted; but he persistently pushed us to push our cases—like the one I persuaded Petersen to not pursue for civil liberties reasons—and never asked any one of us to go easy in prosecuting organized crime cases. It is a wonder to me that this seeming inconsistency existed, but I know it to be so. One can fault him for his surreptitious and potentially compromising endeavors with the CIA, yet conclude—however amazingly—that he never let it get in the way of our Justice Department program.

What about the question of excessive prosecutorial zeal? Mortimer Caplin, a decent and high-minded public servant, had a friendly but very professional relationship with his former student, then boss. "Although he was always considered a very tough guy—the fact that we had the student-professor relationship continued as an important factor . . . We could talk freely to one another." Kennedy told Caplin before they began working together that one of the things he'd be doing as attorney general was taking on organized crime, and asked,

"How do you feel about the IRS getting involved in that?" Caplin thought about the question and discussed it with his own legal lights. "I reached the conclusion that part of our resources could properly be used, but the IRS's role ought to have a specific tax orientation. We shouldn't be there just to help the Department of Justice investigate a drug dealer or gambler. We ought to have a tax crime before us." Caplin rigorously enforced this guideline, however aggressive our joint efforts became through the years, and Kennedy adhered to it. "He agreed with me that the IRS couldn't get involved in those satellite investigations—of cousins of cousins of cousins—just because Justice is running down whoever it's running down . . . we monitored this very carefully . . . We were very much aware of the legal lines that must not be crossed, and there were no winks and secret whispers about it. The whole idea was that we'll be as aggressive as we can here, but we're going to do it on the legal side of the line."

Caplin promised Congress when he took office that he would not exceed the statutory limits of the revenue laws while committing his agency to Kennedy's organized crime drive, and he kept his promise. Caplin agrees that our use of tax laws was, while aggressive and imaginative, not excessive and indeed was productive. When he left office in 1964, Caplin looked back on his experiences and concluded "The record of indictments and convictions of racketeers for tax violations amply supports my pledge and . . . we were able to achieve a year-to-year increase in overall collections of revenue."

Overall the fight was worthwhile if sometimes inexplicable in light of later disclosures. And it couldn't have been fought in a casual, detached fashion. There can be no doubt that the law enforcement world did change in major ways as a result of our efforts, though perhaps at an unexpected and nationally traumatic cost. Prices were paid by our adversaries, and by Kennedy more than anyone. Kennedy took credits, but he paid high prices for them all.

———

The larger question about Robert Kennedy's place in political history continues to engage commentators, critics, historians, and politicians. In a brief but dramatic public career that lasted less than two decades, RFK moved from a short stint as a young Justice Department lawyer ten blocks down Pennsylvania Avenue to become counsel to two news-making, contentious congressional committees, then back to the top of Justice as attorney general, and finally a second time to Congress as a senator from New York. When he was mortally wounded on June 5, 1968, in a kitchen at the Ambassador Hotel in Los Angeles, he was attempting to go sixteen blocks back up Pennsylvania Avenue to the White House. His career was extraordinary, for its pervasive and worldwide impact as much as for the rarefied neighborhood in which it thrived in Washington.

What about the harsh judgments about Kennedy's intellectual abilities and lack of legal experience raised as impediments to his original appointment? *New York Times* columnist Anthony Lewis thinks those who surrounded Kennedy "were crucially placed to further a process of change taking place within him." They were men who were aware of the dangers of abusive power and "their ideas and intellectual connections had their effect on Bobby." Kennedy's former civil rights aide, Burke Marshall, while a dean at Yale Law School, wrote of his former boss's self-education and inspiring working style:

> In dealing with a significant new problem, he steeped himself with information through reading what was suggested to him, and through briefings, and then tested whatever tentative conclusions he reached against the best minds available to him . . . due to the sheer delight, the gaiety, the intellectual thrust of the meetings he held in the process of his self-education on these issues, and the conviction he gave to everyone participating—whatever views they argued for during the meetings—that at the end he had weighed matters properly, understood the legal points thoroughly, and reached a wise conclusion . . . the conduct of those legal debates chaired by the Attorney General . . . were so full of his self-deprecating wit and ego-puncturing humor that pomposity and pedantry could not survive . . . He used to scoff at his training as a lawyer, and his capacity to practice law. But he was wrong about that; it was by no means the least of many abilities.

Even at the end, during his last days in public life, as had been the case when he ran for his Senate seat in 1964, some liberals remained skeptical about Kennedy. When I worked as a speech writer in New

York on his 1964 Senate campaign, most of the people I knew there were cynical about Kennedy (less about the genuineness of his New Yorkness than of his liberalism) and supported his opponent, Kenneth Keating. Lyndon B. Johnson won New York state by a two-to-one majority, while Kennedy won by a 10 percent margin. The Americans for Democratic Action would not endorse him because "his record is not one of a liberal." Leading commentators in the liberal community—James Baldwin, I. F. Stone, Max Ascoli, Gore Vidal, Nat Hentoff, Jules Feiffer—questioned his qualifications. I debated and wrote about Kennedy's credentials then, and he dropped me a droll note commenting, "Anytime I watch television you are defending me."

Some of his earlier critics had noticed major changes in Robert Kennedy during his four years as attorney general. The same *New Republic* that criticized his appointment as attorney general in 1961 wrote in 1964 that "Mr. Kennedy brought first-rate men to the Justice Department and backed them up, that his enterprise in the civil rights fight was both aggressive and astute; that he brought about good reforms in the federal prison system and in the area of juvenile delinquency"; that at the time of the 1962 Cuban crisis his "influence was on the side of restraint, not belligerence"; and finally that "for what it's worth, our judgment is that Mr. Kennedy would make the best senator."

Others agreed. Arthur Schlesinger, Jr., commented that the ruthless, McCarthy stereotype many critics maintained about Kennedy "bears no resemblance to the Robert Kennedy whom the liberals of the Kennedy administration found a strong and faithful ally and on many occasions a leader in the policy debates of 1961–1963, both in domestic and foreign affairs." Schlesinger's thousand-page biography placed Kennedy in a special pantheon of public figures in American twentieth-century history.

The feature that was deemed an impediment when he was first considered for the job, his close relationship with his brother the president, became his strength. Not only did his relationship with the president make Robert Kennedy an extraordinarily powerful attorney general, it also helped him to be an extraordinarily adept politician. Schlesinger who wrote about and knew both men well, remembers that the younger man was "the nerve center of the New Frontier," the one everyone else in the administration turned to with problems. And he used his roving mandate, Schlesinger recalls, "with discretion and imagination to reinforce liberal ideas and initiatives" on diverse national and international subjects. The experience left him "superbly equipped by intelligence, judgment and passion for the great tasks of national leadership . . . He was . . . our nation's most promising leader."

The tough prosecutor whose wry humor, self-confidence, and compassion insiders at Justice came to know was not only intensely saddened but also chastened by the assassination of his brother. The fierce fighter of early days, who one biographer said was "wholly preoccupied by the present," evolved into a politician who cared deeply about his country's future. This beneficiary of a great family fortune became increasingly interested in the country's—indeed the world's—human needs during his Senate years. He seemed to be "on a pilgrimage of self-discovery" his admiring biographer, Jack Newfield, reflected, "a work in progress . . . cut down in transit." *The New Yorker* magazine, commenting at his death about his widening concerns, noted that "Each time we saw him there was more to see. He could never be accurately measured, especially in terms of the past; he was always in the process of becoming."

The sense of moral outrage that had motivated him to fight our adversaries in organized crime would later be channeled toward helping disadvantaged and needy citizens. His fierce commitment became refocused on more benign causes. His priorities evolved from the justice of retribution to the justice of equality. To adapt his favorite quote from the Greek classics, at Justice he had labored "to tame the savageness of man" and later in the Senate he strove "to make gentle the life of this world."

Those of us who worked for him at Justice saw this character evolution in acts of grace under pressure and in revealing incidents even as he fiercely exercised his immense powers against racketeers. In addition to more cosmic, public causes—such as Kennedy's obvious commitment to civil rights—that grew during his tenure as attorney general to meet the rising racial crisis in the South, there were quieter, more private incidents in the department that revealed the human side of this strong yet sensitive public man. I recall one personal experience; I heard of other examples from colleagues.

My book *The Contempt Power* was published in 1963, and though its publication provided a source of personal pride, it also caused me to have a surprisingly painful experience. A major constitutional issue was about to be decided around that time; it concerned the right to trial by jury in criminal contempt cases. Historically, contempt was punished summarily, without the usual procedural protections that surround all other criminal charges. Summary contempt procedures had been attacked as unconstitutional by some scholars and critics, and I was in agreement with court decisions suggesting change.

The timing of the publication was perverse, considering the specific context in which the issue was raised. In 1963, the Department of Justice was in the middle of its historic civil rights struggle, and in two major situations the right to a jury trial in contempt cases had become a very crucial, visible, and contentious issue. The notorious contempt case against Mississippi governor Ross Barnett was wending its way to the Supreme Court, and the evolving Civil Rights Bill (eventually passed in 1964) was being debated in Congress. In both instances, the right to trial by jury became a lightning rod of public debate.

Southern senators who were opposed to integration efforts knew that southern juries were unlikely to convict in civil rights cases; so they seized upon the civil liberties, trial-by-jury issue as a way to beat the law. Governor Barnett's case in the Supreme Court hinged on his claim that he was entitled to a jury trial and had been denied this constitutional right. Southerners filibustering against the proposed new civil rights bill argued that the new law should include a jury trial provision, and they were citing long passages of *my* book into the congressional record as authority for *their* position. No doubt cynics among them were enjoying the ironic twist of citing a liberal Yankee's book against the administration, and at that a book by one of the attorney general's assistants.

Years later, Senator Sam Ervin, the leader of the Southern opposition, told me he had a high regard for my book and its constitutional viewpoints; but at the time I was crushed, and terribly self-conscious about being used perversely by our political enemies in such an important fight.

I asked to see Kennedy about a personal matter when he had time, and one afternoon he invited me to his office. I brought him a copy of my book, apologized for being the cause of any embarrassment, and told him if he wanted, I'd resign. I found it distressing to be causing problems for my colleagues, especially when I was so sympathetic to their cause.

Kennedy asked me about the point of view I advocated in my book: To deny a jury trial in situations where a judge alone could sentence someone to imprisonment was a unique violation of constitutional law and bad public policy. One might like the result in specific situations, I argued, but the practice violates fundamental notions of fair play.

Kennedy listened attentively. To my astonishment, he said he agreed with me, admitting, "It's too bad the timing was so wrong." Then he wished me good luck with my book and asked if I would sign the copy I had brought him. He handed me an autographed copy of his book, *The Enemy Within*. We looked each other in the eye, shook hands, and one anxious young lawyer left his "ruthless" boss, admiring the more that man's principles.

In 1963, a firebrand octogenarian pacifist named A. J. Muste was alleged to have violated federal laws by protesting our country's foreign policies with Cuba. As a result of one of his audacious acts, defying a travel ban against going to Cuba, it had been proposed that he be enjoined and his boat seized. Technically, that course was possible, and immigration officials had proposed the action, and department officials had prepared the paperwork. When the required authorization came to Kennedy to sign, he asked what the case was about. Advised of the background, Kennedy tossed away the papers and tartly asked whether this country really had to worry about an eighty-four-year-old critic's protests. "I'm not going to sign that piece of paper." That was that—an instinctive, private endorsement of First Amendment freedom that impressed the few insiders who knew about it.

In one case where it had been urged that a decorated veteran be denied burial at Arlington Cemetery because he also had been an active Communist Party member, Kennedy demurred. "If the people buried there don't object," he responded, "why do those who are still living?" Similarly, he released Junius Scales, the only Communist imprisoned under the Smith Act, over Hoover's and others' objections to granting clemency because they saw it as a repudiation of the loyalty tests.

Robert Kennedy's press aide throughout his tenure as attorney general, the prizewinning journalist Ed Guthman, remembers numerous private and revealing incidents. Kennedy was disturbed by the shabby District of Columbia public schools existing in the very shadow of the White House in which his brother resided. He told Guthman he wanted to do something about it, and asked that appointments be set up at several schools.

There was no press. Kennedy brought a local sports hero with him, the Washington Redskins' Bobby Mitchell. Kennedy talked to the students about their lives, he asked what they were learning about the Declaration of Independence and the Constitution. At Cardozo High School, he talked with a group of students who told him they were dropping out of school for lack of funds. On the way back to the Justice Department, he asked the superintendent of schools, who was riding with them, about the situation. "We have a program for this," the superintendent told Kennedy. "How many students does it cover?" Kennedy asked. "About fifteen" was the reply. "How many students need help like this?" Kennedy asked. "About four hundred fifty," the superintendent replied.

As soon as he got back to the Justice Department, Kennedy called his key assistants together to tell them, "We have to do something about this." A movie preview was arranged along with a personal appearance by Sammy Davis, Jr. Low-priced tickets were sold throughout the community; $45,000 was raised and it was turned over to be used to hire needy students to work in the schools. The following year there was a repeat event, this time with Ella Fitzgerald. The whole program was run out of the Department of Justice by Kennedy's aides.

Kennedy also visited Shaw Junior High School, where he noted an unused, crumbling swimming pool. Asked why the unused pool was in this condition, Kennedy received the standard "no funds" response. Back at the Department of Justice, the attorney general called the archbishop of the Catholic Diocese, the Episcopal bishop of Washington, and the Jewish Leadership Council and raised $35,000 to repair the pool. "Be sure this pool is maintained," he told the school officials.

Columnist Mary McGrory recalled an event to which she was bringing a group of homeless children. When their transportation became a problem, Kennedy sent Justice Department vans to fetch them. McGrory worried that she'd imposed on Kennedy. "This is what government is for," he replied. Today, there would be an inquiry into misuse of government property; McGrory remembers the incident warmly, three decades later.

Every lawyer who worked closely with Kennedy at Justice has a story like these, private examples of a human side of the public man. So do the journalists who followed his career, and his colleagues in government service. Angie Novello worked for Kennedy for thirteen years, at the McClellan Committee, throughout his years at Justice, and in the Senate thereafter. She saw him up close, nine to nine, under pressure and at play. "People who called Bob ruthless didn't know the man," she reminisced to me. "The personal letters he wrote by hand consoling a grieving low-level staff person, his gentleness with everybody's kids who came to his office, the little courtesies that made you feel valuable as a secretary or staff member, the boat parties on Fridays or the picnics at his house for all the staff, his personal gifts. He was a great guy to work for."

These humane characteristics became more widely perceived after he left Justice. But Kennedy always had an interest in young people and the downtrodden. In the Senate he could focus on the needs of the urban and rural poor, farm workers, people in underdeveloped countries—"the constituency of the powerless," to use Arthur Schlesinger's phrase.

As a result of his civil rights experiences, Anthony Lewis wrote, "Bobby became warmer, more sympathetic, more understanding of humanity's imperfections." It was as if the devotion he had husbanded earlier for his elite and powerful family had opened up and touched the family of man. He became the representative of the unrepresented—the hungry, farmworkers, the hopeless residents of urban ghettos. However lacking in education and sophistication, disadvantaged people particularly sensed an intrinsic element of compassion in Kennedy, a humanism that belied his toughness in other parts of his life.

That combination—one other liberal leaders have not been able to replicate—is what made him appeal to steelworkers in Pennsylvania and factory workers in the Midwest, at the same time that he was adored by disenfranchised blacks in Mississippi and disgruntled urban dwellers in Bedford-Stuyvesant, Brooklyn. His sternness in fighting organized crime was tempered by his empathy with the needs of disadvantaged people.

People today may think that there was a good Robert Kennedy of his Senate years, a public figure reflecting more traditional liberal views of what a public figure should say and do, who was different from the hard-driving official who pressured the mob in his Justice Department years. That assessment is artificial and it is wrong. After Justice, after his war on organized crime, Robert Kennedy moved on to other matters, and he did so with the same intensity and charismatic style as he had always exhibited. The Robert Kennedy at Justice was tough, but he also was humane. The Robert Kennedy in the Senate was humane, and he was also tough. Indeed, it was that rare combination that was the essence of his extraordinary appeal and success.

Can one reconcile the humane Kennedy who was a social engineer with the crusading investigator-prosecutor he also was? Was his goal-oriented zeal a form of persistent demagoguery? Were his compromises, or those ethical standards he overlooked in serving his family as well as his country, fatal flaws, or could they be seen as the inevitable realpolitik of a man of power and action? These are subjective questions; it is my judgment that while Kennedy sometimes crossed uncrossable lines because of excessive prosecutorial tactics, those incidents did not wholly characterize his tenure at Justice. He did not compromise any prosecutions by pulling punches because of any need or desire to protect his brother, his family, or their political or his own personal interests. Indeed, the confounding question I am left with is how he managed to balance what he knew was happening elsewhere in the government concerning some subjects of our work with what he knew we in the organized crime section were doing to them at his urging and with his wholehearted support.

In 1964, when Kennedy's leadership qualities were being questioned by many Democrats, Norman Mailer made a prophetic remark: "I think Bobby Kennedy may be the only liberal about, early or late, who could be a popular general in defense against the future powers of the right wing. For there is no one else around. The Democratic Party is bankrupt, bankrupt of charisma; the right wing has just begun." That his name and likeness was honored at the 1992

Democratic convention demonstrates Mailer's prescience—indeed, Kennedy's unique attraction has grown since he was killed.

Why? Robert Kennedy carried with him both pragmatism and idealism. In dealing with the problems he encountered and cared about, problems that bedeviled America, he exuded a unique and broad-based credibility. What he did was shaped by the times and events he encountered; how he used his power attracted and energized many disparate groups of people as they had not been before and would not be after. Kennedy embraced causes. Harris Wofford described Robert Kennedy's growth and change "from the narrow-minded moralist of the 1950's who would use almost any means to get his ends, to the broad-visioned and strangely transfigured candidate for President in 1968."

Shy about the obvious glamour of his life, he was unabashed in his use of power toward his ends. Kennedy wielded power with a unique combination of assuredness and empathy, of responsibility and individuality, and he communicated these qualities to those around him. These were rare combinations, I would learn in the years after I left Justice and Kennedy left this world. In comparison to a quarter of a century of attorneys general and other nationally prominent politicians, Robert Kennedy grows mightily.

Robert Kennedy tapped into a wellspring of energy and high-minded public service that seems unique in retrospect. Of course, there were people in our regime for whom their job was just a job; and there were some of us who were angling for self-advantage and personal opportunities. But most in our relatively small group at Justice were there to accomplish a task, to follow the goal of a leader in whom we came to believe, and to do something we thought was good for our country. Our experience at Justice exemplified what one astute observer described as "a vast national innocence at a time of unmatched affluence, confidence, and hope . . . for the children of the newly prosperous—college educated, self-involved, itching to do something heroic—self-improvement . . . was about idealism . . . and it was about having smart young people . . . running the country." All young people have that potential quality in them if the right person and message inspires it. For this group of us, "this band of brothers" as Ed Guthman called us, Kennedy and his crusade against organized crime did that.

In the present time of plastic politics—of handlers, and pollsters, and of bites and spins—in such a time particularly, Robert Kennedy's laserlike directness and his genuine commitment to the causes he championed should be viewed as rare commodities. That was not so clear then as it is now with several successive governments and political figures to compare to Robert Kennedy. He grows not in myth but in substance. That man who frightened me in 1961, who assiduously directed our work for four years, imperfect though he was, as unlikely a hero as one could have imagined given his background, was—it is very clear now—an inspiring character, a unique political figure. He was, to use one journalist's artful phrase, the best we had "in a black, dark season in America."

The brash young man who fooled the intellectuals and recited delicate lines from Greek poetry and profound passages from Shakespeare, who saw moral battles in black-and-white terms that are generally obscured by modern politicians, who did not fear to enter the heavy waters of controversy, who never resisted stating the moral imperatives he saw or using them as guideposts for political action, this "soulful man the world thought was ruthless" to use Jack Newfield's phrase, this man of action with the tender heart, as the Reverend Martin Luther King, Jr., described him, was surely unique.

One journalist who knew Kennedy well and watched him closely reflected: "Underneath the exuberance, I thought there was always a fateful quality. He would stand alone, looking into himself, as if he knew that despite all the success and the glamour he had been born under an unhappy star." He had about him, Pete Hamill wrote, "a dark Celtic sense of potential apocalypse."

Kennedy truly reveled in the special legacy of public service; he believed in its importance. As he said in one still relevant speech:

> There is no greater need than for educated men and women to point their careers toward public service as the finest and most rewarding type of life. There is a great danger, not only in politics but in many facets of our nation's social and economic life, that the ethical and moral approach has been reduced to the second rank of importance behind the twin goals of success and prosperity. If this is generally true . . . then our nation is in dire peril.

The brother within Robert Kennedy, the person who emerged from the young man who resisted becoming the attorney general and soon became a bigger-than-life legitimate American political hero, was our brave, imperfect, activist, blossoming leader at Justice. He rejoiced in his life, playing for keeps, and so did we.

Kennedy always wanted to make a difference, and he made those of us who worked for him believe we could make a difference.

Some believe there is nothing one man or one woman can do against the enormous array of the world's ills. Yet many of the world's great movements, of thought and action, have followed from the work of a single man . . .

Few will have the greatness to bend history itself, but each of us can work to change a small portion of events, and in the total of all those acts will be written the history of this generation. It is from numberless diverse acts of courage and belief that human history is shaped. Each time a man stands up for an ideal, or acts to improve the lot of others, or strikes out against injustice, he sends forth a tiny ripple of hope, and crossing each other from a million different centers of energy and daring those ripples build a current which can sweep down the mightiest walls of oppression and resistance.

After Kennedy was elected to the Senate in 1964, I decided it was time to go to work for myself. At a celebratory postelection dinner at a private club in New York City hosted by the senator-elect, I let it be known that I had no interest in working in the Senate. We agreed to keep in touch, and we did meet and correspond from time to time. I started my law firm and wrote the book about the bail system for which he wrote an endorsement. In the Senate, Kennedy became a different political force than he had been at Justice, because he had become the elder Kennedy in politics, because world events (particularly the Vietnam War) thrust him in the role of dissenter to President Johnson's national policy, and because his own personal odyssey and his growing constituency was continuing to evolve.

We talked in his Senate office occasionally, and he asked me for ideas. I recently found a letter I sent him on March 11, 1968. My work on the Presidential Riot Commission had led me to think, I wrote, that our urban dilemma was misperceived by those in power and that the grim life in America's ghettos was growing more troublesome. Our boiling domestic problems were being compounded by the war in Vietnam, and the radical right was breeding, finding these social conditions amenable to its claims.

It all added up to the fact, I urged, that a Johnson-Nixon election campaign would provide no suitable alternative. However uncertain the result might be, he should make a good and respectable try for the presidency; it wasn't too late; and many people like me would respond to his leadership if he ran.

Soon thereafter, of course, he announced that he would run.

On June 6, 1968, when I was called in the middle of the night and told of his death, I wept. Days later, on a hot summer afternoon, my wife and I sat on the grass on a crowded hillside at Arlington National Cemetery, among a sad and silent throng of mourners, ruminating on the death of this young American hero. Neither an intimate of his nor remote from him, I began to realize then what I know now: that my years inside Justice working for this extraordinary man were a unique experience not to be replicated, one that forged me into the person I would become as a citizen of Washington. But a chapter of my life was over.

Kennedy had been warned about this kind of thing happening. The French novelist Romaine Gary had said to Pierre Salinger, "You know, of course, your guy will be killed," and Robert Kennedy admitted to Gary that he believed an attempt on his life would be made sooner or later. Jacqueline Kennedy had told him she feared American hatred would kill him, "but he isn't fatalistic like me." How perverse that it came just as he approached his potential pinnacle of power.

I grieve now when I think of what the country lost when he died, dropped in midstride in his dashing political journey, and how rare a man Robert Kennedy turned out to have been. I agree with the assessment of C. P. Snow that had Robert Kennedy lived, he would have done things as president that no other American could have done.

Writing of the historian Herodotus, Edith Hamilton noted his sympathetic treatment of all humankind. She wrote that "If his heroes are imperfectly great, his villains are never perfectly villainous." To borrow lines from a book that so touched Robert Kennedy seems appropriate for a book about him. Theoretically, it strikes me that the organized crime figures we battled *were* perfectly villainous—they had no redeeming social purpose, to borrow a phrase from the law of obscenity. They were unremittingly criminal and their acts uncondonably antisocial. We who fought them, as enforcers of the social contract, led as we were by one who had a true claim to the title hero, were all imperfect. We erred; we won and lost cases; whatever the provocations or rationales, we were excessive at times. Kennedy himself was part of a process that was for the most part out of everyone else's sight and at least in hindsight subject to serious questioning.

I've wondered often while writing this book, reliving my years in the company and service of Robert Kennedy and discovering parts of his generalship I never dreamed of then, whether he was, in fact, and remains a hero. What is a hero? If it is a perfect person, pure in all he does, Robert Kennedy was no hero. But by such a standard, few would qualify. Real people who can accomplish heroic acts and never transgress in the rest of their lives are few. After all, we are considering heroes, not saints.

Senator Harris Wofford, who worked for the Kennedys, said years later: "In this skeptical age, it is hard to acknowledge heroes, and Americans cannot regain their lost innocence. In classic drama, however, the hero is not one without great flaws; indeed, he usually is brought down by some combination of those flaws and fate, but out of the fall comes new understanding."

Joseph Campbell remarked that "a hero is someone who has given his or her life to something bigger than oneself." If to be a hero one must do that, must perform acts that are extraordinary and have public, rather than personal, influence, of course Robert Kennedy would qualify. In about a decade in public life—from the McClellan Committee to the Justice Department to the Senate—Robert Kennedy grew exponentially, in wisdom, in breadth of influence, in impact for the public good. Few public figures have grown better as their power increased; this Robert Kennedy did. Those corruptions that came with the exercise of that great power were eclipsed by his accomplishments.

Joseph Campbell's ruminations about the nature of heroes are evocative of this Kennedy's life. A hero is one who inspires others to act beyond their ordinary experiences, he stated, to reach farther, do more, affect the public's interest. Campbell noted that the traditional hero is endowed with extraordinary powers from birth, and is one whose central adventure is his life's culmination. Typically, the hero's adventure begins with something being taken from him or lacking to members of society, which the hero seeks to recover. The question in tales of heroism is whether the dangers can be overcome so the hero can serve. By prevailing over oppressors he brings regeneration to society. The dragon he seeks to slay is the status quo. "The moral objective is that of saving a people or supporting an idea. The hero sacrifices himself for something—that's the morality of it."

The archetypal hero, he adds, goes in quest of a new, germinal idea with the potential of bringing something new. Vital people are on journeys to save themselves and, in this attempt, save the world. The hero is fearless of the terror of death and reconciled with the grave. Their deaths only add to the magic of their legends, especially when it comes in the course of their causes, because they have made the ultimate sacrifice. "Show me a hero," F. Scott Fitzgerald wrote, "and I will write you a tragedy."

Heroes portrayed in ancient and contemporary myths from all cultures courageously oppose chaotic forces that threaten the civilized social order, scholars have noted. The hero sees things before others do and, through self-mastery, has the courage "to confront whatever darkness he finds in himself and in the world." The literature of heroes refers to quests, risks, turning points, transformations, and ultimately to the finding of grace—all themes familiar to Robert Kennedy's life.

Where heroes succeed, they provide hope to ordinary man. Psychoanalytically, the ego ideal is the individual's internal version of the hero. People invest their heroes with their personal visions of virtue and sin and thus are able to cope with their own needs and ability or inability to deal appropriately with them. The Indologist Heinrich Zimmer suggested that myths about heros reveal our unconscious selves and provide "a sort of map for exploring and ascertaining contents of our own inner being to which we consciously feel only scantily related."

These thoughts suggest why Robert Kennedy and the so-called Camelot years of the Kennedy administration continue to be so compelling to so many people, and explain why that time and experience is one I continue to cherish and assess. Robert Kennedy provided a spark, set a tone, heightened the spirits, and held together those people who worked for him at Justice. Nicholas Katzenbach recently reminisced: "He inspired in us a high form of public service."

One difference between ancient myths and modern news is that the contemporary observer has so much varied information or "fact" that he or she becomes disillusioned with contemporary heroes. Modern man is capable of heroic acts, but the intensity and pervasiveness of information and disinformation in the modern world bares the human frailties of our heroes as well. The heroic acts of public personalities—politicians or performers, for example—are widely observed, and they have exalted positions in society. However, when their personal weaknesses are revealed—scandals and misconduct—the public becomes disillusioned. That is not the case with mythic heroes. We cannot expect our real life heroes to be perfect, or totally heroic; to perform heroic acts is enough.

And what should be said of villains? Along with their villainous acts, can they not also be credited with acts of goodness? Was Hoffa not useful to the Teamsters, despite his misuse of the powers they provided him? Were Mafia bosses not charitable to their churches and doting on their children and grandchildren, however murderous they were in the rest of their lives? If one recognizes the imperfection of the heroes of this book, why condemn the villains as perfectly evil? Would Herodotus not have had a more balanced view of them? Perhaps. But in the context of this story, weighing the relative character of the combatants in this crusade against one species of criminal offenders, which resulted most frequently in their convictions, it can be said that their imperfection was complete.

Robert Kennedy was not a bad man, Nicholas von Hoffman observed and I agree, but he was a real one. He was not Saint Bobby, as idolaters have suggested; nor was he the constitutional devil his deprecators predicted and some still insist he was. With our program, he changed the nature of national law enforcement for the better, by defining a new and appropriate federal role and providing a model. He was first, fierce, and effective in engaging an important national problem. Whatever its flaws, our program changed reality without doubt for the better. Kennedy's imperfections did not interfere with his heroic war against organized crime.

Might it have been otherwise? Might the heroes have been perfect in their attempts at heroism to match the perfection of the villainy we encountered? Is it ever possible—or necessary—to find a perfect world?

The author

NOTES

CHAPTER 1: THE FATHER WITHIN

p. 3   **"For a Christmas present"**: Robert Thompson and Hortense Myers, *Robert F. Kennedy: The Brother Within*, p. 10

p. 7   **"All of us have worked our tails off"**: Clark Clifford with Richard Holbrooke, *Counsel to the President*, p. 337.

p. 12   **"the flavor of politics"**: Daniel J. Meador, *The President, the Attorney General, and the Department of Justice*, pp. 38–39.

CHAPTER 3: THE EMERGENCE OF ROBERT KENNEDY

p. 37   **"It seems to me imperative"**: Robert Kennedy, *The Enemy Within*, p. 325.

p. 43   **"You grow up with idealistic ideas"**: Jean Stein and George Plimpton, ed., *American Journey, The Times of Robert Kennedy*, p. 52.

p. 45   **"There is wide-open gambling"**: U.S. House of Representatives, 87th Congress, "Legislation Relating to Organized Crime," Committee on the Judiciary, Subcommittee No. 5, Serial No. 16, May 17, 1961, p. 23.

p. 46   **"blow to their operations"**: Ibid., p. 25.

p. 46   **"Justice is going to be involved"**: Ibid., p. 27.

p. 46   **"The face of organized crime"**: Ibid., pp. 28–29.

p. 47   **"these hoodlums and racketeers"**: U.S. Senate, 87th Congress, 1st Session, "The Attorney General's Program to Curb Organized Crime and Racketeering," Committee on the Judiciary, June 6, 1961, p. 17.

CHAPTER 4: LEARNING ON THE JOB

p. 65   **"He personified organized crime in Chicago"**: William Brashler, *The Don: The Life and Death of Sam Giancana*, p. 246.

p. 78   **the lines were clearly drawn:** Ed Reid, *The Grim Reapers, The Anatomy of Organized Crime in America*, p. 231.

p. 78   **"a gawdy-bawdy . . . cowtown":** Ibid., p. 249.

p. 79   **"steady, unseen, incalculable cash":** Brashler, *The Don: The Life and Death of Sam Giancana*, p. 185.

p. 79   **"In each casino there is a counting room":** William Roemer, *Man Against the Mob*, pp. 130–31.

CHAPTER 5: MY TURN, IN NEWPORT, KENTUCKY

p. 85   **"captive of its dark reputation":** Hank Messick, *The Private Lives of Public Enemies*, pp. 110–11.

p. 85   **"supermarket of vice":** Ibid., p. 111.

p. 86   **"publicity mills":** Fred L. Cook, *A Two-Dollar Bet Means Murder*, p. 198.

CHAPTER 6: A RESPITE IN WASHINGTON

p. 137   **"I took Sam's name and wrote it down":** Roemer, *Man Against the Mob*, pp. 189–90.

p. 137   **a Giancana emissary:** Roemer, *Man Against the Mob*, pp. 186, 263.

p. 153   **Valachi "described in intricate detail":** Cartha DeLoach, *Hoover's FBI*, p. 314.

CHAPTER 7: POLITICS IN JUSTICE

p. 162   **Hoover was compromised by crime figures:** Anthony Summers, *Official and Confidential: The Secret Life of J. Edgar Hoover*, p. 331.

p. 171   **"nothing about the Keogh case was routine":** Victor Navasky, *Kennedy Justice*, p. 367.

CHAPTER 8: LABOR AND THE RACKETS

p. 186   **"The tyrant, the bully, the corrupter":** Kennedy, *The Enemy Within*, p. 324.

p. 189   **"Though Beck commanded considerable influence":** Edwin Guthman, *We Band of Brothers*, p. 66.

p. 191   **an antisocial rebel:** Murray Kempton, "Devito Raises Hoffa," *Vogue*, January 1993, p. 225.

p. 192   **"Jimmy had a private system":** Frank Ragano, *Mob Lawyer*, p. 102.

p. 200   **"recognized the devil in Hoffa":** Stein and Plimpton, *American Journey: The Times of Robert Kennedy*, pp. 56–57.

CHAPTER 11: HIDDEN VILLAINS, TRAGIC HEROES

p. 259   **his "flaws perhaps caused their fall":** Richard J. Whalen, *The Founding Father,* p. xi.

p. 259   **The elder Kennedy's mob connections:** Summers, *Official and Confidential: The Secret Life of J. Edgar Hoover,* p. 268.

p. 260   **Sinatra had asked Giancana for help:** Curt Gentry, *J. Edgar Hoover: The Man and the Secrets,* p. 472.

p. 260   **"not getting his money's worth":** Ibid., p. 488.

p. 260   **"We broke our balls for him":** Ragano, *Mob Lawyer,* p. 218.

p. 260   **"They hated Bobby":** *Larry King Live,* "Judith Exner for the Record," CNN, February 4, 1992.

p. 260   **"The Kennedy children were an extension":** Whalen, *The Founding Father,* p. xvii.

p. 261   **"solitary adventurers":** Ibid., p. 491.

p. 261   **markers from Joseph and Jack Kennedy:** Sam and Chuck Giancana, *Double Cross: The Explosive, Inside Story of the Mobster Who Controlled America,* p. 243.

p. 261   **"Bobby is gonna go for the throat":** Ibid., p. 247.

p. 261   **"like a rabbit punch in the dark":** Ibid., p. 294.

p. 261   **"he'd be on top of the list":** Ibid., p. 296.

p. 261   **"It's a brilliant move":** Ibid.

p. 261   **"He'll be your man":** Ibid., p. 230.

p. 261   **"The good thing is":** Ibid., p. 276.

p. 262   **"too far down":** Ibid., p. 277.

p. 262   **"the pressures of the time":** U.S. House of Representatives, 95th Congress, 2d Session, *Report of the Select Committee on Assassinations with Summary of Findings and Recommendations,* 1979, p. xiii.

p. 262   **"U.S. Government personnel plotted":** Ibid., pp. 4–5.

p. 262   **"hairbrained schemes":** Stephen E. Ambrose, *Eisenhower: Soldier and President: The Renowned One-Volume Life,* p. 499.

p. 263   **"never took a nickel":** U.S. House of Representatives, 95th Congress, 2d Session, *Report of the Select Committee on Assassinations with Summary of Findings and Recommendations,* 1979, p. 85.

p. 263   **the Church Committee discovered evidence:** Ibid., p. 71.

p. 267   **CIA officials who testified:** Ibid., p. 102.

p. 269   **he had no animosity:** Frank Mankiewicz, *With Fidel,* p. 168.

p. 270   **"the President trusted him":** Arthur Schlesinger, Jr., *A Thousand Days,* pp. 700–701.

p. 270   "serious suggestion of assassination": Richard N. Goodwin, *Remembering America: A Voice from the Sixties*, p. 189.

p. 270   In McNamara's memoir: Robert S. McNamara, *In Retrospect: The Tragedies and Lessons of Vietnam*, pp. 129–30.

p. 271   "the doctrine of plausible deniability": Christopher Andrew, *For The President's Eyes Only: Secret Intelligence and the American Presidency from Washington to Bush*, p. 263.

p. 271   intimate involvement with the CIA's Cuba plans: Max Holland, "After Thirty Years: Making Sense of The Assassination," *Reviews in American History*, June 1994, p. 195; and Holland, "The Warren Commission Reconsidered," *American Heritage Magazine*, November 1995. See also Holland, "The J.F.K. Files— I: Cuba, Kennedy and the Cold War," *The Nation*, November 29, 1993.

p. 272   "initiatives emanating from MONGOOSE": Scott D. Breckenridge, *CIA and the Cold War*, p. 95.

p. 277   "Hoffa had been thinking": Dan Moldea, *The Hoffa Wars*, pp. 148–49.

p. 277   "Hoffa told Partin": Ibid.

p. 277   The plot: Ibid.

p. 278   a trusted assassin: Benjamin C. Bradlee, *Conversations with Kennedy*, p. 131.

p. 278   "bribes to a key witness": U.S. House of Representatives, 95th Congress, 2d Session, *Report of the Select Committee on Assassinations with Summary of Findings and Recommendations*, 1979, p. 166.

p. 279   "conspiratorial activity in the assassination": Ibid., p. 1.

p. 279   "motive, means, and opportunity": Ibid., p. 3.

p. 280   "any plan to kill the President": Ibid., p. 60.

p. 282   "Oswald was acting": G. Robert Blakey and Richard Billings, *Fatal Hour: The Assassination of President Kennedy by Organized Crime*, p. xi.

p. 283   he'd like to have Robert Kennedy killed: Ragano, *Mob Lawyer*, p. 144.

p. 283   "That fucking Bobby Kennedy": Ibid., p. 135.

p. 283   "It's just a matter of time": Ibid.

p. 283   What if something happened to the president: Ibid., p. 141.

p. 283   Hoffa cursed at Kennedy: Ibid., p. 142.

p. 284   The rest is still more sinister: Ibid., p. 144.

p. 284   "Did you hear the good news?": Ibid., p. 146.

p. 284   **"Bobby Kennedy's just another lawyer now"**: Walter Sheridan, *The Fall and Rise of Jimmy Hoffa*, p. 300.

p. 284   **"a deflection to shield Marcello"**: Moldea, *The Hoffa Wars*, p. 431.

p. 285   **"Johnson is sure as hell going to remove Bobby"**: Ragano, *Mob Lawyer*, p. 147.

p. 285   **"I'll never forget"**: Ibid., p. 151.

p. 285   **"he owes me big"**: Ibid.

p. 285   **he had escaped government retribution**: Ibid., p. 348.

p. 285   **"this man Kennedy is in trouble"**: Charles Rappleye and Ed Becker, *All American Mafioso: The Johnny Rosselli Story*, p. 238.

p. 286   **twisted his earlier words**: Jack Newfield, "I Want Kennedy Killed! Hoffa Shouted . . . ," *Penthouse*, May 1992, p. 36.

p. 286   **"We took care of Kennedy"**: Sam and Chuck Giancana, *Double Cross: The Explosive, Inside Story of the Mobster Who Controlled America*, pp. 329–36.

p. 286   **"Don't worry about that Bobby son-of-a-bitch"**: Rappleye and Becker, *All American Mafioso: The Johnny Rosselli Story*, p. 238.

p. 286   **"the biting would end"**: Ibid., p. 238.

p. 287   **Hoffa used the Mob**: Moldea, *The Hoffa Wars*, p. 432.

p. 288   **"What surely shocked"**: Harris Wofford, *Of Kennedys and Kings: Making Sense of the Sixties*, p. 404.

p. 288   *Onore* required vengeance: Rappleye and Becker, *All American Mafioso: The Johnny Rosselli Story*, p. 237.

p. 289   **"Life in the underworld of crime"**: Judith Exner, *My Story*, p. 299.

p. 289   **"The new administration"**: Ragano, *Mob Lawyer*, p. 358.

p. 289   **"daring the gods of the underworld"**: Peter Collier and David Horowitz, *The Kennedys: An American Drama*, p. 317.

p. 289   **"the secrets of the deep"**: Ibid.

p. 290   **assisting the client in criminal conduct**: *ABA Model Rules of Professional Conduct*, Rule 1.6.

p. 291   **He posits two theories**: Norman Mailer, *Oswald's Tale*, pp. 741–44.

p. 296   **"President Kennedy tried"**: Joseph Califano, *The Triumph and Tragedy of Lyndon Johnson: The White House Years*, p. 295.

p. 296   **"the death of a young president"**: Mark Riebling, *Wedge: The Secret War Between The FBI and CIA*, p. 460.

p. 296   **"There's been so much"**: Guthman, *We Band of Brothers*, p. 244.

p. 297   **Warren Commission report was "a poor job"**: John H. Davis, *Mafia Kingfish: Carlos Marcello and The Assassination of John F. Kennedy*, p. 385.

p. 297   **"mob guy in New Orleans":** Newfield, "I Want Kennedy Killed! Hoffa Shouted . . . ," *Penthouse,* May 1992, p. 104.

p. 297   **"it was organized crime":** Anthony and Robbyn Summers, "The Ghosts of November," *Vanity Fair,* December 1994, p. 190.

CHAPTER 12: JUSTICE AND PASSION

p. 302   **"a suffering that surpassed anything":** Collier and Horowitz, *The Kennedys: An American Drama,* p. 315.

p. 303   **"Mafia effort slacked off again":** Summers, *Official and Confidential: The Secret Life of J. Edgar Hoover,* p. 332.

p. 306   **"a singularly untroubled reign of prosperity":** Ragano, *Mob Lawyer,* p. 320.

p. 309   **Justice Department tactics:** "Nevada Governor Challenges FBI on 'Skimming' Evidence," *Los Angeles Times,* October 28, 1966.

p. 309   **skimming was a media created phenomenon:** Daryl E. Lembke, "Reno and Lake Tahoe Casino Heads Testify," *Los Angeles Times,* August 17, 1966.

p. 315   **"his self-deprecating wit and ego-puncturing humor":** Burke Marshall, "An Honorable Profession: A Tribute to Robert F. Kennedy," *Georgetown Law Journal,* pp. 90, 92–93.

p. 316   **"Mr. Kennedy would make the best Senator":** "Why Robert Kennedy," *The New Republic,* September 19, 1964, pp. 3–4.

p. 316   **the ruthless, McCarthy stereotype:** Correspondence between Ronald Goldfarb and Professor Arthur Schlesinger, which may be found in the author's files.

p. 316   **"the nerve center of the New Frontier":** Pierre Salinger, Edwin Guthman, and John Seigenthaler, eds., *An Honorable Profession: A Tribute to Robert F. Kennedy,* pp. 110–11.

p. 317   **"on a pilgrimage of self discovery":** Jack Newfield, *Robert Kennedy: A Memoir.*

p. 323   **"the narrow-minded moralist":** Wofford, *Of Kennedys and Kings: Making Sense of the Sixties,* p. 5.

p. 324   **"soulful man the world thought was ruthless":** Jack Newfield, *The Village Voice,* June 13, 1968.

p. 324   **"a dark Celtic sense of potential apocalypse":** Pete Hamill, *Good Housekeeping,* September 1968.

p. 324   **special legacy of public service:** Edwin Guthman and C. Richard Allen, *RFK: Collected Speeches,* p. 34.

p. 325   **"the greatness to bend history itself":** Guthman and Allen, *RFK, Collected Speeches,* pp. 243–44.

p. 326   **"heroes are imperfectly great"**: Edith Hamilton, *The Greek Way,* p. 102.

p. 327   **"In this skeptical age"**: Wofford, *Of Kennedys and Kings: Making Sense of the Sixties,* p. 5.

p. 327   **"A hero is someone"**: Joseph Campbell with Bill Moyers, *The Power of Myth,* p. 151.

p. 328   **"The moral objective"**: Ibid., p. 156.

p. 328   **"Show me a hero"**: F. Scott Fitzgerald, *The Crack-Up,* p. 122.

p. 328   **"to confront whatever darkness"**: Dorothy Norman, *The Hero: Myth, Image, Symbol,* p. 5.

p. 328   **myths about heroes**: Ibid.

SELECTED

BIBLIOGRAPHY

Ambrose, Stephen E. *Eisenhower: Soldier and President: The Renowned One-Volume Life.* New York: Simon and Schuster, 1990.

Blakey, G. Robert, and Richard Billings. *Fatal Hour: The Assassination of President Kennedy by Organized Crime.* New York: Times Books, 1981.

Bradlee, Benjamin. *Conversations With Kennedy.* New York: W. W. Norton, 1975.

Brashler, William. *The Don: The Life and Death of Sam Giancana.* New York: Harper and Row, 1977.

Breckenridge, Scott D. *CIA and the Cold War.* New York: Praeger, 1993.

Califano, Joseph A. *The Triumph and Tragedy of Lyndon Johnson: The White House Years.* New York: Simon and Schuster, 1991.

Campbell, Joseph. *The Hero with a Thousand Faces.* New York: Meridian Books, 1956.

Campbell, Joseph, with Bill Moyers. *The Power of Myth,* New York: Doubleday, 1988.

Collier, Peter, and David Horowitz. *The Kennedys: An American Drama.* New York: Summit Books, 1984.

Christopher, Andrew. *For the President's Eyes Only: Secret Intelligence and The American Presidency from Washington to Bush.* New York: HarperCollins, 1995.

Clifford, Clark, with Richard Holbrooke. *Counsel to the President.* New York: Anchor Books, 1991.

Cook, Fred L. *A Two-Dollar Bet Means Murder.* Westport, Connecticut: Breenwood Press, 1961.

Darrah, John. *The Real Camelot: Paganism and the Arthurian Romances.* New York: Thames and Hudson, 1981.

Davis, John H. *The Kennedy Contract: The Mafia Plot to Assassinate the President.* New York: Harper and Row, 1993.

———. *Mafia Kingfish: Carlos Marcello and the Assassination of John F. Kennedy.* New York: Signet, 1989.

DeLoach, Cartha D. *Hoover's FBI: The Inside Story by Hoover's Trusted Lieutenant.* Washington, D.C.: Regnery, 1995.

Exner, Judith. *My Story.* New York: Grove Press, 1977.

Fitzgerald, F. Scott. *The Crack-Up.* New York: New Directions, 1956.

Gage, Nicholas. *The Mafia Is Not an Equal Opportunity Employer.* New York: McGraw-Hill, 1971.

Gentry, Curt. *J. Edgar Hoover: The Man and the Secrets.* New York: W. W. Norton, 1991.

Giancana, Sam, and Chuck Giancana. *Double Cross: The Explosive, Inside Story of the Mobster Who Controlled America.* New York: Warner, 1992.

Goodwin, Richard N. *Remembering America: A Voice from the Sixties.* New York: Little, Brown and Co., 1988.

Guthman, Edwin. *We Band of Brothers.* New York: Harper and Row, 1971.

———, and Richard Allen. *RFK: Collected Speeches.* New York: Viking, 1993.

Hamilton, Edith. *The Greek Way.* New York: W. W. Norton, 1964.

Kennedy, Robert. *The Enemy Within.* New York: Harper and Brothers, 1960.

Kennedy, Robert. *In His Own Words: The Unpublished Recollections of the Kennedy Years.* Edited by Edwin Guthman and Jeffrey Shulman, foreword by Arthur M. Schlesinger, Jr. New York: Bantam, published in cooperation with Twenty-First Century Books, 1988.

Lawford, Patricia Kennedy, ed. *The Shining Hour.* Privately printed, Halliday Lithograph, 1969.

Maas, Peter. *The Valachi Papers.* New York: Putnam, 1968.

Mailer, Norman. *Oswald's Tale: An American Mystery.* New York: Random House, 1995.

Mankiewicz, Frank. *With Fidel.* Chicago: Playboy Press, 1975.

McNamara, Robert S., with Brian VanDeMark. *In Retrospect: The Tragedies and Lessons of Vietnam.* New York: Times Books, 1995.

Meador, Daniel J. "The President, the Attorney General, and the Department of Justice," a paper by Daniel J. Meador and a conference at the White Burkett Miller Center of Public Affairs, University of Virginia. Richmond, Virginia. January 4–5, 1980.

Moldea, Dan. *The Hoffa Wars.* New York: Paddington Press, 1978.

Mollenhoff, Clark. *Tentacles of Power: The Story of Jimmy Hoffa.* New York: World, 1965.

Navasky, Victor. *Kennedy Justice.* New York: Viking, 1971.

Newfield, Jack. *Robert Kennedy: A Memoir.* New York: Dutton, 1969.

Norman, Dorothy. *The Hero: Myth, Image, Symbol.* New York: New American Library, 1969.

Posner, Gerald. *Case Closed: Lee Harvey Oswald and the Assassination of JFK.* New York: Random House, 1993.

Ragano, Frank. *Mob Lawyer.* New York: Scribners, 1994. (Page references are from the advance galleys.)

Rappleye, Charles, and Ed Becker. *All American Mafioso: The Johnny Rosselli Story.* New York: Doubleday, 1991.

Reibling, Mark. *Wedge: The Secret War Between the FBI and CIA.* New York: Knopf, 1994.

Reid, Ed. *The Grim Reapers: The Anatomy of Organized Crime in America.* New York: Bantam, 1969.

Roemer, William. *Man Against the Mob.* New York: Fine, 1989.

Rogers, Warren. *When I Think of Bobby.* New York: HarperCollins, 1993.

Salinger, Pierre. Edited by Edwin Guthman and John Seigenthaler, with an introduction by Kerry K. Cuomo. *An Honorable Profession: A Tribute to Robert F. Kennedy.* New York: Doubleday, 1993.

Schlesinger, Arthur, Jr. *A Thousand Days.* New York: Houghton Mifflin, 1965.

———. *Robert Kennedy and His Times.* Boston: Houghton Mifflin, 1978.

Shannon, William V. *The Heir Apparent: Robert Kennedy and the Struggle for Power.* New York: Macmillan, 1967.

Sheridan, Walter. *The Fall and Rise of Jimmy Hoffa.* New York: Saturday Review Press, 1972.

Sloane, Arthur. *Hoffa.* Cambridge, MA: MIT Press, 1991.

Spoto, Donald. *Marilyn Monroe: The Biography.* New York: HarperCollins, 1993.

Stein, Jean. *American Journey: The Times of Robert Kennedy.* Edited by George Plimpton. New York: Harcourt Brace Jovanovich, 1970.

Strober, Gerald S. and Deborah H. Strober. *"Let Us Begin Anew": An Oral History of the Kennedy Presidency.* New York: HarperCollins, 1993.

Summers, Anthony. *Official and Confidential: The Secret Life of J. Edgar Hoover.* New York: Putnam, 1993.

Thompson, Robert E., and Hortense Myers. *Robert F. Kennedy: The Brother Within.* New York: Macmillan, 1961.

U.S. Department of Justice. *200th Anniversary of the Office of the Attorney General: 1789–1989.* Compiled by the Justice Management Division, 1990.

U.S. House of Representatives, 87th Congress, "Legislation Relating to Organized Crime," Committee on the Judiciary, Subcommittee #5, Serial No. 16, May 16–17, 1961.

U.S. House of Representatives, *Report of the Select Committee in Assassinations, 95th Congress, 2d Session, with Summary of Findings and Recommendations,* 1979.

U.S. Senate, 87th Congress, 1st Session, "The Attorney General's Program to Curb Organized Crime and Racketeering," Committee on the Judiciary, June 6, 1961.

U.S. Senate. *Final Report, Foreign and Military Intelligence: Alleged Assassination Plots Involving Foreign Leaders: An Interim Report of the Select Committee to Study Government Operations with Respect to Intelligence Activities.* 1976.

Whalen, Richard J. *The Founding Father: The Story of Joseph P. Kennedy.* Washington, D.C.: Regnery Gateway, 1993.

Wofford, Harris. *Of Kennedys and Kings: Making Sense of the Sixties.* Pittsburgh, Pa.: University of Pittsburgh Press, 1980.

The following other sources of information were used:

The Cincinnati Enquirer and *The Louisville Courier-Journal* daily reports of the Ratterman Case and other investigations and trials in that area, and the trial and retrial transcripts in *U.S. v. Lester et al.*

The daily reports to the attorney general of the organized crime section's activities for every day Robert Kennedy was attorney general.

The IRS oral history of former commissioner Mortimer M. Caplin, November 18, 19, 25, 1991.

Miriam Ottenberg's records, and particularly her notes regarding major cases of the organized crime section, maintained at the Wisconsin State Historical Society Archives.

The Oral History Collection of Robert F. Kennedy at the John F. Kennedy Library, Boston.

The papers of Victor S. Navasky and Arthur M. Schlesinger, Jr., in the Robert F. Kennedy Collection at the John F. Kennedy Library, pertaining to their books, *Kennedy Justice* and *Robert Kennedy and His Times.*

Earl Johnson's three-part series in the *Journal of Criminal Law, Criminology, and Police Science,* December 1962, March 1963, and June 1963; vol. 53, no. 4; and vol. 54, nos. 1 and 2.

Press clips and other collected papers of the Sheridan group's Teamsters work
  kept by Jack Miller and John Cassidy at their law offices, Washington,
  D.C.
Jack Anderson's syndicated columns on the assassination of John F. Kennedy.
The American Experience, Parts I and II, "The Kennedys," WGBH, August
  8, 1992.
Larry King Live, "Judith Exner for the Record," CNN, February 4, 1992.

INDEX

Abrams, Morris, 246
Accardo, Anthony, 51, 65, 66, 308
Acheson, David, 182
Adlerman, Jerry, 128
AFL-CIO, and Teamsters, 55, 190, 193
Ageuci, Albert and Vito, 127
Agosto, Joe, 79
Aiuppa, Joey, 62
Alderisio, Felix "Milwaukee Phil," 246
Aleman, Jose, Jr., 285–86
Alexander, Cliff, 15
Alexander, Harry, 57, 159, 182–85
Allen charge, 206, 233–34
Allott, Gordon, 14
Alo, Vincent, 130
Amalgamated Workers Union, 201–2
Ambrose, Stephen E., 262
American Experience, The (PBS),
    259–60
American Guild of Variety Artists
    (AGVA), 201
Americans for Democratic Action,
    316
Anastasia, Albert, 31, 67
Anderson, Jack:
    and Castro plot, 269
    and JFK assassination, 256, 268, 269,
    270, 290
Andrew, Christopher, 268, 271
Andrews, Frank "Screw":
    and IRS raid, 107–8, 121
    and Newport corruption, 102, 106
    trial of, 116, 121–22, 136
Army, U.S. Department of, 249
arson, 40
Ascoli, Max, 316
attorney-client privilege, 290

attorneys general:
    appointment process of, 13–14
    functions of, 11–12
    and politics, 161
    priorities set by, 156–58
    see also specific officeholders
Ayotte, Gene, 70

Bailey, Robert, 150
bail laws, 151
Bakery and Confectionary Workers
    Union, 177, 181–85
Baldwin, James, 316
Bankruptcy Act frauds, 61, 67–70, 250
Barbara, Joseph, Sr., 31–32
Barnett, Ross, 318
Bartlett, Charles, 7, 161
Bates, Herb, 44, 49–50, 180
    in Detroit, 67–69, 250–51
    Teamsters' offer to, 67–68
Battaglia, Sam "Teets," 308
Bay of Pigs, 267, 268, 270, 271
Beck, Dave, 37, 55–56, 189
Becker, Ed, 286–87, 292
Beckley, Gil, 223–25
Belli, Melvin, 285
Bellino, Carmine, 43, 55
Bickel, Alexander M., 13
Billings, Richard, 282
Bissell, Richard, 268, 271
Bittner, Bill, 198
Black, Hugo, 16, 17
Black Hand, *see* Mafia
Blakey, G. Robert (Bob), 28, 44, 302
    assessment by, 311
    and Cross case, 183–84
    and Giancana case, 251–52

Blakey, G. Robert (Bob) (cont'd)
  and House Select Committee on
    Assassinations, 278, 279,
    281–82, 284, 286, 287
  and McClellan Committee, 311
Blasingame, Royal, 116
Bonanno, Joseph, 32
Bonner, William, 80
Bradlee, Ben, 278
Breckenridge, Scott D., 272–73
Brennan, Vincent, 225
Bridewell, James, 106
Brownell, Herbert, Jr., 12
Bruno, Angelo, 279
Buccieri, Marty, 92, 104, 110, 112, 114,
    117, 207, 210, 213, 216, 217,
    235–36, 242
Building Service Employees Union,
    202

Cabinet, family members in, 11
Cacheris, George, 165–70
Caldwell, A. B., 87–88, 90
Califano, Joseph, 296
Campbell, Alexander, 165
Campbell, Joseph, 327–28
Canada, narcotics in, 140–42, 151, 250
Cannon, Ken, 132
Caplin, Mortimer, 313–14
  and Gosser, 178
  as IRS commissioner, 48, 314
  on program paying for itself, 246
  on RFK's academic record, 4
Capone, Al, 84
Carbo, Frankie, 51
Carey, James, 159
Carinci, Tito, 242
  conspiracy trial of, 101
  in Ratterman case, 110, 112, 114–15,
    117
  and Ratterman trials, 91, 92, 94–98,
    100, 101, 207–8, 210–11, 215,
    217, 235
Cassidy, John, 55, 57, 77
Castellana, Peter, 69
Castro, Fidel:
  and JFK assassination, 269, 296
  and Mafia, 259, 261–76, 288
  plots to assassinate, 262–76, 296, 313
  and RFK assassination, 269
Catena, Gerardo, 130
Cheasty, Sy, 182
Church, Frank, 262

Church Committee, 262–64, 266,
    267–68
CIA:
  authority of, 270
  and Castro plot, 263–76
  Cold War abuses by, 262, 271
  and Cuba, 267, 295
  vs. FBI, 296
  and Mafia, 261–70, 271–73, 297–98,
    313
  and RFK, 271–73, 313
  and Warren Commission, 295, 296
CIA and the Cold War (Breckenridge),
    272–73
Ciafardini, Patrick:
  and grand jury, 112
  Ratterman arrested by, 101, 104–5
  and Ratterman case, 115, 116, 118
  and Ratterman trials, 97, 207,
    209–10, 217, 235
Citizens for Kennedy, 18, 23
Civello, Joseph Francis, 295
civil liberties, and prosecution, 306,
    313–14
civil rights:
  and the downtrodden, 321
  events and, 23, 157
  in Newport case, 88, 91, 104–5,
    108–9, 112
Civil Rights Act, 88, 104, 161, 318
Clark, Ramsey, 45
Clay, Henry, 12
Clemente, Michelino, 250
Cleveland, Frank, 94, 98, 206, 222–23
Clifford, Clark, 7
Cohen, Bruce, 15–16, 17
Cohen, Mickey, 51
Cohn, Roy M., 5
Cole, Oral, 164
Collier, Peter, 289, 302
Combs, Bert T., 93
Committee on Ballistic Acoustics,
    280–81
confiscation and forfeiture laws, 61
Congress:
  investigative powers of, 13
  laws passed by, 145–46
  and proposed legislation, 45–47, 59,
    62, 64, 73, 311
conspiracy laws, 57
contempt cases, 318
contempt convictions, 73, 117
Cook, Fred L., 86

Cook, Henry, 87, 91, 92, 95–97, 203, 217, 231
Cook, John, 224–25
Coppola, Frank, 141
Corallo, Tony "Ducks," 171–72, 175
Corey, Joe, and Ratterman retrial, 203–5, 207–14, 227, 233, 243
cosa nostra, see Mafia
Costello, Frank, 78, 261
Cox, Archibald, 23, 156, 195
crime syndicates, *see* organized crime syndicates
Crosby, Bing, 137
Cross, James G., 181–85, 246
Cuba:
    Bay of Pigs, 267, 268, 270, 271
    and CIA, 267, 295
    and JFK, 269
    and Khrushchev, 270
    Mafia activity in, 31, 66, 272–73
    racketeering in, 267
    and Task Force W., 272
    Trafficante in, 66–67, 263, 269
    see also Castro, Fidel
Cunningham, Frank, 148, 150
Customs Bureau, and cooperation, 47

Davies, Dan, 115, 120, 214, 220, 226
Davis, John H., 287
Davis, Sammy, Jr., 320
Day, J. Edward, 10
De Carlo, Angelo "Gyp," 137
deportation laws, 61, 63
Desmond, Rita (Noe), 110, 112, 118, 205, 218
Dewey, Thomas E., 18
Dillon, Douglas, 48
Dirksen, Everett, 14, 127
District of Columbia, *see* Washington, D.C.
Diuguid, John, 44
    and Marcello, 73, 74, 76, 145–48, 249
double jeopardy, 275–76
Douglas, William O., 9
Dulles, Allen, 268, 270

Edwards, Sheffield, 267, 268
Eisenhower, Dwight D.:
    and attorney general, 12
    and Castro plot, 262, 268, 271
    and major covert operations, 271

Electrical Workers' Union, 159, 201
Enemy Within, The (RFK), 3
    and Gosser, 180
    idealistic premises in, 37–38, 186–87, 202
    and Seigenthaler, 8, 186
English, Chuckie, 137
Epstein, Edward Jay, 295–96
Erdman, Robert, 172–73, 175
Ervin, Sam, 318
Euripides, 290
Evans, Courtney:
    on Castro plot, 266–67
    as FBI liaison, 56, 265
    on RFK's leadership style, 51
Exner, Judith:
    and Giancana, 260, 265–66, 288
    as JFK-Mafia go-between, 260
    JFK's affair with, 265–66, 287–89

false statement statute, 58
Fawer, Mike, 60, 63
FBI (Federal Bureau of Investigation):
    and Cacheris, 166
    and Castro plot, 263–68, 270
    CIA vs., 296
    and cooperation, 47, 56, 60, 63
    and Giancana, 66, 137–39, 251, 268, 312
    and Gosser, 132–33
    and IRS, 146
    and JFK assassination, 287, 295, 296, 302
    and Justice Dept., 49–50, 51, 56
    and Las Vegas gambling, 308–10
    and local enforcement, 105
    and Mafia, 31, 42, 47, 51, 279, 303
    and Marcello, 287
    politics and priorities of, 161
    and skimming, 130–31
    top-hoodlum program of, 66, 137–38, 250, 308
    see also Hoover, J. Edgar
FCC laws, 58, 63, 73
Feiffer, Jules, 316
Ferrie, David, 74, 147
Fitzgerald, Ella, 320
Fitzgerald, F. Scott, 328
Fitzsimmons, Frank, 199
fixed sentences, 171–73
Fleischer, Arthur, Jr., 15
Flowers, April, 82, 122–23, 194
    and Ratterman case, 117–18

Flowers, April (cont'd)
    and Ratterman trials, 91, 95, 96–97,
        205, 208–10, 218, 220–22, 230
    testimony changed by, 109–12, 117,
        218
Flynn, Jim, 152, 153
Formosa, John, 137
French, Bill, 44
Freund, Paul, 19

Galbraith, John Kenneth, 23
gambling:
    and corruption, 38–40
    and FBI investigation, 308–10
    as interstate activity, 39, 46, 58, 59,
        60, 64, 145–46
    in Las Vegas casinos, 77–81, 129,
        251, 308–10
    lay-off betting, 59, 84, 85
    legalized, 40
    as lifeblood of organized crime, 100,
        247
    in Newport, Kentucky, 84, 100–102,
        106
    and Organized Crime and
        Racketeering Section, 247–49
    in Panama, 249
    and past posting, 60
    as priority, 40–41
    and race wire services, 128–29
    rigged, 108
    skimming in, 78–79, 81, 129–31, 250,
        308–10
    and strong-arm tactics, 38–39
    and taxes, 60, 61, 79, 129–30, 148
    telephone lines in, 39, 59, 60, 148–49
Garrison, Jim, 284
Gary, Romaine, 326
Genovese, Vito, 32, 152
Gettings, Brian, 311
Giancana, Chuck, 261
Giancana, Sam "Mooney":
    and Castro plot, 261, 263–64,
        266–69, 273
    and CIA, 261–70, 297
    death of, 286
    and Exner, 260, 265–66, 288
    and FBI, 66, 137–39, 251, 268, 312
    on JFK assassination, 286, 292–93
    and JFK campaign, 260, 261
    power of, 65–66, 288
    prosecution and release of, 307–8
    RFK and, 274, 276

and Sinatra, 136–37
    and skimming, 130
    and Social Security, 252
Gimbel, Mary Bailey, 289
Giordano, Samuel, 70
Goldberg, Jay, 28, 81, 163–70
Goldwater, Barry, 180
Goodwin, Richard, 270, 297
Gosser, Richard T.:
    arrest of, 178
    and Caplin, 178
    and FBI, 132–33
    and IRS, 132–35, 178–80
    and JFK campaign, 180
    and Lynch, 135, 179, 180–81
    and Pinciotta, 133, 134, 135, 179
    prosecution of, 179
    and UAW, 178, 246
Green, Bill, 159
Green, Bonnie, 97
Greene, Bessie, 26
Grimsley, Frank, 194
Guthman, Ed, 25, 26
    and JFK assassination, 256, 297
    on Keogh case, 170–71, 173
    on RFK as attorney general, 6, 37, 43,
        320

Halpern, Samuel, 271–73, 274, 275
Hamill, Pete, 324
Hamilton, Edith, 290, 326
Harvey, William K., 267, 271
Hatcher, Richard, 169
Hay, Nancy "Granny," 99, 116, 216,
    231
Hayes, Wyn, 50, 57, 245, 247–49
Helms, Richard, 273
Henderson Novelty Company, 308
Hentoff, Nat, 316
Herodotus, 326–27, 329
heroes, definitions of, 327–29
Hodges, Juanita Jean, see Flowers,
    April
Hoffa, James Riddle, 185–202
    conviction of, 199, 310
    disappearance of, 199
    and JFK assassination, 278, 279, 280,
        282–87, 290–92
    and jury tampering, 131–32, 193–98
    and Justice Department, 56, 77, 131,
        158, 200, 312
    and Labor Racketeering Group, 54
    and lawyers' compensation, 192

and McClellan Committee, 4, 5,
182–83
and mail fraud, 131, 196–98
and Nixon, 188, 193, 199
and RFK, 37, 38, 55, 277–78,
283–84, 297, 313
and Teamsters, 131, 177, 185–99
and Test Fleet case, 193–96
and trials, 189–90, 247
Hogan, Frank, 18, 163
Holland, Max, 271, 298
Holovachka, Metro, 163
Hooker, John J., 196
Hoover, J. Edgar:
and Castro plot, 265
and communism, 158
and JFK, 162, 266
and JFK assassination, 256, 270, 295
and LBJ, 295
and Mafia, 31, 42, 47, 51, 162, 279
power of, 48, 49, 161, 295, 303
and RFK, 9, 11, 14, 303
and Warren Commission, 295, 296
see also FBI
Hoover Commission, 5
Horowitz, David, 289, 302
Hosty, James, 295
House Select Committee on
Assassination, 278–82, 284–87,
295
Houston, Lawrence, 266–67
Hughes, Howard, 310
Humphrey, Hubert H., 5, 16
Hundley, Bill, 127, 274, 303
and Cross case, 181
and Hoffa, 195
and Keogh case, 171–75
and Mafia, 149–53, 276
and Miami case, 252–54
and Organized Crime and
Racketeering Section, 170
recruitment of, 42
hung juries, 120

ICC laws, 73
Independent Brotherhood of
Production, Maintenance and
Operating Employees Union,
201
Indiana:
Crime Commission, 163, 168
Lake County, 163–70
Industrial Workers of America, 202

INS (Immigration and Naturalization
Service):
cooperation with, 47, 51, 63
and Marcello, 74, 75–76
and Newport, 100
and Ricca, 250
International Brotherhood of Teamsters,
Chauffeurs, Warehousemen,
Stablemen, and Helpers of
America, *see* Teamsters Union
International Longshoremen's
Association, 201
IRS (Internal Revenue Service):
and Andrews, 107–8, 121–22
and bankruptcy fraud, 68, 250
and Caplin, 48, 178, 314
and cooperation, 47, 51, 60, 62, 63
and FBI, 146
and gambling, 60, 129–30, 148,
309–10
and Gosser, 132–35, 178–80
in Indiana, 163–65
Intelligence Division, 245–46
and Mannarinos, 143–44
and Newport, 100
and tax crimes, 250, 314
Italy, and deportations, 249–50

Jackson, "Action," 29
Jackson, Andrew, 12
JFK assassination, 255–57
acoustical evidence in, 278–81
and Castro plot, 269, 296
and CIA-FBI feud, 296
conspiracy theories of, 270, 278–79,
281, 282–87, 291–97
and end of an era, 301
and FBI/Hoover, 256, 270, 287, 295,
296, 302
Garrison investigation of, 284
and House Select Committee on
Assassinations, 278–82, 284–87,
295
and media, 301
mob benefits from, 281
and mob double-cross factor, 289–90
mob hatred and, 259, 268, 269, 278,
279, 282, 299
mob plans for, 278–80, 282–87,
290–97
and Organized Crime and
Racketeering Section, 258, 310
and Ramsey Committee, 280–81

JFK assassination (*cont'd*)
  and RFK's grief, 276, 290, 294, 297,
    301–2, 317
  RFK's opinions on, 296–97
  and RFK's power, 294
  thesis, 259–76
    conclusion of, 287–90
    conclusions about, 297–99
    credibility of, 290–97
    extension of, 276–87
    two gunmen in, 278–82
    and Warren Commission, *see* Warren
      Commission
Johnson, Earl:
  in Las Vegas, 80–81, 129–30, 309–10
  and new laws, 64
  organized crime studied by, 33–34,
    57
  recruitment of, 28
Johnson, Haynes, 256
Johnson, Lyndon B.:
  election of, 316
  and Hoover, 295
  and Khrushchev, 270
  poverty program of, 304
  and RFK, 283, 284, 285, 294
  and Warren Commission, 294–95,
    296
Jordan, Don, 51
Joyce, Ed, 64, 128
juries, 88, 318–19
  hung, 120
  selection of, 213–14
  tampering with, 131–32, 147,
    193–98
justice:
  philosophical and policy
    considerations in, 156
  and politics, 155–63
  and priority setting, 156–57
Justice Department:
  attorney general in, 11
  and Castro plot, 266
  Civil Rights Division of, 26, 83, 110,
    157, 302
  Criminal Division of, 25, 42, 54, 55,
    294, 306
  emphasis and degree in, 161–62
  and FBI, 49–50, 51, 56
  goals of, 12
  Internal Security Division of, 158, 162
  Labor Racketeering Group in, 54–56
  Lands Division of, 157–58

Organized Crime and Racketeering
    Section of, *see* Organized Crime
    and Racketeering Section
  and playing by the rules, 158–61
  RFK as heart of, 28, 45, 256, 302–4,
    323, 325

Kahaner, Elliott, 171–73, 175
Kastel, Phil, 78
Katzenbach, Nicholas, 173
  as attorney general, 304, 311
  and Newport standoff, 89
  and Oswald, 270
  on RFK as attorney general, 329
  and Warren Commission, 294, 302
Kaufman, Irving, 32
Keating, Kenneth, 316
Kefauver, Estes, 30–31, 42
Kehoe, Bill, 142–43
Kelley, Clarence, 296
Kempton, Murray, 5–6, 191–92, 200
Kennedy, Jacqueline Bouvier, 3, 22, 290,
    326
Kennedy, John F.:
  assassination of, *see* JFK assassination
  and Bay of Pigs, 268, 271
  campaign and election of, 4, 5, 22,
    180, 259, 260, 261, 268
  and Castro, 266, 268, 269, 270–71
  dalliances of, 261, 265–66, 287–89
  and Hoffa, 188–89
  and Hoover, 162, 266
  and McClellan Committee, 4, 7
  Mafia used by, 260–61, 288
  as multimedia president, 301
  presidency of, 20
  priorities of, 189, 262
  and RFK, 3, 256, 298
  and RFK as attorney general, 6–11,
    13, 43, 272
Kennedy, Joseph P.:
  ego and power of, 261
  and racketeers, 42, 188–89, 259, 260,
    261, 288
  and sons' careers, 7, 8, 259–60, 261
Kennedy, Robert F.:
  assassination of, *see* RFK
    assassination
  as attorney general, 6–11, 13–14, 20,
    24, 43, 272, 298–99, 300–304,
    305–6, 310–17, 320–21, 328–30
  background and career of, 4
  and Castro plot, 262, 265–76, 296

and CIA, 271–73, 313
and *Enemy Within*, 3
as heart of Justice Department, 28,
    45, 256, 302–4, 323, 325
and heroism, 327–29
human side of, 317–22, 324
and incorruptibility, 170–71, 175, 181
and JFK assassination, 276, 290, 294,
    296–97, 301–2, 317
and JFK's affairs, 265–66, 288
leadership style of, 24–26, 43–45, 49,
    51, 56, 124, 322–23, 327–29
and Mafia, 262–76, 282, 288–90
and meta diplomats, 274
and Mongoose, 270–74
presidential campaign of, 326
priorities of, 55, 157–58, 161–62,
    176, 177, 189, 200, 202, 262,
    268, 274–76, 298, 313
professional growth of, 157–58,
    314–17, 323
on public service, 324–25
as senator, 317, 321, 322, 325–26
wide appeal of, 321–23
Kennedy family:
    and Mafia double-cross, 289–90
    Mafia hatred of, 283, 297
    in PBS program, 259–60
    and RFK's career, 5, 6
    seductiveness of, 19
    and use of power, 5
Keogh, Eugene, 170, 173, 174, 175
Keogh, J. Vincent, 170–76
Khrushchev, Nikita, 270
King, Larry, 260, 266
King, Rev. Martin Luther, Jr., 23, 278,
    324
Kloeb, Frank L., 179
Komives, Paul, 67
Krause, Allen, 69

labor, *see* unions
Lake County, Indiana, 163–70
Lally, John, 171–73, 175
Lansky, Meyer, 52
    in Miami, 66
    and skimming, 130–31
    and Thunderbird, 78
Las Vegas, gambling in, 77–81, 129,
    251, 308–10
Lausche, Frank, 84
law enforcement agencies:
    action-oriented, 48–49

cooperation among, 47–51, 56–57,
    60–63, 133, 146, 152, 306,
    310
international focus of, 306
legal reforms needed by, 57–64
local vs. federal, 80
and organized crime, 76
see also specific agencies
Lester, Charles E.:
    and appeal, 239–42
    and grand jury, 112
    legal reputation of, 205–6, 224, 225,
        227, 242
    and Newport corruption, 101–2, 136,
        238
    and Ratterman case, 110, 114
    and Ratterman trials, 91, 92, 95–96,
        98, 99–100, 207–10, 216
    sentencing of, 235–36
Levin, Milton, 183, 185
Lewis, Anthony, 5, 47, 315, 321
Licavoli mob, 135
Lombardozzi, Carmine, 32, 71–72
Louis, Joe, 182–83
Luchese, Thomas "Three Finger
    Brown," 137
Lynch, Bill, 28, 107, 109, 163
    and Andrews trial, 116
    career of, 243
    and Gosser, 135, 179, 180–81
    and grand jury, 107, 109
    and Ratterman case, 102, 113–15,
        119, 120–21, 242
Lynch, Francis, 163–64

McBride, Tom, 28, 67, 158–59, 251
McCarthy, Joseph R., RFK's work with,
    4–5, 13, 16
McClellan, John L., 3–4, 9, 14, 55
McClellan Committee (Senate Select
    Committee on Improper
    Activities in the Labor or
    Management Field):
    cases pending from, 54–55, 312
    and corrupt public officials,
        163–70
    and *Enemy Within*, 186
    new and revised laws from, 37, 311
    and racketeering, 5, 42
    and RFK, 3–4, 5, 7, 13, 43, 177
    and union corruption, 4, 5, 55, 181,
        182–83, 189, 201
McCloy, John, 296

McCone, John, 256, 273
McCullough, David, 260
McGrory, Mary, 320–21
McGuire, Phyllis, 65
McIntosh, Brock, 217
McMillan, Dougald (Doug), 136–37
McNamara, Robert S., 10, 270
Madden, Ray, 166, 167
Mafia, 29, 30, 149–53
  arrests of, 31–33
  and assassinations, see JFK
      assassination; RFK assassination
  and Castro, 259, 261–76, 288
  and CIA, 261–70, 271–73, 297–98,
      313
  in Cuba, 31, 66, 272–73
  and deportations, 61
  and double-cross, 288–90
  and FBI/Hoover, 31, 42, 47, 51, 162,
      279, 303
  and JFK election, 259, 268
  and Las Vegas, 78
  and narcotics, 150
  and national crime commission, 66
  and Oswald, 291
  and Teamsters, 186–87, 192
  see also racketeers; specific members
Magaddino, Stefano, 279
Maheu, Robert, 266
Mailer, Norman, 291, 322–23
Mankiewicz, Frank, 269, 296
Mann Act, 90
Mannarino, Gabriel "Kelly," 142–44
Mannarino, Sam, 142–44
Marcello, Carlos, 67, 73–76, 145–48,
      249
  and deportation, 73, 74–75, 312
  and FBI, 287
  and JFK assassination, 269, 278, 279,
      280, 282–87, 290–92, 295
  and Mannarinos, 144
Marcello, Joseph, 76, 146
Marshall, Burke, 26, 173, 302, 315
Marteduzzo, see Hoffa, James Riddle
Masterson, Albert "Red," 93
Meade, N. Mitchell, 90, 110, 225
Meany, George, 193
media:
  and Gosser, 179
  and Hoffa, 198
  and JFK, 301
  and Keogh case, 173
  and Newport, 102, 107

Meli, Angelo, 68
Messick, Hank, 85, 86
Migratory Bird Act, 62
Miller, Herbert "Jack":
  on Castro plot, 265, 266–67, 274
  and Criminal Division, 55
  and Goldberg, 167
  and Gosser case, 180
  and Hoffa, 77, 278
  and JFK assassination, 302
  and Keogh case, 173–74
  and Lombardozzi, 71
  and meetings, 127
  and Miami case, 253
  and Ratterman case, 136
  recruitment of, 25
Minow, Newton, 23
Misslbeck, Jim, 53, 70, 72–73, 168
Mitchell, Bobby, 320
Mitchell, John N., 12
mob, see Mafia; organized crime
      syndicates
Moldea, Dan, 277, 284, 287
Molinoff, Ed, 60
Mollenhoff, Clark, 56, 186, 191
Mollo, Silvio, 254
Mongoose plot, 270–74
Moore, Sandy, 171–72, 175
Morgenthau, Robert, 151, 254–55
Moyers, Bill, 270
Moynihan, Daniel Patrick, 29, 301
Mullaney, John, 143–45, 183
Muste, A. J., 319
mutiny statutes, 61

narcotics:
  heroin traffic, 139–42, 149–52, 250
  and Mafia, 150
Narcotics, Bureau of, 31, 47, 76, 152
National Maritime Union, 61
Navasky, Victor, 8, 171
Neal, Jim, 55, 196
Nerval, Gerard de, 289
Ness, Elliot, 84
Newfield, Jack:
  and JFK assassination, 297
  and Ragano, 282
  on RFK as attorney general, 317, 324
New Frontier, 16, 20, 22–23
  activism of, 26–28, 323
  and changing world, 304
  as illusion, 298
Newport, Kentucky, 45–46, 47

and civil rights, 88, 104–5, 108–9, 112, 161, 226, 239
cleanup of, 92, 93, 122, 136, 311
coordinated law enforcement in, 100, 102, 107
corruption in, 83–84, 91, 100–102, 105–6, 136, 238
Glenn Hotel in, 85, 101
grand jury and, 90, 103, 105–7, 109, 110, 112
and media, 102, 107
Ratterman case in, 82–121, 203–43
and Ratterman trials, 112–20, 203–43
U.S. attorney in, 89–90
whorehouses in, 86, 91, 100, 101, 105
New Republic, 316
Nixon, Richard M., 268
and attorney general, 12
and Hoffa, 188, 193, 199
Noe, Bonnie (Desmond), 218
Nolan, John, 274
Noll, Carl, 74, 76, 146
Northwest Indiana Crime Commission, 163, 168
Novello, Angie, 14, 24–25, 249
and Castro plot, 273
and playing by the rules, 160
on RFK as attorney general, 321

Oberdorfer, Louis, 173, 253–55
obstruction of justice laws, 59
O'Donnell, Kenneth, 257, 265
Olson, Peter, 184–85
Organized Crime and Racketeering Section, 17–18, 27
activity of, 42–43, 51, 199, 245–52, 302–3, 305–6
appeals handled by, 238–41
and Democrats, 160–61
influence of, 309–13
and international diplomacy, 249–50
and JFK assassination, 258, 310
and Kefauver hearings, 30–31
and legislation, 45
and media, 35–36
meetings of, 27, 53, 57, 61, 125–47, 244–52
post-JFK assassination, 300, 301–4, 306
priorities of, 45–47
recruitment for, 15–21, 23–28, 55–56

special assistants in, 47
strike force program of, 310–11
targets of, 18, 201, 246
organized crime syndicates:
and American attitudes, 35–36
and *Enemy Within,* 186–87
features of, 35
history of, 28–32, 41–42
as interstate activity, 45, 47, 64
and law enforcement, 76
regional arms of, 29
scams of, 68–69
scope of, 29, 32, 33–40
see also Mafia
Osborn, Tommy, 132, 196
Oswald, Lee Harvey:
Castro and, 269
and conspiracy theories, 280–82, 291–92, 293, 299
and FBI, 295
and Mafia, 291
Mailer on, 291
Ruby's murder of, 269, 270, 278, 281, 282, 291
Ottenberg, Miriam, 52, 311–12

Pagano, Joe, 69
Paisley, Tom:
conspiracy trial of, 101
in Ratterman case, 103, 110, 118–19
in Ratterman trials, 91, 96–98, 100, 204–5, 209, 211–12, 215–16, 218
Palermo, Blinkey, 51
Palmeri, Matteo, and heroin traffic, 150, 151, 152
Panama, gambling in, 249
Papalia, John, 127
Partin, Edward Grady:
on Hoffa's threats, 277–78, 292
and jury tampering, 195, 197
and Supreme Court decision, 199
testimony of, 197
undercover work of, 131, 194–95, 312
Patriarca, Raymond, 137
Paul, Rony (Scott), 135
PBS Kennedy program, 259–60
Peace Corps, 23, 302
perjury laws, 58–59
Petersen, Henry:
and agency cooperation, 60, 62–63
on Giancana case, 251, 275–76

Petersen, Henry: (cont'd)
  and meetings, 53, 126–27, 144,
    245–46, 249
  and new laws, 64
  on Pagano case, 68–69
  and politics, 159, 168, 180
  and Ratterman case, 237
  and Rivard case, 139–42
Pinciotta, Donald, 133–35, 179
Plumbing and Pipefitting Union, 201, 202
politics:
  as influence peddling, 156–57, 175
  and justice, 155–63
  legal priorities, as opposed to, 156–62
  political influence, 156–57, 162–63,
    175
  and priority setting, 156
  prosecution and, 175
Polizzi, Charlie, 111
Poretz, Abe, 197
Porter, Paul, 229–30
Presidential Crime Commission, 311
Presidential Riot Commission, 325–26
President John F. Kennedy Assassination
    Records Collection Act (1992),
    293
privacy, invasion of, 59, 139
Priziola, John, 68
Profaci, Joseph, 32, 67
Profaci, Sal, 250
prosecution, and civil liberties, 306,
    313–14
Provenzano, Tony, 312
public officials, corrupt:
  and bribes, 39
  contamination from, 36–37
  Democrats, 160–61
  focus on, 127–28
  and gambling, 38–40
  in Newport, see Newport, Kentucky
  organized crime ties of, 34, 37, 41
Purple Gang, 261, 310
Purtschuk, Mike, 15

Quitter, Joseph:
  acquittal of, 235
  and Ciafardini, 209
  and civil rights, 112
  and Ratterman's arrest, 105, 235

Raab, Selwyn, 291, 306
racketeering:
  in Cuba, 267
  and gambling, 38–40
  as Kennedy priority, 262
  labor, see unions
  and Sheridan, 54–55, 57
  see also Mafia
racketeers:
  and Joe Kennedy, 42, 188–89, 259,
    260, 261, 288
  lists of, 50
Rackets Committee, see McClellan
    Committee
Ragano, Frank:
  and Chicago case, 197
  and Hoffa-RFK meeting, 283–84
  and Hoffa's payment system, 192
  and JFK assassination, 260, 282–85,
    287, 290–92
  and Mafia meetings, 67
Ramsey, Norman, 280–81
Ramsey Committee, 280–81
Rand, Sally, 85
Ratterman, Ann, 119, 217
Ratterman, George, 82–121
  arrest of, 83, 87, 99, 100, 101, 107,
    207
  background of, 92
  campaign of, 92–93, 102, 218–19
  civil rights of, 112, 161, 226, 239
  and conspiracy, 103, 104
  election of, 122
  and lie detector, 103–4, 110
  and retrial, 135–36, 203–43
  statement of, 94–95
  trial of, 91, 92, 95–100
  and U.S. v. Lester et al., 112–20
Rayfiel, Judge Leo, 172
Reddy, John, 196
Reeves, Robert, 270
Reid, Ed, 78
Reuther, Walter, 180
RFK assassination, 315, 326
  and Castro plot, 269
  mob hatred and, 259, 260,
    277–78, 279, 283, 286–87,
    299
Ribicoff, Abraham A., 7, 10
Ricca, Paul "The Waiter," 65, 250
Richardson, Elliot, 156
RICO, 311
Riebling, Mark, 296
Rinaldo, Salvatore, 150–52
Rivard, Lucien, 139–42
Roemer, William F., 66, 137, 138

Rogers, William P.:
  on attorney general's job, 9, 167
  and Hoffa, 193
  and organized crime unit, 42
  and transition, 14
Rolf, Judge, 208
Rosselli, John:
  and Castro plot, 263, 266, 267–69
  and CIA, 268
  death of, 266, 268
  and Exner, 265, 288
Rostow, Walt Whitman, 23
Rowan, Dan, 264
Royal Canadian Mounted Police, 63
Rubino, Mike, 70
Ruby, Jack:
  and conspiracy theories, 270, 281,
    282
  and Mafia, 278, 281, 282, 285, 291
  Mailer on, 291
  and Oswald murder, 269, 270, 278,
    281, 282, 291
Rusk, Dean, 9, 10
Russell, Richard, 296
Ruth, Henry, 251
  and civil rights cases, 302
  and Keogh case, 175
  and Presidential Crime Commission,
    311
  recruitment of, 28

Salerno, Ralph, 280
Salinger, Pierre, 326
Sams, Willie, 143–44
Sanfratello, "Big Joe," 252
Scales, Junius, 319
Scalish, John, 130
Schaffer, Charles, 55, 171
Schlesinger, Arthur, Jr.:
  recruitment of, 23
  on RFK as attorney general, 270,
    316–17
  on RFK as senator, 321
  on RFK and Warren Commission, 297
Schulberg, Budd, 186–87
Scopellitti, Rocco, 127
Scott, Neufio (Paul), 135
Seafarers' International Union, 202
Secret Service, 47, 296
Seifried, Christian, 214–15, 231
Seigenthaler, John, 14
  and Byron White, 24
  on Castro plot, 273

and *Enemy Within,* 8, 186
  on JFK-RFK relationship, 298
  and Keogh case, 173–74
  on RFK as attorney general, 5–6,
    8–10, 167
Seith, Mrs. Ellis, 224
Senate Select Committee on Improper
    Activities in the Labor or
    Management Field, *see*
    McClellan Committee
Shannon, William, 170–71
Sheridan, Walter, 14, 201
  and Castro plot, 274–75
  and Hoffa, 54, 77, 131, 193, 194,
    196, 198, 246–47, 278
  on JFK-RFK relationship, 298
  and labor racketeering group, 54–55,
    57
  and postassassination period, 301,
    302
  on RFK as attorney general, 43
Shriver, Sargent, 23, 304
Shur, Gerry, 71–72
Siegel, Bugsy, 78
Silberling, Edwyn:
  and collaborative law enforcement,
    62–63, 146
  and Goldberg, 168
  and Gosser case, 180
  and Keogh case, 173
  and meetings, 57, 61, 81, 126–27,
    136
  and Organized Crime and
    Racketeering Section, 18–20, 27,
    40, 42, 49, 50, 149, 306
  resignation of, 169
Sinatra, Frank, 65, 136–37, 160, 260
skimming, *see* gambling
Sloane, Arthur A., 199
Smith, Ben, 13
Smith, Charles Z.:
  and Beck, 55–56
  and Hoffa, 197–98, 278
  recruitment of, 55–56, 57
  and Sinatra, 160
Smith, Howard K., 296
Snow, C. P., 326
Snyder, Jimmy "the Greek," 248
Sobeloff, Simon, 12
Sorensen, Theodore C., 8, 262
Sprizzo, John, 28, 44, 59–60, 148–49
Staab, Frank, 90, 91
  and FBI, 89

Staab, Frank (*cont'd*)
  and April Flowers, 109–11
  and Ratterman case, 113, 119,
    237–38
  and Ratterman trials, 206–8, 210,
    213, 218
Stacher, Doc, 78
Stassi, Joseph, 139, 141
Steuve, Tom, 114, 120, 214, 215, 218,
    221, 227
Stevenson, Adlai E., 5, 7, 9, 16
Stewart, Potter, 199
Stone, Arnold, 139, 142
Stone, I. F., 316
Subin, Harry:
  and interstate crime, 64
  and Miami case, 253
  and Ratterman retrial, 203–5,
    207–13, 233, 240–41, 243
Sullivan, William, 11
Summers, Anthony, 162, 261, 297,
    303
Supreme Court, U.S., 242
Swinford, Mac, 113, 116, 120–22, 136,
    205–7, 213–16, 223, 226,
    231–36
Swing, General Joseph M., 74–75
Symington, James, 273–74

Taft-Hartley laws, 201–2, 246
Taney, Roger B., 12
Tanzer, Jake, 132–35, 178–80, 302
Task Force W., 272
Teamsters Union (International
    Brotherhood of Teamsters,
    Chauffeurs, Warehousemen,
    Stablemen, and Helpers of
    America):
  and AFL-CIO, 55, 190, 193
  and Bates, 67–68
  and Beck, 56, 189, 190
  cleanup of, 310
  and Hoffa, 131, 177, 185–99
  indictments and, 77, 246–47
  and Las Vegas, 78
  and McClellan Committee, 4
  and Mafia, 186–87, 192
  pension funds, 191, 192, 196–98
  and Test Fleet case, 193–96
Test Fleet case, 193–96
Thomas, Carol, 79
Tocco, William, 68
Tolson, Clyde, 303

Trafficante, Santos, Jr., 260
  and Castro, 263, 267, 268–69
  and CIA, 297
  in Cuba, 66–67, 263, 269
  and JFK assassination, 269, 278, 279,
    280, 282–87, 290–92, 295
  at Mafia meetings, 32, 67
  and Stassi, 139
  in Tampa, 66, 139

Udall, Stewart L., 10
Unione Siciliano, see Mafia
unions:
  corruption in, 4, 5, 32, 41, 159, 160,
    186
  labor racketeering group, 54–55, 57
  and McClellan Committee, 4, 5, 55,
    181, 182, 189, 201
  and rackets, 177–202
  record-keeping by, 61
  see also specific unions
United Auto Workers, 132, 177,
    178–81, 246
United Mine Workers, 201–2
United Nations, 9
U.S. v. Lester et al., 112–20

Valachi, Joe, 149–54, 250
Vidal, Gore, 13, 316
Vincent, Howard, 213, 221, 227
von Hoffman, Nicholas, 329

Wald, Jerry, 187
Walker, Leonard, 114, 120, 205,
    227–28
Walsh, Lawrence E., 31
Warren, Earl, 199
Warren Commission, 293–97, 302
  and alternate inquiries, 278–79
  challenges to conclusions of, 296
  and CIA, 295, 296
  conspiracy testimony ignored by, 279,
    281, 294
  and Dulles, 270
  and Hoover/FBI, 295, 296
  and LBJ, 294–95, 296
  and lone gunman theory, 270, 282,
    295–96
  and Mafia discussions, 278, 295
  and RFK, 294, 295–96, 297, 301–2
Washington, D.C.:
  New Frontier in, 16, 20, 22–23,
    26–28, 298, 304, 323

penal code of, 183
public schools in, 320
Weintraub, Morris, 115, 120, 214,
   220–21, 227
Welfare and Pension Funds Amendments
   Act, 27
Wessel, Milton, 32, 33
Whalen, Richard, 259, 260–61
White, Byron, 173, 174
   and Citizens for Kennedy, 18, 23
   and Lake County cases, 168
   recruitment of, 24
   on RFK as attorney general, 24, 26
   team recruited by, 25, 26
White, Phil, 181
White, Theodore, 25
White, Upshire, 97, 101, 105, 112, 115,
   209, 235
white-collar crime, 40–41
Willens, Howard, 294
Williams, Edward Bennett, 182–83,
   194, 276
Williams, Harry, 256

Wilson, Judge Frank W., 197
Winter, Al, 78
wiretap laws, 59, 265
Withrow, Nancybelle, 99, 104, 116,
   207, 216
Withrow, Thomas, 98–100, 104, 116,
   207, 216, 217
witnesses:
   credibility of, 205–6
   expert, 206
   and immunity laws, 46, 57–58, 73,
      107
   and perjury laws, 59
Wofford, Harris, 26
   and election irony, 260
   on heroes, 327
   on JFK's affairs, 287–88
   on RFK as attorney general, 323

Zambito, Anthony, 145–46
Zerilli, Joseph, 68, 251
Zimmer, Heinrich, 328
Zizzo, Frank, 164

RONALD GOLDFARB was born in 1933 and raised in New Jersey. He received AB and LLB degrees from Syracuse University and LLM and JSD degrees from Yale. He tried numerous courts-martial for the U.S. Air Force for three years, and he was recruited to work as a special prosecutor in the Justice Department's Organized Crime and Racketeering Section. An author and agent, he has practiced law in Washington, D.C., since 1966 while occasionally serving on special assignments for various government agencies and private foundations. He lives in Alexandria, Virginia, with his wife, who is an architect, and has three children.

ABOUT THE TYPE

This book was set in Sabon, a typeface designed by the well-known German typographer Jan Tschichold (1902–74). Sabon's design is based upon the original letter forms of Claude Garamond and was created specifically to be used for three sources: foundry type for hand composition, Linotype, and Monotype. Tschichold named his typeface for the famous Frankfurt typefounder Jacques Sabon, who died in 1580.